DEFENSE 10_

Dear Nikhil,

You are
the best!

Mike

DEFENSE 101

Understanding the Military of Today and Tomorrow

Michael E. O'Hanlon

Dear Kabir,
To the most
amazing and incredible friend
Mr. Mike

CORNELL UNIVERSITY PRESS   ITHACA AND LONDON

First published 2021 by Cornell University Press

Library of Congress Cataloging-in-Publication Data

Names: O'Hanlon, Michael E., author.
Title: Defense 101 : understanding the military of today and tomorrow / Michael E. O'Hanlon.
Description: Ithaca [New York] : Cornell University Press, 2021. | Includes bibliographical references and index.
Identifiers: LCCN 2020042666 (print) | LCCN 2020042667 (ebook) | ISBN 9781501754470 (hardcover) | ISBN 9781501754487 (paperback) | ISBN 9781501754494 (epub) | ISBN 9781501754500 (pdf)
Subjects: LCSH: United States—Defenses. | United States—Armed Forces. | United States—Military policy.
Classification: LCC UA23 .O327 2021 (print) | LCC UA23 (ebook) | DDC 355.00973—dc23
LC record available at https://lccn.loc.gov/2020042666
LC ebook record available at https://lccn.loc.gov/2020042667

To my research assistants over the years at Brookings, including Stacey, Christina, Julien, Sue, Micah, Aaron, Adriana, Nina, Jason, Ian, and Adam, and in memory of Bruce Blair, Janne Nolan, and John Steinbruner

Contents

Acknowledgments

Everyone who has contributed to my education and career deserves thanks for helping, directly or indirectly, with this book. I have been blessed by dozens, even hundreds, of such inspirational figures in my life. But special thanks to my grandfather Ferd, who first sparked my love of science; to my father, Ed, whose military service, while never something he discussed much, helped steer me to the field; and to my mom, Frieda, who was (and is) there every step of the way.

DEFENSE 101

INTRODUCTION
A Primer on the US Military Machine

Modern warfare is a remarkably technical and complex human endeavor. The organizations that carry it out are among the largest institutions on earth. Some of the most sophisticated inventions ever fielded undergird the vehicles, weapons, sensors, communications systems, and other key hardware with which wars are fought. Large fractions of government budgets around the world provide the resources to build military institutions in peacetime and to conduct combat operations during times of war.

The main focus of this book, the American military, is simply a behemoth. Nearly 3 million people work directly for the US Department of Defense (DoD), in uniform or as civilian government employees, across the country and around the world. About 20 million more living Americans have served in uniform in the nation's armed forces in the past. The US military wields some 5,000 nuclear weapons, though they are built and maintained by the National Nuclear Security Administration within the Department of Energy. The Department of Defense and Department of Energy together run research laboratory systems that continue to invent some of the world's most cutting-edge technologies. Together their annual budgets for research, development, testing, and evaluation of new technologies easily exceed $100 billion; the total budget for US national defense is roughly three-quarters of a *trillion* dollars a year. The Department of Defense includes four major military services, each with its own distinct culture, rank system, and command structure. It now also includes a niche "space force" as a fifth military service; the US Coast Guard, although administered within the Department of Homeland Security in peacetime, is a sixth.

1

How to make sense of all of this, without worrying about every insignia, every regimental flag, every small base operated by the American armed forces, or each and every dollar spent defending the nation? How to understand the basics of war—and the most important characteristics of the military that are relevant to core matters of US national security? These are the central questions that motivate this book.

The book is designed less to address immediate policy issues than to provide some of the basic knowledge and analytical tools that will be relevant regardless of which security problems become most acute in the years ahead. We know that matters of war and peace will always be important in the modern world, as they have been throughout history. We can also be sure that military budgets will be large for most countries for years to come, and therefore that methodologies for making them as efficient as possible will be central to good public policymaking. Thus, this book is intended first and foremost as a primer and textbook in a field of enduring importance, not as a policy tome to address a particular problem of the day.

That said, I should also speak to several contemporary security debates of major importance for the nation and the world. One crucial matter is that, if history is a guide, policymakers may again forget the risks and likely costs of war. Doing so is usually incorrect, and always dangerous. It is too easy, during times of rapid technological and strategic change like today, for leaders to persuade themselves that new weapons and new concepts of warfare will greatly improve the prospects for rapid victory by a technologically superior country. Such hubris could affect the decision making of the United States, and perhaps other countries, in unfortunate ways in the years to come.

A second major debate that the information and methods presented here can help illuminate concerns America's proper global security role. This debate is happening at a time when projected trillion-dollar annual federal deficits, now further increased by COVID-19, stretch as far out as the eye can see—constituting an insidious threat to US economic prosperity and thus national security themselves. In this context, policymakers need better tools to understand the implications of various possible visions of US grand strategy for the size and shape of the US defense budget. "Grand strategy" is a somewhat arcane and grandiose term that inevitably requires adjustment when theory meets real-world crises and circumstances. Even so, it is important to have a general concept of how a country seeks to protect its security as well as its broader interests when designing a defense program and budget.[1] Third, while hawks and doves are important in today's US debate, challenging each other's core assumptions and logic, there are some dangerous strands of thinking on both the left and the right. Über-hawks believe that American military preeminence of the type enjoyed in, say, the 1990s is again attainable if we only put our minds to it and spend enough; given technological realities and trends, as well as China's rise, I do not think that is a realistic position. And some doves believe that American defense budgets and technologies are so predominant that the United States can afford big and even somewhat indiscriminate cuts in military spending. Such thinking ignores the fact that adversaries can often challenge the United States asymmetrically, especially on or near their own territories, even when spending far less on their armed forces. I challenge such misconceptions—or at least discuss the kinds of tools that can help others to do so.

There is, unquestionably, an art of war—as Sun Tzu wrote millennia ago, and as many other great scholars and historians over the years have underscored. There is also a politics of war, where human passions intersect with the interests, institutions, and group or national identities of key peoples and their leaders—as great writers from Thucydides to Machiavelli to Clausewitz have dramatized over the centuries. The politics of war includes the hugely important subject of civil-military relations, as well as matters of bureaucratic and organizational performance. And, of course, there are troves of important studies on military history, which also demand attention from anyone who is serious about the military profession and national security policymaking today.

This book, building in part on a text I wrote a decade ago, is, however, not about the art, politics, or history of war, but instead the *science* of war. By that expression, I mean a subdiscipline of defense analysis that, beginning with a foundation of basic facts and figures about military organizations and operations, uses analytical methods to tackle key questions in the national security field. Those methods include simple computational algorithms for assessing military effectiveness and predicting combat outcomes. They include study of defense budgets and economics, as well as efforts to understand the physics and technology of military weapons and operations today.

If there is a science of war, it is admittedly an inexact one—and this reality is what makes me want to underscore the message of caution just noted. Great precision in predicting combat outcomes, or even in accurately estimating defense budget requirements to achieve a given mission, is generally not possible. Initial expectations for the expenses of new weapons are often off by 50 percent. Predictions about the costs, casualties, and outcomes of war are generally off by even more than that. One central theme of this book is that such uncertainties are inherent in the business. Those believing they have a great capacity for clairvoyance about the future of military matters follow in the footsteps of previous generations of Pollyannas who have usually been wrong—often deadly wrong. It is important to remember, and seek not to emulate, those who have predicted military "cakewalks" (as with the invasion of Iraq in 2003) or quick summertime campaigns that would have the boys "home before the leaves fall" (as in World War I).[2] A proper understanding of the science of war can give tools to bound predictions about future military outcomes, while also making us humble about what we do not and indeed cannot know.

The rest of the introduction discusses many of the ABCs of the US armed forces. It also explains the evolution of American grand strategy—the theory of the case for how the nation should ensures its safety, prosperity, and survival—that these forces are designed to undergird. Chapter 1 dissects the US defense budget, as well as various matters in the broader field of defense economics. It also provides methodologies for understanding how different defense strategies and military force postures affect that budget. This introduction and chapter 1 are primarily about the United States—though because America's armed forces are so global in presence and in reach, they have considerable relevance for other audiences as well.[3]

Chapters 2 through 4 have a more ecumenical and universal scope. Chapter 2 discusses wargaming, combat modeling, and simulation, as well as force sizing and other issues related to military operations and warfighting scenarios. Chapters 3 and 4 examine various areas of defense technology, with a philosophy that might be described as "physics for poets." My goal is to make these important subjects accessible to a general audience, suggesting methods by which nonspecialists can make inroads into understanding them.

Most of the rest of this introduction describes the US Department of Defense. But first, to set the stage, I sketch out characteristics of today's global security environment in broad brush.

Today's Global Security Environment

There can be little doubt that military force remains relevant in today's world—both for waging war and for attempting to keep the peace. But in a book on modern defense analysis, it is valuable to make this case explicitly with a brief tour of sorts around the globe.

The current international security environment is complex, with numerous positive and negative features. The latter get most of the press, though—from Eastern Europe, to the Western Pacific, to much of the broader Middle East region, to parts of Africa. So it is worth beginning with a few of the positives. There are no great-power wars today and have not been, in any meaningful sense, in more than half a century. The few interstate wars that have occurred since 1945 have been primarily within South Asia, East Asia, and the Middle East; the Western Hemisphere, Latin America, Europe, and Africa have been largely spared this particular scourge.

There are still more than 10,000 nuclear warheads on earth. Even though that number has been reduced substantially since Cold War days, when combined inventories exceeded 50,000, it is still enough to put human civilization itself at risk in the event of war. The United States and Russia account for more than 90 percent of the total. The United Kingdom, France, China, India, and Pakistan each likely possesses from 150 to 300, with Israel's unconfirmed arsenal totaling almost 100 bombs. North Korea probably has a couple dozen nuclear weapons, with enough fissile material to make a few dozen more.[4] That said, the situation is not entirely grim. While nuclear proliferation continues, and nine countries are known to possess nuclear weapons, the fear once expressed by John F. Kennedy that at least a couple dozen countries could have the bomb by the twenty-first century has not panned out.[5]

The United States, although not universally popular in the Donald Trump era (or any other), continues to find itself at the center of a system of alliances and security partnerships involving more than sixty countries, which collectively account for some two-thirds of world gross domestic product (GDP) and military spending. Table I.1 presents a running tally of worldwide military spending, starting with the United States and then the rest of the impressive western alliance system. This alliance network is the end product of three-fourths of a century of a US grand strategy that has viewed the security of the Western Hemisphere, Western Europe, East Asia, and much of the Middle East as integral to America's own well-being and ultimately its safety and security. The experience of the world wars, which broke out when no such globally minded grand strategy guided American military or foreign policy, created a consensus that it was better to engage in these regions to prevent large-scale war rather than to intercede only after it erupts. The Cold War solidified that consensus further—and led to the creation of many of the key American alliances that still survive today—out of fear that Communist expansionism could ultimately threaten core American interests if not checked early in distant regions. The end of the Cold War, combined with various changes in America's economic trajectory and internal politics, may by now have weakened this consensus somewhat. But a grand strategy of forward engagement has nonetheless persisted even through a period in which the nation's forty-fifth president, Mr. Trump, has openly questioned much of the underlying logic behind it.

America's annual national defense budget, which totaled nearly $746 billion in 2020, translates into spending of about 3.2 percent of the nation's pre-COVID projected GDP (though it turned out to be a slightly higher percent than that, in actuality, given that GDP was temporarily reduced due to the coronavirus-induced recession). In inflation-adjusted 2020 dollars, that is more than $200 billion above the Cold War average. Yet as a percentage of GDP, national defense spending constitutes a relatively modest burden by comparison to recent decades.

TABLE I.1. Global Distribution of Military Spending, 2019

COUNTRY	DEFENSE EXPENDITURE (BILLIONS OF US $)	FRACTION OF GLOBAL TOTAL (PERCENT)	ROUGH CUMULATIVE PERCENTAGE	PERCENT-AGE OF NATIONAL GDP
United States	684.5	39.5	39.5	3.2
NATO				
Canada	18.7	1.0	40.5	1.1
France	52.2	3.0	43.5	1.9
Germany	48.5	2.7	46.2	1.2
Italy	27.1	1.5	47.7	1.3
Spain	12.9	0.7	48.4	0.9
Turkey	8.1	0.4	48.8	1.0
UK	54.7	3.1	51.9	2.0
Rest of NATO[a]	65.6	3.7	55.6	
Total NATO, excluding U.S.	287.8	16.6		
Total NATO	972.3	55.6		
Rio Pact[b]	54.5	3.1	58.7	
KEY INDO-PACIFIC ALLIES				
Japan	48.5	2.7	61.4	0.94
South Korea	39.7	2.2	63.6	2.44
Australia	25.4	1.4	65	1.8
New Zealand	2.7	0.1	65.1	1.3
Thailand	7.1	0.4	65.5	1.3
Philippines	3.4	0.2	65.7	0.9
Total key Indo-Pacific allies	126.8	7.3		
OTHER SECURITY PARTNERS				
Israel	19.2	1.1	66.8	5.8
Egypt	3.3	0.2	67	1.5
Iraq	20.4	1.2	68.2	9.1
Pakistan	10.3	0.6	68.8	3.6
Gulf Cooperation Council[c*]	95.2	5.5	74.3	
Jordan	1.6	0.1	74.4	4.6
Morocco	3.6	0.2	74.6	3.0
Mexico	5.0	0.2	74.8	0.4
Taiwan	10.9	0.6	75.4	1.8
India	60.5	3.4	78.8	2.0
Singapore	11.2	0.6	79.4	3.1
Total	241.2	13.7		

TABLE I.1. (continued)

COUNTRY	DEFENSE EXPENDITURE (BILLIONS OF US $)	FRACTION OF GLOBAL TOTAL (PERCENT)	ROUGH CUMULATIVE PERCENTAGE	PERCENT-AGE OF NATIONAL GDP
OTHER NATIONS				
Non-NATO Europe, minus Russia	23.6	1.4	81	
Other Middle East and North Africa[d]*	13.35	0.8	82	
Other Central and South Asia[e]*	9.0	0.5	83	
Other East Asia and Pacific[f]	12.1	0.6	83.6	
Other Caribbean and Latin America[g]*	0.4	0.0	83.6	
Sub-Saharan Africa	17	1	84.6	
Iran	17.4	1.0	85.6	3.8
North Korea[h]	5	0.3	85.9	
Syria/Venezuela*	3.0	0.0	85.9	
China[i]	181.1	10.4	96.3	1.3
Russia	48.2	2.7	99	2.9
Indonesia	7.4	0.4	99.4	0.7
Other nations	337.55	19.1		
TOTAL	1,732.4		100	

Sources: International Institute for Strategic Studies, *The Military Balance 2020* (New York: Routledge Press, 2020), 529–534; World Bank, *GDP (current US$)* (Washington: World Bank, 2020), available at https://doi.org /10.1080/04597222.2020.1707977.

a. Albania, Belgium, Bulgaria, Croatia, Czechia, Denmark, Estonia, Greece, Hungary, Iceland, Latvia, Lithuania, Luxembourg, Netherlands, Norway, Poland, Portugal, Romania, Slovakia, Slovenia.

b. Argentina, Bahamas, Bolivia, Brazil, Chile, Colombia, Costa Rica, Dominican Republic, Ecuador, El Salvador, Guatemala, Haiti, Honduras, Nicaragua, Panama, Paraguay, Peru, Trinidad and Tobago, Uruguay

c. Bahrain, Kuwait, Oman, Qatar, Saudi Arabia, United Arab Emirates

d. Algeria, Lebanon, Libya, Mauritania, Tunisia, Yemen

e. Afghanistan, Bangladesh, Kazakhstan, Kyrgyzstan, Nepal, Sri Lanka, Tajikistan, Turkmenistan, Uzbekistan

f. Brunei, Cambodia, Fiji, Laos, Malaysia, Mongolia, Myanmar, PNG, Timor-Leste, Vietnam

g. Antigua and Barbuda, Barbados, Belize, Guyana, Jamaica, Suriname, Cuba

h. North Korea value is an author estimate

i. Some estimates for China are $30 billion to $50 billion higher, including that of DoD

* At least a portion of the total cost cited here is from earlier years because 2019 data are not available.

Corresponding levels were typically two to three times as high during most of the Cold War, and 4 to 4.5 percent of GDP in the early years of this century. US national defense spending constitutes more than 35 percent of the global total—a fact that some see as wasteful, while others find it comforting. Most of America's allies, with a few exceptions like South Korea, do not devote nearly as large a fraction of their GDPs to their armed forces as does the United States— with twenty of twenty-nine North Atlantic Treaty Organization (NATO) allies falling clearly below the alliance's formal defense spending goal of 2 percent, for example. Only the United States, the United Kingdom, Greece, Poland, and the three Baltic states now reach or exceed it, as of 2019/2020, with France and Romania quite close to the goal (though ironically, COVID may at least temporarily increase the number meeting the goal, by shrinking GDP and thereby *increasing* the ratio of military spending to GDP for many countries). But because most American allies are wealthy, the resulting military budgets and spending levels are quite substantial even if defense resources are modest relative to GDP.[6] Whether this constellation of allies and alliances is on balance more of a burden and responsibility for the United States, with its obligations to help defend these countries in times of war, or a huge strategic advantage, given their wealth and power, is of course a matter of ongoing intense debate. But the consensus view among scholars and policymakers is still the latter, reflecting the country's ambitious and muscular grand strategy.

America's nearest defense spending competitor, China, spends only about one-third as much as does the United States, with most estimates in the rough range of $200 billion to $250 billion (once a standard definition of military spending, rather than China's own understated official figures, are used).[7] Saudi Arabia ranks third in spending at just under $80 billion (as of 2019, in that case, with all figures converted into US dollars), followed by India at $60 billion.

The next tier of military spenders is made up of five countries with annual budgets around $50 billion. Four are American allies—the United Kingdom, France, Japan, and Germany. Russia is the other country in this overall league, though the amount has fluctuated a good deal in recent years largely due to currency valuations. South Korea rounds out the world's top-ten list of military big spenders at $40 billion in 2019. Brazil, Italy, and Australia are next in the pecking order, in the general range of $25 billion to $27 billion each, followed by Iraq, Israel, Canada, and Iran in the ballpark of $20 billion apiece.[8]

In terms of military personnel, the US armed forces include 1.35 million active-duty troops. That number is actually rather modest by historical and international standards. They total fewer than the uniformed personnel in China's armed forces and are only modestly more numerous than North Korea's or India's.[9] They represent less than 7 percent of the total of 20 million uniformed active-duty military personnel worldwide.[10]

Globally, army forces constitute nearly three-fourths of all active-duty military personnel.[11] However, given the nation's geography and grand strategy, the American armed forces have proportionately larger naval and air forces. The air force, navy, and marine corps together constitute almost two-thirds of the active-duty forces of the American military, with the space force likely less than 1 percent of the total, and the army the remainder. (The army's share of active-duty troops, about 36 percent, grows to 47 percent if one includes active-duty forces as well as the reservists of all the military services in the calculation.)

Major US security relationships include NATO; bilateral alliances with Japan, South Korea, Australia, New Zealand, the Philippines, and Thailand in the Asia-Pacific; strong security partnerships with Singapore and Sweden, as well as most Arab countries and Israel; and the Rio Pact. China has only the Democratic People's Republic of Korea as a formal ally. Russia has only Armenia, Belarus, Kazakhstan, Kyrgyzstan, and Tajikistan as formal allies, within the Collective Security Treaty Organization.[12] Both Russia and China are members of a group that falls well short of a working alliance, the Shanghai Cooperation Organization (SCO), the other members of which are Kazakhstan, Kyrgyzstan, Tajikistan, Uzbekistan, India, and Pakistan.[13]

Yet even if defense budgets and international military alliance fundamentals align well for the United States and its allies, other characteristics of the global security environment are not so favorable. Great-power rivalries are heating up in the Western Pacific region as well as in Central and Eastern Europe. Swaths of the Middle East and North Africa regions are in conflict, and there are additional acute hot spots in Korea, the Persian Gulf, and South Asia.

Indeed, there have been and continue to be more than thirty active conflicts at any given point during much of the twenty-first century. More than ten have typically qualified as "wars," using the standard threshold for such a designation of 1,000 or more battle deaths a year. (By this methodology, there could be multiple wars in a given country, such as Syria.)[14] This remains a higher figure than in much of the twentieth century.[15] Estimated aggregate fatalities in recent wars total in the many tens of thousands annually, according to the Peace Research Institute in Oslo and Uppsala University in Sweden.[16] (For the sake of comparison, there have been more than 400,000 annual homicides worldwide in recent times—and more than 1 million fatalities globally from car accidents.)[17]

There were fourteen United Nations peace operations globally as of 2019, involving a grand total of some 100,000 personnel, including troops, police, civilians, and specialists. Most UN operations are in the broader Middle East and northern and central Africa, with additional missions in Cyprus, Kosovo, South Asia, and Haiti. The annual combined cost of these operations is now about $7 billion.[18] Historically, peacekeeping operations have a mixed track record, failing to keep the peace about 40 percent of the time. Some conflicts are just too deeply rooted, or the world's collective capacities (and will) are too lacking, to do better than that. This is not an argument against such missions—which do in fact succeed in whole or part some 60 percent of the time, and which are far cheaper than American-led military operations of the type witnessed recently in Iraq and Afghanistan.[19] For example, Lise Howard of Georgetown University documents the dozen multidimensional missions since the end of the Cold War that have succeeded in achieving much or most of their respective mandates: in

Namibia, Cambodia, Mozambique, El Salvador, Guatemala, East Slavonia and Croatia, Timor Leste, Sierra Leone, Burundi, Timor Leste again (underscoring that "success" does not necessarily mean an end to all problems), Cote d'Ivoire, and Liberia. By contrast, about a half dozen of these complex missions have been unsuccessful: in Congo (in the 1960s), and then since the 1990s in Somalia, Angola, Rwanda, Bosnia, and Haiti.[20]

Terrorism has increased dramatically in this century by comparison with the latter decades of the twentieth century.[21] Al Qaeda affiliates remain active in dozens of countries. ISIS, or ISIL as some prefer, has now gained adherents from Nigeria and Libya to the Sinai to Afghanistan while continuing to attract many recruits to the Middle East—and to inspire terrible attacks around the world.[22] There has been some reported reduction in terrorism in recent years, but violence levels are still far above those of any decade preceding that of the 2010s, with fatalities in the low tens of thousands annually (most within the contexts of civil wars in the broader Middle East and Africa).[23]

COVID and its associated economic effects now add a further layer of disruption and difficulty to the international security environment, though it is too early to say how they will shape the course of conflict around the world. Adding it all up, while there are certainly some hopeful elements in trends in global security, the famous adage attributed to Trotsky still applies. To paraphrase, we may not have an interest in war, but war may still have an interest in us. It has mutated in some ways over the course of modern history, but it certainly has not gone away.

A Quick Historical Sketch of the American Military

America's Department of Defense dates back only to 1947, but most of the nation's military services date back to the eighteenth century. Article I, Section 8 of the 1789 US Constitution, which gives Congress the power to declare war, also entrusts it to "raise and support Armies" and "provide and maintain a Navy." That same section entrusts Congress to raise militias when needed—in effect, a precursor to today's National Guard. Both the army and the navy had existed before 1789, going back to 1775.[24] The marine corps too dates back to the beginning of the Revolutionary War, with its official birthday also in 1775 (and its official birthplace a tavern in Philadelphia!).[25] The Department of War was created by Congress in 1789, but it wound up primarily overseeing the Army during most of its existence, until 1947, with the Department of the Navy overseeing maritime military matters largely independently.[26] The coast guard has roots going back to 1790, though it did not acquire its name or its full suite of current responsibilities until the twentieth century.[27]

Throughout its first 150 years or so, the United States was wary of a large military, seeing such institutions as the epitome of the European imperialist nation-states that many immigrants to America had fled. It sustained a somewhat romanticized image of the gentleman soldier, or the farmer-soldier, who only takes up arms when his country's security demands it, returning to civilian life once the shooting stops.

This image fits with the life of the nation's first commander in chief and president, George Washington. General Washington resigned his military commission after the Revolutionary War and resumed life as a private citizen. His preference for the plow over the sword earned Washington the nickname of the American Cincinnatus, after the Roman farmer-soldier who also returned to his fields after battle.[28] Washington's example helped foster and reinforce the historical theme of a United States disinterested in Europe's wars of the eighteenth and nineteenth centuries, as typified in John Quincy Adams's admonition in 1821 about championing freedom abroad without actively seeking to impose it.[29] Washington's Farewell Address had a similar theme:

> Hence, likewise, they will avoid the necessity of those overgrown military establishments which, under any form of government, are inauspicious to liberty, and which are to be regarded as particularly hostile to republican liberty. In this sense it is that your union ought to be considered as a main prop of your liberty, and that the love of the one ought to endear to you the preservation of the other.[30]

This attitude led to the rapid demobilizations of the nation's armed forces after the Revolutionary War. One result was the poor preparedness of the nation for the War of 1812, when the army had fewer than 10,000 soldiers at the outbreak of hostilities.[31] Similarly, at the outbreak of the Civil War, the US Army numbered just 17,000.[32] After the Civil War, during which some 3 million Americans were ultimately at arms, mass demobilization occurred again.[33] From the 1870s until the Spanish-American War, the full-time army numbered less than 30,000 soldiers.[34] During most of this time, the US military focused on battles against Native Americans, Mexico, and Spain.[35] At the outbreak of World War I, the US Army was only about 100,000 strong. It built up during that war but, just as surely, dismantled most standing forces in the aftermath. Even as Europe again lurched toward war, that remained the case; in 1938 the US Army was only 165,000 strong, nineteenth largest in the world.[36]

In the late nineteenth and early twentieth centuries, new thinking emerged about naval and, eventually, aerial combat. Alfred Thayer Mahan, with his book *The Influence of Sea Power upon History* (1890), advocated a network of overseas bases, as well as naval capability sufficient to defeat any enemy's fleet, so as to gain control of the oceans. He influenced a young Theodore Roosevelt—as well as President McKinley, who seized the Philippines and annexed Hawaii during the Spanish-American War of 1898 and its aftermath. A few decades later, Billy Mitchell articulated his belief in airpower and the importance of a military service focused on that new domain of warfare.[37] But even as these debates picked up steam, American naval power and airpower lagged considerably behind those of the European powers—a situation that did not really change until World War II.[38] The US Air Force was created in 1947.

The evolution of the US Marine Corps followed a broadly similar path to that of the army. It was a tiny force throughout the nineteenth century, generally in the range of 1,000 to 3,000 marines in total at any time, not even exceeding 4,000 during the Civil War. Then it began its upward trajectory early in the twentieth century, reaching about 10,000 uniformed personnel by 1910, temporarily growing to about 75,000 during World War I, and then averaging in the 50,000 range in the 1920s before its rapid growth in World War II to nearly half a million marines.[39] Since 1952, its force structure has been mandated by law to include three divisions and three air wings (though the definition of divisions and wings was not formalized legally).[40] In recent decades its strength has varied from 170,000 to 200,000 active-duty uniformed personnel.

In the nation's first 140 years of independence, militias were arguably more central to American military life and strategy than was the army, navy, or marine corps. The Constitution made militias permanent and explicitly codified their independent standing separate from the army. Quite often, combined militia strength was far in excess of regular army strength. At the onset of the Spanish-American War, for example, the sum total of all militias exceeded 100,000 personnel, or about four times the total number of soldiers in the active army.[41]

All that changed with the world wars, of course. In World War II, in particular, US military forces became gargantuan. They reached about 12 million active-duty troops—about 6.2 million in the ground-combat army, 2.0 million in the army air forces (the air force did not yet exist as a separate service), 3.3 million in the navy, and 500,000 in the marine corps. The national defense budget reached a whopping 35 percent of GDP.[42]

After the war, while demobilization obviously occurred, America did not revert to its time-tested preference for a small standing military. With the descent of the "Iron Curtain" over much of Eastern and Central Europe in the late 1940s, the fall of China to communism in 1949, and the North Korean invasion of South Korea in 1950, the nation geared up for a cold war and for numerous regional hot wars. As a result, during the four decades of the Cold War, US military spending averaged more than $500 billion annually, ranging roughly between 5 and 10 percent of GDP (typically closer to 10 percent in the 1950s and 1960s, and less thereafter).[43]

The National Security Act of 1947 and subsequent legislation created and formalized the Department of Defense, the air force, and the Central Intelligence Agency (CIA). In its early years, however, DoD as such was rather weak, and the military services continued to dominate much of defense policymaking.[44] Only with the era of Robert McNamara under President Kennedy and President Johnson did the civilian leadership of DoD truly begin to assert itself. Since that time, DoD has continued to evolve, and civilian leadership as well as central military leadership have continued to strengthen, culminating in the 1986 Goldwater-Nichols Department of Defense Reorganization Act, described in greater detail later.

A brief word on post–World War II military strategy: During the Cold War, the United States prepared principally for a large war against the Soviet Union, especially in Europe. It relied in large part on nuclear weapons to underwrite that strategy, given the proximity of Soviet and Warsaw Pact armies to America's NATO allies. Depending on the decade, it also planned for the possibility of a second, simultaneous war against China. Throughout, it also sought the capability to conduct smaller regional wars, as in Korea and Vietnam—since it was those kinds of wars it was actually fighting.[45] However, it rarely made such conflicts central to its force planning, weapons acquisition, doctrinal development, or training, and partly as a result, it struggled in them mightily.[46] Nor did it officially designate these conflicts as wars in the US Constitution's sense of the word; Congress has not formally declared war since 1941. Sometimes in this period, scholars referred to a "2 ½ war" capability as the goal for American force planning. The Soviet bloc, China, and a smaller threat like North Korea were the presumed adversaries in conflicts that could overlap in time. During other periods, especially after the height of the Vietnam War, a less ambitious "1 ½ war" construct was employed. This paradigm was based in part on the conviction that fighting one big and one medium-scale conflict simultaneously was already a fairly conservative way to do defense planning. In addition, such a goal was more attainable than a 2 ½ war capability, given the size of military budgets that the nation was prepared to sustain.

After the Cold War ended, and Operation Desert Storm took place against Iraqi forces in 1991, the United States focused its military planning efforts primarily on smaller, "rogue" states, including most notably Iraq and North Korea. After the attacks of September 2001, it engaged in hot wars in Afghanistan and Iraq, which led to some modifications to force structure but only gradual adjustments in overall strategy. As before, the main contingencies against which US forces were sized featured simultaneous, or overlapping, conflicts of some type against smaller countries with extremist governments (and with possible possession of weapons of mass destruction, though generally not the capacity to hit the United States with nuclear-tipped long-range missiles).[47]

Throughout all these periods, the US Navy and US Marine Corps contributed to backstopping war plans. But they also conducted regular deployments in the Western Pacific, the Persian Gulf region, and the Mediterranean Sea, as well as other places, with an eye toward maintaining deterrence of adversaries and reassurance of friends and allies in those regions. They also sought to ensure control of the sea lanes that are so crucial to the global economy.[48]

Especially in the post–World War II era, there have been important distinguishing characteristics—and often rivalries—within the Department of Defense. For example, the air force and navy have been the services most focused on the strategic nuclear deterrent mission; they have also tended to focus the most on technology. The army and marine corps have had cultures focused more on the individual trooper or warrior, as RAND scholar Carl Builder and others have explained. Of course, all of the services have lots of high-tech equipment, and all care about their people. But there are notable differences. For example, in the 2019 budget, the air force received about $40 billion for research, development, testing, and evaluation, the navy almost $20 billion, and the army just over $10 billion (with another $25 billion or so for joint and ecumenical efforts). These figures, not unlike those for other years, together constitute a telling indicator of the relative importance the different military services place on technological innovation compared with their other responsibilities (since, as discussed further in chapter 1, the army, air force, and navy all have budgets of roughly similar overall magnitude).[49] As for the rivalries, sometimes they produce redundancy and waste, as more than one service seeks to develop more or less the same capability. But a degree of competition is healthy as a means of driving innovation, and a certain amount of redundancy is useful. Not all military technologies, or concepts and tactics, wind up working as well on the battlefield as they do in the laboratory or on the test range.

In the early post–Cold War decades, another key aspect of US defense policy included numerous efforts to engage Russia and China in cooperative activities. These took place in areas such as nuclear threat reduction, peace operations, humanitarian relief, counterpiracy patrols, and military-to-military dialogue. These efforts have yielded some progress, but a number have slowed down in more recent years.[50]

Fast forward to today. Over the course of the 2010s, thinking about China and Russia has changed considerably. These countries have increasingly come to be seen as strategic rivals and as top-tier concerns for military planners. In his first term, President Obama undertook a "rebalance" to the Asia-Pacific theater. Although that initiative was not focused primarily on warfighting strategy, it was nonetheless informed and influenced by China's general rise, as well as the more assertive behavior by the People's Republic of China in the East China Sea and

South China Sea. Obama's rebalance did have some military elements, such as an increase in the fraction of the US Navy devoted to the broader Pacific region (from the historic norm of 50 percent to about 60 percent).[51] Then, after Russia's aggressions against Ukraine beginning in 2014, the United States also became more vigilant about great-power threats to Europe. By the latter Obama years, the Pentagon was beginning what it called a "third offset" strategy. (The "first offset" was the potential use of US nuclear weapons to counter Soviet conventional forces early in the Cold War; a "second offset" employed US precision weapons and Air-Land Battle doctrine to check Soviet conventional threats to Europe later in the Cold War.)

The new strategy places greater emphasis on those areas of military capability and modernization relevant to possible conflict with Russia or China. Under the Trump administration, Secretary of Defense Jim Mattis's 2018 National Defense Strategy completed the shift, declaring that great-power competition and deterrence had become the primary concerns of the Department of Defense.[52] The chief of staff of the US Air Force, General David Goldfein, gave a crisp explanation in 2019 of how DoD had concluded it must size and shape its military capabilities: "Defend the homeland, [maintain a] safe, secure, effective nuclear deterrent, defeat a peer, deter a rogue, maintain campaign momentum [against ISIS]. You've got to be able to do those five things simultaneously. And so the Force we need is designed against those mission sets."[53] That is roughly where things stand today.

The Secretary, the Joint Chiefs, the Services, and the Commands

With nearly 3 million total employees, the US Department of Defense is one of the two largest organizations on earth, along with China's military. That tally of 3 million does not include the many hundreds of thousands of contractors— employees of large private firms that enter into contracts to provide goods or services to DoD. Yet today's DoD, big as it is, is now only about two-thirds its size from latter Cold War years, and less than half as big as it was in the Korea and Vietnam eras.[54]

Somewhat confusingly, in terms of lexicon, the Department of Defense includes three separate and individual military departments—the navy, air force, and army. The marine corps is a separate military *service*, but it is part of the Department of the Navy. The coast guard is a military service, too, as noted earlier; it is located within the Department of Homeland Security but reverts to DoD operational control in time of war. The space force will now become the sixth military service, within the Department of the Air Force (at least initially).

The Department of Defense has a host of additional and separate agencies within it too, such as the Defense Logistics Agency and Defense Intelligence Agency, as can be seen in more detail in the accompanying organizational chart in figure I.1, from 2008 (and thus missing the Space Force, Space Command, and Cyber Command).

The national defense budget includes virtually all of the funding for the US intelligence community as well. However, organizations like the CIA and the National Security Agency are run separately; they are not part of the Department of Defense.

Nuclear weapons production and stewardship responsibilities are also assigned to an organization outside DoD—in their case, to the National Nuclear Security Administration of the Department of Energy. The associated annual costs of more than $20 billion are therefore not part of the DoD budget. However, the Department of Energy nuclear costs are counted within the broader "national defense" budget function (or "050" account, to use the formal designation employed by the Office of Management and Budget), as explained in more detail in the next chapter.

The services are constitutionally and legally responsible for raising, training, and equipping the men and women of the US armed forces. Thus, they command the big budgets that together constitute the bulk of the overall Department of Defense budget, as discussed further in chapter 1. Together, as mentioned earlier, they currently employ about 1.35 million active-duty troops—the military's "active component" or AC. The armed forces also include 800,000 reservists spread

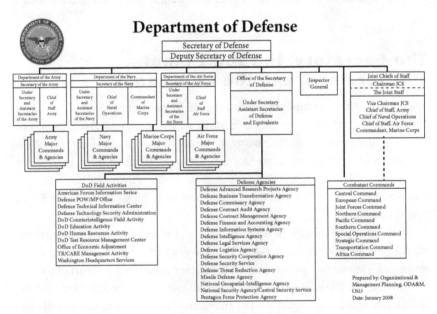

FIGURE I.1. Department of Defense organizational chart.

Source: *Organizational and Management Planning, ODA&M, OSD (Department of Defense, 2008), www.defenselink.mil.*

across six organizations. Each of the four major services has a reserve. The army and air force each also have national guard elements, under day-to-day control of the respective states where they are based. Each state's top national guard officers are chosen by the state's governor or legislature.[55]

The army is easily the largest service, with about 485,000 active-duty soldiers in 2020. It has about 525,000 soldiers in its reserve component—the Army National Guard and Army Reserve. Thus, counting everyone, there are more than 1 million soldiers in the US Army. At the other extreme, the marine corps is the smallest of the four main DoD services, with some 185,000 Marines and almost 40,000 reservists. The air force has about 334,000 active-duty uniformed personnel and almost 180,000 reservists (in the Air Force Reserve and Air National Guard, combined); a few thousand will now move to the space force. The navy has about 342,000 active-duty sailors and 60,000 reservists.[56]

The Department of Defense also has just over 750,000 full-time civilian government employees. In addition, as noted previously, there are the legions of contractors—individuals who are building weapons, maintaining equipment or bases, supporting deployed forces abroad—whose salaries are paid by private companies doing business with, and being paid by, DoD. This figure is in the range of 2 to 3 million, the exact count depending on how one codes individuals whose work is split between DoD business and other, nonmilitary contracts that their companies enter into.[57]

Like the organization he or she oversees, the position of secretary of defense dates back to 1947. That official has responsibilities to run DoD and to be a key member of the president's cabinet and National Security Council. The first secretary of defense was James Forrestal; James Mattis was the twenty-sixth, and, as of this writing, Mark Esper is the twenty-seventh.[58]

The secretary of defense also has a deputy, traditionally thought of as the "building manager." That is, while secretaries of defense focus on matters such as cabinet meetings, wartime strategy, international relationships, and Congress, the deputy traditionally stays closer to home in order to administer, manage, and supervise. David Packard fit this model in the early Nixon years, under Melvin Laird, for example—as did Donald Atwood under Dick Cheney in the first Bush administration; John White and John Hamre under Secretary Perry and Secretary Cohen in the Clinton administration; Bill Lynn under Bob Gates and Leon Panetta in the early Obama period; and Patrick Shanahan under Jim Mattis in the first two years of the Trump administration. Sometimes, the deputy takes a particular interest in technology and innovation, as with Robert Work in the latter years of the Obama administration. That said, there are exceptions to this informal distribution of labor. Paul Wolfowitz was probably more of a policy adviser to Donald Rumsfeld than a manager or administrator in the Bush administration. And Bill Perry, a long-standing champion of military innovation and technology advancement, was Les Aspin's deputy for a year in the Clinton administration but then ascended to a more strategic role as secretary of defense himself from 1994 through 1997.

There are also, at present, six under secretaries of defense who specialize in policy, in intelligence, in personnel and readiness, in research and engineering, in acquisition and sustainment, and in financial management. Each has a deputy. There are also thirteen assistant secretaries of defense, most working for one of these under secretaries. There are civilian secretaries as well for the army, air force, and navy—that is, for each of the military *departments*—and each one has one or more under secretaries or assistant secretaries, too.[59]

The position of chairman of the Joint Chiefs of Staff was also created in 1947. The chairman's job is to provide military advice to the president, as well as to the secretary of defense, the Homeland Security Council, and the National Security Council on three central matters: the use of force, the state of the military, and the modernization of the armed forces.[60] He or she may also advise the Congress. The first chairman was General of the Army (five-star) Omar Bradley; the nineteenth, marine corps general Joseph Dunford, served through the summer of 2019 before being replaced by the twentieth, army general Mark A. Milley. There is no formal "sharing" or rotation of the position across the four military services, but officers from each have served as chairman (and in the twenty-first century to date, the position has gone from army to air force to marine corps to navy to army to marine corps to army again).

The other members of the Joint Chiefs of Staff are the vice chairman, the chief of naval operations, the chief of staff of the army, the chief of staff of the air force, the commandant of the marine corps, and the chief of the National Guard Bureau.[61] They too may offer their military advice to the secretary of defense, president, National Security Council, Homeland Security Council, and the Congress. All of this is formalized and codified under Title 10 of the US legal code.

At the working level, a joint staff of some 2,500 individuals supports the chairman and vice chairman with analysis, information, and management. Responsibilities include global integration of military activities that may cross over boundaries of the various regional commands. This is an increasingly likely possibility in an era of great-power rivalry and competition, since Russia and China also operate globally and have important worldwide interests, assets, and vulnerabilities. The Joint Staff also helps the chairman and vice chairman establish priorities about the deployment of resources if there are competing demands on scarce assets from the various regional combatant commanders—as is often the case.[62]

Although their preference is generally to avoid it, sometimes there is dissent among the chiefs on key issues of national security, which can lead them to give conflicting advice to civilian leaders. Modern-day examples of contentious issues include the debate about surging combat forces in Iraq in 2007 (under President Bush), and then in Afghanistan in 2009 (under President Obama). Another prominent modern case occurred when the chief of staff of the army, General Eric Shinseki, told Congress prior to the Iraq War in early 2003 that several hundred thousand troops could be needed to stabilize Iraq after Saddam Hussein was overthrown. He wound up in a public disagreement with the civilian leadership of the Department of Defense as a result.[63] Sometimes the chiefs disagree with the secretary of defense or the president, as in the Shinseki case; sometimes they disagree with each other. In some cases, they resign or are relieved of command as a result of the disagreement. Contrary to popular lore, however, General Shinseki was not fired—his four-year term as chief ended soon enough after the public disagreements over Iraq that he simply retired a few months later, as previously scheduled.

Civil-military relations seem generally good and consistent with the US Constitution in today's America; most notably, there is clear acceptance among military leadership about the principle of civilian control of the military, and of the nation's foreign policy. That said, there are good reasons to stay vigilant. One challenge is that, given the relatively small size of today's military and its all-volunteer character, too few Americans may have the kind of knowledge of the military that provides appreciation for its inherent strengths as well as its limitations.[64]

Moreover, civil-military relations are destined to remain complex in many ways. It is implausible that military and political aspects of any crisis or war can be neatly separated into their own distinguishable compartments, with military officers providing advice on technical matters of warfare only after reaching consensus among themselves on those subjects.[65] In fact, as the great Prussian strategic thinker Carl von Clausewitz wrote some 200 years ago, war is best understood as a continuation of politics, not an entirely separate and purely technical undertaking. Even in conflicts where it might seem otherwise, such as World War II, in which the United States and its allies chose to pursue the unconditional surrender of enemies, highly complex and political issues were intertwined with technical matters of military planning and operations. Should the United States and allies demand that very unconditional surrender (which now seems so obvious, but was actually an enormously consequential decision)? Should they prioritize the Atlantic or the Pacific theater? Should the atomic bomb be dropped on Japan? The same is true of counterinsurgencies in places such as Vietnam, Iraq, and Afghanistan. One cannot reduce the missions to purely military tasks. Strategic and political decisions about how much of the nation's blood and treasure to invest in such missions must inform military decisions, and vice versa. Even on their own terms, the tasks associated with counterinsurgency and many other complex missions involve elements of economics, diplomacy, and politics.

There is also a robust debate on whether retired generals, admirals, and other military personnel should engage in partisan politics. Clearly, George Washington, Ulysses S. Grant, and Dwight Eisenhower did so—presumably to the nation's net benefit. So presumably there is *some* allowable and desirable role. There is no consensus, however, on what that role should be. There is probably some degree of agreement around the general notion that any role should be restrained in its rhetoric, polite in style, and substantive in content. Consider the 2016 presidential race as one recent example. Although I should note that I work for him, in my view retired general John Allen attempted to meet these standards in his July 2016 speech at the Democratic National Convention, in which he focused almost exclusively and positively on Hillary Clinton's character and abilities. By contrast, retired lieutenant general Michael Flynn, with his encouragement of "lock her up" chants at Trump campaign rallies, did not. But even Allen's approach was controversial in many quarters.[66] Joint Chiefs' Chairman General Mark Milley created controversy when, wearing combat fatigues, he accompanied President Trump on a walk near the White House that challenged demonstrators after the killing of George Floyd in the spring of 2020. But Milley later recanted and apologized, recognizing the sensitivity of the situation, as well as the importance of upholding his oath to the Constitution and its protections for free speech.

In any case, the United States has worked hard in the post-1947 era to make the process of active-duty military advice and dissent as systematic and disciplined as possible. There have been numerous reforms to the process of providing military advice, as well as to Pentagon organization and command authority, over the years.[67] Most notably, the landmark 1986 Goldwater-Nichols Department of Defense Reorganization Act strengthened the relative role of the chairman as the nation's key military adviser to the president, encouraging that person in that position to speak his or her own mind and not simply relay the least-common-denominator points of agreement among all the chiefs. Goldwater-Nichols also clarified that, for combat operations, the military chain of command did not in fact involve the service chiefs. Instead, orders go from the president to the secretary of defense, then through the chairman to the so-called combatant commanders at joint-service headquarters like Central Command or Indo-Pacific Command. This streamlining was partly a reaction to the tragic attempted Iran hostage rescue of 1980, together with the somewhat troubled invasion of Grenada in 1983 and the marine barracks bombing tragedy in Lebanon in 1983. Too many four-stars were involved in planning and oversight of such operations, increasing confusion and weakening accountability.[68] (It might be noted in passing that the existence of the Joint Chiefs as a body predates the creation of the position of chairman, the former being created in 1942 to improve coordination in World War II.)[69]

Service chief jobs are usually held for four years. The terms of service for the chairman and vice chairman are two years, typically renewed once, again making for a total of four years in the position. Legally, even though it has not happened, it is actually possible for a chairman to serve six years in that position—and even longer in principle during wartime, when the president can waive limitations.[70] And sometimes the chairman serves less than four years. The George W. Bush administration chose to seek a new chairman after just two years when it decided in 2007 that the incumbent, General Peter Pace, had not been sufficiently innovative in thinking about the Iraq War.[71] Sometimes, combatant commanders at places like Central Command are asked to step down after just two years instead of the more common three, for reasons that may or may not reflect any real disagreement with civilian authorities. Often, when this occurs, it is reported that they have been "fired." But, in reality, there is usually enough play in the expected time duration for many of these positions that such a stark term is often not appropriate.

The chairman, service chiefs, combatant commanders, and other higher-ranking military officers require Senate confirmation after being nominated by the president. For such high military ranks, the secretary of defense and the White House are highly involved in the nomination process. As an example, Secretary of Defense Jim Mattis reportedly recommended two possible successors to General Dunford as chairman, air force chief of staff General David Goldfein and army chief of staff General Mark Milley. President Trump interviewed both top candidates and chose General Milley as his nominee for the Senate to consider (he was of course later confirmed).[72] For lower ranks, the military services typically handle most of the promotion process themselves.

Many top leaders are based at the Pentagon, completed during World War II, and one of the world's largest office buildings—with 17.5 miles of corridors and three times the office floor space of the Empire State Building.[73] There are, however, six regional military "combatant" commands that are *not* located within the Pentagon, or anywhere close to Washington, D.C. They include the recently renamed Indo-Pacific Command, plus Central Command, European Command, Southern Command, Northern Command, and Africa Command (the last two both having been created during the Bush 43 presidency). Between the six, as seen in Figure I.2, virtually every inch of the planet's surface (and seas and skies) is under some degree of American military vigilance—if not necessarily for major combat operations in all cases, then for surveillance and monitoring, for search and rescue, and for protection of key assets based in or transiting a given region.[74]

Northern Command (NORTHCOM) covers Canada, Mexico, the Bahamas, and the United States. It would coordinate military responses, for example, in the event of a missile attack against the homeland or in support of civilian authorities

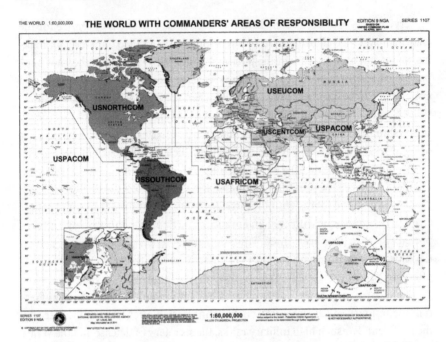

FIGURE I.2.   Map of combatant commands; USPACOM is now US Indo-Pacific Command.

Source: The National Geospatial-Intelligence Agency.

after a massive disaster or terrorist strike on US soil. Southern Command (SOUTHCOM) has responsibility for the Caribbean as well as Central and South America and surrounding waters.

European Command (EUCOM) covers much of the North Atlantic maritime region. On land, its purview ranges over the entire European continent, including NATO countries as well as neutral states; over Russia and other former Soviet republics in Europe; and to Georgia and Armenia and Azerbaijan in the east as well as Israel, Turkey, and Cyprus to the southeast. Africa Command (AFRICOM) covers the entire African continent except Egypt; the latter is within the area of responsibility of Central Command (CENTCOM), which extends eastward to cover the entire Arabian Peninsula (and surrounding waters), the Levant (except Israel), Iran, Afghanistan, Pakistan, and the five "stan" nations of the former Soviet Union.

The area of responsibility for Indo-Pacific Command reaches down to Australia, New Zealand, and Antarctica, over to Indonesia and India and points in between, and up through the South China Sea and Association of Southeast Asian Nations (ASEAN) regions to China, Mongolia, Japan, and the Koreas. There, the commander of combined US-ROK forces is an American four-star officer who is, despite his or her equal rank, subordinate to the four-star Indo-Pacific commander.

Of these combatant commands, only two are based abroad—EUCOM and AFRICOM, both in Stuttgart, Germany (to be a little closer to the African continent). Indo-Pacific Command is in Hawaii (though Combined Forces Command, which directs American and South Korean armed forces, is in the Republic of Korea). Northern Command is based in Colorado; CENTCOM and SOUTHCOM are in Florida. Traditionally, Indo-Pacific Command is led by a navy admiral, Korean Combined Forces Command (in South Korea) by an American army general, and AFRICOM (so far at least) by a marine or army officer. But, in general, these commands can have commanders from any service.[75] They all have staff from each of the military services, as well as from DoD's civilian and contractor ranks.

These commands run operations in their respective theaters, but they depend on the services and thus on Washington for the means to do so, since they have few if any dedicated forces "of their own." The military commands typically have headquarters staff numbering up to roughly 1,000 to 2,000 personnel each, including civilians and contractors.[76] By the standards of headquarters, these are large organizations. By comparison with the overall size of the Department of Defense, however, they are very small—typically, each constituting less than 0.1 percent of the total direct DoD payroll. They include subordinate component commanders for each of the services as well, at the three-star or four-star level. For example, there is an army command within Indo-Pacific Command, and so on for the other services. The combatant commanders, who have considerable authorities and resources at their disposal, are important elements of US foreign policy in their respective theaters.[77]

There are five additional unified commands that serve functional rather than regional purposes and complement the six geographic combatant commands. They are Strategic Command, Special Operations Command, Transportation Command, since 2018 Cyber Command, and since 2019 Space Command (which had previously existed from 1985 to 2002).[78] Their responsibilities are global. They are headquartered in Nebraska, Florida, Illinois, Maryland, and Colorado, respectively. The substantive responsibilities of each are addressed in various places throughout this book, in discussions of nuclear weapons issues, satellites, missiles and missile defense, and digital technologies.

As one illustration of how these functional commands work, and are structured, consider Special Operations Command (SOCOM). In terms of structure and composition, it has some 57,000 active-duty uniformed military within its broader purview, as well as reservists and civilians, making for a grand total of some 70,000 personnel. But while SOCOM may have its own (modest) budget and service-like responsibilities to train and equip its people, the uniformed personnel also belong to their parent services. Delta forces and Rangers are in the army; SEALS are in the navy. In addition, SOCOM contains important subordinate commands—for example, the storied Joint Special Operations Command (at Fort Bragg, North Carolina).[79]

Each of the regional and functional commands is run by a four-star officer—a general or admiral. The service chiefs and their vice chiefs are four-star officers as well; so, of course, are the chairman and vice chairman, as well as the head of the National Guard Bureau. A comparable number of additional four-stars run individual commands within the various services, such as Air Combat Command or Army Materiel Command. Altogether, to take a recent and typical snapshot, as of late 2018, there were 39 four-staff officers in the US armed forces (general or admiral), with 14 in the army, 8 in the navy, 5 in the marine corps, and 12 in the air force. There were also 149 three-star officers across the four DoD services, 292 two-star officers, and 440 one-stars, for a grand total of 920 "general and flag officers."[80]

Table I.2 shows some of the basic formations associated with the combat elements of the army, air force, and navy. (Marine corps ground formations are not unlike those of the army, though sometimes the nomenclature is different, as with greater use of the term "regiment" rather than "brigade.") Somewhat counterintuitively, however, the military services are *not* primarily made up of combat

TABLE I.2.   Standard US Military Combat Units

NAME	NUMBER OF PERSONNEL	NUMBER OF SHIPS OR AIRCRAFT	RANK OF LEADER
ARMY			
Squad	4–10 soldiers	Not applicable	Staff Sergeant
Platoon	16–40 soldiers, 3+ squads	n.a.	Lieutenant
Company	100–200, 3+ platoons	n.a.	Captain
Battalion	500–800, 3+ companies	n.a.	Lieutenant Colonel
Brigade	3,000–4,000, 3+ battalions	n.a.	Colonel, Brigadier General
Division	10,000–18,000, 3+ brigades	n.a.	Major General
Corps	50,000+, 2+ divisions	n.a.	Lieutenant General
AIR FORCE, NAVY, MARINE CORPS, ARMY AVIATION			
Flight	20–100	4–6	Captain
Squadron	100–300	7–16	Lieutenant Colonel, Major
Group	300–1,000	17–48	Colonel
Wing	1,000–5,000	48–100	Colonel, Brigadier General
Numbered Force		2+ wings	Major General, Lieutenant General
NAVY SHIPS			
Squadron		3–4 warships plus support	Rear Admiral (lower half)

Source: Judith Hicks Stiehm, *The U.S. Military: A Basic Introduction* (New York: Routledge, 2012), 35–37.

forces. That may come as a surprise. After all, is it not true, as the old saying goes, that "every marine is a rifleman?" At one level, it is indeed the case that all marines receive basic training in core infantry skills and marksmanship, and the marine corps culture continues to properly emphasize basic, traditional skills. Other services retain "warrior cultures" as well.[81] But, in a broader sense, the modern American armed forces do not, and could not, consist primarily of "trigger pullers," given the nature of modern military operations. In fact, most uniformed personnel provide support of one type or another—in transport, logistics, construction, equipment repair, medical care, communications, intelligence, and many other crucial activities that make the combat forces effective.

For those parts of the armed forces that are organized into combat forces or other large operational units, one can present them as what is often called an "order of battle"—a detailed force structure typically consisting of several categories of units within each service. Each unit is itself individually numbered and often named as well. At higher levels of organization, the marines keep it simple, with the 1st, 2nd, and 3rd Divisions. When combined with airpower and other elements, they become the 1st, 2nd, and 3rd Marine Expeditionary Forces. The army, mostly for reasons of history and tradition, is somewhat more complicated—with the 82nd Airborne Division and the 101st Air Assault Division, and the 25th Infantry Division, for example. But it also has the 1st Armored Division, as well as the 1st and 2nd and 3rd and 4th and 7th and 10th Infantry Divisions, so it too has endeavored to make its organizational structure somewhat more decipherable in recent times. There are also echelons of flexible size above the division—as with the 3rd Corps based in Texas or the 8th Army in Korea (the names often having as much historical significance as anything).

For the air force, the squadron is the most basic standard building block of force structure. Today's air force has some 312: 53 for airlift, 40 for tankers, 9 for bombers, 27 for combat search and rescue, 20 for special operations forces, 16 for space, 40 for command/control/communications/intelligence/surveillance/reconnaissance, 18 for cyber, 55 for fighters, 9 for missiles, and 25 for remotely piloted aircraft.[82] Larger elements of organization are referred to as wings or, simply, air forces. For example, the "7th Air Force" includes all American air force capabilities in Korea, notably the 8th and 51st Air Force fighter wings. (Somewhat confusingly, the air force has many constituent "air forces," many of them much smaller than the 7th—including the 1st, 3rd, 4th, 5th, 7th, 8th, 9th, 10th, 11th, 12th, 14th, 18th, 20th, 22nd, 24th, and 25th.)[83] The air force also organizes capabilities into multipurpose deployable structures known as air expeditionary wings—like the 455th Air Expeditionary Wing, for example.

In its turn, the US Navy has "fleets." The 2nd Fleet focuses on much of the Atlantic Ocean, the 3rd on much of the Pacific, the 5th on the Central Command theater, the 6th on Europe including the Mediterranean Sea, and the 7th on the western Pacific Ocean.[84]

Each of the services has its own major types of capabilities, organizations, cultures, and subcultures. For the army, the latter include armor, infantry, artillery, aviation, and special forces, on the combat side of things, as well as a slew of logistics, transport, engineering, medical, legal, finance, and other support specialties. Like the other services, it also has various types of internal organization that cut across the order of battle and combat force structure. These include Materiel Command, Training and Doctrine Command, Forces Command, and the newly created Futures Command, as well as subordinate elements for the various regional combatant commands, plus special operations and space and missile defense.[85] For the navy, chief subcultures include the submarine force, the carrier force with associated aircraft (as well as navy aircraft flying over water but off land bases), and surface combatants and their surface warfare officers. For the air force, specialties include bombers, fighters, transport, electronic warfare, and—formerly, until the creation of the space force—space operators.[86]

A brief word on the intelligence community: Even though most of it is outside the DoD organizational purview, virtually all of it is funded within the Department of Defense budget. In 2018, total funding for the intelligence community exceeded $80 billion. That includes resources for seventeen separate agencies, notably the CIA, the Defense Intelligence Agency, the National Geospatial-Intelligence Agency (NGA), the National Reconnaissance Office (NRO), and the National Security Agency (NSA). Each of the military services has its own intelligence organization, as do other federal departments (Treasury, Energy, Homeland Security, Justice with the FBI, State, and the Drug Enforcement Agency). Of that total funding, almost $60 billion in 2018 was for the "National Intelligence Program," and $22 billion was for the "Military Intelligence Program," the latter focused more narrowly on intelligence units supporting operational military commands.[87]

So much about the organizations and structures. What about the actual people? Who is in today's American armed forces, and what are their careers and their lives like?

The People and Personnel Policies of the Military

Who are the men and women (and families) who make up the US armed forces today? To begin, they are a small fraction of our nation's population—less than 1 percent, even if one includes active-duty personnel and reservists, plus full-time civilian employees of the Department of Defense. Only about 0.1 percent of the population joins the uniformed military in any given year (active and reserve combined). Extrapolated into the future, this means that considerably less than 10 percent of the population will likely ever serve. These facts are not bad in and of themselves. One would presumably not wish for a more dangerous international environment that in turn required a substantially larger and more expensive US military. But this set of circumstances has downsides. Relative to the Cold War years, fewer and fewer wear the uniform or work for the national security enterprise in some other capacity. Therefore, fewer and fewer Americans have a firsthand sense of what military service actually entails.

As for those who do serve, they are a remarkable bunch. Retired General David Petraeus describes them, in fact, as America's new "greatest generation"—in a riff on Tom Brokaw's apt description of the cohort of Americans who won World War II before going on to build the most powerful modern economy on earth.[88]

Military personnel are a well-educated group on the whole. More than 90 percent of all enlisted personnel in the military have a high school diploma; nearly 99 percent have either a high school diploma or an equivalency degree. About 95 percent of officers have at least a bachelor's degree.[89]

About 15 percent of US military personnel are commissioned officers. Just over 1 percent are "warrant officers," drawn from the enlisted ranks and typically having important technical skills and responsibilities. The remaining 84 percent are enlisted personnel.[90] Thus, some 200,000 individuals, out of today's active-duty force of just over 1.3 million uniformed personnel, are officers.

Officers can earn commissions through their respective service academies— as midshipmen at the US Naval Academy at Annapolis for sailors and marines, or as cadets at the US Military Academy at West Point for soldiers, or as cadets at the US Air Force Academy in Colorado Springs for airmen (generally the term used for both men and women within the air force). They can also enter the military through the Reserve Officers' Training Corps (ROTC) program at many other universities. Despite the name, many ROTC graduates go into the active-duty forces after graduation, not the Reserve or National Guard. Yet another path to commission is through officer candidate school.

Officers headed for senior leadership usually need to complete two years of midcareer education as well. This usually happens at one or more of the military's advanced educational facilities. These include the Marine Corps War College in Quantico, Virginia; the US Army Command and General Staff College at Fort Leavenworth, Kansas; the US Army War College in Carlisle, Pennsylvania; the Naval War College in Providence, Rhode Island; and the Air War College in Montgomery, Alabama.[91] (Under the terms of the 1986 Goldwater-Nichols Department of Defense Reorganization Act, officers also need a tour in some kind of joint-service position such as a combatant command headquarters to qualify for more senior promotions.)[92] A modest number go to other places, including think tanks and nonmilitary civilian universities.

The war colleges and other institutions that are part of the services' and DoD's broader educational and research ecosystem write official military doctrine too. These are essentially textbooks for military operations of various kinds, such as the well-known US Army and Marine Corps *Counterinsurgency Field Manual* first published in 2006 under then lieutenant general David Petraeus and then lieutenant general James Amos.[93] That latter manual, written by more than one service, is an example of what is considered joint doctrine. Other doctrine is written by individual services for their own needs and personnel.

There are ten levels of seniority for officers for each service, with minor exceptions (there have been no five-star officers, who are in effect at an eleventh level, since World War II, and the warrant officer career path has just five levels). For the army, marine corps, and air force, the progression for officers is as follows:

O-1: second lieutenant
O-2: first lieutenant
O-3: captain
O-4: major
O-5: lieutenant colonel
O-6: colonel
O-7: brigadier general (one star)
O-8: major general (two stars)
O-9: lieutenant general (three stars)
O-10: general (four stars)

For the navy and coast guard, the order is ensign, lieutenant junior grade, lieutenant, lieutenant commander, commander, captain, rear admiral lower half, rear admiral upper half, vice admiral, and admiral.[94]

There are typically twelve ranks for enlisted personnel. All the services have somewhat different nomenclature, but to use the army as an example, the promotion path goes as follows: private E-1, private E-2, private first class, corporal or specialist, sergeant, staff sergeant, sergeant first class, master sergeant, first sergeant, sergeant major, command sergeant major, and sergeant major of the army. Starting with corporal or specialist (that is, the fourth rank, or E-4), enlisted soldiers are also referred to as noncommissioned officers (NCOs)—what many consider the real backbone of the American military.[95]

Military personnel can choose from a multitude of Military Occupational Specialties. For example, in the army, combat specializations include infantry, field artillery, air defense, aviation, special forces, and armor. Counting active-duty forces, National Guard, and Army Reserve, these categories account for some

400,000 soldiers out of America's total of about 1 million.[96] But beyond those combat specialties, a soldier can also focus on fields such as engineering, communications, electronic warfare, psychological operations, transportation, chemicals (to be clear, however, the United States no longer has chemical weapons), intelligence, military policing, law, civil affairs, financial management, public affairs, medicine, dentistry, petroleum supply, logistics/quartermaster operations, and handling of dangerous materials like ammunition.[97]

Military personnel typically commit to tours of active duty lasting from three to four years in today's all-volunteer force. Many renew for one or more additional tours; the average duration of a military career is about six years. The system is still largely centered on the "up or out" concept of career advancement, and continuous service is still the norm (very rarely do people leave the military, then return later).[98]

In modern times, about 17 percent of military personnel (though about half of all officers) reached the twenty-year threshold at which they became eligible for a rather generous retirement package. Anything short of twenty years' service yielded no pension until recently, but that has changed under reforms made after the 2015 report of the Commission on Military Compensation and Retirement Modernization. The system is now somewhat less generous for a twenty-year retirement than previously (40 percent of peak pay, roughly speaking, rather than 50 percent as it used to be). But the system is now much more inclusive, offering some pension to all who complete their service honorably, even after just a few years in service.[99]

"Regular military compensation," defined as basic pay plus housing and food allowances plus tax benefits, is fairly robust in the United States today when evaluated against comparison groups in the civilian economy. This is true for officers and enlisted personnel, and for those with high school degrees, as well as for those with some college or bachelor's or advanced degrees. Specifically, if one compares cohort by cohort, enlisted personnel in the military earn more than 90 percent of all those in the civilian economy with comparable age, skills, and experience. Officers on average make more than 83 percent of cohorts in the nonmilitary economy. There are some exceptions for certain job categories, as with computer technicians and pilots. Overall, however, the all-volunteer force is compensated better than are most other workers in the US economy today (even before retirement and health care benefits, or Veterans Affairs benefits like those under the GI Bill, are included).[100] Military veterans tend to do comparably well compared with their cohorts in their postmilitary careers, in terms of employability and compensation—though that can vary from one type of military specialty to another, and also of course depending on the mental and physical well-being of the veteran.[101]

This is not to say that all is well with every element of compensation, however. For example, recent investigations and surveys have found that one-third of military families who live on base have significantly substandard housing.[102] Moreover, largely because of frequent moves, some 30 percent of military spouses who want to work report that they are unemployed, and of those who do work, more than half consider themselves underemployed. Finding good child care after frequent moves is difficult for military families, too.[103]

Today's military is much more integrated along gender lines than at any time in the past. Women are no longer excluded from certain types of combat missions; they are pilots, vehicle drivers, mechanics, and infantry officers too.[104] But while the US military has never had a higher fraction of women than it does today, women still constitute just 16 percent of the total force (with their representation lowest in the marine corps, at about 8 percent of the total, and highest in the air force, at about 19 percent).[105]

In terms of racial diversity, the armed forces are similar to the country as a whole. Some 43 percent of its recent male enlisted recruits are Hispanic or members of a racial minority, and 56 percent of its recent women recruits are Hispanic or members of a minority. Recruits come from all fifty states, as well as Puerto Rico and other territories and the District of Columbia, of course—and a small number even come from abroad, on pathways to eventual US citizenship. On a per capita basis, they are most likely to come from southeastern, mountain West, extreme northeastern, or extreme northwestern states. They come less often from the mid-Atlantic states, the Great Lakes region, and California.

A few more facts and figures: The median age of enlisted personnel is in the late twenties for all the services except the marines, for which it is the early twenties. The median age for officers is in the early thirties across all the services.[106] About half of all US military personnel are married, and 39 percent have children; single parents make up about 6 percent of the total armed forces. About 5 percent of military personnel are married to another member of the armed forces.[107]

In terms of their family income backgrounds, there is fairly equal representation across all five quintiles of US income distribution. But there is modest overrepresentation from the three middle classes or quintiles, and modest underrepresentation from the top and the bottom income brackets.[108]

In regard to politics, the military leans somewhat conservative, but there is considerable variance across its demographic distribution. Military women may lean Democratic, for example. And in regard to their views on policy, as scholars Peter Feaver and others have shown, those who have served are more reluctant about using US military power in the first place than is the general population—but they also favor fewer restrictions on *how* it is used once a conflict begins.[109]

Recruiting and retention have generally been fairly strong in modern decades in America's all-volunteer military. There are challenges facing the all-volunteer military, however, including a somewhat excessive dependence on recruits from military families, given the limited appeal of military service to the general population. This has resulted in occasional shortages of up to several thousand recruits in the modern era.[110] In fact, some 60 percent of army recruits now come from military families, according to Colonel Deydre Teyhen of the US Army's Walter Reed Army Institute of Research. And the number of military families as a percentage of the population is dwindling with time, as the nation moves further away from the Cold War period, when the armed forces were substantially larger (and the overall US population substantially smaller) than today. With only 15 percent of American youth now having parents who have served, this may become a problematic dependence on multigenerational military families.[111] In addition, as of 2018, the army recruited 50 percent of its enlisted soldiers from just 10 percent of the nation's high schools, suggesting too much of a geographic dependence on the areas mentioned earlier. Today's army leadership is trying to change this situation, but the effort will surely take time.[112]

The strains on US military forces from two decades at war are palpable. Divorce rates are roughly similar to those for comparable age cohorts in the general American population.[113] But tragically, after rising substantially in the early years of this century, suicide rates among active-duty forces and veterans are at least 20 percent greater than in the overall population.[114] Women in the military services also continue to suffer high rates of sexual assaults from their male counterparts.[115]

On balance, while America's impressive military personnel are outstanding, and while the state of the all-volunteer force is strong, there are also chinks in their collective armor, and much still to repair or improve.

Finally, it is worth emphasizing that Americans hold the military in very high regard. More than 70 percent of respondents consistently say they have a great deal or quite a lot of confidence in the US armed forces, another 20 percent or so express "some" confidence in the military, and only about 5 percent say they have "little" regard for the institution.[116]

Domestic Bases and Places

Moving from people to property, any survey of the US military should take stock of the vast empire of land under the auspices of the American armed forces. All of this real estate not only is important in mechanical, budgetary, and tactical military terms but also undergirds America's overall concept of overseas engagement, forward presence, alliance solidarity, and deterrence that has been at the heart of US national security and grand strategy since World War II.[117]

The Department of Defense is a very big property owner. Its bases cover 27 million acres worldwide, with the vast preponderance in the United States, of course, with a total value of property and structures of nearly $1.2 trillion. The 2018 DoD Base Structure Report lists a total of 4,775 DoD sites, not even including properties worth less than $10 million or smaller than 10 acres. Of those nearly 5,000 substantial locations worldwide, 4,150 are in American states, 111 are in American territories, and 514 are overseas. Of the grand total, 148 are considered "large sites," with value exceeding $2 billion, and 112 are of medium size, with value between roughly $1.1 billion and $2 billion.[118] The others are "small," but that is a relative term.

Breaking down the numbers further, by military service, of the 4,775 sites, a total of 1,807 are army installations, 970 are navy properties, 1,710 are air force locations, 213 are marine corps sites, and 75 are joint or headquarters-related.

Table I.3 lays out the economic effects of the domestic US military presence, combined with the economic effects of defense industry. Generally speaking, most of the large defense-spending states tend to be located near seacoasts. But there are exceptions, and not every littoral state has a large defense spending footprint.

As noted earlier, the US military used to have a huge role in the American economy. It skyrocketed to 35 percent of GDP during World War II; in the Cold War,

TABLE I.3.   Top States for Defense Spending (2018)

STATE	AMOUNT (BILLIONS)	PERCENTAGE OF STATE GDP
California	$57.7	1.9
Virginia	$56.2	10.3
Texas	$50.8	2.8
Maryland	$25.2	6.0
Florida	$24.1	2.3
Washington	$16.2	2.8
Pennsylvania	$16.1	2.0
Connecticut	$15.9	5.7
Alabama	$15.4	6.9
Arizona	$15.2	4.3

Note: The top ten states ranked by defense spending as a percentage of their respective gross state products are Virginia (10.3%), Hawaii (7.7%), Mississippi (7.2%), Alabama (6.9%), Alaska (6.4%), Maryland (6.0%), Connecticut (5.7%), the District of Columbia (5.2%), Kentucky (5.2%), and Missouri (4.7%).

Source: Department of Defense, "Defense Spending by State—Fiscal Year 2018" (Washington, D.C.: Office of Economic Adjustment, 2020), pp. 3, 8, https://www.oea.gov/sites/default/files/defense-spending-rpts/FY2018-Defense-Spending-by-State-Report_0_0.pdf

it still constituted roughly 5 to 10 percent of GDP for four decades. In many parts of the country, and in many technology sectors, defense spending did much to provide jobs and spur innovation. The United States, with its strong commitment to the free market, has never had a formal industrial policy. But during World War II and the Cold War, areas of economic activity that were related to the priorities of the US armed forces were given huge boosts by the federal government, whether that was the intended effect or not.

All of this is less so today. Currently, defense spending represents just over 3 percent of GDP, and about 15 to 16 percent of federal spending—substantial figures, but not nearly as dominant as previously. As discussed earlier, the US national defense enterprise accounts for at least 5 million jobs—almost 3 million in direct DoD employment (more than 1.3 million active-duty troops, some 750,000 full-time civilians, 800,000 members of the six reserve organizations), and as noted earlier, 2 to 3 million more in the private sector, plus tens of thousands in the Department of Energy's nuclear weapons work.[119]

The concentration of US military spending within the fifty states does not follow a simple "red state/blue state" pattern, or an east-west breakdown either. If there is one overall theme, it may be that northern states tend to have less military spending relative to their economies, on average. But that is just an overall tendency, not a firm rule. Indeed, Washington State, Alaska, and most of New England have substantial concentrations of defense-related activity. By contrast, a number of southern states have modest to low military spending relative to the size of the state economy.

More specifically, the top ten states with the most DoD spending in 2017 included the following in this order: California, Virginia, Texas, Maryland, Florida, Washington State, Connecticut, Georgia, Pennsylvania, and Alabama. For defense spending as a fraction of state GDP, the order goes like this: Virginia, Hawaii, Connecticut, Alaska, Maryland, Alabama, District of Columbia, Mississippi, Maine, and Kentucky. The greatest concentrations of military personnel are based along the Eastern Seaboard of the United States (from New York southward); in Ohio, Texas, and Colorado in the nation's center; and in California, Washington, and Hawaii in the Pacific region.[120] America's base structure has not been changing much in recent years, and so these numbers and ranks remain very similar today.

When sizing up the impact of a defense presence on a nearby community, there is also a defense spending multiplier effect to bear in mind. For every civilian or military job that might be created (or lost) in a given area through a change in military spending of some type, one would expect an additional gain or loss of about half a job in the surrounding community.[121]

Additional spending related to national security, but *not* found within the defense budget and *not* included in the figures provided here, comes from the more than $200 billion a year the nation spends on its veterans and their families through the Department of Veterans Affairs. Much of this is for health care for those who are hurt or disabled. Much is for compensation for disabilities, or survivor benefits. Other spending is for former military families with programs such as the GI Bill for college education.

Overall, the Department of Defense is estimated to have about 20 percent more domestic base capacity than its current force structure requires. Such math seems roughly correct for the simple reason that the Cold War force was reduced by some 40 percent over the last thirty years, yet the base infrastructure over that period was reduced only around 25 percent. The army and air force have the most estimated excess capacity today—each more than 30 percent. The reductions to base infrastructure over the last three decades have happened through the base realignment and closure (BRAC) process, with five separate rounds in the years 1988, 1991, 1993, 1995, and 2005. This process was an innovative concept for circumventing parochial pressures in the Congress that often made it hard to close or restructure bases, as individual members of Congress and senators would generally oppose such changes within their own districts and states. With the BRAC process, by contrast, Congress ultimately votes up or down on an entire list of proposed changes to DoD's base infrastructure that is developed by an independent panel of experts. Unfortunately, after four impressive rounds in 1988 through 1995, the 2005 process proved less effective at saving money in a timely way (savings from BRACs always take a few years to be realized, due to factors such as construction and cleanup costs associated with changes and closures in base infrastructure, but the 2005 round was much worse in this regard). For that and other reasons, the process has bogged down since that time; Congress has not agreed to any additional BRAC rounds of late, even though the Pentagon has frequently requested them.[122]

The US Military's Global Reach

Many believe that what separates the US armed forces from all others is technology—space assets, advanced fighters, stealth bombers, quiet submarines, precision munitions, unmanned aircraft, a large nuclear arsenal, missile defenses, and the like. All that is significant, to be sure. So are America's warriors. But arguably just as important is the US military's ability to deploy, operate, and sustain itself abroad. With the partial and very limited exceptions of Britain, France, Russia, and increasingly China, no other country in the world can conduct major operations anywhere except on or near home territory. This capacity for overseas operations is a function of foreign bases combined with strategic transport and mobile logistics capabilities.

Of course, and not coincidentally, no other great power is so far removed from major possible threats to its own territory. The United States lives in a hemisphere that, while hardly safe for individuals, given typical crime rates, is generally free of international conflict. Certainly, the United States, as far and away the Western Hemisphere's greatest military power, is effectively impervious to traditional attack by any of its neighbors. Thus, it can pursue a more overseas-oriented kind of preventative grand strategy, buttressed by a forward-defense policy, that most other countries have neither the luxury nor the desire to undertake.

Of the 514 US military bases that are located abroad, the service-by-service breakdown goes like this: 202 are army posts, 123 are navy bases, 166 are air force facilities, and 23 are marine corps properties. Across the 514 bases, 24 are considered "large sites," and 21 are "medium" in size.[123]

The key unified military command for addressing military transportation and logistics is US Transportation Command, headquartered at Scott Air Force Base in Illinois. As noted previously, it is one of eleven unified commands in the US military, and perhaps the most unsung and underappreciated. It prioritizes and coordinates the global use of American strategic lift assets that move US military forces around the world and keep them supplied and supported wherever they operate. Sometimes, it also helps move and support allied forces, or provides assistance for various types of humanitarian relief missions—especially when rapid action is required, as well as when circumstances are dangerous or austere.

As shown in table I.4, the United States has military personnel abroad in many dozens of countries and at hundreds of locations. However, there is a clear pecking order. In three countries the size and capacity of US bases rise clearly head and shoulders above all others—Germany, Japan, and South Korea, each of which hosts tens of thousands of GIs (a nickname that originated in World War II with all the "government issued" labels that accompanied American troops around the world). Then, there are several countries where the US presence is in the broad range of 10,000 to 15,000 uniformed personnel, most notably Italy and the United Kingdom in Europe, and Qatar in the broader Middle East/Central Command theater. The Afghanistan figure is declining (and the totals in Germany may do so soon as well).

There are another eight countries where the US military presence exceeds 1,000 troops at present.[124] The list includes Iraq; it also includes Bahrain, Kuwait, and Djibouti in the broader Middle East/Horn of Africa region. There are another three countries in Europe with at least 1,000 GIs: Belgium, Spain, and Turkey. About 5,000 U.S. troops are also on rotational deployment in Poland.

TABLE I.4. US Troops abroad by Country (as of late 2019)

COUNTRY OR REGION	NUMBER OF TROOPS
EUROPE	
Belgium	1,046
Germany	35,275
Italy	12,902
Spain	3,658
Turkey	2,500
United Kingdom	9,254
EAST ASIA AND PACIFIC	
Japan	55,245
Korea	26,525
NORTH AFRICA, NEAR EAST,	
Bahrain	7,000
UAE	5,000
Jordan	3,000
Qatar	13,000
Saudi Arabia	3,000
SUB-SAHARAN AFRICA	
Djibouti	88
WESTERN HEMISPHERE	
Cuba (Guantanamo)	776
CONTINGENCY OPERATIONS SUPPORT	
Afghanistan	14,000 (and declining)
Kuwait	13,000
Iraq	5,200
Syria	800

Sources: Miriam Berger, "Where U.S. Troops Are in the Middle East and Afghanistan, Visualized," *Washington Post*, January 4, 2020, https://www.washingtonpost.com/world/where-us-troops-are-in-the-middle-east-and -could-now-be-a-target-visualized/2020/01/04/1a6233ee-2f3c-11ea-9b60-817cc18cf173_story.html?arc404 =true; "DoD Personnel, Workforce Reports and Publications" (Washington, D.C.: Department of Defense, September 2019), www.https://www.dmdc.osd.mil/appj/dwp/dwp_reports.jsp; Thomas Gibbons-Neff and Mujib Mashal, "U.S. Is Quietly Reducing Its Troop Force in Afghanistan," *New York Times*, October 21, 2019, https://www.nytimes.com/2019/10/21/world/asia/afghanistan-troop-reduction.html?module=inline; Dan De Luce, Courtney Kube, and Mosheh Gains, "Trump Admin Sending Thousands More Troops to Saudi Arabia," NBC News, October 11, 2019, https://www.nbcnews.com/news/mideast/trump-admin-sending-thousands-more -troops-saudi-arabia-n1065051; "U.S. Will Keep 500 or 600 Troops in Syria to Counter ISIS," *The Guardian*, November 10, 2019, https://www.theguardian.com/world/2019/nov/10/us-troops-syria-isis-turkey-erdogan -white-house; Corey Dickstein, "Pentagon Deploys Raptors to Qatar amid Iran Tensions," *Stars and Stripes*, June 29, 2019, https://www.stripes.com/news/middle-east/pentagon-deploys-raptors-to-qatar-amid-iran -tensions-1.588073.

These major basing countries for US troops play different kinds of roles. Japan is a regional and global hub, also hosting major combat forces from all services except the army. US armed forces in Korea are dominated by army and air force capabilities, focused specifically on the defense of the peninsula. Diego Garcia in the Indian Ocean, a British territory, is a crucial hub, particularly for getting to and from the broader Middle East. Bahrain hosts the navy's Fifth Fleet; Qatar hosts the Middle East region's major US Air Force base known as al-Udeid; Kuwait provides logistics capabilities, many of them army-focused, for US forces in Iraq. Facilities in Djibouti provide a mix of capabilities across the services. Spain and Italy host US naval capabilities; Italy also has air force and army personnel in considerable numbers. Turkey's Incirlik base is an important US Air Force facility. US bases in Britain are principally air force installations; Germany hosts large contingents of both army soldiers and air force personnel.[125]

All told, the United States typically has about a quarter million uniformed personnel abroad or in forward overseas waters at any given time. They are found in roughly equal aggregate numbers in three main regions—Europe (mostly Western Europe); Northeast Asia together with the Western Pacific; and the broader Middle East, including South Asia, the Persian Gulf, and nearby waters. US forces are sometimes located on facilities shared with the host government, but often on bases that the United States effectively controls itself.

Table I.5 shows the several dozen major US military facilities abroad that rank as medium or large sites according to official Department of Defense metrics.

Even with all its overseas bases and deployed forces, however, most US forces will not be in the right place at the right time when a crisis erupts. It is not possible that they could be. Even though American military deployments and bases abroad dwarf those of any other country, they still constitute only a bit more than 10 percent of total US military power. In a major crisis or conflict, reinforcements will generally need to be sent from the United States. Thus, it is important to see how the US base network combines with the transport and logistics assets of the American armed forces to create a capacity for global power projection.

How does one move the equivalent of a midsize city halfway across the world, quickly yet safely, and then supply and sustain it? That is effectively what the United States does when it goes to war—since Korea, Vietnam, Iraq, and Afghanistan each involved from 100,000 to 500,000 or more personnel at their peak levels of intensity. (In World War II, the scale of the effort was even greater—more like moving and then supplying a small state's worth of Americans.)[126] In Operation Desert Storm in 1991, for example, the United States moved half a million people, more than 100,000 vehicles, and about 10 million tons of supplies in the war to liberate Kuwait (more than 6 million tons were petroleum products). The numbers would have been even larger absent Saudi host nation support—each

TABLE I.5. Major US Bases Abroad

COUNTRY	NAME OF BASE	US MILITARY SERVICE
Diego Garcia (United Kingdom)	Naval Support Facility	Navy
Djibouti	Camp Lemonier	Navy
Germany	East Camp Grafenwoehr	Army
Germany	Hohenfels Training Area	Army
Germany	Ramstein Air Base	Air force
Germany	Smith Barracks	Army
Germany	South Camp Vilseck	Army
Germany	Spangdahlem Air Base	Air force
Germany	Wiesbaden Army Airfield	Army
Greenland	Thule Air Base	Air force
Cuba	Guantanamo Bay Station	Navy
Italy	Aviano Air Base	Air force
Japan	Akasaki Depot	Navy
Japan	Camp Courtney	Marine corps
Japan	Camp Foster	Marine corps
Japan	Camp Foster Housing	Air force
Japan	Camp Hansen	Marine corps
Japan	Camp Kinser	Marine corps
Japan	Camp Schwab	Marine corps
Japan	Camp Zama	Army
Japan	Sasebo Navy Base	Navy
Japan	Yokosuka Navy Base	Navy
Japan	Ikego Housing Area	Navy
Japan	Iorizaki Depot	Navy
Japan	Kadena Air Base	Air force
Japan	Kadena Ammunition Annex	Air force
Japan	Futenma Air Station	Marine corps
Japan	Iwakuni Air Station	Marine corps
Japan	Misawa Air Base	Air force
Japan	Atsugi Naval Air Facility	Navy
Japan	Sagami Depot	Army
Japan	Yokose Depot	Navy
Japan	Yokota Air Base	Air force
Kuwait	Camp Arifjan	Army
Portugal	Lajes Field	Air force
South Korea	Camp Carroll	Army
South Korea	Camp Casey	Army
South Korea	Camp Humphreys	Army
South Korea	Kunsan Air Base	Air force
South Korea	Osan Air Force Base	Air force
South Korea	Yongsan Garrison	Army
Spain	Rota Naval Station	Navy
Turkey	Incirlik Air Base	Air force
United Kingdom	Lakenheath Air Field	Air force
United Kingdom	Mildenhall Air Field	Air force

day, the Saudis provided a quarter million meals and 2 million gallons of potable water.[127] Regional partners also provided up to 15 million gallons of fuel per day for the air force alone (about 50,000 tons).[128] Table I.6 provides some key facts and figures of relevance.

Supplies also need to be moved about within a combat theater after they have arrived on intercontinental or strategic transport. This theater-level transport typically employs assets like C-130 transport aircraft, large helicopters, and trucks.

As noted, most brigades require several hundred tons of supplies a day, and trucks typically have payloads of five to ten tons. Thus, roughly 100 trucks per day are needed to supply a given brigade in combat, especially once the brigade's typical support units are also accounted for. A large military operation involving twenty brigades, plus associated support elements, would therefore require 1,000 to 4,000 truckloads of logistics support a day in round numbers, depending on the amount of combat and the amount of movement the typical unit is conducting. If these supplies need to move on roads, given the topography in question, bottlenecks can develop. A single major artery might be able to handle 2,000 truckloads of supplies a day, but only if it is possible to send out a fresh armed convoy including twenty supply trucks every fifteen minutes and maintain that pace continuously. The United States has enough trucks to maintain such a pace

TABLE I.6. Weights and Logistical Needs of Key Military Units[1]

WEIGHTS OF UNITS

- 17,000 tons for the vehicles and other equipment of a light division (11,000 troops)
- 27,000 tons for the 82nd Airborne Division (just over 13,000 people)
- 36,000 tons for the 101st Air Assault Division (nearly 16,000 soldiers)
- 110,000 tons for an armored or mechanized division (18,000 soldiers)
- 99,000 tons for an army corps structure, for the command and coordination and general support of several divisions in the field (22,000 troops)

SUPPLY REQUIREMENTS

- 600 tons of supplies per day for a heavy army brigade of 3,100 soldiers in combat (roughly 300 tons of fuel, 130 tons of water, 85 tons of dry stores, and 60 tons of ammunition)
- 300 tons per day for an airborne brigade of about 3,400 soldiers in combat (roughly 85 tons of fuel, 50 tons of dry stores, 145 tons of water, 10 tons of ammunition)
- 400 tons per day for a Stryker medium-weight brigade of about 3,900 soldiers (110 tons of fuel, 170 tons of water, 70 tons of dry stores, 40 tons of ammunition)[2]

1 Rachel Schmidt, *Moving U.S. Forces: Options for Strategic Mobility* (Washington, D.C.: Congressional Budget Office, 1997), 80.

2 Robert W. Button, John Gordon IV, Jessie Riposo, Irv Blickstein, and Peter A. Wilson, *Warfighting and Logistic Support of Joint Forces from the Joint Sea Base* (Santa Monica, Calif.: RAND, 2007), 77–85. The main equipment in a heavy brigade includes 58 M1A2 tanks, 109 Bradley Fighting Vehicles, 43 armored personnel carriers, 45 HMMWVs, 23 recovery vehicles, 451 utility trucks, and 218 cargo trucks. The main equipment in an infantry brigade includes 75 HMMWVs, 16 heavy trucks, 25 medium tactical vehicles, 13 light tactical vehicles, and 263 utility trucks. The main equipment in a Stryker brigade includes 302 Stryker vehicles, 381 utility trucks, and 158 cargo trucks.

in its inventories.[129] Still, this scale of resupply is generally feasible only if vehicles are in very good shape (since frequent breakdowns will interfere with movement), if roads do not need to be shared with heavy civilian traffic, if key infrastructure like bridge networks is robust (and defensible), if weather is not a major factor, and if engineering and maintenance crews and equipment can keep the roads in acceptable driving condition.

For movement of air force units, most of the combat platforms themselves are inherently self-deploying. They generally require refueling, however, in the air, on land bases, or both. Fuel, munitions, and base support assets—fuel distribution systems, aircraft maintenance equipment, runway repair equipment, radars, missile defenses, and command and control systems—do need to be moved and can be quite heavy. Spare parts impose additional demands. Supply requirements for a combat wing of seventy-two fighter aircraft (which might involve about 1,500 to 2,000 people) are roughly as follows:[130]

- 1,000 to 2,000 tons of ground-support equipment
- 100 to 200 tons per day of ammunition expenditure
- 500,000 to 1 million gallons of fuel, or up to 3,500 tons, a day

What is needed to move all these people and their supplies? There are three main elements of the "strategic transport triad"—airlift, sealift, and prepositioning. Prepositioned supplies, which can be on ships or on land, can then be married up with troops flying from the United States or elsewhere to form operational units.

Airlift can be subdivided into several categories. One type is dedicated military lift, generally used for cargo, especially higher-value equipment such as advanced munitions, radars, command and control equipment, and helicopters. Another is a fleet of commercial planes that the government can access, by prior agreement with the airlines, in times of crisis or war, largely to move people or lighter supplies and equipment. Other aircraft play the role of aerial tankers to provide fuel to aircraft in flight and en route; some of these tanker aircraft can instead carry supplies if necessary. There are also large fleets of small passenger jets owned by the armed forces. Some of these exist for the necessary purpose of moving senior commanders quickly, and keeping them plugged in to chains of command, in times of war. Others are perhaps less essential than that, and more about stateside convenience, in peacetime as well as wartime.

Sealift can be subdivided into two main categories: ships for moving equipment and ships for moving petroleum. The former type of sealift can be further broken down into two broad categories. The first is ferry ships that are easy to load and often called "roll-on/roll-off ships," as well as marine corps amphibious ships. The second is made up of normal vessels that require cranes for loading and unloading in port (some of these are owned by the military; others are privately owned and rented when needed).

Prepositioning is concentrated in the Western Pacific, the Indian Ocean, the broader Persian Gulf region, and Europe. The stocks include vehicles and weaponry, such that a whole combat unit can be formed out of them—typically a brigade-sized force for the army or marine corps. They also contain supplies like munitions, fuel, and base support equipment to sustain units in combat, including airpower as well, in the early days or weeks of a possible campaign. For example, the marines have two such brigade stocks, each with seven ships to store the necessary equipment, including thirty days of combat supplies. One is at Guam/Saipan, and the other at Diego Garcia; the marines also have equipment ashore in Norway. The army has prepositioned weaponry and supplies in the Western Pacific, at Diego Garcia, in Kuwait and Qatar, and in Italy.[131] The air force itself has forward-based stockpiles of key weaponry and other equipment such as advanced munitions.

These assets were built up throughout the Cold War and, importantly, in the early post–Cold War decades. In the modern era of great-power competition, however, they may need to be changed. In particular, the services may seek to rely less on such large ships and large fixed warehouses on land, given their likely vulnerability to anti-ship missiles and other precision-strike capabilities.[132]

The key factors for understanding the respective transport capacities of planes and ships are their speeds, their payloads, their dependability/availability, and their time needed for loading as well as unloading. For all major US planes, average speeds are about 500 miles per hour, and average loading and unloading times are about three to four hours at each end of operations (with the C-17 slightly faster than others). Average payloads and average aircraft utilization rates per day were estimated by the Congressional Budget Office several years ago as follows:[133]

- 61 tons and 8.1 hours for the C-5
- 45 tons and 12.5 hours for the C-17
- 33 tons and 8.6 hours for the KC-10

For shorter-range transports such as the V-22 Osprey tilt-rotor aircraft and CH-53 helicopter, typical payloads are about ten tons.[134] The payload of the C-130 propeller aircraft, the workhorse of intratheater airlift for the US military, is about fifteen tons, and its range typically varies from 1,000 to 2,000 miles at normal payload depending on the version of the aircraft. But aircraft range depends on how much cargo is carried because the latter limits fuel loadings. As one example, the C-130H variant of that plane flies 300 knots per hour and consumes 5,000 pounds of fuel per hour. Thus, if the cargo payload were to weigh 25,000 pounds, 45,000 pounds of fuel could be carried, allowing about nine hours of flight or about 2,700 nautical miles of range. If the payload were reduced by 10,000 pounds, to 15,000 pounds total, then 10,000 more pounds of fuel could be loaded aboard—translating into two more hours and 600 more nautical miles of flight.[135]

Roll-on/roll-off ships can typically be loaded in three to four days and unloaded in two to three. Their speeds vary from 25 to 30 miles per hour for the SL-7 and large medium-speed roll-on/roll-off (LMSR) ships to 15 to 18 miles per hour for many ships in reserve. Most roll-on/roll-off ships have average payloads of about 15,000 to 20,000 tons. However, their capacity is often constrained more by square footage; SL-7 ships have about 150,000 square feet of space, LMSRs about 250,000. Ships requiring cranes to move equipment on and off (including container ships) can take four to ten days for loading and a comparable amount of time for offloading. Their payloads vary greatly.[136]

Putting all these numbers together, it typically takes two to six large roll-on/roll-off ships to move an entire division, depending on the division's size and weight. Alternatively, if it is to be flown (virtually never the approach taken for a whole division), the total number of flights required would notionally be 1,000 to 3,000, or more.[137]

The United States has roughly 330 large airplanes for carrying troops and equipment (and another couple hundred available via the civil reserve air fleet program). It also has about thirty large roll-on/roll-off ships, each capable of carrying 15,000 to 20,000 tons of equipment (equipment and initial supplies for a heavy division weigh about 100,000 tons), as well as various other sealift ships. Altogether, its transportation assets create a theoretical capacity for a sustained average movement of about 30,000 tons of military equipment a day to a typical overseas destination.[138]

However, logistics are rarely smooth, which is why the adage about how generals dwell on it is so telling and correct. Bottlenecks often develop at ports and airfields, particularly abroad. Many airfields have very limited space for loading and unloading aircraft, for example—their "MOG" numbers, for maximum aircraft on the ground, are often just a few at a time. Many have limited refueling capacity as well. Even at a reasonably large, modern airfield, it is generally difficult to deploy and unload much more than 1,000 tons of equipment and supplies a day.[139] For example, in Operation Desert Storm, with several pristine and uncontested Saudi airfields available to it, the United States peaked at an airlift delivery rate of 3,600 tons per day in January 1991.[140] Because Saudi Arabia is about 8,000 miles away from the typical American base, that represented a pace of just under 30 million ton-miles per day (often abbreviated MTM/D), only half the theoretical potential of the US air fleet of the day. And that was for an uncontested effort benefiting from some of the finest facilities in the world. In practice, therefore, the United States could need a few weeks to deploy a division-sized force and a few months to deploy a large force to most parts of the world, even if theoretical rates might be two to three times as fast.[141]

Conclusion: The American Military Juggernaut

The US military establishment is enormous. There is no other way to describe it. It also spans widely across America, with tentacles reaching out to East Asia, the Middle East, Europe, and the world at large. It reflects the diversity of America in its personnel, even if only a modest fraction of the population displays much proclivity to serve. It certainly exemplifies the very best of its people and their qualities, as well. It is organizationally complex. It is wasteful in some ways, yet remarkably efficient and well-honed in others. Its budget is very large by most absolute measures, yet also modest relative to GDP, as discussed more in chapter 1.

With all these facts, figures, and statistics in hand, the rest of the book now turns primarily to understanding the nature of today's American armed forces and of modern military operations. The general goal is to develop analytical methods that are powerful and accurate enough to provide meaningful insight into key issues and policy choices yet simple enough to be widely accessible and easily usable. Chapter 1 focuses on budgetary and economic matters and methods, with a primary focus on the United States. Chapter 2 discusses how to model and analyze combat, and also how to estimate the necessary sizes of forces for various types of operations. Chapters 3 and 4 consider the science and technology of modern warfare.

DEFENSE BUDGETING AND RESOURCE ALLOCATION

Does the United States spend too much, or perhaps too little, on defense? Where and how does it spend that money—and to achieve what missions, in the context of existing US grand strategy and national security policy? Regardless of whether the overall budget is excessive, or adequate, how can proposals for new types of military capabilities be properly evaluated, weapon by weapon and unit by unit? Only by understanding the components of the defense budget can these kinds of questions be seriously addressed.

This chapter attempts to place the US defense budget in broad international and historical perspective, and then to break it down into useful, analytically meaningful components that can help answer such questions. While its clear focus is on the US defense budget, some of the methods and tools are relevant to other modern Western armed forces—in particular, those with similar cost structures, personnel systems, and military technologies.

Here is another way to think of the purpose of this chapter. Imagine that one is helping a presidential candidate with a different view of the world, and different set of American national security priorities than the incumbent administration, develop an alternative defense plan and budget. Perhaps that candidate believes the United States should no longer assume security responsibilities in the broader Middle East, or Korea, or even NATO—whether due to belief in a fundamentally different vision for US grand strategy like "offshore balancing," or a more narrow challenge to existing strategy focused on certain specific interests and allies. How does one link strategy and policy to forces and budgets? What are the consequences of the former for the latter?

Answers to these questions are frequently oversimplified in the American political debate, often by those with a predetermined agenda of making the defense budget seem either high or low. For example, many who wish to defend the magnitude of Pentagon spending often point out that in recent decades its share of the nation's economic output has been modest by historical standards. During the 1950s, national defense spending was typically about 10 percent of gross domestic product (GDP). In the 1960s, it averaged 8 to 9 percent of GDP, again including war costs and nuclear weapons costs. In the 1970s, it began at around 8 percent and wound up at just under 5 percent of GDP. During the Reagan buildup of the 1980s, it reached 6 percent of GDP before declining somewhat as the Cold War ended. In the 1990s, it then went down further, to about 3 percent of GDP. During the first Bush term, the figure reached 4 percent by 2005 and grew to 4.5 percent by 2009, due largely to the wars in Iraq and Afghanistan. National defense spending gradually declined over most of the Obama presidency. It has ticked upward slightly in the early Trump years, and again exceeded 3 percent of GDP—though budget projections as of early 2020 would see it drop below 3 percent in the coming years. As is standard when talking about the national defense budget, these figures include costs for the wars, costs incurred by military reservists as well as active-duty troops, and the Department of Energy's expenses for nuclear weapons activities. They do not include the spending of the Department of Veterans Affairs of more than $200 billion. Seen in this overall light, current levels seem moderate.[1]

By contrast, those who criticize the size of the Pentagon budget often note that it constitutes more than one-third of all global military spending, and three times that of the number two global military power, China. Or they note that estimated 2020 national defense spending will exceed the Cold War inflation-adjusted average of around $525 billion by roughly $200 billion (expressed in 2020 dollars, as are all costs in this chapter). Or critics note that national defense spending dwarfs the size of America's diplomatic and foreign assistance accounts, as well as its homeland security activities. Each of these latter two categories of federal spending that are relevant to overall national security, but *not* formally part of the national defense budget, costs currently in the rough vicinity of $50 billion to $60 billion a year.[2]

These observations are all simultaneously true. But they are contradictory, and thus inconclusive, in the aggregate. The US defense budget is and will remain large relative to budgets of other countries, other federal agencies, and even other periods in American history. Yet, at the same time, it is modest as a fraction of the nation's economy in comparison with the Cold War era or even the first decade of the twenty-first century. As such, while informative on one level, these observations are of little ultimate utility in framing defense policy choices for the future. We must look deeper.

Only by looking more carefully at how defense dollars are spent can we decide if the budget is either excessive or insufficient. The ultimate test is, of course, adequacy for key missions the US military may be asked, often in conjunction with allies, to carry out—and wars it is expected to deter or, if necessary, to win.[3]

This chapter explores various ways the defense budget can be categorized, broken down, and defined. The chapter also explores issues like military readiness—how the Department of Defense ensures that its forces are ready-to-go for crises that may emerge quickly. It examines the economics of military bases, at home and abroad. Finally, it also discusses military acquisition, modernization, and innovation.

The Big Picture: Broad Definitions and Budget Processes

In 2020, before COVID struck, US federal spending was projected by the Trump administration to reach about $4.7 trillion, out of an economy it projected would reach $22.4 trillion in size. The deficit was expected to total $1.1 trillion, and the cumulative debt held by the public (including from all previous years) would reach $18.1 trillion. COVID then blew up the deficit and debt numbers in 2020, and reduced gross domestic product—meaning that publicly-held debt has now grown so much that it equals GDP. State and local expenditures currently constitute roughly another $3 trillion of GDP across the United States each year. Together, these figures mean that all types of government spending add up to almost 35 percent of GDP without the effects of COVID. The Trump administration's projected national defense spending in 2020 of somewhat more than $700 billion constitutes just over 15 percent of total federal government spending in the pre-COVID budget, or about 10 percent of all types of US government spending combined.[4]

As noted, by official definitions, this US national defense budget does *not* capture all major government activities that in fact do influence American security. It includes neither diplomacy, nor foreign assistance, nor Department of Homeland Security operations, nor the Department of Veterans Affairs. It does, however, include the Department of Defense, the intelligence community, and the Department of Energy's nuclear weapons–related activities, as well as war costs and DoD's role in activities such as disaster relief.

The national defense budget is officially known as the 050 function in the federal budget. The Department of Defense's (dominant) part of that is the 051 function. International affairs programs including diplomacy and foreign assistance are labeled as the 150 account; veterans' benefits are found within the 700 function; homeland security is distributed among a range of accounts.

Because defense budget semantics can be confusing, it is essential to be precise. Sometimes, the nuances in wording are subtle enough that it is best to clarify them explicitly, rather than to assume they have been used precisely by whoever is employing the various terms. For example, the *defense budget* is often used to refer to funding for the Department of Defense only—now typically well over 95 percent of the total 050 budget. But the *national defense budget* also includes the nuclear weapons activities of the National Nuclear Security Administration within the Department of Energy. These latter costs, about $25 billion in the 2020 budget, are for monitoring and maintaining the nuclear weapons stockpile (which has been done without nuclear tests ever since 1992), sustaining the nation's naval nuclear reactors, and carrying out overseas nonproliferation activities. The Department of Energy also cleans up radioactive sites that were severely contaminated during the peak nuclear production years of the Cold War.

On Capitol Hill, the annual budget appropriations process funds most DoD operations each year through a *defense appropriations bill*—but that bill contains somewhat *less* than the full DoD budget. That is because there are separate, smaller defense appropriations bills for military construction and family housing; altogether, these bills fund the entirety of the Department of Defense.

It is also important to know the distinction between budget authority and outlays. This distinction exists for all forms of federal spending, including within the national defense budget. Outlays amount to actual spending—checks written by the Treasury and cashed by individuals or corporations. Budget authority, by contrast, is new legal power to enter into contracts, granted to DoD by the Congress through appropriations bills. It can loosely be thought of as putting money into the Pentagon's hands, which is then gradually committed and spent over the ensuing months and years, as contracts are signed and products delivered. Budget authority that is provided for a given fiscal year may be spent very quickly, as with salaries for troops. Or it may be spent slowly, as with contracts for aircraft carriers and other large types of equipment (which take years to build and are paid for in installments).[5]

A given year's national security budget authority tends to exceed outlays when defense budgets are rising, and to fall below outlays when budgets are declining. For example, for 2020, the Trump administration requested discretionary budget authority of $750 billion and projected that outlays would be $726 billion. (Congress ultimately approved $746 billion out of the $750 billion request, when all emergency funding is included.) Put more simply, not all money that is authorized and appropriated for a given year is spent that same year, and thus changes in outlays lag those in budget authority. (On rare occasions, money that is authorized and appropriated may not be spent at all, if a given program is canceled partway through—though in such situations, the funds will often be reallocated to other programs intended to provide analogous capabilities.) It is outlays that are relevant in calculating the nation's deficit in a given year.

Another nuance: most defense funding is considered *discretionary*, meaning it must be provided each and every year by the Congress. It is not *mandatory* spending, such as Social Security, Medicaid, and Medicare entitlements (which do not need to be approved afresh each year). However, modest amounts of defense funds, of the order of a few billion dollars a year, do count as mandatory spending and thus do not require annual reauthorization. Sometimes they can even be negative for a given year, since they include certain kinds of trust funds and user fees.

Each year the Department of Defense builds a new detailed budget proposal, for the following budget year, as part of the annual congressional budget process. That process was essentially developed in modern form with the passage of the Congressional Budget and Impoundment Control Act of 1974. (But in fact the obligation for the executive branch to submit a budget proposal to Congress each year dates back to the Budget and Accounting Act of 1921. The obligation for Congress to fund the government dates back, of course, to Article I of the US Constitution.)

In principle, this is roughly how the budget process is supposed to work—though there are many exceptions and imperfections to the system, which has functioned much less smoothly in recent years.[6] Early in the calendar year, the president submits a budget request for the entire government to the Congress for the fiscal year that will begin that same October (for example, the request for fiscal year 2020, beginning October 1, 2019, was submitted in March 2019). That presidential request often places particular emphasis on the discretionary accounts, since it is those that must be passed by October 1 to prevent a government shutdown (sometimes averted through temporary funding even in the absence of proper yearlong budgets).

In principle, action next turns to the congressional budget committees in each house. Then, the full House and Senate approve their own separate resolutions setting broad government funding levels by category; they then agree on a compromise resolution to guide each going forward. These budget resolutions do not have the force of law, however, and are not always employed.

Attention then turns to the authorization committees and appropriations subcommittees. (Across the whole government and budget, there are total of twelve appropriations subcommittees in each chamber, which receive technical aid in the process of writing their bills by the Congressional Budget Office [CBO] as well.)[7] The appropriations bills actually provide the money. Authorizing committees, by contrast, provide the legal foundation for the appropriations, as required by law (though, in some cases, authorizations are provided on a multiyear basis or at a different point in the calendar year than appropriations). The House Armed

Services Committee, Senate Armed Services Committee, House Defense Appropriations Subcommittee, and Senate Defense Appropriations Subcommittee are the key players at this stage. Then, each chamber passes its own overall defense bills, after which the House and Senate seek to compromise on any differences with each other in conference committees. If successful, their merged bills are approved again in each chamber, then sent to the White House. The president can sign or veto the authorization and appropriations bills that Congress creates; Congress can override a veto with a two-thirds majority vote in each house.[8]

Unlike other federal agencies and departments, DoD also includes budget projections over a half-decade time horizon in a document called the Future Years Defense Program (FYDP). The annual practice of creating such a document began in the Robert McNamara years of the 1960s and is called the planning, programming, budgeting, and execution system (PPBES). Informed conceptually by the National Security Strategy, National Defense Strategy, and National Military Strategy, the services employ the PPBES process not only to undergird budgetary requests to Congress but also to develop detailed road maps for maintaining and improving their forces, facilities, and weaponry with the money that Congress does provide.[9]

When attempting to understand the complementary roles played by the executive branch and the Congress in defense policymaking, it is important to underscore the vast difference in scale of personnel. A given congressional committee typically has dozens of staff, with comparable numbers in the personal offices of key representatives and senators, and several dozen analysts at places such as CBO who contribute as well. By contrast, the planning, budgeting, and management staffs of the military services number in the thousands—indeed, the tens of thousands—of personnel. While Congress does the authorizing and appropriating, therefore, it cannot do so without considerable help from the executive branch.

The Department of Defense also publishes unclassified information on its major weapons programs though documents such as the selected acquisition reports (SARs), discussed in more detail later in the section on acquisition. These show total cost projections and planned numbers of equipment purchases for several dozen of the Pentagon's largest acquisition programs over an even longer time horizon than five or six years (extending as far out as the relevant acquisition program is expected to continue).

A few more details on the PPBES process are important to understand. In the first, or planning, phase of the PPBES process, documents called the Defense Planning Guidance and the Guidance for the Development of the Force are written (there is also a Guidance for the Employment of the Force, which is more operationally focused). These documents prioritize certain military missions and begin to translate broad strategy into more concrete concepts.[10]

Then, in the second, or programming, phase, specifics really emerge. The services and defense agencies take the lead at drafting program objective memoranda (POMs) during this phase, subject to the all-important budget ceilings provided by the Office of Management and Budget. The POMs are then vetted and revised by the office of the secretary of defense and are used to produce the FYDP, as noted earlier.[11]

As mentioned earlier, this process produced a request by the Trump administration to Congress for discretionary budget authority of $750 billion in 2020 (plus another $10 billion or so in mandatory defense programs). The $746 billion that Congress then authorized compares with $716 billion in 2019, $701 billion in 2018, and $634 billion in 2017, the last Obama budget. The $713 billion in projected outlays for 2020 contrasts with earlier respective figures of $674 billion, $623 billion, and $590 billion. Despite the big recent increases, future budgets are projected to grow only at roughly the rate of inflation in the years to come, according to the 2021 (pre-COVID) Trump budget proposal.[12] In 2020, of the total for national defense, or "budget function 050" budget authority, $33.4 billion was for the Department of Energy and other agencies.[13]

Congress has never wished to provide the executive branch with carte blanche, or extra funding in advance, to carry out new operations with which Congress may or may not agree. Hence, it has jealously guarded its power of the purse under Article I of the Constitution, requiring DoD to ask for additional funds for any contingency operations. Some mock this process, saying that DoD's budget is already huge, "and then you have to pay extra if you actually want to use the military." But Congress, which otherwise fears losing its clout in the budgetary and warmaking process, wants it just that way, for constitutionally understandable reasons having to do with checks and balances in government.[14] This concern is amplified by the fact that the United States has not declared war formally since World War II, dramatically reducing Congress's role in the initiation of hostilities. (Congress has only formally declared war, which requires a majority vote in both houses, a total of eleven times in the context of five different conflicts: the War of 1812, the US-Mexico War of 1846, the Spanish-American War of 1898, World War I, and World War II.[15] It has also authorized military operations on eleven other occasions, including a number of times since World War II: over Formosa/China in 1955, the Middle East in 1957, Vietnam/Southeast Asia in 1964, Lebanon in 1983, Iraq in 1991, counterterrorism in 2001, and Iraq again in 2002.)[16] Congress attempted to regain some leverage in the War Powers Act of 1973, demanding the right to approve combat operations within two months of their initiation, but presidents have not recognized the constitutionality of this law.[17]

For 2020, the Department of Defense requested $66.7 billion for overseas contingency operations (OCO) expenses and another $9 billion for emergencies that might occur closer to home, such as rebuilding after Hurricane Florence and Hurricane Michael. The figure of $66.7 billion contains two main pieces. One, $25.4 billion, is for the direct costs of combat operations that are expected to end when the wars end. The other, $41.3 billion, is for enduring costs related to the broader war on terror (and other challenges) but expected to continue even after current combat operations in places like Afghanistan cease. That latter figure should invite scrutiny and debate, however, as it is not obvious why costs that were incurred to address Syria, Iraq, Afghanistan, and elsewhere should still have to be borne even after the operations are over.[18] Ultimately, the Congress provided just over $71 billion in OCO funds for 2020, plus another $8 billion or so for the border wall with Mexico through DoD accounts.[19]

As a historical note, Congress has also used supplemental appropriations frequently and generously in the past—in the 1970s, for example. Thus the current habit, while not considered good fiscal practice, is not entirely without precedent, either.[20]

Typically, most OCO funding is for operations and maintenance (O&M). To take one snapshot, in 2019, of the $69 billion total for OCO, $50 billion was for O&M; almost $13 billion for procurement; almost $5 billion for military personnel; just over $1 billion for research, development, testing, and evaluation (RDT&E); and just under $1 billion for military construction. Broken down by department that year, the army received $33 billion, the air force $18 billion, the navy (including the marine corps) $8 billion, and defense-wide activities nearly $10 billion.[21]

Returning to an issue noted earlier, for the 2020 budget, the Trump administration also initially requested roughly $98 billion for base-budget activities to be funded out of the OCO account. This request was a pure and simple workaround to get the Department of Defense more money than the 2011 Budget Control Act (BCA), in effect through 2021, would otherwise allow. The BCA limits base budgets, not emergency or OCO funds. That 2011 piece of legislation, passed in the aftermath of the "Tea Party Revolution" of 2010, reflected Congress's desire to curtail federal spending and deficits—though it left out any significant changes to entitlement accounts or the tax code in the process. By placing binding caps on two large categories of discretionary budgets—defense and nondefense—the BCA inadvertently created an incentive for the Pentagon to migrate some normal, peacetime base costs into the OCO account, where they could be funded without constraint. (The alternative would be to hold defense spending below where most Democrats and Republicans thought it should be—perhaps through the indiscriminate mechanism of "sequestration," by which most parts of the budget are cut proportionally and indiscriminately to achieve a given reduction in overall spending levels—as occurred for part of 2013.)[22] The Trump

administration tried to take advantage of this loophole in 2020 even more bla-
tantly and unapologetically than had previously been the case. That said, Congress considered this latest proposed use of OCO funding to be excessive even by
the permissive standards of modern times and rejected it, instead legislating another onetime exception to the limitations placed by the 2011 legislation.

A more fortunate aspect of Trump administration defense budget policy occurred in 2019, when for the first year since 2009, the Department of Defense got
its budget on time. In the previous decade, DoD operated under a continuing
resolution (CR), rather than a new budget, for at least seventy-six days of each
fiscal year (and, in four cases, for roughly six to seven months).[23] Continuing resolutions are employed when Congress and the executive cannot agree on a new
budget yet wish to keep DoD operating more or less normally on an interim basis. But with a CR—effectively an autopilot or extrapolation of the previous
year's budget into the next fiscal year—new programs cannot be started, and big
changes in existing programs cannot be undertaken either. Although routine pay
and training and maintenance activities can generally continue under a CR, the
Department of Defense operates considerably less efficiently in such circumstances. The Department of the Navy estimates that it effectively lost $4 billion
over the last decade due to such budgetary practices.[24] Unfortunately, this new
good habit of Washington policymakers—getting budgets done on time—did not
survive into the 2020 fiscal year, when authorization and appropriations bills were
only finalized and signed into law the week before Christmas.

Breakdowns of the US Department of Defense Budget

The US government, in its official budget documents, breaks down the Department of Defense budget in several ways. Two basic methods show resources by
appropriations "title" and by military department. (Neither includes DoE nuclear
costs.) These categories remain very broad and large, and as such they are generally not detailed enough to carry out meaningful examination of policy alternatives. But they are still important for establishing broad context.

Consider first the taxonomy that employs appropriations titles. Within that
framework, the military personnel account pays salaries, housing allowances, military health care fees, and retirement accrual for active-duty uniformed personnel and reservists. Procurement buys equipment, whether weaponry or not, and
whether big-ticket items or smaller and less expensive hardware. Research, development, testing, and evaluation budgets pay for the relatively inexpensive basic science research of interest to the Pentagon that is done at a plethora of labs

and universities around the country. They also fund advanced development, prototyping, and testing of new weapons systems or other advanced technologies. (The three subcategories of the RDT&E budget called basic research, applied research, and advanced technology development together make up just over $15 billion of the annual RDT&E budget; subsequent development, prototyping, and testing phases make up the rest of the $100 billion.)[25] The most complex title is known as operations and maintenance. It funds everything from the salaries of all DoD civilians, to recruiting costs, to basic training and more advanced training, to DoD's military hospital system, to the maintenance and upkeep of bases, to maintenance and fuel costs for equipment.

The other broad budgetary approach mentioned earlier is focused on military departments. It includes marine corps costs within the navy's budget—since, as discussed in the introduction, the marine corps is a separate service but is not a separate military department. Many intelligence community costs, and now the expenses of the space force, are found within the Department of the Air Force budget, since it launches and operates many of the rockets and satellites used in intelligence.

Yet another method of parsing the defense budget, devised in the McNamara years, subdivides spending by what are called major force programs. Rather than allocate the defense budget based on military service, or procurement versus personnel and so forth, Robert McNamara's Pentagon defined broad categories in terms of the overall national security functions they served. They include strategic nuclear capabilities, main combat forces, transportation assets, administrative and related support activities, National Guard and reserve forces, intelligence, and several smaller areas of expenditure. This method, however, has major limitations as well. Many military forces are usable for both nuclear and conventional operations, for example. Should they be coded as strategic nuclear capabilities or main combat forces? And how to allocate expenditures for equipment first bought for active forces but later transferred to the reserves? Moreover, these categories are sufficiently broad that, even if accurate, they may have only modest bearing on informing a policy choice.

Tables 1.1 through 1.3 show the authorized and appropriated budget for the Department of Defense in 2020, including all supplemental funding for the OCO and emergency accounts.

The Pentagon puts out reams of annual detailed budgetary documentation, found at www.budget.mil and https://comptroller.defense.gov/Budget-Materials. For example, within the military personnel accounts, information can be found on the costs of officer pay versus enlisted pay, of salaries versus accrual financing for the future retirement of current troops, of active versus reserve compensation, and of travel and moving allowances, to name but a few subcategories. Within

TABLE 1.1. DoD 2020 Budget Authority by Title (Discretionary Funding, Rounded to the Nearest Hundred Million Dollars)

Military personnel	154.7
Operations and maintenance	289.6
Procurement	143.8
Research, development, testing, and evaluation	104.5
Military construction and family housing	18.2
Management funds, transfers, receipts	1.8
TOTAL	712.6

Source: Office of the Under Secretary of Defense (Comptroller), "2021 Defense Budget Overview," Washington, D.C., February 2020, A-1 through A-10, https://comptroller.defense.gov/Portals/45/Documents/defbudget/fy2021/fy2021_Budget_Request_Overview_Book.pdf.

TABLE 1.2. DoD 2020 Budget Authority by Service (Discretionary Funding, Rounded to the Nearest Hundred Million Dollars)

Army	178.4
Navy	209.0
Air force	205.4
DoD-wide	119.8
TOTAL	712.6

Source: Office of the Under Secretary of Defense (Comptroller), "2021 Defense Budget Overview," Washington, D.C., February 2020, A-1 through A-10, https://comptroller.defense.gov/Portals/45/Documents/defbudget/fy2021/fy2021_Budget_Request_Overview_Book.pdf.

the procurement budgets, there are subcategories for aircraft, vehicles, ammunition, missiles, and other groupings of assets by each military service. Annual budget support materials also include the "P-1" and "R-1" documents that give copious detail on procurement and RDT&E budgets. There are similar tomes for personnel and for O&M. Every four years, there is a review of military compensation.

Which budgetary taxonomy is most useful for understanding a given policy challenge or framing a given policy choice depends on the issue at hand. For example, imagine that someone wishes to know if the country should move to a smaller but more mobile military. One notional way to create this might be to double the budget for US mobility forces, using savings from a smaller combat force structure to fund the expanded transportation programs. McNamara's categories shown in table 1.3 would give a sense of what fraction of the combat force

TABLE 1.3. DoD 2020 Budget Authority Request by Major Military Program (Total Obligational Authority, Rounded to the Nearest Hundred Million Dollars)

Strategic forces	15.0
General purpose forces	287.4
Command, control, communications, intelligence, and space	97.5
Mobility forces	17.8
Guard and reserve forces	47.5
Research and development	68.3
Central supply and maintenance	27.1
Training, medical, and other	90.0
Administration	24.1
Support of other nations	9.1
Special operations forces	19.6
Space	14.6
TOTAL	717.8

Source: Under Secretary of Defense (Comptroller)/Chief Financial Officer, "Defense Budget Overview," Department of Defense, Washington, D.C., March 2019, p. A-1, https://comptroller.defense.gov/Portals/45/Documents /defbudget/fy2020/fy2020_Budget_Request_Overview_Book.pdf. Here the figures add up to a slightly different total because what is presented is total obligational authority, not budget authority. The difference in these two concepts is quite small for our purposes, but it has to do with the possibility that some funds and some obligations can carry over from one year to the next (or lapse or be eliminated before being obligated), creating a slight difference between budget authority and total obligational authority in any given year. See Under Secretary of Defense (Comptroller), *National Defense Budget Estimates for FY 2021*, pp. 104–105,https://comptroller.defense .gov/Portals/45/Documents/defbudget/fy2021/FY21_Green_Book.pdf.; and Allen Schick, *The Federal Budget: Politics, Policy, Process* (Washington, D.C.: Brookings, 2007), 57.

structure might have to be cut to make this possible. The same table could help one estimate how much a deep cut in nuclear programs might save. In doing so, one would have to remember that DoE nuclear warhead costs, and many missile defense costs, are not captured in that department's strategic forces category. (Historically, nuclear-related costs were far higher than today. They typically reached or exceeded $90 billion a year in 2020 dollars, as the nation built its huge Cold War arsenal of warheads, intercontinental ballistic missiles (ICBMs), bombers, and submarine-based missiles as well as the command, control, communications, and intelligence networks that tied them together.)[26]

Or if the question was how a 5 percent across-the-board increase in military compensation would affect the defense budget, the information in table 1.1 could provide a rough framework for starting to answer the question. (Civilian pay for DoD employees, which as noted is found in the O&M budget, totals about $85 billion a year at present.)[27] Most of DoD's $50 billion a year in health care spending is in the O&M account, too. So if one posited slowing DoD's health care cost growth by some percent, that figure could be used to estimate associated savings over time.

The Acquisition Budget

Roughly one-third of the Department of Defense budget is usually devoted to acquisition of equipment. An entire set of organizations and cultures is involved in this effort, including government agencies, defense contractors big and small, university research laboratories, and other players.

The United States does not have a government-owned arsenal system for building armaments. Weapons are generally produced by private defense firms, starting with the "big five" of Lockheed Martin ($37.8 billion in all types of DoD spending in 2018), Boeing ($26.2 billion), Raytheon ($17.9 billion), General Dynamics ($14.4 billion), and Northrop Grumman ($13.8 billion). The next five are Huntington Ingalls ($7.1 billion), United Technologies ($7.0 billion), BAE Systems, ($6.9 billion), L3 Technologies ($6.2 billion), and Humana ($5.4 billion). There are thousands of smaller firms and subcontractors that contribute to the effort as well. Contractors also perform many support functions for DoD, outside of the acquisition process; all told, somewhat more than half of all defense dollars are spent through contracts with private companies, with about two-thirds related to acquisition and just over one-third to services including maintenance.[28] Of course, numbers change a bit year to year, but the basic pecking order of these firms is fairly well established at this juncture.

The Pentagon does business with these companies through various financial mechanisms that it consistently seeks to adjust and improve. Harvey Sapolsky, Eugene Gholz, and Caitlin Talmadge describe the various tools as "all the imperfect types of contracts," underscoring that each major type has its advantages and disadvantages. It is often difficult to agree to a fixed-price contract for technology that is still being developed when contracts are negotiated. Usually, some method is needed to account for uncertainty and for unexpected costs or complications. A number of approaches have been attempted, and, depending on the ripeness of a given type of technology, one or another may be invoked for a given purchase. Cost plus percentage contracts (CPPCs) reimburse a contractor for all documented expenses and then add a profit margin of some set percentage on top of that. But because CPPCs incentivize companies to build more expensive weapons (profit is a percentage of total costs), other approaches have been developed too. They include the cost plus fixed fee (CPFF) contract and the cost plus incentive fee (CPIF) contract. The first is self-explanatory. The second ties a company's profit to achieving less costly (or higher-performing, or more quickly acquired) weapons. It works best if a realistic baseline can be established in the planning, competition, and contracting process—in other words, if the benchmark goals for cost, performance, and schedule are not too far divorced from the reality of what is achievable once actual development and production occur.[29]

Although the private sector builds weapons, DoD supervises the process. Most of this is done through the individual military services, as acquisition programs move through their various milestones—called, very simply, A, B, and C. For large programs, the under secretary of defense for acquisition and sustainment plays a role in the milestone approval process as well. The first milestone authorizes moving a program into what is called the technology maturation and risk reduction phase, the second into full-bore engineering and manufacturing development, and the third into production and deployment.[30]

At various stages, decisions are informed by inputs from other Pentagon entities, such as the Office of Cost Assessment and Program Evaluation (CAPE) as well as Operational Test and Evaluation (OTE). The Office of the Secretary of Defense and the chairman and vice chairman of the Joint Chiefs of Staff together with their Joint Staff also have roles. Programs that have multiple-service implications are prioritized and coordinated through the Joint Requirements Oversight Council, run by the vice chairman of the Joint Chiefs of Staff.[31]

Basic research activities, as well as certain types of development and testing work, take place at a broad range of institutions. These include many private universities, such as the massive Johns Hopkins University Applied Physics Laboratory near Baltimore, Maryland. Much of the research is overseen, catalyzed, and supported by the Defense Advanced Research Projects Agency (DARPA). Basic research also occurs at more than 100 more specialized institutions and facilities within the purview of the individual military services, such as the US Naval Surface Warfare Center and the army's Aberdeen Proving Ground in Maryland, the army's White Sands Missile Range and the air force's Directed Energy Directorate in New Mexico, and Edwards Air Force Base in California. A great deal of DoD-related work also takes place at Department of Energy laboratories, including Sandia and Los Alamos in New Mexico, as well as major facilities in Oak Ridge in Tennessee, Lawrence Livermore in California, Argonne in Illinois, and a dozen other locations.[32]

All of this effort produces remarkable technology that will be discussed throughout this book. Often, of course, that technology winds up being quite expensive, and sometimes it does not work as intended. But, on balance, America's edge in weaponry and technology is among the nation's chief competitive advantages—even if it is increasingly under challenge from China and Russia. Among the areas of greatest American military technological preeminence are undersea warfare, as with the extremely quiet Los Angeles-class attack submarines; America's stealth aircraft, including the F-22 and F-35 and B-2 bomber and soon the B-21 bomber as well; its aircraft carriers, including the Nimitz-class and now the new Ford-class of ships; robotics, including unpiloted aircraft as well as autonomous sea and ground vehicles; and the nation's remarkable space and nuclear systems. The cyber domain is an area of both national strength and considerable vulnerability. Missile defense systems feature impressive technology, as with the shipborne Aegis-radar-based ships and the Terminal High-Altitude Area Defense (THAAD), but must contend with a global missile threat that is daunting in scale and capability.

Table 1.4 shows all US weapons systems now in development or production for which the Trump administration requested $1 billion or more in funding for the 2020 budget of the Department of Defense (dollars in billions, rounded to the nearest tenth). They are listed by category as DoD does in its budget documents.[33]

It might be noted that, in table 1.4, at least ten of the Pentagon's most expensive systems are not lethal weapons. Instead, they are support assets—to provide capabilities for activities such as moving forces around the world and the battlefield, and for stitching them together with an elaborate and robust command and control network.

The Wars and the Wartime Supplementals

As noted earlier, in the American budgetary system, costs for fighting wars are generally appropriated separately from standard, peacetime, core costs of the Department of Defense. Because these costs often wind up being quite high, in budgetary and of course in human terms, it is worth examining them separately.

Take the nation's most recent large conflicts. Through 2020, the United States will have spent $1.0 trillion on the Iraq War and $1.0 trillion on the Afghanistan campaign, in round numbers and expressed in 2020 dollars.

By comparison, it may be of interest to know that, in 2020 dollars, the Revolutionary War cost almost $3 billion as best as can now be estimated, the War of 1812 just under $2 billion, the Mexican War of 1846–1849 just under $3 billion, the Civil War more than $90 billion for the two sides combined, and the Spanish-American War about $10 billion. In more modern times, World War I cost the United States about $400 billion, World War II about $4.8 trillion!, the Korean War about $400 billion, and the Vietnam War $850 billion.[34] Desert Storm cost about $115 billion—paid primarily by other countries.[35]

Those estimates of $1.0 trillion per recent war are inexact. One reason is that, starting in the latter years of the decade of the 2000s and then the early 2010s, increasingly flexible rules were employed to define what DoD could count as OCO costs.[36] As a result, not all "war costs" have really been for the wars, and these numbers could be 10 to 20 percent too high in one sense.[37]

Arguably, however, the costs of the Iraq, Afghanistan, and related campaigns since 2001 should be viewed as much *higher* than the preceding figures, not lower.

TABLE 1.4. Major Weapons Systems in 2020 Budget Request (Billions of Dollars); Quantities Not Shown

AIRCRAFT AND RELATED SYSTEMS—JOINT SERVICE

F-35 Joint Strike Fighter 11.2

V-22 Osprey tilt-rotor aircraft 1.3

C-130 Hercules transport aircraft 1.6

MQ-9 Reaper unmanned aerial system 1.0

MQ-4C/RQ-4 Triton/Global Hawk unmanned aerial system 1.0

AIRCRAFT AND RELATED SYSTEMS—US ARMY

AH-64E Apache attack helicopter 1.0

UH-60 Black Hawk helicopter 1.7

AIRCRAFT AND RELATED SYSTEMS—US NAVY AND MARINE CORPS

F/A-18 Super Hornet combat aircraft 2.0

E-2D Advanced Hawkeye aircraft 1.3

P-8A Poseidon maritime surveillance aircraft 1.5

CH-53K heavy lift helicopter 1.5

AIRCRAFT AND RELATED SYSTEMS—US AIR FORCE

B-21 Raider bomber 3.0

KC-46A tanker aircraft 2.3

F-15 Eagle combat aircraft 2.1

CRH combat rescue helicopter 1.1

COMMAND, CONTROL, COMMUNICATIONS, COMPUTERS, AND INTELLIGENCE

Cyberspace joint system 2.8

GROUND SYSTEMS—JOINT SERVICE

Joint Light Tactical Vehicle 1.6

GROUND SYSTEMS—US ARMY

M-1 Abrams tank 2.2

MISSILE DEFEAT AND DEFENSE PROGRAMS—JOINT SERVICE

Ground-based Midcourse Defense system 1.7

Aegis ballistic missile defense system 1.7

MISSILES AND MUNITIONS—JOINT SERVICE

Joint Direct Attack Munition (JDAM) 1.1

MISSILES AND MUNITIONS—US ARMY

Guided Multiple Launch Rocket System 1.4

MISSILES AND MUNITIONS—US NAVY

Trident II ballistic missile 1.2

SHIPBUILDING AND MARITIME SYSTEMS—US NAVY

Gerald Ford-class aircraft carrier, advance payment 2.6

Columbia-class ballistic missile submarine, R&D 2.2

Virginia-class attack submarine 10.2

Arleigh Burke-class destroyer 5.8

Guided Missile Frigate 1.3

John Lewis-class fleet replenishment oiler 1.1

SPACE-BASED SYSTEMS—US AIR FORCE

National Security Space Launch system 1.7

Global Positioning System (GPS) III 1.8

Space-Based Overhead Persistent Infrared System 1.6

Satellite communications projects 1.1

The Watson Center at Brown University has made estimates for years that attempt to be more comprehensive than standard DoD accounting. Although some aspects of its methodology can be disputed, the Watson Center's argument for adding about $1.5 trillion in ongoing and expected future costs for the Department of Veterans Affairs related to casualties from these conflicts is rather compelling. Recall that the Department of Veterans Affairs has a budget exceeding $200 billion a year, with many of its costs from taking care of the often still-young veterans of Iraq and Afghanistan. Such costs can be projected into the future to estimate the future legacy costs of the wars in terms of medical expenses and disability payments. They will be high for decades to come as a result of injuries that have already been suffered. These are, by any reasonable accounting, part of the real and direct costs of the Iraq and Afghanistan campaigns.

American casualties in Iraq have been greater than in Afghanistan to date—more than 4,400 and more than 2,200 fatalities, respectively, as of early 2020, with more than 30,000 wounded in Iraq and more than 20,000 wounded in Afghanistan. Thus, of the Watson Center's $1.5 trillion overall estimate, it should be roughly correct to attribute nearly $1 trillion of that total to the Iraq conflict and somewhat more than $500 billion to Afghanistan. (The Watson Center's contention that another $1 trillion should be added to overall war costs for homeland security since 2001 conflates missions that might be better understood separately, so I do not find that part of its methodology as persuasive. Homeland security costs would have gone way up even if we had not waged the Iraq and Afghanistan campaigns, once the 9/11 attacks occurred; indeed, had the Afghanistan war in particular not taken place, homeland security costs might have had to go up even more to deal with a still-potent Al Qaeda that continued to enjoy sanctuary in South Asia.)[38] Thus, by my assessment, the Iraq War might be estimated to have cost nearly $2 trillion to date, and the Afghanistan war some $1.5 trillion.

In these recent wars, the incremental costs per troop deployed to conduct operations in Iraq or Afghanistan have been very high. They have averaged around $1 million per deployed trooper per year, above and beyond the expenses for basic salaries and equipment that are already accounted for in the normal, peacetime defense budget—several times what was initially projected. They have been higher than expected.

These wars did not represent the first time that the Pentagon has failed to predict accurately the cost per troop per year in a major operation—quite apart from inevitable uncertainties over how long a mission would last or how many troops it could require. The Department of Defense has been notorious for a failure to understand deployment costs accurately in the recent past. For example, in the Bosnia mission, initial estimates for the cost of deploying 20,000 troops to the region for a year were $1.5 billion to $2 billion, but actual costs were at least twice the upper bound (in other words, at least $200,000 per deployed troop per year).[39] This is a good case study in how even sophisticated defense analysis tools are often crude, and therefore in how generalists armed only with fairly simple methodologies can often be nearly as accurate as Pentagon planners.

A question that sometimes arises in regard to wartime operations is this: Can the Pentagon save money in wars by using contractors rather than its own soldiers for certain tasks? The answer is that it all depends. Savings may be achievable when contractors are able to hire lower-wage non-Americans for some support tasks, for example. Moreover, in short wars, contractors can save the government money because they need not be paid when operations end. By contrast, comparable numbers of uniformed personnel would generally be retained in the force structure even after an operation was over, and only gradually scaled back. However, some types of contractors cost more per person than uniformed personnel, particularly if they have to be lured to accept the risks of dangerous assignments in war zones by generous compensation packages. American contractors are generally not individually cheaper than government employees, according to a recent study by the Office of the Director of National Intelligence, and in fact may be at least 50 percent more expensive.[40] On balance, contractors do have an important role for the US military. But this fact is already being exploited, since in recent wars the United States has typically used one contractor for every uniformed man or woman—2.5 times the highest rate of any previous large conflict.[41]

Budgeting by Overseas Region

Clearly, the amounts of money spent or already committed to this century's wars in the broader Middle East are staggering—more than $3 trillion by any reasonable reckoning (a good chunk of it, as noted, outside the defense budget, within Department of Veterans Affairs accounts). However, in the first two decades of this century, more than $14 trillion will have been allocated to national defense (in this case, *not* counting the Department of Veterans Affairs—but counting nuclear weapons expenses within the DoE budget, plus of course the intelligence budgets embedded within DoD accounts).[42] In other words, most defense spending has not been directly in support of wartime operations. Is there any way to apportion this total among the various overseas commitments of the United States, from the Western Hemisphere to the Asia-Pacific to the Middle East to Europe, such that one can estimate which foreign commitments are most expensive?

The short answer is, no, there is neither an official algorithm nor a widely accepted unofficial methodology for divvying up the defense budget theater by theater. Resource allocations toward each major continent or alliance system cannot be associated with a precise figure, such that the sum total equals much or all of the total defense budget. Most American military forces are flexible and fungible by theater of use. They can go to where they might be needed. Even if some conduct training with a most-likely region of the world in mind, they could easily be repurposed, especially in the event of large-scale hostilities.

Nonetheless, a defense analytical giant, the late Bill Kaufmann, attempted such a breakdown. His thinking was that specific threats and contingencies do indeed drive American defense planning, even if not in an easily calculable way. Kaufmann was motivated by the fact that often, in debates on burden sharing or grand strategy or some other issue, it is desirable to have at least ballpark figures for such allocations, based on probabilities of where forces could most likely be used in large numbers.

Some military assets are indeed designed primarily for one type of operation in just one or two places. During the Cold War, Europe was the primary theater where the United States prepared for large-scale air-ground operations, making it logical to attribute the costs of most army and tactical air force units to that region, for example. But that same case reveals the challenge of this kind of calculation; it turned out that most fighting during and right after the Cold War occurred in Asia, not Europe (in Korea, Vietnam, and the Persian Gulf region). Forces developed and intended mostly for the Fulda Gap in Germany wound up being used primarily elsewhere. So, again, any such attempt at budgetary breakdowns needs to be taken with a grain of salt.

The last time that Kaufmann provided an estimate of where and how DoD spends its money abroad was in 1992. He used, as a starting point, the first Bush administration's plan for a post–Cold War US military that was called the "Base Force." The early 1990s were a time when the Pentagon still worried about a possible Russian resurgence and the resulting hypothetical danger to countries like the Baltic States, even though they were not yet within NATO. The Department of Defense also worried about post–Desert Storm Iraq, where Saddam Hussein was still in power and still defiant; the United States would, in fact, undertake a policy of "dual containment" of both Iraq and Iran in following years. However, the Department of Defense had not yet focused much on the People's Republic of China in the way it has more recently. So Kaufmann estimated that a substantial fraction of the overall defense budget was for the defense of Europe, and another large share for the broader Middle East. His numbers for East Asia were quite modest; they would presumably increase if Kaufmann were to redo his estimates today. It is also worth noting that the nuclear estimates would increase if DoE's nuclear weapons activities were part of the overall math in table 1.5 (Kaufmann's estimates were for DoD only).

TABLE 1.5. Kaufmann Estimates of DoD's Spending by Geographic Region under the "Base Force" of the First Bush Administration (Percent)

Strategic nuclear deterrence	15
Tactical nuclear deterrence	1
National intelligence and communications	6
Northern Norway/Europe	5
Central Europe	29
Mediterranean	2
Atlantic sea lanes	7
Pacific sea lanes	5
Middle East and Persian Gulf	20
South Korea	6
Panama and Caribbean	1
United States	3

Source: William W. Kaufmann, *Assessing the Base Force: How Much Is Too Much?* (Washington, D.C.: Brookings, 1992), 3.

Despite the inherent and inevitable imprecisions, these kinds of figures can be useful. For example, one might ask, how much does the United States spend each year defending Persian Gulf oil? Some rough answer to this question might be important for comparing the subsidies that are effectively provided today to the oil economy and comparing those with any federal help that might be provided to renewable or nuclear energy. Answering such a question requires some simplifying, and potentially controversial, assumptions. Is the main driver for US interest in the Persian Gulf region hydrocarbons? Partly, yes. However, the US commitment to Israel's security and its commitment to check global terrorist movements also motivate America's interest in the broader Persian Gulf and Central Command region.

In addition to Kaufmann's approach, another way to estimate force allocations and budgetary expenditures by region could note that, at present, the Persian Gulf theater represents one of the three main areas for which the Pentagon has built its combat force structure (the other two are Europe and East Asia). Under the 2020 defense budget, if one excludes war costs for actual operations and focuses just on the underlying core budget, the United States will allocate a bit more than $650 billion to its military. Roughly one-third of that total, or about $200 billion, is for costs not easily attributable to any one potential combat theater—intelligence, research and development, homeland defense, and central headquarters. That implies, in very broad brush, a bit more than $450 billion for the three main theaters of overseas interest, or an average of around $150 billion per year for each. That is only a rough estimate, but it may be useful for broad conceptual and strategic policy debates. (It is worth emphasizing that the United States does not really envision fighting three simultaneous big wars. So, as a practical matter, if war did erupt in the Western Pacific, Europe, or the Middle East, the Department of Defense would have many of its worldwide forces to draw upon for that conflict, and not just one-third of the total.)

Then there is Kaufmann's approach. He estimated in 1992 that the United States spent 20 percent of its peacetime DoD budget on defense of the Persian Gulf and broader Middle East (see table 1.5). Applying that same percentage today to the $650+ billion figure for core DoD costs would also suggest an expense of defending the broader Persian Gulf region in the rough ballpark of $130 billion a year.

Yet another way to estimate US military costs by potential combat theater would be to assume some force package that might be required for a major operation there. One could start with, say, the six-plus ground combat divisions used in Operation Desert Storm in 1991, or the roughly four divisions used in Operation Iraqi Freedom in 2003, together with corresponding amounts of airpower and naval power. Then, using the methodologies presented at the end of this chapter, one could estimate the average annual cost of that combination of forces. For example, if one assumed fifteen brigades of land power and fifty squadrons of airpower, the annual costs of keeping that much military power in the US force structure could reach $100 billion (see tables 1.6 and 1.7 later in the chapter).

These figures are, as noted, for normal peacetime spending. One can also then add the expenses incurred in actually fighting wars in the broader Middle East since 9/11.

A word of warning about such figures, however. It is important not to think that, if the US interest in a given part of the world were somehow abandoned, the defense budget would automatically decline by whatever amount one attributes to that theater. In fact, the resulting implied decline in the defense budget would generally be less than Kaufmann's method suggests. That is because some of the forces he allocated to a given region are in fact also important for other regions, if not in a primary role then at least as a strategic reserve, so some of them would likely have to be kept even if their primary mission went away.

The Economics of Overseas Basing

The preceding analysis focuses on grandiose questions of grand strategy. But more mundane, down-to-earth issues also frequently arise about America's overseas bases. Leaving aside broader debates, what are the nuts-and-bolts costs of foreign presence? Even these matters can have major consequences for force planning and for alliance relations. For example, in 2019 and 2020 the Trump administration sought a fivefold increase in the roughly billion-dollar annual contribution that South Korea was making to defer some of the costs of stationing 30,000 US troops on its territory. Was Seoul right that $1 billion a year was already pretty generous—or was President Trump right that $5 billion would be a fairer contribution, above and beyond the 2.5 percent of its GDP that South Korea devoted to its own military forces?

The key points are these. Permanently stationing US forces in countries with modern, industrial economies is not very expensive relative to basing those same forces in the United States (the numbers behind this conclusion are discussed in more detail later). But deploying and operating forces in war zones in places such as Iraq, Afghanistan, and the Balkans is quite a bit more expensive than keeping them at established, permanent facilities in the United States or in countries like South Korea, Japan, Germany, Italy, and Britain.

Start with the first issue—the costs of having US forces based for long periods in nations with strong economies. To understand the math, it is useful to break down the Pentagon budget into three relatively equal main chunks, with the appropriations titles as a starting point. One is for acquisition—research and development and testing of equipment, then procurement of that equipment. One is for the salaries of US military and civilian employees of the Department of Defense; this category includes the military personnel appropriations title, plus some of O&M funding. The last is for operations, maintenance, contractor support, and base infrastructure.

Of these three categories of cost, the first changes negligibly if forces are based in Europe or Northeast Asia rather than at home. Either way, the Pentagon buys them basically the same equipment. The second varies a little, but not that much. In terms of personnel costs, home or abroad, US personnel are paid the same salaries; the only differences in compensation are relatively minor ones for things like travel and slight differences in housing allowances. The third category of expense varies a bit more, but still not much. Operating from relatively cramped locations in densely populated South Korea, Japan, or Germany may entail somewhat higher costs than stationing forces in Texas or the Carolinas, but not radically so. To good approximation, the cost differential from stationing forces abroad is roughly 0 percent for acquisition, no more than 5 percent for personnel, and perhaps 10 to 20 percent for O&M as well as military construction activities. Averaging across all three categories, costs per troop might go up 5 to 10 percent for stationing abroad. The typical total cost of the US military per active-duty member is in the range of $300,000 to $400,000 a year. So the added costs of forward stationing per GI typically are measured in the low tens of thousands of dollars a year.

More detailed analysis backs up these hand-waving estimates. RAND has estimated that added annual costs of basing forces in a Northeast Asian or European allied nation total $10,000 to $40,000 per soldier, sailor, marine, or airman/airwoman.

Thus, for the 150,000 or so US forces stationed abroad but not in war zones, overseas basing adds perhaps $4 billion to $6 billion a year in total costs.[43] Most of those added costs are offset by contributions made by Seoul, Tokyo, Berlin, and others, which total some $4 billion of that amount.

The preceding is a very narrow dollars-and-cents calculus. In fact, in a broader sense, overseas basing can save the United States money. Stationing forces abroad often provides cheaper presence than sending reinforcements quickly during a crisis—if one takes as a given that the United States should be committed to the defense of a given region or ally (admittedly a debatable proposition in grand-strategic terms).

Take one slightly oversimplified example: the US air and naval bases in Japan. Today, the United States bases about two wings of air force fighter aircraft in Japan, with a third wing flying off a US aircraft carrier based near Tokyo (and marine corps airpower as well). Each wing consists of roughly seventy-two combat aircraft. If Washington did not have access to these Japanese bases, yet still believed that its interests in Korea and the Western Pacific required maintaining that same level of tactical airpower constantly on station in the region, its only real choice might be to keep two more aircraft carriers plus associated escort ships in Western Pacific waters most or all of the time. That would be one way to compensate for the loss of US Air Force bases. Given the tyranny of distance and the need for rotations to avoid excessively long deployments, keeping two more carriers on station continuously could require at least eight more in the fleet.[44] (At present the United States has ten aircraft carriers in the navy's fleet, only four to five of which typically focus on the Western Pacific.) That would be a whopping requirement—and expense.

This deployment math is due to the fact that, for a typical carrier battle group, long deployments occur for only about six out of every twenty-four months over a two-year operational cycle. For the other eighteen months, the carrier is otherwise preoccupied with various types of preparation. For the first six months of any two-year cycle, new crews are formed and trained in basic skills (given normal personnel patterns, at any given time about 15 percent of the US military is made up of first-year "rookies" who have just joined the armed forces). In the second six-month period, the ship's crew works up to short training deployments at sea, integrating operations across different subunits and subspecialties. The third phase is for the actual deployment, and indeed even some of that is consumed in ocean transit. The last six-month interval can be consumed by additional maintenance on equipment, if problems develop, or the ship and crew can be on standby, in effect.

But for the sake of conservatism, assume that just six carrier battle groups, rather than eight, would be enough to sustain two more on forward station. How much would an additional six aircraft carrier battle groups cost today's military? An aircraft carrier, plus planes and escort ships, now costs almost $30 billion to acquire. Averaged out over typical equipment lifetimes, that translates into about a billion dollars a year. The carrier battle group then costs more than $2.5 billion annually to operate, according to CBO, as discussed in more detail later. That makes for an average annual total of some $3.5 billion. Thus, the average annual cost of adding six carrier battle groups to the standing US military force structure would be more than $20 billion. Of course, in the absence of US bases in Japan, the United States might make other decisions about how much combat power to maintain on continuous station in the Western Pacific, so the preceding calculation is notional and illustrative. But it is still telling about the potential value of bases.[45]

Military Readiness

Military readiness is defined by the Joint Chiefs of Staff as the ability of the armed forces to deploy quickly and perform effectively for certain assigned types of military missions.[46] It should be distinguished from military innovation and modernization, which concern longer-term issues of preparing for new types of warfare and new potential missions.

Maintaining high military readiness is time-consuming and expensive. It can therefore compete with resource requirements for modernizing the military of the future. Emphasizing the latter requires that money and time be devoted to research and development, to professional military education, and to experimentation with new warfighting concepts and technologies.[47] Dollars spent on research and development cannot be spent on fuel or ammunition; officers' time devoted to running future-oriented exercises and experiments is not available for drilling forces for near-term missions; units trying out new concepts are not as able to practice on more immediate tasks or potential tasks. So it is important to think in terms of trade-offs between readiness, on the one hand, and innovation as well as modernization, on the other.

Military readiness has often been a political football. In the 1970s, America's military was widely believed to have gone "hollow." A fairly large force structure existed, but it did not benefit from adequate numbers of the right people, equipment, spare parts, or training exercises. At various points since the Cold War ended, military readiness has been said to suffer, and perhaps even to be "broken."[48] What are these criticisms about? What do terms like "hollow" and "broken" even mean in the context of military preparedness? One guideline in evaluating readiness is to be specific, and quantitative, as much as possible. Sweeping terms like "broken" and "hollow" tend to do more to obscure, and politicize, readiness than to diagnose accurately or to repair it.

A few analytical principles should be kept in mind in regard to this subject. Readiness for one mission can compete with readiness for another. The Balkans wars were seen as distractions from "real" warfighting priorities and readiness requirements in the 1990s, for example, since formal war plans were focused on Northeast Asia and the Persian Gulf. The Afghanistan war was not anticipated or planned very well before it occurred, in part because of the preoccupation with readiness to handle what were considered more important threats. The US military was much better prepared for the invasion phase of the Iraq War than for what came next, suggesting that training had emphasized maneuver warfare at the expense of counterinsurgency and stabilization missions. And in the first fifteen years of the twenty-first century, ensuring readiness for counterinsurgency and counterterrorism took priority over focusing on great-power conflict, though that has been changing in the latter Obama and the Trump years.

Readiness also requires a balancing act in the pace of training and deploying forces. Too little of the latter, and units clearly cannot be sharp. Too much, however—too high of an "operational tempo," whether from deployments abroad or even from training exercises on and near home base—and people and equipment can wear down.

Some debates about ensuring readiness arise from changes in technology. One concerns the growing role of simulators. As simulators become much more realistic, to what extent can they replace the need for true training? Military personnel need to work with real weapons to acclimate to the pressures and the fear of combat. That said, do we really know for a fact that tank crews need 800 miles a year of driving their vehicles (rather than 600, with many more hours on simulators)? Or that pilots need 20 to 24 hours in the air per month, the late Cold War norm, rather than today's 14 to 18?[49] If excellent simulators can mimic combat conditions in most ways, surely at least a 5 or 10 or 20 percent reduction in actual driving or flying should be achievable without any degradation of combat readiness. But, of course, one could overdo it, so there need to be ways of assessing the abilities of those who have had varying degrees of different types of preparation, as new standards are evaluated and established.

Many problems with readiness are not really as serious as they may first appear when examined out of context. A salient case was in the late 1990s and 2000, when the Clinton administration was accused of insufficient purchases of cruise missiles. But, in fact, at that time, DoD had almost ten times the number of cruise missiles used in Operation Desert Storm. Nonetheless, because this total was below the "requirement" set by Pentagon planners, it was seen as inadequate. A similar dynamic may be behind President Trump's dubious claim that the American armed forces were somehow short on ammunition when he became commander in chief.[50] That popular DoD term "requirement" should in fact always be viewed with a jaundiced eye, or at least suspicion; it typically means more of an educated guess about optimal requirements for future combat than any obligatory minimal threshold for adequate military readiness. As another example, in the late 1990s, two entire army divisions were deemed "unready" because they had each sent one brigade to the Balkans. In fact, each still had two brigades that were available for other missions.[51] But a division's overall readiness was determined to be best represented by its single weakest attribute. As such, since a division was officially judged to require three brigades, the absence of one of them on short notice translated into a failing grade. By the early years of the 2000s, the US Army focused its attention on individual brigades more than divisions—so at that point, it would have judged the original division to be roughly two-thirds ready for combat, corresponding to how many brigades could be quickly mustered. But in the 1990s, the grade for the entire unit was effectively an F. This was largely capricious and misleading.

Or consider equipment. How important is a shortfall in which "mission capable" equipment inventories drop by a certain moderate amount, say 10 to 15 percent, relative to nominal requirements for tanks or trucks or ships? At what point does the cohesion of a tank unit—its ability to carry out basic operations such as maneuver and attack in a coordinated fashion—truly suffer as a result? As a broad rule of thumb, the military's own collective judgment and official rating systems tend to suggest that shortfalls in the range of 5 to 15 or 20 percent of most types of equipment are tolerable, but that larger deficits become of serious concern. Yet even these rules of thumb are notional and rough, not scientific or exact.

Inevitably, the military will have certain shortfalls relative to ideal readiness—and to what it defines as "requirements." Not every shortfall amounts to a crisis; many can be worked around, at least to a degree.

It is always possible to find readiness metrics that make a predetermined political case—that seem to suggest that the military either is in fine shape or that it is falling apart. Richard Betts, a professor at Columbia University, aptly subtitled one chapter in his seminal book on the subject of readiness "Lies, Damn Lies, and Readiness Statistics."[52]

It is therefore not particularly helpful when the Pentagon limits its public discussion of readiness metrics to a few categories that it selects, especially when it fails to present a historically significant time period to provide perspective on these categories. For example, in recent years, the Pentagon has often given data for just a few categories of readiness.[53] This trend began in the early years of the 2000s under Secretary Donald Rumsfeld, did not improve in the Obama years, and has intensified in some ways in the Trump years, with less and less readiness information routinely available. Neither the military nor any other organization or political leader should be trusted to cherry-pick individual statistics to serve some policy agenda. Only by viewing a wide swath of readiness data across a number of years can meaningful comparisons be made.

Waiting for the next war to evaluate a new readiness initiative or take stock of what traditional efforts have accomplished is not a preferred, or a reliable, way to evaluate readiness. At that point, it may be too late. As such, other more mundane methods must be employed. They typically begin with dividing the subject into three broad categories: personnel, training, and equipment. Within these broad categories, one can then evaluate readiness by examining several dozen individual line items—say, marine corps attack helicopter mission capable rates, or recruiting and retention statistics by military service (including, for example, the quality of military personnel based on various aptitude tests relative to past trends). Then, the individual analyst can construct an overall assessment and debate with others who may form different assessments from the same data about their respective conclusions.

The best practices for keeping readiness debates data-focused, concrete, and nonpolitical are probably to present readiness data in a relatively raw form, to use consistent standards over time in evaluating them, and to avoid sweeping generalizations about "passing" and "failing" readiness grades. Generally it is best to show statistical trendlines over time.

With many readiness problems, specific policy actions can provide remediation. For example, when the military services wind up with shortages of pilots, perhaps because the civilian airline industry is booming and offering generous salaries to those who leave the military to fly aircraft for them, pilot bonuses can be increased, or the number of pilots trained in any given year can be augmented as well.[54] It is for this reason that readiness problems can often be most usefully viewed as specific resourcing challenges, and addressed accordingly when problems arise.

The Main Show: Costs of Individual Combat Units

With all these broad perspectives in place, the conditions are now set to turn to the core of this chapter—understanding the costs of DoD's force structure by type of unit. Ultimately, this is probably the core of defense budgeting methodology for those seeking to understand the fiscal implications of a given defense strategy and force structure.

The logic of the analytical process works something like this. Grand strategy as reflected in the nation's national security strategy helps assess where interests are important enough to be worth fighting for, if necessary. Determinations about where and how one might need to fight—and about how many places one might need to be prepared to fight at once—then allow an analyst to develop a corresponding force posture. This is where the National Defense Strategy, National Military Strategy, and ensuing plans like the FYDP then come into play. Knowing the types and numbers of combat and support units thus required, one can estimate their annual cost.

Again, Bill Kaufmann's pathbreaking work provides a natural starting point. His approach was to subdivide the overall defense budget according to main combat force structure. These included army and marine corps divisions (active and reserve), special operations forces, air force and marine corps tactical air wings, navy carrier battle groups and amphibious ships and sea control forces, airlift, sealift and prepositioning, strategic nuclear forces including submarines, bombers, land-based ICBMs, missile and air defenses, and early warning assets, and national intelligence and communications systems. Again, as with his geographic allocation scheme, Kaufmann's goal was to create a meaningful yet simple tool, so he sought to avoid excessive complexity. His approach was to assign all DoD costs to these categories so that they added up to exactly the overall size of the defense budget. He then divided the cost for a given category of combat capability by the number of units within that category to provide a cost per unit.

This is a somewhat oversimplified approach to defense budget analysis. There are in fact dozens of forces designed to support combat formations, such as those focused on logistics, intelligence, administration, air defense, other specialized weaponry, electronic warfare, and the like. Kaufmann's logic, however, was that in the end such capabilities exist only to support combat formations. As such, associating a certain proportionate number of support capabilities with each main combat formation, and allocating costs accordingly, is a reasonable way to create a good framework for policy choices. It allows a rough answer to the question of how much the country would save (or expend) if, for example, we cut (or add) an army division or an air force wing to the military force structure.

This approach, while imprecise, does a much better job of capturing the real cost implications of many policy alternatives than do most official Pentagon numbers. For example, if the Department of Defense were asked how much it could save by cutting an army division out of its force structure, it might give (and often has given) a very modest figure. Army divisions have only about 16,000 to

18,000 soldiers in them in general, and in making an estimate of savings, the army would probably focus on personnel and operating costs (not equipment), since the former are often the only guaranteed expenses for a given military formation in a given year. However, in fact, some 40,000 soldiers are typically associated with a given army division once support units are included, and of course over time the army will save a certain amount in reduced equipment expenditures when reducing force structure (even if savings in a given year cannot be specified exactly). So Kaufmann's method would often show a cost about five times greater for a unit such as an army formation than would DoD estimates. There is little doubt that Kaufmann's estimate would be in general more accurate, at least to indicate potential savings after full implementation of any cutback over a period of at least several years.

Still, the Kaufmann approach has its limitations. It is somewhat idealized. Not all defense expenses can be proportionately allocated to main combat formations. Some military costs such as research and development of new technology, strategic intelligence operations, and combat headquarters operations are to a large extent independent of the size of the force structure. Therefore, cutting the number of combat units does not reduce the former costs proportionately (if at all). Yet Kaufmann's method would often allocate such costs proportionately to combat force structure, implying greater savings than reality would allow.

In addition, Kaufmann's method ignores economies of scale. Buying more of a given type of weapon, or operating more of a given type of unit, generally provides efficiencies that reduce average cost. For example, the cost of operating a given type of military aircraft varies, most clearly and notably, with the size of the relevant fleet of planes. Smaller fleets have higher operating costs per plane. That is because they do not benefit from economies of scale associated with maintenance, repair, and other activities. Thus, cutting a given fleet of aircraft by some percentage, say 25 percent, will not typically reduce operating costs by as large a percentage. This nonlinear effect is most notable for aircraft fleets numbering fewer than 150 planes or so (if fleets are substantially larger than that, the percentage of operating savings may in fact approximate the percentage cut in the number of aircraft).[55]

For all these reasons, Kaufmann's figures may overestimate actual savings from any force structure cuts by 20 to 30 percent, roughly speaking. To see why, we can examine army force structure as one example. It has historically been divided into three relatively equal groups—combat units, deployable support units, and nondeployable or institutional units. The combat units are often called "tooth," and the support units, somewhat pejoratively, are called "tail," And the United States is sometimes criticized for having too low of a "tooth-to-tail" ratio in its armed forces. But, in fact, the latter have as much to do with the American military's excellence as the former; they are what give the nation the ability to deploy and sustain forces in faraway locations far better than any other country on earth.

Most support units can be cut proportionately when main combat forces are reduced. But the link between combat forces and institutional capabilities—research and development laboratories and institutions, major headquarters, intelligence units, and the like—is much less direct.[56] So Kaufmann assumes comparable savings in all three types of costs, when in fact major savings are likely to prove quickly possible only in two of the three.

Despite the limitations of Kaufmann's methods, they are typically the most accurate way to get back-of-the-envelope estimates. Indeed, in a recent major report on DoD force structure and associated costs, CBO adopted a very similar approach. It insisted that, beyond the direct costs of combat units, a proportionate share of each service's total numbers of deployable support units (for transport, maintenance, engineering, and so forth) should be attributed to each combat unit. Then it went further, assuming that almost all kinds of overhead—for training, doctrine development, headquarters, and the like—should also be proportionately divvied up and associated with a part of the combat force structure.[57] This logic has the advantage of simplicity, but it also has flaws.

All that being said, the CBO figures are highly useful, well organized at a very appropriate level of detail, and systematically and consistently computed, so they provide the backbone of the cost estimates provided in this chapter. Figures for the annual costs of keeping such units in the force structure—that is, operations and support (O&S) costs, which include military personnel as well as O&M—are shown in table 1.6.

These annual costs will likely grow faster than inflation in the future, just as they have in the past. Over recent decades, O&M costs on a per troop basis have grown about 1.3 percent annually in real terms, according to CBO.[58] The rate of growth varies, from period to period and service to service. But it is always greater than inflation, and it has a fairly steady trajectory. In recent decades, health care and environmental cleanup costs associated with base closures have been among the largest drivers of increased O&M expenditures. Aging weaponry contributes, too; a recent CBO study found annual cost growth of 3 percent to 7 percent (each year, in a cumulative and ongoing way).[59] While it is not a given that such cost-growth trends will continue, absent a radical change in management methods they probably will.

To do a complete unit-by-unit costing, we need to complete one more step—estimating the costs of acquiring weaponry and other equipment for each unit. Typically, O&S costs represent about two-thirds of the Pentagon budget. Acquisition and construction costs represent the other third. Again, they include RDT&E, as well as procurement, military construction, and family housing.

TABLE 1.6. Annual Cost for Operations and Support for Key US Military Units

	ANNUAL COST PER UNIT (MILLIONS OF 2020 DOLLARS)			
	DIRECT	INDIRECT	OVERHEAD	TOTAL
DEPARTMENT OF THE ARMY				
Active-component armored brigade combat team	530	890	1,360	2,770
National Guard armored brigade combat team	190	410	250	870
Active-component Stryker brigade combat team	530	840	1,360	2,700
National Guard Stryker brigade combat team	200	390	250	850
Active-component infantry brigade combat team	480	800	1,280	2,560
National Guard infantry brigade combat team	150	370	230	740
Active-component aviation brigade	590	0	440	940
Reserve-component aviation brigade	170	0	50	210
Army special operations forces	3,380	0	4,260	7,640
Rest of the army	2,120	0	1,250	3,370
DEPARTMENT OF THE NAVY				
Aircraft carrier	500	190	560	1,250
Carrier air wing	350	210	410	970
Arleigh Burke-class destroyer (DDG-51)	60	20	60	150
Ticonderoga-class cruiser (CG-47)	40	20	40	120
Littoral Combat Ship	40	20	30	110
Zumwalt-class destroyer (DDG-1000)	40	20	40	110
Attack submarine	70	40	30	150
Amphibious ship	120	40	130	290
Active-component Marine corps infantry battalion	150	150	500	780
Reserve-component Marine corps infantry battalion	70	50	370	500
Marine corps aircraft complement	170	150	230	550
Ballistic and guided-missile submarines	70	40	50	180
P-3 and P-8 maritime patrol aircraft squadron	120	70	160	350
Seabee construction engineers	760	0	1,220	1,970
Navy special operations forces	1,110	0	1,410	2,510
Marine corps special operations forces	220	0	300	520
Rest of the navy	3,700	0	3,240	6,940
Rest of the Marine corps	170	0	64	240
DEPARTMENT OF THE AIR FORCE				
A-10 attack aircraft squadron	90	60	100	350
F-15 fighter aircraft squadron	110	90	130	320
F-16 fighter aircraft squadron	70	50	110	230
F-22 fighter aircraft squadron	127	170	200	500
F-35 fighter aircraft squadron	140	220	240	600
B-52 bomber attack squadron	290	180	320	780
B-1B bomber attack squadron	290	240	330	860
B-2 bomber attack squadron	710	520	720	1,950
C-130 cargo aircraft squadron	120	90	180	380
C-5 cargo aircraft squadron	140	120	200	460

TABLE 1.6. (continued)

	ANNUAL COST PER UNIT (MILLIONS OF 2020 DOLLARS)			
	DIRECT	INDIRECT	OVERHEAD	TOTAL
C-17 cargo aircraft squadron	100	60	120	290
KC-135 tanker aircraft squadron	120	100	160	380
KC-10 tanker aircraft squadron	190	170	270	620
KC-46 tanker aircraft squadron	90	10	90	190
MQ-1 Predator UAS squadron	40	10	20	70
RQ-4 Global Hawk UAS squadron	200	110	150	470
MQ-9 Reaper UAS Squadron	50	40	70	170
Minuteman III missile squadron	140	100	170	400
Red Horse construction engineers	700	0	1,610	2,300
Air force special operations forces	1,950	0	2,000	3,950
Rest of the air force	6,530	0	4,070	10,600
Special Operations Command	5,690	0	0	5,690
Defense Health Program for retirees	15,600	0	0	15,600
Classified defense funding	15,412	0	0	15,410
Rest of the defensewide organizations	4,300	0	0	4,300

Source: Congressional Budget Office, Appendix B: Reconciling CBO's and DOD's Five-Year Tallies of Funding and Personnel, "The U.S. Military's Force Structure: A Primer" (July 2016), https://www.cbo.gov/publication/51535.

The simplest—but extremely crude—way to account for acquisition spending, if O&S spending figures are available, would be to multiply O&S figures by about 1.5 to get a total cost that also captures acquisition. That is based on the simple, long-standing accounting reality that, on average, O&S costs represent about two-thirds of the DoD budget, and acquisition costs represent one-third. So, on average, smoothed out over time, the acquisition costs associated with a given kind of combat or support unit will be about half of the O&S costs. But, of course, this approach makes no allowance for whether a unit is manpower-intensive or technology-intensive, so it is only a way to get a rough estimate, not a precise one.

A better approach is to identify the big-ticket items in a given type of military unit and figure out what they cost to acquire. Then, knowing how long they tend to last, and how many are needed per unit, one can estimate the annualized cost over the lifetime of the equipment. The Congressional Budget Office assumes most equipment will have a lifetime of 30 years, except fighter and attack aircraft, which are assumed to have a lifetime of 20 years, and Virginia-class submarines, for which longevity is assumed to be 33 years.[60] This approach tends to be easiest for the air force and navy, for which just a few types of expensive items dominate most procurement budgets, and harder for the army and marine corps. After calculating weapon-by-weapon costs for big-ticket items, one then accounts for the costs of minor equipment, which normally make up 40 to 50 percent of the total acquisition expense of outfitting a given unit.[61]

Data for conducting these calculations can be found in a couple of fairly handy sources. Each year the Department of Defense provides extensive documentation on the major weapons it is still buying. In using these databases, one must be careful to understand if the acquisition costs include RDT&E expenses (prorated across the number of weapons purchased, typically). One must also be careful to note whether costs are given in inflation-adjusted, constant dollars. Finally, one must take note of whether procurement costs are in effect "flyaway" costs that include only the bare-bones essential equipment for a given system, or if they also include some standard allocation of support equipment and spare parts in what is considered a more comprehensive or total cost.[62] A useful annual document for large programs is DoD's *Selected Acquisition Reports*. These show total quantities and total program acquisition costs for major platforms. Unfortunately, the unclassified summary documents do not break out RDT&E costs separately, so if one wishes that kind of information, one must look elsewhere. Good places to find it include the Government Accountability Office's *Weapon Systems Annual Assessment*, as well as more specific studies on individual weapons programs by the Congressional Budget Office, the Government Accountability Office, and the Congressional Research Service.[63]

Calculations of average annual costs can be made for various weapons and military systems using the O&S data in table 1.6 and the acquisition cost data in table 1.7. (Table 1.8 estimates the number of military personnel associated with various types of units.) Note that, for systems currently in development or production, table 1.7 prorates or distributes RDT&E costs among the expected number of platforms that will ultimately be purchased. But for weapons that have completed their RDT&E cycles as well as production runs, the table shows only their procurement costs (since the RDT&E costs are all truly "sunk," and since the best available data sources use this approach themselves).[64]

Whether or not a military system is still in production, it is important to ask if RDT&E should logically be included in an analysis of policy options. If the question is not whether to buy a system at all but rather how many to buy, RDT&E costs may not be relevant to the computation in any event. They would generally have to be incurred in full regardless of the size and scale of the ultimate production run. Thus, they should be removed from the cost-benefit calculation to the extent possible, and the focus should be on how procurement as well as O&S costs would vary for different choices about the size of a given force structure.

In addition, if one is cutting forces, near-term savings may not be as great as first anticipated. It may take time to shut down a unit, its base, and its associated support units. Also, many weapons for that unit might already have been purchased,

TABLE 1.7. Acquisition Costs of Selected US Defense Systems Still in Production (In Millions of Constant, Inflation-Adjusted 2020 Dollars, Rounded to Two Figures)

WEAPON SYSTEM (OR OTHER PLATFORM)	AVERAGE UNIT COST, RDT&E PLUS PROCUREMENT
ARMY	
AH-64E Apache helicopter	33
CH-47F Chinook helicopter	32
Joint Light Tactical Vehicle	0.42
PAC-3 MSE missile	5.3
UH-60M Black Hawk helicopter	21
NAVY (INCLUDING MARINE CORPS)	
Launch and arresting gear, Ford-class aircraft carrier	1,700
CVN-78 Ford-class aircraft carrier	12,000
Amphibious Combat Vehicle	7.9
AGM-88E Advanced HARM missile	1.2
AIM-9X Block II Sidewinder missile	0.62
CH-53K King Stallion helicopter	150
DDG 51 destroyer	1,500
E-2D Advanced Hawkeye aircraft	309
EA-18G Growler aircraft	110
MQ-4C Triton Long-Range UAV	230
P-8A Poseidon aircraft	310
SM-6 Surface-to-Air missile	5.0
SSBN 826 Columbia class submarine	8,900
SSN 774 Virginia Class submarine	3,100
Trident II nuclear-tipped missile	110
V-22 tilt-rotor aircraft	150
AIR FORCE	
AMRAAM missile	1.6
AWACS upgrade	100
C-130J aircraft	100
Evolved Expendable Launch Vehicle	370
GPS III satellite	610
JASSM Joint Air-to-Surface Standoff Missile	1.6
JDAM Joint Direct Attack Munition	0.32
KC-46A aircraft	240
MQ-9 Reaper UAV	32
SBIRS High satellite	1900
Small Diameter Bomb II	0.27
JOINT	
F-35 Lightning II aircraft (average across A/B/C)	125
F-35 Lightning II engine	25
ADDENDUM: COSTS FOR CERTAIN OLDER SYSTEMS (PROCUREMENT ONLY)	
MX ICBM missile	170
Ohio class nuclear-armed SSBN submarine	2,400
B-2 stealth bomber	1,200

(continued)

TABLE 1.7. (continued)

WEAPON SYSTEM (OR OTHER PLATFORM)	AVERAGE UNIT COST, RDT&E PLUS PROCUREMENT
B-1 bomber	340
Tomahawk sea-launched cruise missile	3.4
A-10 Warthog aircraft	17
F-15A-D aircraft	70
F-15E aircraft	85
F-16A-D aircraft	35
F-117 stealth fighter aircraft	170
A-6E Navy aircraft	60
AV-8B Harrier Navy aircraft	52
F-14 Navy aircraft	85
F/A-18A-D aircraft	68
LHD-1 amphibious assault ship	1,800
LSD-41 dock landing cargo ship, Whidbey-class	450
LCAC Landing Craft, Air Cushion	45
Littoral Combat Ship	580
LHA-6 amphibious assault ship	4,100
LPD-17 amphibious transport dock, San Antonio-class	1,700
Equipment for 1 army division and associated support (averaged across heavy and light divisions)	10,000
Equipment for 1 heavy army division and support	13,000
OH-58D Kiowa Warrior Helicopter	14
C-17 transport aircraft	270
Large Medium-Speed Roll-On/Roll-Off Ship, LMSR	630
Delta IV medium-lift rocket (hardware/total launch)	130/260
Atlas V medium-lift rocket (hardware/total cost)	130/260
Delta IV heavy-lift rocket (hardware/total cost)	255/450
M-1 Abrams tank	6.3

Notes: To calculate average annualized costs, divide most aircraft costs by 20 years of expected service life and most ships by 30 years, though submarines are sometimes assumed to last 33. Clearly, many systems last longer than 20 or 30 years—but they typically will undergo service-life extension programs or major modifications in such cases. As one indicator of typical cost growth, the following estimates for the F-35 were offered in 1997: the Department of Defense estimated an average acquisition cost per plane of $85 million, in 2020 dollars (when it expected to buy 3,000), and CBO predicted about $110 million. These costs include those for the engines.

Sources: Department of Defense, "Department of Defense Comprehensive Selected Acquisition Reports for the December 31, 2017, Reporting Requirements as Updated by the President's Fiscal Year 2019 Budget," Washington, D.C., December 31, 2017, https://www.acq.osd.mil/ara/am/sar/SST-2017-12.pdf. See also Ray Hall, David Mosher, and Michael O'Hanlon, *The START Treaty and Beyond* (Washington, D.C.: Congressional Budget Office, 1991), 139; Lane Pierrot and Jo Ann Vines, *A Look at Tomorrow's Tactical Air Forces* (Washington, D.C.: Congressional Budget Office, 1997), xiii, 3, 86; Michael Berger, *Moving the Marine Corps by Sea in the 1990s* (Washington, D.C.: Congressional Budget Office, 1989), 35; Eric J. Labs, *An Analysis of the Navy's Fiscal Year 2013 Shipbuilding Plan* (Washington, D.C.: Congressional Budget Office, 2012), 17; Eric J. Labs, *The Future of the Navy's Amphibious and Maritime Prepositioning Forces* (Washington, D.C.: Congressional Budget Office, 2004), 41; Adam Talaber, *Options for Restructuring the Army* (Washington, D.C.: Congressional Budget Office, 2005), xvii, 85; Kevin Eveker, *Modernizing the Army's Rotary-Wing Aviation Fleet* (Washington, D.C.: Congressional Budget Office, 2007), 5; Frances M. Lussier, *Budgetary and Military Effects of a Treaty Limiting Conventional Forces in Europe* (Washington, D.C.: Congressional Budget Office, 1990), 34; David Arthur, *Options for Strategic Military Transportation Systems* (Washington, D.C.: Congressional Budget Office, 2005), 42; and Federation of American Scientists, "M1 Abrams Main Battle Tank," Washington, D.C., 2000, available at https://fas.org/man/dod-101/sys/land/m1.htm.

TABLE 1.8. Uniformed Personnel for Key US Military Units

	NUMBER OF UNITS DIRECT IN 2020	MILITARY PERSONNEL PER UNIT		
		INDIRECT	OVERHEAD	TOTAL
DEPARTMENT OF THE ARMY				
Active-component armored brigade combat team	9	4,200	9,090	4,160	17,450
National Guard armored brigade combat team	5	4,140	9,090	1,210	14,440
Active-component Stryker brigade combat team	7	4,440	8,590	4,150	17,180
National Guard Stryker brigade combat team	2	4,450	8,590	1,190	14,230
Active-component infantry brigade combat team	14	4,230	8,090	3,920	16,250
National Guard infantry brigade combat team	19	3,560	8,090	1,060	12,720
Active-component aviation brigade	10	3,020	0	1,280	4,300
Reserve-component aviation brigade	12	2,520	0	230	2,750
Army special operations forces	n.a.	32,370	0	12,730	45,100
Rest of the army	n.a.	8,860	0	3,710	12,570
DEPARTMENT OF THE NAVY				
Aircraft carrier	11	3,200	760	2,620	6,590
Carrier air wing	10	1,630	1,300	1,930	4,860
Arleigh Burke-lass destroyer (DDG-51)	72	340	100	290	720
Ticonderoga-class cruiser (CG-47)	20	250	90	220	550
Littoral Combat Ship	24	190	70	170	430
Zumwalt-class destroyer (DDG-1000)	3	220	80	200	500
Attack submarine	51	190	50	150	390
Amphibious ship	35	710	170	580	1,450
Active-component Marine corps infantry battalion	24	1,490	1,990	2,300	5,780
Reserve-component Marine corps infantry battalion	8	2,070	560	1,740	4,370
Marine corps aircraft complement	24	760	890	1,090	2,750
Ballistic and guided-missile submarines	18	320	80	260	660
P-3 and P-8 maritime patrol aircraft squadron	8	630	500	750	1,890
Seabee construction engineers	n.a.	8,550	0	5,650	14,200
Navy special operations forces	n.a.	9,900	0	6,550	16,440
Marine corps special operations forces	n.a.	2,130	0	1,410	3,530
Rest of the navy	n.a.	22,860	0	15,120	37,990
Rest of the marine corps	n.a.	460	0	310	770
DEPARTMENT OF THE AIR FORCE				
A-10 attack aircraft squadron	6	350	440	400	1,190
F-15 fighter aircraft squadron	25	430	590	520	1,540
F-16 fighter aircraft squadron	46	450	370	420	1,250
F-22 fighter aircraft squadron	13	430	1,150	810	2,390
F-35 fighter aircraft squadron	10	430	1,510	1,000	2,940
B-52 bomber aircraft squadron	4	1,310	1,220	1,300	3,830
B-1B bomber aircraft squadron	4	940	1,680	1,350	3,980
B-2 bomber aircraft squadron	1	2,120	3,600	2,940	8,660

(continued)

TABLE 1.8.   (continued)

	NUMBER OF UNITS DIRECT IN 2020	MILITARY PERSONNEL PER UNIT		
		INDIRECT	OVERHEAD	TOTAL
C-130 cargo aircraft squadron	24	800	590	720	2,120
C-5 cargo aircraft squadron	3	780	820	830	2,430
C-17 cargo aircraft squadron	16	450	460	470	1,390
KC-135 tanker aircraft squadron	27	610	660	650	1,930
KC-10 tanker aircraft squadron	3	900	1,170	1,060	3,140
KC-46 tanker aircraft squadron	5	640	70	360	1,070
MQ-1 Predator UAS squadron	0	90	80	90	260
RQ-4 Global Hawk UAS squadron	3	470	750	630	1,840
MQ-9 Reaper UAS squadron	27	340	270	310	920
Minuteman III missile squadron	9	690	650	690	2,040
RED HORSE construction engineers	n.a.	12,780	0	6,560	19,340
Air Force special operations forces	n.a.	15,900	0	8,170	24,070
Rest of the air force	n.a.	32,370	0	16,630	49,010
Special Operations Command	n.a.	0	0	0	0
Defense health	n.a.	0	0	0	0
Program for retirees		0	0	0	0
Classified defensewide funding	n.a.	0	0	0	0
Rest of the defensewide organizations	n.a.	0	0	0	0

Note: For consistency, the Congressional Budget Office focused in this analysis on notional squadrons of 12 aircraft each.
Source: Congressional Budget Office, "The U.S. Military's Force Structure: A Primer" (July 2016), available at: https://www.cbo.gov/publication/51535.

meaning that a decision to eliminate it might come too late to save any big procurement dollars for the foreseeable future.

Even if production runs can be scaled back, savings might not be proportionate to reductions. That is because economies of scale would generally be lost as fewer weapons were purchased for acquisition, as well as operations and support (as noted earlier).[65] According to CBO, a 50 percent reduction in the annual rate of production for aircraft typically increases unit production costs by roughly 10 to 35 percent—depending in part on whether the lower rate of production remains above the "minimum economic rate" range or drops below it. These figures vary somewhat from one type of military system to another. For example, a 50 percent reduction in the production run for aircraft typically increases unit costs by 15 to 30 percent. A 50 percent reduction in the production rate for army vehicles generally implies a 25 to 40 percent increase in unit cost, roughly. For missiles, the typical unit cost increase historically has been in the range of 15 to 50 percent.[66]

Weapons also grow in cost because of their complexity and difficulties in figuring out how to build and efficiently manufacture them. For this reason, even if production runs are not cut back, weapons typically cost more to acquire than the Pentagon initially anticipates. For example, space vehicles and army ground combat vehicles both tend to cost 70 percent more to develop, and ground vehicles also typically cost 70 percent more to produce, than initially estimated. On the other end of the spectrum, ships typically cost about 15 percent more to develop than first projected and 10 percent more to produce (after adjusting for any changes in numbers of weapons bought). Using such information, CBO can crudely estimate cost growth for each weapon based on where it stands in its overall development and production cycle. On average, weapons cost around 20 to 50 percent more to acquire than initially forecast—in both the RDT&E and the procurement phases.[67]

The Congressional Budget Office also has weapons-specific models, most notably for fighter aircraft, that predict cost based on weapons performance characteristics. For fighter aircraft, cost estimates are based on aircraft weight, maximum speed, the amount of advanced materials in the airframe, the number of contractors involved in the effort, the technological maturity of software, the maximum airflow through the engines, engine thrust-to-weight ratios, specific fuel consumption, and avionics. The basic concept is to look at previous aircraft, take their performance characteristics for all these key attributes, run a regression to create a mathematical formula, and then plug in the expected performance features of the new plane to calculate expected costs.[68]

Conclusion: Defense Budgeting and Grand Strategy

To tie together the ideas and methods discussed in this chapter, imagine how two different concepts of grand strategy and/or military policy might be translated into force structure, weapons acquisition, and budget plans. Going back to the hypothetical presidential candidate mentioned at the beginning of the chapter, who wishes to promote a much different kind of grand strategy and national security policy for the United States, how might that candidate determine the budgetary implications?

One possible alternative concept might spring from a less activist foreign policy vision for the United States, based on a grand strategy of "offshore balancing" or "restraint." This worldview would reject much of the basic consensus that has guided US foreign policy since World War II and the start of the Cold War. The consensus has been premised on the notion that the United States cannot be indifferent to security conditions in key regions of the world like Europe and East Asia, and that it is better off trying to shape security conditions in those theaters continuously rather than "come to the rescue" only when major conflict erupts. But one could, at least in theory, argue that such an approach is no longer required in a post–Cold War world, or no longer possible for a gradually weakening United States (if in fact the United States is in relative decline), or no longer as necessary in a world with nuclear weapons and nuclear deterrence. Such a candidate might suggest fewer US alliances, fewer American troops deployed abroad in peacetime, and a smaller military (especially smaller ground forces) under normal peacetime conditions. That candidate might claim that such a grand strategy, and military budget, could save money and reduce the proclivity of the United States to wind up in foreign wars (though both those claims, especially the latter, might be contested).[69]

Another alternative approach might take overall grand strategy, including existing alliances and American overseas commitments, essentially as given. But a candidate might seek to develop and deploy new military technologies in more rapid and transformative style than would current strategy, in effect trying to create what is sometimes called a "revolution in military affairs," in order to take advantage of new opportunities, and perhaps also to mitigate new vulnerabilities, before an adversary could do so.[70]

Consider how each of these big ideas might be translated into more concrete material and budgetary terms. The approach of restraint might lead a candidate to believe it possible to cut the US Army by a substantial amount, as noted earlier. That conclusion might follow from the argument that while the United States has a constant interest in protecting the global sea lanes, airways, and orbital zones of outer space, it can afford to stay out of most foreign ground wars—only getting involved if truly essential, in the event that a rising great power begins to conquer large swaths of territory (particularly in Eurasia).[71] One estimate is that, with such a grand strategy, the United States could eliminate 40 percent of its active-duty brigades (perhaps temporarily building up again in the event that it did have to engage in a future major foreign ground campaign).[72] What might that particular interpretation of offshore balancing mean for the defense budget?

Today, the army has some thirty active-duty brigade combat teams and ten active-duty combat aviation brigades. Cutting 40 percent of each would remove twelve brigade combat teams and four aviation brigades from the force structure. Once this is fully implemented, annual recurring savings in O&S would be about $36 billion, consulting table 1.6. However, it is also possible that CBO is too optimistic about these savings, since it assumes almost all overhead and support in the defense budget can be reduced proportionately whenever force structure is scaled back. In that event, a more realistic figure might be only 70 to 80 percent as great, or roughly $25 billion to $30 billion (and even that figure might take several years to reach, as personnel ranks were gradually reduced and excessive bases at home and abroad were gradually closed).

Over time, acquisition cutbacks could contribute to the savings as well. As noted, averaged across all of DoD, acquisition costs are usually about half of O&S costs, implying added annual savings of $12 billion to $18 billion. But the army is not quite as technology-dominant a service as the air force and navy. Consulting table 1.7, we see that the average cost for acquiring all the equipment in a division (roughly three brigades) is about $10 billion. For four divisions, that makes $40 billion; adding in the costs of helicopters for the aviation brigades could drive the figure to $50 billion to $60 billion. Assuming average equipment lifetime of twenty years—a conservative number for aircraft and ground vehicles, with thirty years being a better estimate for ships—then implies an average annual procurement savings of only about $3 billion.[73]

Thus, we have a range of plausible values. For a lower-bound estimate, annual steady-state savings might be $25 billion in O&S and $3 billion in procurement, or close to $30 billion. For a higher bound, savings might exceed $50 billion, accounting for higher O&S and higher acquisition costs. So the answer might be framed as a range of roughly $30 billion to $50 billion a year, once the policy has been fully put in place (and smaller savings in the early years). Where in this range the actual savings would land would be a function largely of the details of just how the policy was implemented.

As for the second big idea, an attempt to expedite a military revolution and radically transform much of DoD's force structure, one could approach this goal in several ways. One might be to begin with a proposal for a reduction in large-unit ground forces of the type already considered earlier, since they are sometimes considered anachronistic by proponents of military revolutions, and perhaps add to the list several other systems that are frequently deemed obsolescent, often because they are assessed to be increasingly vulnerable. Aircraft carriers and short-range combat jets might be placed on such a list. Then, savings from all of these reductions could be used, perhaps in a budget-neutral way (as one possible approach), to dramatically increase resources available for research and development, prototyping, experimentation, and rapid fielding of various new concepts and capabilities as they show promise.

Starting with the $30 billion to $50 billion in eventual annual savings from the ground-force cuts discussed earlier, and adding in savings from reductions in aircraft carriers and short-range fighters, the math might go roughly as follows. First, if the carrier fleet were cut from 11 to 6 ships, and carrier escorts (often about

4 ships per carrier group) as well as the aircraft that fly off them were also reduced proportionately, annual savings might total $3.5 billion a year per carrier battle group, or almost $18 billion.

Assume that the air force's tactical aircraft squadrons were to be reduced by say twenty, out of fifty-five in the force structure today. The typical squadron of older aircraft involves around $250 million to $350 million in annual O&S costs. Thus, one might save another $6 billion in O&S costs, and some $10 billion overall in annual spending, once the changes were fully phased in.

Putting the pieces together—savings from cuts to main ground combat forces, aircraft carrier battle groups, and short-range air force combat jets—implies an annual defense budget savings of $60 billion to $80 billion. Again, however, it should be underscored that savings take time to realize. It should also be underscored that achieving the higher end of savings usually requires additional tough decisions—regarding base closures, headquarters efficiencies, and other management matters—beyond the initial choice to make reductions to force structure. More often than not, the lower end of such a range is a better prediction of attainable savings than the upper end, and that is especially true in the early years after a policy is put into effect.

Would that much money suffice for the task at hand? It is difficult to calculate any "right answer" as to how much money is needed to spark a revolution. Coming up with the right ideas can be relatively inexpensive, as with the US Navy's decision to develop the aircraft carrier during the lean budget years before World War II. But taking them to scale can be enormously expensive (recall that the US defense budget reached 35 percent of GDP by the latter World War II period). The range of numbers calculated here could allow, for example, that the Department of Defense's RDT&E budget grow by more than 50 percent, which would in fact be a dramatic change.

GAMING AND MODELING COMBAT

This chapter discusses methods for predicting how various combat scenarios will unfold. The endeavor is centrally important for purposes of planning wars, deciding whether to undertake or continue them, and shaping defense postures as well as budgets.

Clearly, predicting outcomes in war is a fraught business. There are potentially calamitous results for those who do it badly—and who then act on their incorrect assumptions. From the Redcoats at Lexington and Concord, to Union forces early in the American Civil War, to leaders in Europe as they started World War I in August of 2014 expecting to have forces home by fall, to Hitler and his generals as they hoped blitzkrieg could work as well against the Soviet Union as it had against Poland and France, to the United States in Vietnam and Iraq, there is a tendency toward overconfidence. That overconfidence can arise from the personal arrogance of leaders, jingoism of a nation, breathless enthusiasm among political and military elites about their country's new military capabilities or battle plans, or a lack of imagination about how the enemy might respond to attack. As Clausewitz underscored, given the high stakes it involves and the powerful passions it incites, war turns out typically to be a highly complex and unpredictable undertaking. Even the simplest things become hard. Human passions as well as national pride make most people more likely to double down and fight tenaciously than to capitulate at the first sign of trouble.

The ultimate purpose of wargaming and modeling is not to write detailed war plans; that is a separate enterprise. Rather, it is to help a country like the United States decide what kind of military, and military budget, it needs—as well as when and how to decide to use force. Certain types of more focused modeling can also help evaluate different types of individual weapons systems, through various cost-benefit-risk assessments, helping a military establishment estimate the optimal mix of weapons for achieving various battlefield outcomes.

Because most participants in policy debates will not have access to classified war plans or modeling results developed by the Pentagon, other methods are needed. Decisions about war and peace are among the most important any state can make. A democracy needs to make them through an inclusive process, even when that is not the executive branch's preference—as it often is not. And since the executive branch generally controls access to Pentagon models even when they are *not* classified, it is doubly important that outside analysts have methods of doing their own assessments.[1]

These modeling methods are often fairly simple. Sometimes, that simplicity limits their accuracy to an extent. But quite often their very simplicity can prove to be an advantage because it keeps the focus on the big assumptions and big ideas involved in any military engagement or combat scenario. It also avoids creating a false sense of precision about matters that generally cannot be forecast with great accuracy regardless of the methodology that is utilized. Such straightforward methods were central, for example, in designing the "two-regional-war" frameworks for the post–Cold War US military.[2] They were also used by some scholars to predict likely costs, casualties, and combat dynamics in conflicts such as Operation Desert Storm of 1991 as well as Operation Iraqi Freedom starting in 2003. They can be useful as well in analyzing hypothetical wars of the future, such as another Korean war, combat against Russia after Moscow decides to attack a Baltic state, or an attempted Chinese invasion of Taiwan. Complex models certainly have their uses, too. But it is beyond the scope and capacity of this book to explore them in detail—and, as noted, they should not always be the preferred instrument of analysis in any case.

Whether using simple or complex models, computations about combat depend greatly on variables that are often very hard to quantify. These include the quality of leadership, the effectiveness of any surprise, and the performance of new weapons systems or military operational concepts not previously tested in battle. In many situations, the politicization of a military may degrade its effectiveness, as well.[3] Depending on how the factors play out, a given operation may succeed or fail, and a given battle may be won or lost. Little if anything about war is preordained.[4]

Moreover, whatever the outcome of a specific battle, the factors that go into determining the winner of a *war* are often much different from, and broader than, those determining the outcome of a given engagement. As a former North Vietnamese officer memorably put it to the strategist and author Colonel Harry Summers, the United States may have won all the key battles in the Vietnam conflict, but it still lost the war. The tactical, theater-wide (or "operational"), and strategic levels of combat are distinct.[5] Models focus mostly on the former. Wargames and tabletop exercises are typically more flexible and effective in integrating analyses of individual battles into a larger picture. Modeling tends to involve simple arithmetic, and it works best when extrapolating from relatively recent and similar kinds of military engagements for which data are already available. Wargaming tends to be more qualitative and to focus on big-picture questions, though it can also incorporate modeling to examine specific engagements or battles. Thus, the two approaches are complementary and are sometimes even used together. Both are discussed here.

History suggests that even if one country or alliance is clearly stronger than another according to various military metrics, such as overall manpower or weaponry or both, it is still very hard to make high-confidence predictions about which side will win. Data gathered by the US Army Concepts Analysis Agency during the Cold War show that for countries with roughly comparable military capabilities—with neither side having more than a 50 percent edge against the other in military inputs—the attacker won 142 out of 230 battles, or 58 percent of the total.[6] Even though the attacking country usually won, it was far from assured of doing so. Just as important, there was no tendency toward stalemate (only 7 percent of all cases).[7] Put differently, relatively even "balances of power" do not produce peace by virtue of making the likely outcome of war a stalemate.

If the attacking side had a larger advantage—between 50 and 200 percent—it won some 63 percent of the time. It prevailed in 74 percent of all cases when having an even greater edge.[8] So even when military balances seem to clearly favor one side in a battle, outcomes are far from preordained.

These conclusions help explain arms race dynamics. It is not easy to measure a military balance accurately. Correlations of forces always depend on specifics of when and where a war is fought. Outcomes also depend on leadership, on initiative, on the creativity of war plans, and on other factors—many of them intangible.

So, if the business of predicting the results of war is very challenging, why bother with it at all? One reason is that, in military analysis as well as other disciplines, understanding what we *do not* or even *cannot* know is important in its own right. If a large body of human experience strongly suggests that warfare is an inherently risky and unpredictable business, the onus will be on policymakers who propose engaging in warfare to explain why it is necessary—and to explain how they have taken every reasonable precaution to minimize the chances of being surprised by the course of events. A good case in point is the Bush administration's decision to engage in what some have called a "war of choice" to overthrow

Saddam Hussein in 2003—and, even more, its decision to do so with smaller forces than recommended by military officers or other analysts, and without a well-developed plan for restoring order after Saddam was toppled. Greater care in preparation, and less confidence about the probable course of battle, would have been appropriate. This is especially true when war involves stabilizing a foreign country, not simply achieving a combat outcome. As the United States has repeatedly seen from Vietnam to Iraq to Afghanistan, translating battlefield wins into actual victory in war is extremely difficult.[9]

When analysis identifies areas of major uncertainty, be they technical or political, this is also useful for planning purposes. It helps underscore where a military organization may wish to develop backup options in case something goes wrong, and where it may choose to buy more insurance (in the form of redundant capabilities to achieve a given outcome, for example) as a hedge.

Modeling does not always produce pessimistic forecasts. But it does tend to temper overconfidence, especially if lower and upper, or optimistic *and* pessimistic, estimates are always generated as a matter of proper professional practice. For example, when one of my former colleagues at the Congressional Budget Office, Lane Pierrot, presciently argued in 1990 that it was possible US aircraft loss rates in Operation Desert Storm would be as low as peacetime training rates, she was making the sophisticated yet also straightforward argument that American countermeasures and flying practices might be good enough to counter much of the Iraqi air defense network. (It is worth noting that peacetime training, for pilots as well as other military personnel, is not exactly safe. Even in the safest years of the 1980s, more than 1,600 American military personnel lost their lives annually—and at least 1,000 of these each year were from accidents, including those during training. Even in the safest parts of the 1990s, toward decade's end, about 800 US personnel died each year, with 400 or more from accidents, and the rest mostly from illness or suicide. Fatality figures have been similar but slightly higher in the late 2010s.[10] Two to three dozen fatalities per year have occurred from flight operations.)[11]

But back to Operation Desert Storm: Pierrot foresaw that American airpower might render the latter air defenses largely powerless except when coalition aircraft had to fly low to go after certain targets or to penetrate particularly dense air defense bastions. Pierrot also realized that losses could be much higher. She wound up accurately prognosticating the results in part because she did not seek to be *too* accurate but focused instead on establishing plausible lower and upper bounds for expected losses. This is an important lesson about the proper way to model combat.

The Pierrot example also shows that the more elaborate models are not always better. Getting the fundamentals of a given battle or war right is the most important thing, and simplicity in method can sometimes help keep an analyst's eye on the eight ball. Sophisticated computer simulations attempt to capture the use of multiple weapons over complex terrain, in variable weather conditions, and with numerous possible assumptions about the performance of airpower, logistics systems, and other key determinants of battlefield outcomes. But they may lack some key data about weapons that perhaps have not been employed previously in battlefield conditions. Moreover, they cannot realistically capture all the intangible and human elements of warfare.[12] As my colleague Tom Stefanick notes, they also cannot truly capture the vulnerabilities of sophisticated command and control systems in the modern era—given all the threats that everything from cyberattacks, to physical strikes on key command nodes and communications arteries, to electronic warfare and nuclear-induced electromagnetic pulse can pose to those sophisticated yet highly fragile networks. Even the analyst working deep in the bowels of the Pentagon with all sorts of top-secret information at his or her beck and call should probably use simpler methodologies as "sanity checks" against the results of complex and classified computations.

Moreover, elaborate models are usually classified, and usually controlled by the executive branch of government. That means that the release of their results for general public debate is often controlled and at times even subject to politicization.

Simple models cannot easily capture all uncertainties of battle themselves, of course. But at least they do not claim or imply otherwise. Thus, while it is generally optimal to have recourse to *both* types of models—the detailed and the simple—the outside, independent analyst should generally not be intimidated into silence just because he or she lacks access to sensitive information and complex algorithms.

To take a prominent recent case, as discussed later in more detail, simple calculations about the likely course of Operation Desert Storm in 1991 by numerous independent analysts were generally more accurate than sophisticated Pentagon computer runs. While virtually all were too pessimistic, outside analysts generally estimated that US fatalities would total around 1,000 to 3,000. More elaborate models reportedly projected American deaths up to several times as numerous. (Actual combat losses were 148, including both Operation Desert Shield and Operation Desert Storm. Including accidents as well as other noncombat losses, nearly 400 Americans lost their lives.)[13] Outside analysts focused less on minute details of force levels and weapons performance, and more on higher-level aspects of the war. Were the Iraqi forces well trained? Were they likely to fight hard? Could they be largely isolated by a technologically dominant adversary who faced little to no time pressure in launching a ground operation, and could bomb for weeks if so desired?

The elaborate models, by contrast, were often jury-rigged adaptations of models built for hypothetical NATO–Warsaw Pact showdowns during the Cold War. Because the software code was complicated, it could not quickly or easily be rewritten from scratch in a matter of weeks. So existing models, even if designed for a different theater and scenario, were used. But Iraqi forces, even if they possessed Soviet equipment, did not fight nearly as well as Warsaw Pact units likely would have done. Because the complex modeling did not anticipate such a dynamic, its results were therefore quite inaccurate.

This chapter employs several different frameworks for gaming and modeling combat. All are rather simple, though all involve some arithmetic and some historical data. They also require making rough estimates about how certain types of modern military technology will perform on the battlefield, based on past wartime experience, recent live-fire exercises, and the performance of weapons on test ranges. They are distinct from manuals for troops, like the *Ranger Handbook* and many other documents, which describe how to perform certain military tasks and operations correctly, because they focus on a much more aggregated level of warfare and attempt to predict rather than prescribe.

The discussion begins with wargaming. Such efforts often involve multiple teams of players acting as various parties to a conflict, as well as a control group that writes out a scenario, sets parameters for the players, and introduces new exogenous elements to a given wargame at various points in the process. A wargame can focus more on tactics or more on broader strategy. Either way, it is particularly good for challenging core assumptions when there are major complexities and uncertainties associated with a possible war. Wargames can also be used in conjunction with computational models of individual battles. The wargames can link the latter into a broader assessment about the likely course of an overall campaign or war, combining qualitative and strategic judgment with quantitative assessment.[14]

The discussion then turns to what I call "micromodeling." This kind of computation typically assesses a very limited use of force, or a discrete element of a broader combat operation. Its purpose may be to estimate the effectiveness of one type of weapon versus another. It could also be to estimate budgetary costs. Such calculations might be done, for example, within the planning arms of the military services, or the Office of Cost Assessment and Program Evaluation (CAPE) in the Pentagon, or the independent Congressional Budget Office, as they seek to develop and evaluate options.

Then, I examine simple models of combat, starting with Lanchester equations, derived by a British engineer early in the twentieth century. The Lanchester equations are a good starting point to understand how combat modeling is done. However, they do not account well for most types of modern warfare, so the discussion next considers other models. For simplicity, I emphasize an approach modified from that of the late Trevor Dupuy, focused on air-ground combat.

The chapter's focus then turns to naval combat, including amphibious assault and blockade operations. Nuclear exchange calculations are discussed as well. The chapter concludes with a framework for analyzing progress, or the lack thereof, in counterinsurgency operations like those in Iraq and Afghanistan.

Wargaming

Wargaming means conducting a simulation exercise with the use of multiple "players" who take on the roles of various parties to a hypothetical crisis or conflict. Sometimes physical representations of various actors, forces, and geographic features are used, in which case it is often described as a "tabletop exercise" as well.

Wargaming can focus on political uncertainties and variables as much as military ones. Often, it is employed in such a way as to allow participants to focus on both—within the limits of the knowledge and creativity of the writers of the scenario, the control team overseeing the endeavor, and the players themselves. Even when such matters cannot be easily understood or foreseen, wargaming can stretch the imagination of players, challenge key assumptions, and help anticipate dynamics that might not be evident prior to the outbreak and development of a given scenario.

The modern concept of wargaming has origins in the nineteenth century but came fully into its own in the early twentieth century. For example, the US Navy conducted numerous wargames and tabletop exercises, often at the Naval War College, in the 1920s and 1930s to develop new concepts of aircraft carrier warfare that later influenced operations in World War II. It often took many of the ships and concepts of World War I, such as from the Battle of Jutland between Britain and Germany in 1916, and then introduced new or improved technologies to see how optimal tactics might change under different circumstances.[15] It led to a greater appreciation for the importance of the aircraft carrier in naval combat, and also gained tactical insights, such as the value of massing aircraft for attack.[16]

Hitler's officers also used wargaming to prepare their blitzkrieg attack against France, among other innovations. They focused their attention on matters such as logistics, deceptive feints, and the likely reactions—and reaction times—of French decision makers, who were represented in the games by individuals with knowledge of France's leaders of the era.[17]

After World War II, wargames were used to explore ideas such as the use of helicopters—a new invention—on the modern battlefield. Sometimes, ideas that grew out of games were then tested with real equipment and mock battlefields.[18]

To give an example from the modern era, a Brookings wargame on Iraq in 2006, when most hope seemed lost in that war, asked fundamental questions about an alternative approach that would envision a controlled US withdrawal. By forcing players to accept a new premise, and then by tasking different participants with various roles including those of Iran and other regional nations, it was able to look several steps down the path toward a new possible policy. Games like this generally play out over many hours and even several days, leading to a more thorough examination of second-order, third-order, and subsequent consequences of a given policy than the typical analyst's mind would otherwise likely explore.[19]

A RAND wargame in 2016 examined how NATO might respond to a Russian invasion of the Baltics. Here, as with similar games and studies, the emphasis was on logistics and geography. In such games, there is generally an attempt to make the dynamics reflective of realities on the ground such as the actual capacities of road networks, rail lines, ports, and airfields. In such scenarios, NATO's decision-making methods also can be factored into the dynamics. So can uncertainties about how command and control networks will perform under various stresses or attacks. So can the proclivity of various actors to consider limited types of nuclear strikes as an escalatory move—perhaps if they find themselves losing in a conventional fight.[20]

Looking forward, a wargame might explore scenarios in which Russia and China cooperate in some sense against the United States and allies. It might attempt to envision how new technologies like quantum computing and artificial intelligence could affect the future battlefield (though of course, the fidelity of any such assumptions will only be as good as the creators and players of the game—so the purpose of this method for understanding such futuristic technologies is less to make confident predictions than to explore different possibilities). It could test how different types of force postures, and different warfighting strategies, might fare in a given set of circumstances—and what kinds of successful outcomes, or unpleasant choices, might eventually result.[21]

Micromodeling

Shifting from the big picture, with wargaming, to the specific, with micromodeling, let us consider one illustrative problem: What, for example, might be the most economical way to destroy 100 fixed aimpoints within a given country? This is the kind of question that a simple set of arithmetic calculations, if informed by a correct framing of the problem and reasonably good data, can often help answer. As is often the case, for the problem at hand, there would likely not be a single correct answer to this question across all types of scenarios. So we will have to make more assumptions to reach a verdict for a specific case.

To simplify the problem, let us focus on one particular choice: whether to use a stealthy, "penetrating" bomber like the B-2 (carrying cheap, "dumb" bombs) to attack targets directly, or whether to use aircraft from standoff distances that do not penetrate the airspace in question, but instead use cruise missiles launched from an aircraft like a B-52. This comparison only makes sense if both the bombers and the cruise missiles can successfully reach their targets. If some losses are expected, the respective expected costs of replacing the losses should be factored into the calculation. So, of course, should the implications of losing bomber pilots—or having them captured.

Since the United States already has B-2 and B-52 bombers, this example is somewhat contrived. But it could still be relevant in deciding what type of plane, and what types of munitions, to buy or to keep in the future.

To simplify, assume that the B-52-like aircraft can carry ten cruise missiles and the B-2 bomber can carry twenty bombs (say, an inexpensive short-range guided munition such as the joint direct attack munition [JDAM], which is terminally guided by GPS). Further assume that the cruise missiles and bombs are equivalent, in terms of expected effect on the target—their explosive power and their accuracy are comparable, so the same number of weapons must be used on each target regardless of which ordnance is selected. (In fact, assume that two weapons must be dropped on each target.) If the targets must all be destroyed on the first sortie of planes, to maximize the shock value and prevent the enemy from recovery and prompt retaliation, we need a way to deliver 200 weapons to target in a single salvo. By the preceding assumptions, that would require either ten B-2 bombers or twenty B-52/747 aircraft.

To complete the calculation, some information on costs is needed. Assume that the marginal production cost of buying B-2s is $850 million per airplane (assuming that the research and development of the plane was already completed, meaning that such costs are "sunk" and as such are no longer relevant to future policy choices). And assume the cost of a B-52 or 747 carrying cruise missiles to be $250 million, again not far off from reality. Cruise missiles are assumed to cost $1 million each in the following discussion; JDAM bombs $20,000 apiece.

So buying ten B-2 bombers and 200 JDAMs would cost about $8.505 billion, whereas buying twenty B-52/747 aircraft and 200 cruise missiles would cost $5.2 billion. Clearly, if only one mission of this type were expected over the lifetime of the aircraft, the B-52/747 option would be cheaper. Factoring in estimated operating costs over a thirty-year lifetime, the answer would not change fundamentally. The added cost per plane of maintaining the B-2 would be partly, but not completely, canceled out by the fact that more B-52s would be needed to accomplish the same mission, according to assumptions about likely weapons payload.

However, one can see from the structure of the computation that, to the extent many more bombs had to be delivered, at some point things would change. Given how often the United States engages in combat operations, multiple missions should probably be expected in the next twenty to thirty years as well. In that event, the math would swing back in favor of the B-2 as the more economical platform.

The Lanchester Equations

The Lanchester equations were formulated more than a century ago by a British engineer, Frederick Lanchester, who gave them their name. There are several forms of these equations, but two are of particular note: for direct fire (such as rifles aimed at specific individuals) and for indirect fire (such as artillery fired into a broad area where enemy forces are known to be located, even if they are not individually visible and targetable).

Of course, modern war has elements of both direct and indirect fire, as well as many different types of weapons in the mix. A complex model would include many types of weapons, each with its own coefficients for lethality, rates of fire, and survivability, among other things. In that sense, a complex model is often built out of individual component elements that resemble the Lanchester equations, so it is doubly useful to understand these building blocks.

Direct Fire Equation

Imagine two rows of eighteenth-century soldiers lined up firing at each other. Assume they are not quite shoulder to shoulder but instead have some spacing between them (making it very unlikely that one soldier will be hurt by a weapon fired at another soldier). Assume further that there is no issue of concealment; all soldiers on both sides are within sight, and weapons range, of each other.

This model of combat may be a relatively good way to understand naval gunfire exchange at sea (more on that appears in a subsequent part of this chapter), certain types of aerial combat in the skies, and general warfare in which there is little subtlety or complexity to the battlefield—enemy forces see each other and try to destroy each other in a fairly straightforward exchange of gunfire.

With this image of combat in mind, and two armies represented by $A(t)$ and $B(t)$, the basic mathematics of the Lanchester equation are simple to derive. (They involve a small amount of very basic calculus; those unable to follow it need not worry, since the result can be understood just through arithmetic.) $A(t)$ and $B(t)$ are the total numbers of soldiers on each side still unwounded and capable of fighting at a given time; $A(0)$ and $B(0)$ are their initial values. Clearly, $A(t)$ will diminish faster the larger the number of enemy soldiers on the other side and the more effective that side's weapons. Weapons effectiveness, which can be simplified as the multiplicative product of the rate of fire, the accuracy of the weapon, and the lethality of the weapon, is condensed into a single term for each side (represented by a and b, respectively, for army A and army B). In mathematical form, assuming a simple linear relationship, this can be written as follows (those uninterested in the derivation or put off by the calculus can simply skip a few lines to the actual formula):

$$dA(t)/dt = -bB(t)$$

Similarly, for $B(t)$, we have:

$$dB(t)/dt = -aA(t)$$

In other words, A's forces decline faster to the extent that B has a larger army firing more lethal weaponry at them, and vice versa. By the chain rule, $dA(t)/dt$ can also be written as:

$$dA(t)/dt = [dA(t)/dB(t)][dB(t)/dt]$$

Substituting the term on the right into the first equation, we get: $[dA(t)/dB(t)][dB(t)/dt] = -bB(t)$

Further substituting for $dB(t)/dt$ from the second equation above yields:

$$[dA(t)/dB(t)][-aA(t)] = -bB(t)$$

Rearranging terms and canceling out the respective minus signs, we get:

$$a[A(t)][dA(t)] = b[B(t)][dB(t)]$$

Integrating, and expressing for the time $t = T$, we get:

$$A^2(T) - A^2(0) = [b/a][B^2(T) - B^2(0)]$$

As one example, assume army A starts with ten soldiers and army B with twenty (at time $t=0$), and assume weapons effectiveness to be the same on both sides. How many soldiers will army B still have standing when A's force has been wiped out (at time $t = T$)? This boils down to solving the following arithmetic problem:

$$0^2 - 10^2 = B^2(T) - 20^2$$

10^2 is of course 100, and 20^2 is 400, so this becomes:

$$-100 = B^2(T) - 400$$
$$300 = B^2(T)$$
$$B(T) = \sqrt{300} = 17 \text{ (roughly)}$$

That is, army B loses just three soldiers in annihilating all ten of A's soldiers. The Lanchester direct fire equation gives a great premium to numerical superiority, other things being equal. (Every soldier in B's army on average faces only half the fire of one soldier on the other side; every soldier in A's army by contrast is being shot at on average by two soldiers from B, explaining why A is at such a disadvantage in this engagement.)

Indirect Fire

At least two things are unrealistic about the scenario behind the direct-fire Lanchester equation. First, at least for all eras since the eighteenth century, enemy forces will take cover to get out of the way of weapons. Second, many weapons are fired in a way to barrage an area rather than directly strike a specific individual or vehicle. Pure musket-fire exchanges no longer tend to occur in warfare.

The indirect-fire version of the Lanchester equations corrects for these problems. It does so at the price of going to the other extreme and eliminating any role for direct-fire weaponry. But it is still instructive to see how the math changes, and how the predicted battlefield results can also therefore change. If nothing else, this helps us appreciate the stark differences between battlefield dynamics for wars dominated by direct fire and those dominated by indirect fire. (Capturing both direct and indirect fire in a single Lanchester equation is of course more realistic, but also more complicated mathematically. In fact, when trying to capture such complex dynamics, I do not employ Lanchester equations, but other types, as discussed further later in the chapter.)

In the Lanchester indirect-fire equations, the likelihood that one's forces will suffer losses becomes proportionate to three terms. Two are as before, the effectiveness of the enemy's weapons and the number of enemy forces. The third term is the density of one's *own* forces on the battlefield. Having more people means having more targets, increasing the chances that an enemy weapon fired more or less randomly at a broad area will by chance strike soldiers in that area upon detonation. The resulting formula is:

$$A(T) - A(0) = [b/a][B(T) - B(0)]$$

With this formulation, there is much less benefit to numerical superiority, as having more troops on the battlefield gives one more shooters but also provides the enemy more targets. Mathematically, the number of one's own forces is taken only to the first power, and not squared, as a result. As one simple example, if A and B have equally effective weapons, and A starts with 10 soldiers while B begins with 20, they will lose personnel at the same rate. A will have 5 people left when B has 15 left; A will run out of soldiers when B has 10 still standing. Again, B wins, but less dramatically than in the direct-fire case. And in a situation where A had somewhat better weapons than B, say 2.1 times as good, it could win. By contrast, in the direct-fire equations, it would need to possess a huge (more than fourfold) advantage in weaponry in order to compensate for its fewer forces and prevail in the engagement.

Modeling Air-Ground Combat

Although the Lanchester equations can be used to model modern air-ground combined warfare, other methods are probably better in light of the complexities of such combat. Prior to Operation Desert Storm in 1991, a number of scholars, using models and databases developed largely for assessing the NATO–Warsaw Pact military balance during the Cold War, estimated the losses likely to result in a war to expel Iraqi forces from Kuwait. Virtually all these estimates were too high, but they were also generally more accurate than those produced by the Pentagon before the US-led war against Iraq began. Indeed, they were virtually all correct in predicting a short, decisive conflict in which US casualties would be far less than American losses in the Vietnam War or the Korean War. In that sense, the flawed estimates were still useful.[22]

Epstein's Adaptive Dynamic Model

One of these methods was Joshua Epstein's adaptive dynamic model. It is more sophisticated than the famous, century-old Lanchester equations, which as noted require simplifying assumptions about the nature of weaponry that apply much better to eighteenth-century musket fire, nineteenth-century battleship duels, or World War I artillery exchanges than to the modern battlefield.[23] It is less complex than the detailed, and classified, computer models such as "TACWAR" and "Janus" used by the Pentagon community to predict combat outcomes. But it offers simplicity and accessibility.[24] That helps avoid the "garbage in, gospel out" fallacy, by which one can be hypnotized by seemingly rigorous computer outputs even if they depend on badly flawed data inputs or other limitations.

Epstein's model, created when he was at the Brookings Institution, explicitly accounts for the roles of airpower, ground power, and maneuver in modern warfare. Specifically, it focuses on armored units and ground-attack airplanes, and requires a user to estimate key performance parameters for each side in a given battle. It is an attrition model—with the opposing armies pitted against each other directly, grinding down each other's initial strength as the combat unfolds day by day.

Epstein's approach challenges the popular idea that a sufficient "force-to-space" ratio ensures a viable defense. That force-to-space ratio is typically cited as one armored division equivalent (ADE) per twenty-five kilometers of front according to believers in such an approach. (An ADE is essentially defined as a modern American heavy division, and other countries' forces are then evaluated relative to this standard; for example, an Iraqi division with somewhat smaller size and inferior equipment relative to a US division might rate as 0.5 ADEs.) However, some estimates suggest an ADE can cover twice as much frontage—underscoring the imprecision of this rule of thumb, a point that Epstein also emphasizes.[25] Epstein further rejects the "3:1 rule"—the view that a defense can fend off an attacker if it prevents the latter from gaining a 3:1 force advantage in the sector of attempted breakthrough.[26] In fact, as noted earlier, attackers have often succeeded historically when roughly equal to, or even smaller than, the defender.[27]

In the computations, an "exchange ratio" based on the quality of the opposing forces is used to estimate the relative loss rates due to ground combat. For example, for every attrition of 0.1 ADEs of the superior military, the inferior force would lose 0.2 ADEs if the exchange ratio is 2:1 against it. Invoking historical data, Epstein's model assumes that rate of attacker losses per day is usually 1 percent to 5 percent for a division-sized force, though, of course, those numbers can vary even more depending on the specific circumstances of battle.[28] Epstein's model allows the defender to reduce this intensity of battle by staging an orderly tactical retreat, trading space for time, perhaps in order to allow an opportunity for reinforcements to arrive.[29]

As noted, the model also specifically incorporates a role for ground-attack aircraft in the close-air support role. They are assumed to be capable of dropping a given number of munitions per sortie and flying a given number of sorties per day (with a given probability of being shot down on each mission). Each munition is assigned a "kill probability" to reflect the likelihood it will strike and destroy a major ground vehicle. Knowing the number of such ground vehicles per division, typically 1,200 for a modern American division (though closer to 3,000 if one includes trucks and other support vehicles),[30] one can translate the attrition from aerial attacks into armored division equivalents, thereby linking the ground and air wars conceptually and mathematically.[31]

There are limitations to the fidelity of these kinds of models in their ability to capture all the important dynamics of modern warfare. For example, airpower is of course used against many targets besides vehicles in the field.[32] In Desert Storm, for example, while just over half of all strike missions were against fielded Iraqi forces, the remaining 43 percent focused on targets like airfields, SCUD missile launchers, surface-to-air missile sites and other air defense infrastructure, strategic lines of communication including bridges and port facilities and train lines, military industry, suspected weapons of mass destruction sites, telecommunications, electricity grids, oil assets, and leadership targets. More than 1,000 US attack aircraft (plus another 250 or so from allies such as Saudi Arabia and Britain) flew an average of more than 2,000 missions a day and dropped more than 200,000 munitions, not quite 10 percent of them precision-guided.[33] Epstein's model and others like it do not allow a role for such strategic airpower.

Incidentally, and by way of comparison, it might be of interest that in NATO's 1999 air war against Serbia, Operation Allied Force, the United States and allies dropped munitions against roughly 7,600 fixed targets and 3,400 mobile targets. A total of about 1,000 NATO aircraft were ultimately employed in the conflict, including strike planes and air superiority fighters and support aircraft, flying nearly 40,000 total sorties. Against those 11,000 aimpoints, they dropped some 28,000 munitions, of which about 83 percent were American. A total of nearly 30 percent were precision-guided. Incidentally, the proportion of "smart bombs" went up to nearly 70 percent in Afghanistan in 2001, and then to nearly 100 percent in NATO's 2011 campaign in Libya.[34]

Operation Desert Storm

How did this type of model do in estimating the outcome of Operation Desert Storm? Like other independent scholars working with similar models, Epstein accurately predicted rapid, decisive victory by coalition forces, with considerably higher casualties on the Iraqi side than the American side. Epstein predicted weeks of combat and a US-coalition casualty range of 3,000 to 16,000 (dead and wounded combined).[35] The calculations assumed that a coalition combined-arms counteroffensive would follow a relatively short air campaign, given what was known about likely Pentagon war plans at the time. As it turned out, the coalition waged a fairly long air campaign of more than a month, prior to undertaking ground operations.[36]

The Department of Defense, despite knowing its own war plans in advance, and despite having legions of sophisticated computer modelers at its beck and call, appears to have done a much less accurate job of forecasting the fight. Press reports suggested that the Pentagon was prepared for at least 30,000 or more US casualties in the war, implying perhaps 5,000 dead and 25,000 wounded based on recent historical ratios.[37]

In the actual event, losses were less than forecast. By official count, a total of 382 Americans died in the southwest Asian theater in the combined course of Operation

Desert Shield, which began in August 1990, and Desert Storm, as that operation was renamed in January 1991. That count includes prewar and postwar fatalities as well. Of the total, as noted previously, 148 US troops died in combat, including 35 killed accidentally by so-called friendly fire. Others died in accidents of various types, on and off the immediate battlefield.[38] Considering allied forces as well, and using round figures, the coalition suffered about 240 combat deaths and about 1,500 total casualties.[39]

Epstein's predictions, like those of Barry Posen, Richard Kugler, and Trevor Dupuy, were quite good. Yes, the actual coalition losses were fewer than the lower bound of most of these analyses. But getting the essence of the battle right, and estimating a likely range of casualties that nearly encompasses the actual outcome, is impressive prescience, compared with what can realistically be forecast about human combat. Had they known that coalition forces would bomb Iraqi positions for more than a month before starting the ground campaign, these scholars could probably have done an even better job of estimating likely casualties in Desert Storm.

Why was the outcome of Operation Desert Storm even more lopsided in the coalition's favor than had been predicted? High technology explains much of it. For example, the tactic of "tank plinking," in which laser-guided bombs were dropped on Iraqi armor (often in the early evening, when the desert sands cooled more quickly than Iraqi armor, revealing the locations of the latter to infrared sensors), was developed in the course of the war. The ability of coalition aircraft to undertake that and other effective tactics from high altitude, out of range of Iraq's man-portable surface-to-air missiles, was also not foreseen—even by war planners, who had coalition pilots fly low for the first days of battle. The United States had new reconnaissance technologies, such as the Joint Surveillance and Target Attack Radar System (JSTARS), that made it much easier to detect moving Iraqi vehicles.[40] American forces also benefited from their supporting superstructure—intelligence, communications, equipment maintenance, and logistics support—even more than expected.[41]

In addition, Iraqi forces performed less well than predicted. Stephen Biddle has enumerated many of the basic mistakes the Iraqis made in engagements like the Battle of 73 Easting on February 26, 1991. Among other things, they failed to post advance guards ahead of their dug-in positions and failed to remove dirt from the vicinity of those positions to keep the locations of dug-in forces secret.[42] As a result of all these factors, the American-led victory over Iraq was far more decisive than Israeli victories in previous wars against Syria, Jordan, and Egypt, in which the Israeli advantage in quality per troop or unit usually turned out to be three to five times greater than the adversary.[43] It was enormously more decisive than NATO's assumed advantages against the Warsaw Pact. Thus, the more modeling efforts tended to focus on history, analogy, and recent experience in the Middle East in particular, the better they tended to do at predicting outcomes. This again underscores the importance of keeping the math simple when possible, so that it does not swallow up more intuitive discussions and debates about the capabilities and likely performance of different armies, in ways that the independent analysts just mentioned as well as scholars like Kenneth Pollack, Caitlin Talmadge, and Anthony Cordesman so wisely emphasize in their respective work.[44]

One can get the gist of what happened in the air war with simple calculations. In broad brush, Iraq had about 1 million individuals under arms, perhaps a third of whom were in position to fight in the general Kuwaiti theater. Iraq began the fight with about 10,000 pieces of heavy weaponry in theater, amounting to roughly ten divisions or about five ADEs once allowance is made for their lower quality relative to US forces. (These adjustments use what was called the WEI/WUV system during the Cold War, as well as the TASCFORM methodology. The former acronym stands for "weapon effectiveness indices/weighted unit values," and the latter a "technique for assessing comparative force modernization.") Coalition forces had about 7.0 ADEs plus a slew of high-tech airpower operating from land and from ships in the Arabian/Persian Gulf.[45]

Iraq appears to have lost a cumulative total of roughly 3,000 to 4,000 tanks, armored personnel carriers, and large-bore artillery tubes during the air war. It lost almost as much equipment again during the ground campaign, which is discussed later.

As for personnel, though these figures are even more uncertain than those for weaponry, Iraq probably had about 340,000 personnel in the broader Kuwait theater at the start of hostilities, plus or minus several tens of thousands perhaps.[46] Iraqi casualties probably numbered in the low tens of thousands. Somewhat more than 2,000 Iraqi civilians are also believed to have died in the course of the conflict.[47]

In the air war, most Iraqi equipment losses resulted from use of up to 10,000 precision-guided air-to-ground munitions (PGMs), including Maverick and Walleye air-to-surface missiles and laser-guided bombs.[48] Airpower used by itself was probably more effective in this situation than in most combat environments given the open terrain and the static and isolated targets, and thus the availability of tactics such as tank plinking.[49] Coalition air forces may have destroyed a grand total of as many as 6,000 to 8,000 vehicles of all types, given typical ratios of heavy weapons to support vehicles in modern armies.[50] That implies better than a 60 percent kill probability per weapon—a very high figure, compared with historical norms.[51]

The Dupuy Model for Ground Combat

For combined-arms maneuver warfare such as Desert Storm, and also for urban or infantry combat, a simplified version of the model of the late US Army colonel Trevor Dupuy can be quite useful. The Dupuy method focuses on troops, not ADEs, as the core independent variable for analysis. Like Epstein's approach, it is an attrition model that effectively pits the two sides in a battle (or larger war) directly against each other and calculates daily losses for both sides. Also like the Epstein model, the Dupuy method requires the user to input data to reflect the quantity as well as the quality of each side's troops and equipment.

Dupuy's methodology is informed by a very detailed dataset on past conflicts. It incorporates coefficients for a wide range of factors such as weather, surprise, and terrain that require subjective interpretation to employ, but that allow for more explicit consideration of these elements of combat than some other models. It does not, however, have a specific and separate way of considering the role of airpower.[52]

Dupuy's methodology is a bit hard to follow in its detail, but sensible and logical in its main framework. I simplify it here somewhat. He begins by translating the number of troops fielded by each side into a total power figure, P. In my modified approach, P is the product of three terms: the size of the fielded force, its quality, and a situational factor. The advantages of airpower and other advanced technologies are incorporated through the quality term. The situational term addresses the degree of surprise achieved in the early days of battle (for an attacker) and also accounts for the benefits of any concealment, complex terrain, and prepared positions (for a defender), as well as weather and time of day or night.

Using these power figures to calculate relative casualties requires use of detailed, lengthy tables that reflect Dupuy's experiences with a wide body of combat data from many past battles. In essence, each side's daily casualties are estimated to be the product of three main types of terms: total troop strength, times a daily maximum casualty rate, times a factor accounting for the power differentials between the two sides.[53]

In mathematical form, the terms for the attacker and defender are:

$$P_{ATTACKER} = (N_{ATTACKER})(Q_{ATTACKER})(S_{ATTACKER})$$
$$P_{DEFENDER} = (N_{DEFENDER})(Q_{DEFENDER})(S_{DEFENDER})$$

Again, for the attacker, the first term is the number of its troops, the second term is the relative quality of its troops, and the third term represents situational factors of direct relevance to the nature of the attack. For the defender, the quality term can be set equal to 1 for simplicity, since what matters mathematically is just the relative quality of the two sides. Then the attacker's Q term will be more than 1 if it is considered the better force, and less than 1 if it is inferior.

Often the quality factor for the stronger side can be three to five times greater than the quality of the weaker side. Such ratios would apply, for example, to most Israeli-Arab wars of recent decades. In an extreme case, the quality advantage for the superior force can even be greater, as seen later in the discussion of Operation Desert Storm.

The situational factor would generally range from 1 to 2, depending on the degree to which the attacker is aided by surprise or the defender by weather, terrain, and prepared defensive positions. (Each of the individual terms—for weather, for terrain, for the nature of prepared positions—can typically vary by about 50 percent, meaning that its mathematical representation might vary from 1 to 1.5 on average. They are then multiplied together to create the overall effect or score for S, as I have simplified the approach, in general keeping with Dupuy's own formula.) Dupuy's books provide detailed estimates of what the various factors might be for different types of defensive positions, varying types of weather, and surprise.[54] Essentially, he did the equivalent of regressions, but without the formal statistical methods—developing through trial and error a system that could explain, reasonably accurately, the historical battles for which he had gathered data.

The terms for daily casualties might then be as follows. In the calculation, I take 1 percent losses as the standardized attrition constant for both sides; this coefficient should be the same for both sides, since it is simply a gauge of the overall intensity of the fighting, and disparities in the two sides are entered through the other factors:

$$C_{ATTACKER} = (0.01)(N_{ATTACKER})(P_{DEFENDER}/P_{ATTACKER})$$
$$C_{DEFENDER} = (0.01)(N_{DEFENDER})(P_{ATTACKER}/P_{DEFENDER})$$

It should be noted that, especially for large armies where many units will be out of range of the enemy on any given day, a daily attrition constant of 0.01 might be too high. One simple modification is simply to keep the normalizing constant of 0.01 (which, again, should always be the same for both sides), but then to reinterpret the formula as generating *weekly* rather than daily attrition estimates.[55]

The simplicity of this equation (like all others considered here) is both its strength and its weakness. There is clearly some arbitrariness in the calculation of each side's power. However, Dupuy's books give some historical perspective as to how the qualitative factors can be reasonably estimated. Certainly Dupuy's own personal track record was rather good in using historical analogy and instinct to estimate such factors. It can be harder for someone else with less experience trying to use his approach, but the extensive databases in his books make the process somewhat tractable.

The Dupuy method, with its focus on foot soldiers, seems best suited to infantry battle. However, Dupuy also applied his model to predicting Desert Storm casualties, with accuracy comparable to that of the other models discussed earlier in this chapter.[56] And for mixed cases involving heavy combat as well as infantry battle, it can be useful, too. I apply it here to the US invasion of Panama in 1989 and Operation Desert Storm in 1991.

Panama

In Operation Just Cause of December 1989, US forces overthrew Panamanian strongman Manuel Noriega and defeated his armed forces. About 20,000 American personnel were part of the overall mission, including navy Seals, army Rangers, and many of the 10,000 American troops stationed in Panama. The operation involved simultaneous nighttime airborne operations against more than two dozen objectives throughout the country. Special forces infiltrated key sites shortly before the airborne assaults to take down Panamanian communications and interfere with any attempts at sustained resistance. In the battle, 23 Americans died, as did about 300 Panamanian military personnel (with nearly 500 more detained). Total US casualties including wounded were about 350; total Panamanian casualties including killed, wounded, and detained totaled some 850 according to reports (though I would not be surprised if the true figure was substantially higher).[57] Some 200 to 600 Panamanian civilians died as well.[58]

As explained previously, Dupuy's approach begins with a calculation of the power of the two sides. With US combat forces somewhat more than 20,000 strong, if they are accorded a quality advantage of 3:1 over Panama's military, and assumed to enjoy a 15 percent benefit from surprise, multiplying these factors together gives them a power score of almost 70,000. Counting paramilitary units, Panama may have had about 8,500 troops available, though the number who were truly engaged in combat may well have been less. The fact that they fought on the defensive and in complex terrain might be assumed to give them a doubling of capability, for a total power of about 17,000. Again, these numbers are rough. The resulting US power advantage would be about 4 (which shows up as the inverse of 4, or 0.25, in the first equation below).

American daily casualties can then be estimated at:

$$(20,000 \times 0.01 \times 0.25) = 50$$

Over two days, US casualties would be about 100, with about 20 killed.

For Panama, flipping over the power ratio term, we get: $(8,500 \times 0.01 \times 4) = 340$

Over two days, Panama's casualties are estimated at 680, with about 170 killed. These results track reasonably well with the actual outcome.[59] A more accurate estimate would result from either increasing the US quality advantage or reduc-ing the estimated number of Panamanian personnel involved in combat (or lengthening the presumed duration of the conflict). A reasonable alternative might be to accord US forces a 6:1 quality advantage, in light of technology, airpower, and night-vision capability and the like, and a 50 percent benefit from surprise. American forces would then have about a 10:1 overall advantage in power. That would lead to an estimate of daily US casualties of about 20, and daily Panama-nian losses (killed and wounded) of about 800.

Operation Desert Storm Revisited

Returning to Operation Desert Storm, we know from the preceding discussion that Iraq lost about one-third of its military strength originally deployed to the theater in and near Kuwait due to the coalition air campaign that preceded the ground war. One way to represent this mathematically is to assume that one-third of the 340,000 or so Iraqi troops who had been deployed there initially were rendered dead, wounded, or combat ineffective due to loss of equipment and unit cohesion. That leaves roughly 225,000 Iraqi forces to take on 700,000 from the US-led coalition in the combined air-ground fight that ended the war.

For a pessimistic calculation for the coalition, one might assume just a 3:1 qual-ity advantage for US and UK and other coalition forces, and a doubling of Iraqi power due to the advantages of being dug in, on the defensive (even though, after the fact, we now realize that these advantages did not prove so important). Thus, the power term for coalition forces would be 2.1 million and for Iraqi forces, 450,000.

Coalition daily loss rates would then be roughly $(0.01)(700,000)(450,000/2,100,000) = 1,500$.

Iraqi daily loss rates would be estimated at $(0.01)(225,000)(2,100,000/450,000) = 10,500$.

Most militaries cease to function effectively after absorbing 30 to 50 percent attrition. So if this pace of combat and losses played out for, say, ten days, Iraq could be assumed to be defeated, having suffered close to 100,000 losses by then (the numbers of forces lost per day would decline with time, since losses of a given percentage would come against a declining total number of troops, due to the cumulative effects of each day's attrition). Over that same time, the coalition would suffer about 15,000 total casualties, with some 2,500 estimated as fatali-ties. (Again, this calculation could be done more exactly by subtracting out each day's losses before conducting the calculations for the following day, but the pre-ceding approach provides a rough sense of how things would ensue.) These numbers are broadly consistent with how Epstein, Posen, and others calculated their upper-bound loss estimates before the war.

For a more optimistic calculation, and especially knowing what we know now about the coalition's air campaign, its subsequent "left hook," Iraq's inability to make good use of its defensive advantages, and the remarkable additional benefits provided by assets such as the US JSTARS aircraft, we might give the Iraqis no situational advantage at all. Also, we might assign coalition forces a 6:1 advantage in quality, going well beyond the Israeli advantages in its wars against Arab armies. Thus:

$$\text{US/coalition daily loss rate} = (0.01)(700,000)(225,000/4,200,000) = 375$$
$$\text{Iraqi daily loss rate} = (0.01)(225,000)(4,200,000/225,000) = 42,000$$

After some three days of combat at this pace of losses, the battle will be over, and the coalition will have suffered just over 1,000 casualties, with 150 to 200 dead. That turns out to be roughly the result that was observed.

Some might question my use of the 700,000 figure for coalition forces in the war. After all, many of these forces were far removed from contact with the enemy; undoubtedly, some of them were not essential to the war effort, either. At the time of the Iraqi invasion of Kuwait, the United States still effectively had a Cold War–sized military with few competing operational demands upon it; as such, Washington could overinsure in the fight against Iraq. These points are valid, but it is hard to know where to draw the line between forces deployed efficiently and contributing importantly to a given fight, and those that are in some broad sense supporting the main effort yet perhaps secondary or even redundant. It is also worth emphasizing that modern militaries are built to have lots of support, for transportation, other logistics, intelligence, and so on—functions that are essential to the combat performance of armed forces like those of the United States. Indeed, it would be fair to note that even some forces based in the United States or Europe contributed support to the combat effort. Alternatively, one could also use the 700,000 figure for the optimistic estimate (from the US perspective), and a smaller number for the pessimistic one.

Modeling Naval Combat

Naval combat in today's world is very complex. It typically occurs on, above, and below the surface of the water. It can take place on the open oceans or in waters near a country's shores. The latter cases can include amphibious assaults, intended to establish positions on enemy territory and ultimately to seize and control parts of it. They can also include blockades. Missile attacks, to and from not only ships and airplanes but also locations on proximate land, can also be part of many engagements. This section of the chapter thus considers a number of cases and types of naval warfare.

Amphibious Assault

The heyday of amphibious assault was undoubtedly World War II, in the Pacific and Normandy and Italy and elsewhere, though there were also important examples of amphibious operations in World War I at Gallipoli, Turkey, as well as in Inchon, Korea, in 1950 and in the Falklands/Malvinas War of 1982. The modern era of precision strike has made some doubt whether amphibious assault really has a future. The US military's decision not to try to fight ashore in Kuwait in 1991 (largely out of concern over simple Iraqi mines at sea) reinforced the theory that perhaps amphibious operations had become too difficult in current times. But the US Marine Corps, while currently rethinking its tactics and equipment, still takes the amphibious mission quite seriously (maintaining a sealift capacity to put two-thirds of a division ashore in the face of hostile fire, and purchasing amphibious vehicles and tilt-rotor aircraft designed largely if not primarily for such operations). And there may be situations where amphibious assault is contemplated for the simple reason that it may be the only way to take a given objective. Certainly China's aspirations to reunify Taiwan with the mainland come to mind in this context.

Amphibious assault involves several distinct phases, though these may overlap in a given instance. The following framework, which I developed (with considerable help from generous marine corps officers) some twenty years ago, is designed less to predict an outcome than to help gauge the basic feasibility of an amphibious assault operation for a given military balance.[60]

To succeed in amphibious assault, an invader has generally first needed air superiority, and preferably outright air dominance or supremacy to keep a defender's own airpower at bay. Such mastery of the skies is needed to prevent attacks against the invader's ships as they approach shore. Second, benefiting from this airpower advantage as well as maneuver and surprise and brute strength, the attacker has needed to land troops in a place where they initially outnumber defenders in troops and firepower. As the earlier discussion of data gathered by Trevor Dupuy, the army's Concepts Analysis Agency, Joshua Epstein, and others shows, it is in principle possible to win battles when outnumbered. But in the case of amphibious assault, that is difficult, given the exposed positions in which an attacker finds itself in this phase of the operation. Third, if successful in creating a foothold, the attacker has then generally tried to strengthen its initial lodgment faster than the defender can bring additional troops and equipment to bear at the same location, in preparation for a breakout maneuver.

As table 2.1 shows, attackers can succeed without enjoying all three advantages. But in the cases considered here, they did not succeed without at least two of them.

A methodology based on such historical cases may actually understate the difficulty of amphibious assault in modern times. For example, the capabilities of modern sea mines outstrip those of mine-clearing technologies for the most part, especially in shallow waters. Sensors have proliferated, making it harder and harder to fool a defender's warning systems as ships approach shore. Precision-guided anti-ship missiles have also spread widely and probably outpaced improvements in defenses (see chapters 3 and 4 for more detail). Thus, the era of precision strike makes it very hard for large assets, notably ships, to approach a defender's shores if the defender has any reasonable combination of prepared defensive positions and some reconnaissance assets.[61] That said, if the defender has allowed vulnerabilities to grow in its command and control networks, a cyberattack or a strike with precision ordnance against key headquarters and communications infrastructure may leave it reeling. Those technology trends may help the attacker and may partially offset the way that most technology trends seem to be favoring the defender.

It is easiest to think through these complex issues with reference to a specific example. Given the importance of this scenario, as noted earlier, a good case for

TABLE 2.1. Key Elements in Amphibious Assaults

CASE/ATTACKER	AIR SUPERIORITY	INITIAL TROOP ADVANTAGE AT POINT OF ATTACK	BUILDUP ADVANTAGE AT POINT OF ATTACK
HISTORICAL SUCCESSES			
Okinawa, 1945/US	yes	yes	yes
Normandy, 1944/US, allies	yes	yes	yes
Inchon, Korea 1950/US	yes	yes	yes
Falklands, 1982/UK	no	yes	yes*
FAILED ATTEMPTS			
Anzio, 1943/US and UK*	yes	yes	no
Gallipoli, 1915/UK, allies	no	yes	no
Bay of Pigs, 1961/Cubans	no	marginal	No

*British forces were outnumbered on East Falkland Island, but they managed to build up their lodgment successfully and move out from it without opposition. At Anzio, although the forces there ultimately contributed to Allied victory in Italy in the spring of 1944, their initial objective of making a quick and decisive difference in the war during the previous winter was clearly not met; thus, the operation is classified here as a failure.

scrutiny is that of a possible Chinese attack on Taiwan. China rejects the idea of Taiwan's permanent separation from the mainland, whereas Taiwan has been seeking to expand its role as an autonomous entity in global affairs, and many Taiwanese feel that the island should be independent. China has also continued to make military investments, reforms, and reorganizations in recent years that prioritize, and substantially improve its capacity for, effective action against Taiwan.[62] The potential exists for a political crisis that could lead to war—and a war that might ultimately even engage the United States. Even if not likely, such a conflict is important to analyze and understand given the huge stakes.

As noted, the first step in successful amphibious assault, both conceptually and chronologically, is usually to establish air superiority—and ideally air *supremacy*, where the enemy is virtually unable to use the skies itself. China would wish to ground Taiwan's air force early in any war. Otherwise, even the occasional Taiwanese attack aircraft sortie could cause serious losses to PRC ships approaching Taiwan's shores in an amphibious assault, given the accuracy and lethality of modern aerial ordnance.[63]

China's ballistic and cruise missiles with enough range to reach Taiwan from their positions on Chinese shores are numerous, totaling well over 1,000 and perhaps as many as 2,000. More notably still, they are now accurate enough to conduct effective attacks against airstrips as well as associated infrastructure.[64] This is a huge qualitative change compared with the relatively recent past. Now, instead of lobbing large numbers of missiles toward small targets, in the hope that one would reach its mark by serendipity, the odds are squarely in China's favor. Such is the calculus of using missiles with expected miss distances, or "circular error probable" (CEP), of five to twenty-five meters, and warheads with "lethal radii" of, say, fifty meters. This situation stands in stark contrast to that of the 1990s and early years of the 2000s when China's missiles had typical CEPs of hundreds of meters.[65] With such improved CEPs, China could now effectively bisect Taiwan's dozen or so military-grade runways with relatively modest salvos of missiles.

Assume that each Chinese missile has a reliability of 90 percent and a CEP roughly comparable to its lethal radius. Then, with just eight missiles, the attacker could have a 99 percent chance of shutting down the runway by cutting it in half, rendering each segment too short to afford any aircraft an opportunity to take off.[66]

The math here is quite simple. Again, assume conservatively (from the point of view of a Chinese planner) that a missile's CEP is comparable to the lethal radius of its warhead. Specifically, in a recent landmark study, RAND scholars assumed that an effective lethal radius for a missile carrying submunitions might be about fifty meters. Then any one shot has roughly a 45 percent chance of doing serious or lethal damage to its target, once reliability is factored into the mix. Put differently, the target has a 55 percent chance of *surviving* that shot, but as the number of offensive attempts increases, the chances of survival dwindle because the target must separately survive *each* shot. The calculation goes like this, multiplying chances of survival together:[67]

> Chances of survival after one shot $= 1 -$ single-shot kill probability $= 1 - (0.5 \times 0.9) = 0.55$
>
> Chances of survival after two shots $= 0.55 \times 0.55 = 0.30$
>
> Chances of four shots not damaging/destroying target: $0.55 \times 0.55 \times 0.55 \times 0.55 = 0.09$, or just under 10 percent—and, thus, just under 1 percent after eight shots

This slightly oversimplifies the math for a situation in which there is not a single target to destroy with one large munition, but a swath to damage with multiple submunitions. Thus, to be conservative, an attacker might target aimpoints on the left and right sides of a given runway to ensure complete coverage of its width. Perhaps something closer to 16 missiles rather than 8 would be required. The basic point remains the same: a country with more than 1,000 accurate missiles can surely shut down a dozen unprotected airfields for hours or days, using repeated attacks as necessary.[68]

If the airfields are defended by effective interceptor missiles, the attacker must first saturate the target with enough incoming missiles to exhaust the defense's supply. But in an era in which defenses require one interceptor for each incoming threat—and where, to be safe, two or more interceptor missiles might in fact be required for high probability of intercept—the advantage is generally to the offense.

In the days when airfields are damaged and nonfunctional, the attacker might then seek to destroy aircraft in hardened bunkers with larger laser-guided bombs dropped by attack aircraft. Taiwan's ability to have *any* survivable air capability thereafter would then be a function of how well hardened shelters could be defended from such follow-on attacks, how well they could survive any strikes that did occur, whether Taiwan could disperse aircraft to remote operating locations in advance of the initial attack, and/or whether Taiwan had acquired enough helicopters (with anti-ship missiles) such that vertical-lift planes could substitute for jets in attacks against incoming ships.[69]

The next stage in the battle, the actual amphibious assault, is largely a question of how fast transport ships can be loaded, sailed, and unloaded. It is, of course, also a function of how fast a defender's force can be mobilized and sent to fighting positions, and of how well the defender can attack approaching ships before and as they unload troops and equipment.

China has the capacity to transport up to 15,000 troops with some heavy armor by amphibious lift. Interestingly, that figure is not dramatically different from what it was a decade or more ago; modernization has focused more on improved capability than on raw capacity.[70] Some estimates are twice as high, but it is not clear that China has completed the shipbuilding program needed to move such a force.[71] Regardless of where in this range of 15,000 to 30,000 troops Chinese amphibious capacity really lies, the question is this: Could the number of arriving troops rival the number of Taiwanese defenders that would likely be able to arrive at a comparable time? If so, my analytical framework suggests that China will have satisfied one more prerequisite to *possible* success in its overall operation.

To defend effectively, Taiwan would need to mobilize forces and position them appropriately before Chinese forces arrived. It would have numerous advantages, starting with the fact that its own reconnaissance capabilities and those of the United States would surely pick up Chinese preparations for the assault well before ships left PRC ports. In fact, by the assumptions of this scenario, it would have been struck with a surprise attack against its airfields, providing obvious warning. The only truly plausible reason that it might not respond promptly has to do with the vulnerability of its command and control network. If key technical systems were knocked out, physically or through cyberattack, and/or if some top political and military leaders were assassinated or kidnapped, Taiwan's response could be delayed. This underscores the importance of redundant command and control as well as clear procedures for maintaining the chain of command when it is under attack.

If Taiwan's command and control and communications systems largely survived the opening attack, China could find itself on the horns of a dilemma. With a large military and a relatively small land mass to defend, as well as a good road network, Taiwan would have advantages that not every such defender would enjoy. Note that Taiwan possesses roughly:[72]

- 165,000 active-duty forces, of which almost 90,000 are ground troops
- 1.5 million more ground-force reservists
- a coastal perimeter of about 1,500 kilometers

So, in theory, Taiwan could deploy roughly 1,000 defenders per kilometer of coastline along all of its shores if it wished. Over any given stretch of ten to fifteen kilometers, a tactically relevant distance, fully mobilized Taiwanese defense force would be able to deploy as many troops as China could deploy there with all of its amphibious fleet. (An attacker would want to seize a shoreline of at least that length, to create areas safe from enemy fires of various sorts.)[73]

The preceding presupposes rapid Taiwanese mobilization, including of reservists, but no advance knowledge by Taiwan about where the PRC intended to come ashore. In reality, unless completely blinded and paralyzed by China's preemptive attacks against airfields, ships, shore-based radars, other monitoring assets, and command centers, Taiwan would see where ships sailed and be able to react with at least some notice. The United States would likely be willing to provide Taiwan with satellite or aircraft intelligence on the concentration of China's attack effort, as well.[74]

Although the strait is typically only 100 miles wide, Taiwan itself is about 300 miles long. Ships traveling twenty knots would need more than half a day to sail its full length, and could not credibly threaten all parts of the island at once.

In addition, amphibious assault troops cannot come ashore just anywhere. Only about 20 percent of the world's coastlines are considered suitable for amphibious assault. On Taiwan's shores, the percentage is even smaller, given the prevalence of mudflats on the west coast and cliffs on the east. Thus, to establish acceptable initial defensive force densities, Taiwan would perhaps need only its active-duty forces and some 10 to 15 percent of its reservists, for the lower end of the range of China's amphibious ship capacity, and 20 to 25 percent for the higher end.

Taiwan also has at least two airborne brigades that it could use to react rapidly where China attacked.[75] They would allow it to counter China's airlift capabilities (estimated at two brigades of paratroopers as well).[76] Some of Taiwan's air-mobile forces could be shot down by Chinese fighters, but PRC paratroopers or troop-carrying helicopters over Taiwan would themselves be at great risk from Taiwanese surface-to-air missiles, antiaircraft artillery, and any surviving and operational fighters. Paratroopers in fixed-wing transports are particularly vulnerable in situations in which the attacking force does not completely dominate the skies and in which the defender has good ground-based air defenses.[77]

Even with all of its modernization efforts of the last two to three decades, China probably still does not possess the ability to generate the second element of most successful amphibious attacks as shown in table 2.1. For this requirement of successful amphibious assault, its expected effectiveness might not be dramatically different or better than it was twenty years ago. Its maximum likely deployment of initial forces would at best be comparable to Taiwan's activation of defensive forces in the same landing zone.

Victory (and Defeat) at Sea

The preceding analysis does not even include expected attrition to Chinese incoming forces. In reality, such losses would be large if Taiwan adequately prepared its defenses, both in the initial assault and in subsequent reinforcement operations. Large transport aircraft are vulnerable when operating near modern air defense systems. The standard means of protecting them—landing them in locations out of range of ground-based radars and interceptors, for example, as NATO might do in reinforcing its easternmost allies against hypothetical Rus-

sian attack[78]—would be difficult to employ against a hardened, densely populated, and well-armed island polity like Taiwan. Many of the ships crossing the
strait would never make it to land. They could be attacked through a combination
of advanced minefields in coastal waters, as well as widespread use of anti-ship
missiles launched from various hidden platforms and sites, not to mention more
modern capabilities like drones.[79]

Retired captain Wayne Hughes Jr. provides a very simple and useful algorithm
for understanding one reason that exposed ships at sea are highly vulnerable. As
he points out, given the lethality of modern anti-ship missiles, ship defenses are
best viewed as filters—taking out a certain percentage of incoming threats—rather
than reliable protectors. Defense generally relies on a finite number of interceptor missiles that can be exhausted by a salvo. Attackers can concentrate their fire
in salvos of several shots at a time, saturating the defense, as noted earlier in regard to possible attacks on airfields. And modern ships are often incapacitated
after just a couple hits.

To take an example, if 8 shots are fired at a given ship, and 6 are correctly aimed
toward target, only 1 or 2 might be intercepted. That means 4 or 5 might strike
their targets, and often 2 to 4 would be enough to incapacitate a given ship—so
in this kind of example, the attacked ship would almost surely be sunk.

Captain Hughes's "salvo equation" can be written in simplified form as follows. Assume that there are two fleets, with A the number of ships in the first and
B the number in the second. $B(0)$ is the initial number of ships for B, and $B(t)$ is
the number at a subsequent time, t, after it has taken losses.[80] Those losses are:

$$B(0) - B(t) = [aA(0) - bB(0)]/s$$

Here a is the number of accurate shots fired by A per ship, b is the number of
missiles intercepted by B's defenses per ship, and s is the survivability of the typical ship in B's fleet. Put differently, this equation simply says that B's losses are
equal to the total number of good shots fired by A, minus the number intercepted
by B, then divided by the number of shots typically required to put any given ship
out of commission. So if A has 5 ships each shooting 4 accurate missiles, for a
total of 20 incoming missiles, and B has 5 ships each capable of intercepting 2
missiles on average (for a total of 10 intercepts), then 10 missiles will get through
defenses. If 2 hits are needed to sink the typical ship in B's fleet, then 5 ships will
be sunk, assuming that the missile shots are well distributed:

$$5 = [(20 - 10)]/2$$

The formulas can be used to show the effects of attacks on an approaching fleet
by a land-based force, as in the case of Taiwan. The product of the two terms aA

can simply be interpreted as the number of successful shots at fleet B, wherever and whatever their origin might be. Even if Taiwan's air force is rendered largely impotent for the opening days of war, and perhaps beyond, anti-ship missiles launched from shore batteries, fast patrol craft at sea, and helicopters could be devastating to large troop ships approaching well-defended positions.

In the late twentieth century, more than 90 percent of missiles fired at undefended ships reached their targets (with 54 ships sunk or otherwise put out of action with just 63 missiles fired). About 68 percent of missiles fired at ships that had partial or imperfect defenses reached their targets (with 19 ships sunk or put out of action using 38 missiles). Against ships employing their defenses, about 26 percent of missiles fired reached their mark, with 29 ships incapacitated in one way or another by a total of 121 missiles fired.[81] Of course, there is variation from case to case, but the overall trends are telling about the difficulty of defense and survivability at sea regardless.

As one telling case, consider the Falklands War of 1982.[82] There, the British lost 5 ships to missiles and aircraft and had up to another 11 damaged, out of a 33-ship task force—and they did not generally have to approach any closer than 400 miles from the Argentine mainland during the conflict.[83] That amounts to an effective attrition rate of roughly 15 percent (50 percent, if all damaged ships are considered to be "casualties" too) during blue-water operations against an outclassed Argentine military that only owned about 100 aircraft and five Exocet anti-ship missiles.[84] The PRC's losses would likely be greater against a foe whose anti-ship missile capabilities substantially exceed Argentina's in 1982, provided that Taiwan makes adequate preparation to launch those missiles from a number of platforms (and not just vulnerable fixed-wing aircraft), and provided that Taiwan's command, control, and communications systems function properly even in the face of attack.

All told, if Taiwan makes smart investments in anti-ship missiles fired from multiple platforms, the PRC would likely lose at least 10 percent of its forces just in approaching Taiwan's coasts and fighting ashore each time it attempted another trip. This means that after five trips it would be down to 60 percent (or less) of its initial fleet, and after ten trips it would be down to 35 percent.

The situation would get no better over time for China even if it could somehow establish an initial toehold on the island. In other words, it could not satisfy the third criterion for successful amphibious assault described earlier, either. As the battle wore on, Taiwan's internal lines of communication would help even more, and its ability to reinforce its defensive position at the chosen point of PRC attack would improve further in relative terms, even as China tried to reinforce its attacking legions. China could probably deploy no more than 10,000 more troops per day to Taiwan by sea and air combined, in days 3 through 10 of the operation. This assumes that the average ship can do a round trip to Taiwan at least every other day, on average, including time for loading and unloading. And for days 11 through 20, the average daily flow would be only half that due to ship attrition, given the assumed ship loss rate.

By contrast, Taiwan could probably mobilize and deploy another 50,000 troops a day to the location where China was seeking to establish a toehold.[85] And its means to continually reinforce would not be nearly as vulnerable to interdiction as would China's.

Might the PRC use chemical weapons in this part of its attack? China would presumably want to use a nonpersistent agent, like sarin, so that its troops could occupy the area within a short time without having to wear protective gear. The effects of the weapons on Taiwan's defenders would depend heavily on whether they had gas masks handy, the accuracy of Chinese attacks, weather conditions, and the speed with which Taiwan could threaten the PRC ships doing the damage.[86] Historical experiences with chemical weapons suggest that China should not expect these weapons to radically change the course of battle, however. Even in World War I, when protective gear was rudimentary, chemical weapons caused less than 10 percent of all deaths; in the Iran-Iraq War, the figure has been estimated at less than 5 percent.[87] China would also need to worry that, if its timing and delivery were not good, its own mobile and exposed troops could suffer larger numbers of casualties than the dug-in defenders.[88] Still, the threat bears watching, and Taiwan should be sure to exercise in chemical gear at times.

Could the PRC use its fishing fleet to put tens of thousands of troops quickly ashore on Taiwan? Some have raised this possibility, but there are several important reasons to be very skeptical. The ships could not carry much in the way of landing craft or armored equipment. Moreover, Taiwanese shore-based coastal defense guns and artillery, as well as Taiwanese aircraft, small coastal patrol craft, and mines (not just advanced anti-ship missiles), might well make mincemeat of many of the unarmored ships, which would have to approach very close to shore in order for the disembarking soldiers not to subsequently drown.

Some of these challenges facing any amphibious attacker China could address. It could build a great deal more amphibious shipping. It could, and will, continue to improve the accuracy of its missile force and its air-delivered munitions to improve capacities against Taiwan's air force in particular. It could continue to learn more about how to disrupt Taiwan's command and control networks. So Taiwan's defensibility is not guaranteed to endure. Still, vulnerability to blockade and barrage seems likely to remain much greater than vulnerability to invasion, as discussed in the next section.

Barrage and Blockade versus Anti-submarine Warfare and Air and Missile Defense

While Taiwan and its friends should certainly be vigilant about a possible Chinese attempt to seize the island directly, an attempted amphibious assault would be a huge risk, with no easy going back if the effort failed. Two less fraught, and therefore more likely, ways that China might threaten Taiwan include missile attack and naval blockade. The two techniques might also be combined in a single operation.

China has more than 1,000 short-range ballistic and cruise missiles, equipped with conventional warheads, in the southeastern part of its country near the Taiwan Strait. The missiles could be used in a number of ways that go well beyond what happened in the mid-1990s when they were fired into the sea near Taiwan. They could be aimed at remote farmland or mountains, to minimize the risk of casualties. If only a few missiles were used, in a strictly symbolic way against such sites, it is plausible that no one would be killed, though of course China could not be sure in advance. Given these missiles' improved accuracy, they could be aimed very close to land such that they would be visible to residents when their warheads exploded. If a crisis intensified, successive missile strikes might be aimed closer to shore and closer to cities, or perhaps at key infrastructure. Missiles could also be directed at military installations, if China wished to avoid civilian casualties yet wanted to cause real damage (as in the Iranian attack against US military facilities in Iraq in January 2020, after the killing of Qassem Soleimani).

Such attacks would be no silver bullet, necessarily. These types of strikes, while perhaps unlikely to cause many casualties, would also be unlikely to achieve much direct and lasting military or even economic effect. Escalating to use them against cities would be seen as a brutal terroristic act that could do more to unify the people of Taiwan—and the world—against China than to achieve Beijing's war aims. At least, that has been the historical norm when cities have been bombarded in the modern era, whether by airplanes in World War II or ballistic missiles in the Iraq-Iran and Persian Gulf wars.[89] For these reasons, missile strikes might be a logical way for China to begin any use of force, but it would probably need a backup option in case they failed.[90]

A naval blockade could offer more appeal to China. It need not stop all ship voyages into and out of Taiwan. It would simply need to deter enough ships from risking the journey that Taiwan's economy would suffer badly. The goal would probably be to squeeze the island economically to a point of capitulation. This solution could seem quite elegant from Beijing's point of view—it could involve only modest loss of life, little or no damage to Taiwan itself, more terror than harm suffered by the people of Taiwan, and the ability to back off the attack if the United

States seemed ready to intervene or if the world community slapped major trade sanctions on China in response. Additionally or alternatively, the capabilities needed to carry it out, most notably submarines as argued later, could also help deter and complicate any American naval intervention to come to Taiwan's aid.[91] How to analyze such a blockade attempt?[92]

Perhaps the greatest worry for Beijing would be its likely inability to distinguish one country's merchant ships from another's. But if Beijing announced to the world that those shipping anything toward Taiwan were aiding and abetting its enemy, and gave fair warning, it might consider itself to have done enough to justify attacking any ship approaching Taiwan. It might offer countries the option of first docking in a PRC port for inspection (if it decided to allow humanitarian goods through, for example, or ships from certain friendly countries but not others) and then being escorted safely to Taiwan. Since this strategy might require it to sink just a few ships to achieve the desired aims, it might believe that it was threatening the lives of only a few dozen commercial seamen. Given the perceived stakes involved, Beijing could well consider this a reasonable risk.

The PRC submarine force is steadily improving. Although its submarines' abilities to coordinate with each other and reconnaissance aircraft may be limited or impeded by American and allied action, that might not matter greatly for the purposes of a "leaky" blockade. Even if they had to find commercial ships individually by sonar or by sight, such submarines could maintain patrols over a large fraction of the sea approaches to Taiwan. It could take Taiwan weeks to find the better PRC submarines, particularly if China used them in hit-and-run modes. Given the lethality of modern torpedoes and anti-ship cruise missiles for any PRC submarines carrying the latter, the existence of these submarines in important waterways near Taiwan would constitute a major threat.

To break the blockade, the United States and Taiwan would probably need to deploy enough forces to the Western Pacific to establish a safe shipping lane east of Taiwan. In addition, they would have to heavily protect ships during the most dangerous part of their journeys when they were near the island. To carry out that mission, the United States, together with Taiwan, would need to establish air superiority throughout a large part of the region, protect ships against Chinese submarine attack, and cope with the threat of mines near Taiwan's ports.

Establishing air superiority has become much harder for the United States and Japan in these kinds of scenarios because of the modernization trends in the People's Liberation Army (PLA) Air Force in recent years, combined with the limited options for basing US aircraft in the region. Fortunately, modern US stealth or "fifth-generation" aircraft are still far superior to Chinese planes. Unfortunately, China now has close to 1,000 "fourth-generation" fighters roughly comparable to US aircraft such as the F-15 and F-16, and it can base perhaps 1,000 aircraft within several hundred miles of Taiwan. A RAND simulation estimates that China might be able to devote about 600 planes, including air-to-air fighters or escorts and ground-attack jets, to the attack, surging about half of them into the air at a time if so inclined. Using a basic model and some simplifying assumptions, RAND estimates that the United States could prevent such a surge force from reaching most of its targets only by continuously keeping some two wings or about 150 aircraft airborne near Taiwan. In effect, RAND's model assumes that with enough survivable American aircraft on patrol, wielding enough air-to-air missiles, they will detect, acquire, and shoot down most Chinese aircraft that attempt to reach the defended region. The model assumes a high degree of effective surveillance by US (and any effective Taiwan) aircraft in this engagement. There is little presumed danger of a Chinese aircraft somehow slipping through the protected zone. The United States and its partners would likely succeed in such an effort because, according to RAND's model, the United States' fifth-generation aircraft—F-22s and F-35s, and to a lesser degree F/A-18E/F Super Hornets—could have almost 50 percent more lethality and up to 90 percent less vulnerability than even relatively modern Chinese combat jets.[93]

But the success would come at a price, and only with considerable effort and difficulty. China could choose the time and place of its surge, and the United States (with any allies) would therefore have to be vigilant at all times. It would need to keep fighters airborne near Taiwan essentially for as long as the crisis endured. It would also need the continued presence of airborne warning aircraft in the vicinity. Bases on Okinawa are about 750 kilometers away from Taiwan, or about an hour of flight time; aircraft carriers might be kept roughly that close too. But other bases in the area—Misawa Air Base on Japan's main Honshu island, Andersen Air Force base on Guam—would be 2,500 kilometers or more distant, meaning some three hours of flying each way to get to station and then return after flying a patrol, assumed to last two hours on station. If we assume, as did RAND, that aircraft and crews are limited to a daily flight average of about six hours a day, then jets from Okinawa could average 1.5 sorties per day, and those from the more distant bases about 0.75 sorties per 24 hours. That would translate into 3 hours a day on station flying from Kadena and 1.5 hours a day flying from Guam or Honshu. Put differently:

> Eight aircraft (plus or minus) based on Kadena would be needed to sustain one on station near Taiwan.
>
> Sixteen aircraft or so based at Misawa or Andersen Air Force Base would be needed to keep one on station near Taiwan.

Keeping two wings (about six squadrons) of fighters aloft at a time could require about ten to twelve times that number being based in the region, or twenty to twenty-four wings—more than half the total US military aggregate. (The RAND study actually estimates that fourteen to thirty would be needed, depending on specific assumptions; I have simplified the analysis.)[94]

Moreover, the United States could lose a number of aircraft in this process, perhaps even dozens. China could lose dozens or even hundreds. The backdrop would be set for escalation. Both sides would be increasingly tempted to attack the land bases and aircraft carriers from which planes operated.[95] Ballistic missiles and ballistic missile defense would be important in this kind of engagement, too. China now has missiles, such as the medium-range DF-21 in the Dong-Feng series, that are capable of being fired from its homeland and reaching ships east of Taiwan. It is not clear whether the United States could blind China's sensors adequately to deprive the PLA of targeting information. Any PLA attack against military facilities in a place like Okinawa therefore could well shut down runways for at least some stretch of time and destroy aircraft or ordnance and fuel stocks not in underground areas or hardened shelters, as discussed earlier.[96] And none of this even considers the possibility of Chinese nuclear attacks.

But the greatest difficulty for US and Taiwan forces would probably arise in trying to counter Chinese submarine operations. The ASW effort against these subs would have multiple aspects but probably could not prevent significant losses.

As one element of the ASW operation, the United States would surely be tempted to deploy its own attack submarines as close as possible to China—certainly in the Taiwan Strait, maybe just outside PRC ports. This approach would provide American submarines a good prospect of destroying PRC subs at their source, before they were in a position to fire on commercial shipping (or US aircraft carriers) in more distant waters. However, this type of ASW would be extremely delicate strategically, especially if it involved attacks against Chinese ships in Chinese territorial waters.

Whatever happened near Chinese shores, there would surely be additional layers of American ASW further out to sea. Ships and aircraft would use sonar to listen for approaching submarines, and for the sound of any torpedoes being fired. Some of the ships would be larger destroyers or cruisers, such as those equipped with advanced Aegis radars, to detect any use of cruise missiles and attempt to defend against them.

The United States would probably deploy significant numbers of surface combatants and airplanes like P-3s and P-8s to the region for this mission. Some would help protect US aircraft carriers, of which perhaps four or more might deploy east of Taiwan in the event of any conflict. Others would provide additional protection to merchant ships or mine warfare vessels as they operated near Taiwan's shores. US minehunters and minesweepers would of course operate near Taiwan's ports and the main approaches to those ports. Land-based or ship-based helicopters might assist them. So might robotic submersibles deployed from ships near shore.

If China then used its submarines in attacks on shipping, or if direct hostilities began in another way, the United States would almost surely begin to search for and fire upon Chinese submarines as a matter of normal operations. Any Chinese submarine wishing to fire at a merchant ship or aircraft carrier would then first have to run quite a gauntlet. It would have to evade submarine detection as it left port, avoid any open-water search missions that the United States and Taiwan established, and then somehow penetrate the defensive ASW perimeter of whatever convoy it was attacking as it approached its target. To survive the overall engagement and return to port, it would of course then need to successfully negotiate all of this in the other direction.

During the Cold War, the effectiveness of ASW operations was commonly assessed at 5 to 15 percent per "barrier." (Cold War barriers were more linear and literal perimeters than would be likely here, but the fact remains that Chinese subs would have to survive perhaps three types of pursuers at three different parts of their journey to or from home base.)[97] Assume that the United States (and Taiwan and possibly Japan) can create the equivalent of three barriers any attack submarine trying to fire on a convoy would have to traverse before firing. (There would then be three more barriers the submarine would have to survive before reaching port to rearm and refuel.) So, to get off its first round of shots or torpedoes, a submarine would need to transit three barriers successfully, with an expected survivability of $0.85 \times 0.85 \times 0.85 = 0.61$. To get off a second volley, it would need to transit nine barriers. To get off a third volley, it would need to survive running an ASW gauntlet fifteen times, and so on. Assume further six torpedoes per submarine, each with a kill probability of 50 percent for newer submarine-torpedo combinations and 25 percent for older ones.

Modern submarines can also carry a dozen or more anti-ship missiles, which could pose an additional threat to ships. For simplicity, I focus on torpedoes, since a submarine can operate autonomously in firing them and since a ship's air and missile defenses are not relevant against them. To the extent that missiles are factored into the computation, they could of course change the specific numbers, but they would only reinforce the two main points, namely, ships are vulnerable to submarines and are especially vulnerable to modern submarines carrying advanced weapons.

So, focusing on the torpedo threat, the math would then go something like this:

OLDER SUB

Probability of getting into firing position without being destroyed, on first
sortie = 61%

Probability of getting into firing position on second sortie = 23%

Probability of getting into firing position on third sortie = 9%.

Thus the typical older submarine would manage to fire on a convoy of ships
only once or twice before meeting its own demise.

Kills per sub = 1 or 2 sorties per sub per lifetime × 6 torpedoes per sortie × 0.25
success rate per torpedo = (1 or 2) × 6 × 0.25 = 1.5 or 3 successful
torpedo attacks per sub

If we assume further that it will sometimes take two hits to sink a ship, the
typical older Chinese submarine might destroy one to two ships before itself being destroyed. If we assume roughly one US Navy ship for every four cargo ships,
that translates into 0.2 to 0.4 navy ships sunk per older submarine. Should China
devote thirty older submarines to this operation, it might sink six to twelve US
Navy (or allied) naval ships as a result.[98]

The same basic kind of math could then be applied to attempted attacks by
modern Chinese submarines, as follows:

MODERN SUB

Probability of getting into firing position without being destroyed on first
sortie: 86%

Probability of getting into firing position on second sortie:
0.86 × 0.86 × 0.86 = 63%

Probability of getting into firing position on third sortie:
0.63 × 0.86 × 0.86 = 46%

Probability of getting into firing position on fourth sortie:
0.46 × 0.86 × 0.86 = 34%

Probability of getting into firing position on fifth sortie:
0.34 × 0.86 × 0.86 = 25%

According to these calculations, a typical submarine would survive long enough
to carry out perhaps two to four separate attacks with six torpedoes each, twice
the norm for the older subs—translating into 0.4 to 0.8 navy ship kills per submarine. A more elaborate recent RAND analysis also concludes that a given submarine, especially if able to receive targeting information from aircraft or
satellites, might have several opportunities to sink a ship such as an aircraft carrier before itself being destroyed.[99]

Before 2000, when almost all of China's submarines were noisy and obsolescent, the PLA might have been able to sink a couple of US Navy ships in a US-led counterblockade contingency near Taiwan. Today, with the PLA using a mix of, say, thirty older and new submarines, the total might be twenty US Navy ships or more. By 2040 the figure might approach thirty. These numbers are admittedly notional and approximate. But they suggest the pace at which circumstances are probably changing in the early decades of the twenty-first century—especially since China is likely to be able to improve the performance of its submarine fleet faster than the United States and allies can improve their ASW capabilities because of the relative maturity of the technologies underlying the ASW mission today.[100] Moreover, China has been netting these submarine forces together with more elaborate sensor and command and control and communications networks in recent decades as it has placed a higher premium on the role of information in modern war, meaning that its chances of acquiring targets successfully on any given mission have also grown considerably.[101]

And, of course, the threat goes beyond torpedoes. Hypersonic anti-ship cruise missiles are becoming more common and are extremely difficult to defend against, even for high-performance US Navy ships with advanced Aegis radar systems. The ranges of PRC cruise missiles are now reaching or exceeding 150 miles. To make these weapons more effective, China can be expected to try to improve its targeting and communications systems too. For example, it is putting into orbit more satellites capable of detecting large objects on the oceans.[102] With the information from satellites, guidance systems on the cruise missiles could then direct them to the vicinity of their targets, where terminal seekers on the missiles themselves could finish the navigation job.[103] The only truly reliable way to protect ships against such threats is to minimize the number of missiles that can be fired at them by depriving the missile-carrying aircraft or ships of information on, and proximity to, their would-be targets. The United States would have a good chance to do this successfully against China, but the PRC's submarines would complicate the task and cause a real risk of significant American losses in the course of battle.

China could also attempt to deploy advanced minefields near Taiwan's main ports. Past experience in the Persian Gulf and elsewhere suggests that even advanced minehunting capabilities can clear only a few dozen mines a day at best—and the rate could slow for advanced mines with more sophisticated fuzing mechanisms (and perhaps with robotic features that allow them to reposition themselves autonomously). Individual minehunting ships typically average a mine or two cleared per day, in relatively fast operations, since the process of disabling a given mine typically takes concerted and focused effort even once the threat is located.[104] As such, if China is able to lay minefields with submarines, and then find a way to lay them again, it might be able to further impede Taiwan's ability to restore shipping. However, this seems a method that may work best the first time, when China can perhaps do it clandestinely at the outset of a blockade operation. (It could work more effectively, over a longer duration, when Taiwan is laying mines in its own waters to fend off an invasion attempt, as noted previously; in this case, Taiwan would have the natural advantage in deploying the mines given the geography of the situation.)

Artillery Barrages against Population Centers

A very specific, but tragically frequent, type of military attack is the use of artillery against exposed civilian populations in cities. To take a concrete example, what could North Korea do to Seoul and environs by way of artillery bombardment? If its capabilities were sufficient, South Korea might in theory be intimidated into some type of appeasement prior to hostilities, knowing what would happen if war began (and fearful that North Korea might be willing to run the risks, given its extremist regime).

With such attacks, North Korea could do serious harm.[105] Several hundred of North Korea's roughly 13,000 artillery tubes are within range of Seoul in their current positions. Most artillery can fire several rounds a minute. Also, the initial speeds of fired shells are generally around half a kilometer per second. That means that even if a South Korean counterartillery radar some ten kilometers away picked up a North Korean round and established a track on it within seconds, a counterstrike would not be able to silence the offending North Korean tube for at least a minute (and probably closer to two minutes). On average, such a tube could therefore probably fire two to five rounds, and quite possibly a dozen or more, before being neutralized or forced to retreat fully into its shelter.

Altogether, at least several thousand rounds could detonate in Seoul no matter how hard the allies tried to prevent or stop the attack. The lethal radius of a typical artillery shell is typically 30 to 50 meters (for standard 81-mm and 155-mm rounds in the US arsenal, with anywhere from 7 to 25 pounds of explosive). That reference point as well as historical precedents from conflicts such as the Bosnian civil war of 1992–1995 suggest that an average single round detonating in a city could cause tens of casualties and considerable physical destruction, depending of course on whether people had taken shelter prior to most rounds being fired. The end result could be up to tens of thousands of civilian casualties, with 10 to 20 percent of those fatalities. Attacks against Seoul would be even worse if they involved chemical weapons.[106]

Nuclear Exchange Calculations

Although they may seem a vestige of the Cold War, nuclear exchange calculations still influence Russian, American, and possibly other nations' nuclear force planning decisions. These exchange calculations typically focused on a nuclear-armed "triad" of forces that the Soviet Union and the United States maintained during much of the Cold War—and that Russia and the United States maintain today, at lower force levels. The triad consists of intercontinental ballistic missiles (ICBMs), placed in the ground in hardened concrete silos or made mobile to complicate the enemy's targeting; submarine-launched ballistic missiles (SLBMs) on submarines that deploy to sea to enhance their survivability against attack; and bomber-launched nuclear munitions (bombs or cruise missiles), delivered by planes that can if necessary be placed on runway alert or even on airborne alert, again to enhance survivability.

A central goal of nuclear force planners for much of the Cold War was to ensure that their own country's forces could survive any plausible attempt by the enemy to disarm them in an all-out surprise first strike. At the same time, force planners also sought to deny the adversary a survivable second-strike force of its own, or at least to minimize the forces that an adversary could expect to have survive after such an attack. This competitive dynamic was recognized as dangerous by many, and helped spur on a number of arms control accords—yet was never truly abandoned by military planners on either side.[107]

In assessing whether they had achieved their core defensive goal of creating survivable forces (and in also assessing whether they could destroy much of an enemy's nuclear assets through "counterforce" strikes), nuclear planners employed exchange calculations. The basic question was, assuming one side might be willing to launch an all-out zero-warning attack on the other, how well might it do?

The scenarios generally went something like this. First, hardened below-ground ICBM silos would be attacked by the other side's most accurate and lethal ballistic missile warheads. Typically, two warheads would be used against each silo, to account for the imperfect reliability and accuracy of the incoming warheads. (Bombers would generally not have been useful to attack ICBM silos. By the time an attacker's bomber forces could drop bombs, the attacked side would have had hours of warning, allowing the latter to launch its ICBMs before they could be struck.)

Second, submarines carrying SLBMs but located on submarines in their ports would be destroyed by warheads carried on long-range missiles. This was considered a fairly straightforward proposition, since submarines are not very hard relative to ICBM silos. Deployed submarines would be hunted down by the other side's attack submarines to the extent possible (this was probably something that only the United States ever had the capacity to do).

Finally, bomber bases could be barraged, again by warheads from ballistic missiles. Bombers on the ground or in the air very close to the airfield would be destroyed. Any bombers that managed to escape such attacks would stand a chance of being shot down by air defenses as they approached or reached the defender's territory. This was the basic picture of any first strike.

Several key assumptions were built into many nuclear-exchange models—and not all of them were necessarily right. One assumption was that neither side would launch its ICBMs and SLBMs in the fifteen to twenty minutes it might have available, between when it likely detected the other side's massive launch of missiles and when the incoming warheads would begin to detonate. A second assumption was that the command and control and communications systems of each side would survive initial attacks and be capable of ordering and coordinating retaliation; otherwise having one's forces survive might be of little benefit.[108]

In planning forces in this way, both sides effectively assumed that keeping forces on alert would not lead to a high risk of accident that would trump the strategic benefits of deterrence.[109] They also tended to believe, or at least hope, that any conventional war preceding the nuclear exchange would not create the misimpression that nuclear attacks had begun. Otherwise, one or both sides might "retaliate" against the other, believing that they were responding with nuclear weapons to a nuclear attack by the other.[110] Again, inadvertent nuclear war could result.

Calculations were done with certain additional assumptions and simplifications. For example, it was assumed that two warheads could be detonated near a single silo nearly simultaneously, without the shock wave or X-rays or debris cloud from the first destroying the second (in a process known as "fratricide").[111] It was further assumed that missiles would perform the same way on flight trajectories over the North Pole as they had on test ranges. It was also assumed that, while ballistic missiles might individually fail, there would be no systemic problem with warheads detonating—even though those warheads would never have been tested under truly realistic conditions before, after surviving atmospheric reentry at high speed, and even though many warheads would share a common design.

Keeping these potentially flawed assumptions in mind, this is how the exchange calculations then proceeded for some typical weapons involved. Assume that a Soviet SS-18 missile, carrying ten warheads, was used to attack American Minuteman ICBM missile silos. The warhead yield was estimated at 500 kilotons, or half a megaton. The hardness of the US silo was estimated to protect against up to 2,000 pounds per square inch of overpressure from the blast wave of the nuclear blast. These numbers could be combined to calculate a "lethal radius"—the distance from the point of detonation out to which a silo might be destroyed—of 290 meters for an SS-18 warhead against an American ICBM silo. The following formula assumes that the yield of the warhead is expressed in megatons and the hardness of the silo in thousands of pounds per square inch:

$$\text{Lethal radius} = (460)(Y/H)^{1/3} \text{ meters}$$

The average miss distance (or "circular error probable") of a warhead launched by an SS-18 was estimated at 150 meters—much less than the lethal radius of the warhead. Thus, most SS-18 warheads would in fact destroy the silo they were aimed at, since most would land within 290 meters of their aimpoints, given their typical miss distance of only half that distance. For any missile that fired correctly, and a warhead that detonated correctly, the likelihood of destroying the target was 93 percent; assuming 85 percent reliability of the missile and warhead produced a net estimated reliability of 79 percent per shot. My suspicion is that such estimates should have been couched as *at least* 10 percent uncertain in either direction, but the tendencies of the Cold War literature were to treat such estimates as precise and robust.

Nonetheless, it was probably true that as the Cold War progressed, fixed silos increasingly became sitting ducks. The main hope for a silo surviving a nuclear strike, by this methodology, would be that any and all missiles launching warheads at it would fail. Thus, as noted, an attacker was assumed to use two warheads per silo. Assuming two different missiles were used to launch the two warheads directed at each silo—a practice that complicates targeting, of course, but hedges against the failure of any given rocket—implies a 95 percent kill probability per silo.[112]

For submarines, the math was simple. For either country, all SLBMs stuck in port would be destroyed. All US SLBMs deployed at sea would survive the nuclear attack (in other words, neither side could locate the other side's subs in real time accurately enough to undertake successful nuclear strikes). Soviet SSBNs that were deployed at sea, for their part, might or might not survive for any duration depending on how well US attack submarines and other anti-submarine warfare (ASW) capabilities were able to do their jobs in finding the Soviet subs carrying the SLBMs.

For bombers, all bombers on the ground would be assumed to be destroyed, and all those well into the air before the attack would survive (and then stand some chance, perhaps 50 to 90 percent, of successfully penetrating enemy air defenses as they approached their targets). Only for those trying to get off the ground as warheads started to explode around them would the math be complicated, as the attacker might have sought to barrage the airspace around the runways, creating enough overpressure to knock planes only just getting off the ground out of the sky. Roughly speaking, a warhead of roughly 500 kilotons' yield could likely destroy aircraft out to about three to five kilometers distance—though there is considerable uncertainty in this estimate and it could easily vary by a factor of two or even more, either way.[113]

Typically, exchange calculations showed that either superpower might retain 20 to 50 percent of its initial forces after an enemy first strike during most of the latter decades of the Cold War. Each would still have retained a great deal of redundancy or "overkill" in its nuclear forces, clearly. The situation might not be so simple, however, for smaller nuclear weapons states with less survivable forces. Effective missile defenses, if built at a scale approaching that of survivable second-strike forces, could also change the calculus in important ways.

Assessing Counterinsurgency and Stabilization Missions

In this brief overview of analytical methods for assessing and modeling various uses of military force, one final topic merits mention: How to evaluate counterinsurgency (COIN) operations? In conventional warfare, it is relatively straightforward to define the terms and conditions of victory. Movement of the front lines, relative attrition rates, industrial production of war matériel, and logistical sustainability of forces in the field provide fairly obvious standards by which to assess trends—even if the trends can, of course, change over time. But counterinsurgency and stabilization operations are different, more complex, and more political. Even if, from an American perspective in dealing with a faraway country, our own goals seem modest—preventing a given country from again becoming a sanctuary for extremists, for example—the task is inevitably complex. For such a goal to be achievable, one must help a foreign government develop the capacity to control its own territory. That requirement inevitably leads toward what is frequently called "nation building"—though a more precise term is probably "state building," to underscore the central importance of building functioning security forces, judicial institutions, and economic systems. How to measure progress, and how to recognize success or failure, in such a situation?

First, a warning: it is easy to misuse and abuse metrics in such assessments. In Vietnam, for example, the United States was convinced that there would be a "crossover point" in attrition of the Viet Cong. If US military forces could manage to kill enough of them, say 50,000 a year, their recruiting efforts would not be able to keep pace, and combined American and South Vietnamese forces would ultimately prevail. This argument was based in part on the conviction that successful counterinsurgency requires ten government soldiers for every insurgent—a simplifying assumption that, while partly validated by history, gave American policymakers too much confidence that a given number of US troops could produce victory. That approach led to General William Westmoreland's famous search-and-destroy concepts for ground operations. It resulted in a focus on massive firepower that killed huge numbers of innocents as well as combatants, and also failed to achieve its military objective. The conviction that the Viet Cong needed hundreds or thousands of tons of supplies daily led to additional bombing of the Ho Chi Minh Trail and ultimately Cambodia—though it turned out that the Viet Cong in South Vietnam needed little outside help.[114] The US focus on supporting a government with strong anticommunist credentials led to dependency on a corrupt regime with limited legitimacy among its people. American hopes that GDP growth in Vietnam could win "hearts and minds" were dashed because the country's economic successes accrued only to a small fraction of the population and did nothing to discourage the Viet Cong in any event. Finally, Washington's focus on enlarging and equipping South Vietnamese security forces could not compensate for their qualitative deficiencies and in many cases their questionable reliability.[115]

Moreover, the traditional counterinsurgency emphasis on winning hearts and minds needs considerable rethinking—and has received a good deal of it in recent years. It is not enough that a government and/or occupying force provide good governance and a better quality of life to most citizens. A counterinsurgency campaign also typically needs a degree of *legitimacy* among most or all major groups in a population so as not to incur resistance for political or sectarian reasons. (As a partial alternative to true legitimacy, it may be able to buy off the allegiance of others.) It also likely needs a given amount of *power* so as to crush, or at least contain, elements that may have no interest in having their hearts and minds won over. It needs to protect civilian allies physically so that they will continue to support, and provide intelligence to, counterinsurgent forces. And it requires a certain amount of political time and space as well, since counterinsurgency operations typically take years to succeed.[116]

One more warning: it is not enough to size a stabilizing force correctly and resource it adequately. To be sure, having enough soldiers or police helps a great deal. According to modern American counterinsurgency doctrine, stabilizing a given region should ideally involve twenty to twenty-five military or police personnel for every thousand indigenous citizens.[117] Put differently, that is at least one peacekeeper for every fifty citizens. Such ratios have sometimes been achieved, notably in post–World War II Germany, in Bosnia and Kosovo in the 1990s, and in Iraq during the surge of 2007–2008, if one counts foreign as well as Iraqi forces together.[118]

But this is not a hard-and-fast rule. Even a more modest approach that accepts somewhat greater risk suggests deploying one peacekeeper for every 100 members of the civilian population.[119] In relatively benign postconflict environments with an exhausted or thoroughly defeated population (Japan in 1945, Namibia in 1989, El Salvador in 1991, Mozambique in 1993), it has been possible to make do with only one peacekeeper for every 200 or more citizens of the host nation.[120] Indeed, once a peace accord is reached in a conflict, UN peacekeeping missions with even lower troop densities tend to improve the prospects of peace quite considerably—by as much as 55 to 75 percent, perhaps even more, relative to cases in which there are no third-party forces.[121] The peacekeepers do so largely by providing monitoring, confidence-building, and arbitration capacity, as well as persuasion and economic incentives, even when they do not have capacity or mandates to impose an end to any violence that might ensue.[122]

Nor does a certain amount of force guarantee a successful outcome. History contains numerous examples of failures even when theoretically adequate forces were deployed, as with the French experience in Algeria from 1954 to 1962 (about 40 troops per 1,000 indigenous citizens) and the US experience in Vietnam (about 85 troops per 1,000 Vietnamese). But being wary of the importance of force numbers is one thing; totally ignoring their relevance is something else. Without adequate forces it is impossible to protect the population, and in fact counterinsurgents often fall back on excessive use of firepower to compensate for their lack of presence.[123]

So what *does* work in such missions? Bearing in mind the warning about focusing just on hearts and minds, successful counterinsurgency and stabilization missions in places such as the Philippines and Malaya did in fact tend to place a premium on tracking trends in the daily life of the typical citizen. How secure were they, and whom did they credit for that security? How hopeful did they find their economic situation, regardless of the nation's GDP or even their own personal wealth at a moment in time? Did they think their country's politics gave them, and their communities and political or ethnic or sectarian groups, a voice and a share of the spoils of power?[124] Again, these kinds of metrics need to be balanced with assessments of hard power—how well can a counterinsurgent force identify, target, and contain or attrit its enemy?

The marine corps tended to focus on population-centric metrics in Vietnam and developed an approach called the Combined Action Program (CAP) to help protect the population in "ink spots" that would gradually expand with time. In fact, the marine CAP concept applied more broadly would have led to fewer overall American forces than were actually deployed, suggesting that the 10:1 rule was in fact *not* the optimal way to gauge US force requirements. But the marine corps did not carry the day with this concept for the US military overall.[125] The US military finally moved toward this type of thinking, combined with ample elements of hard power and combat capability, in Iraq. However, it did not do the former in general until 2007 (though the marine corps had been pushing similar ideas in Anbar Province in 2006, and army officers including David Petraeus and H. R. McMaster had applied elements of such thinking sooner, too).[126]

Gauging whether a counterinsurgency campaign is working is difficult. Many considerations enter into this question, which helps explain why the Iraq Index at Brookings, created by Adriana Lins de Albuquerque and myself in late 2003, included more than fifty key indicators.[127] Even when some indicators are going well, others may not be, and it is difficult to know how to weight their relative importance. Information is also typically imperfect, of course. Take Iraq from roughly 2003 through 2006. Some things went well after the overthrow of Saddam: availability of consumer goods to a much larger fraction of the population, proliferation of media, opening up of political debate, restoration of services like electricity that had suffered during the brief invasion, initial boost to the economy from the large presence of foreign troops and workers. All these positives gave hope. Violence rates, at least as measured, were initially low. But lurking beneath these positive indicators were brewing problems that turned out to be lagging indicators of big trouble ahead. Even if measured violence rates were low, crime was spreading, starting with the widespread looting right after the removal of the Baathist regime. The nation's economic foundations were not really improving, even if the economy was enjoying some short-term stimulus, and as a result jobs were scarce in many places. Most of all, disaffected Sunnis felt angry about their new place in the political order, and political parties were aligning largely along sectarian lines in nefarious ways that portended big cleavages ahead.

Sometimes it is much easier to tell how things are going. For several years in Iraq, violence rates kept going up, very significantly. Then, during the surge, violence went down even faster and more dramatically. By 2008, Iraq's rate of violence had declined by 80 percent relative to the 2006 peak. With US troop fatality rates down by 60 to 80 percent by mid-2008 as well, and Iraqi Security Force casualties reduced by more than half too, the overall trajectory of the war was clearly good by 2008—just as it had been bad in 2006, and probably for the two years before that.

The progress from the surge did not happen overnight. Even as the "surge brigades" arrived from the United States over the first half of 2007, and Iraqi security forces continued to grow at a rate of almost 10,000 uniformed personnel a month, violence remained very high for several months. That is because those larger US and Iraqi forces were going on the offensive, rendering themselves visible and vulnerable in dangerous areas. By 2008, however, violence rates were hugely improved.

The next question, however, was, would it last? Would Iraqis themselves take more ownership of the successes of the surge and sustain them as American forces gradually drew down? These kinds of questions required gauging political trends—

an even murkier business than tracking quantifiable metrics. In 2007, there was some progress: in purging extremists from government jobs, in Baghdad sharing more resources with Iraq's eighteen provincial governments, and in the Iraqi government allowing deployment of its forces to places where they could support the US-led surge.

My own confidence in the new strategy grew greatly after a trip to Iraq in mid-2007, but the data themselves were not totally conclusive at that point. It was the combination of some encouraging data trends with a general sense that the United States and Iraq had developed a proper counterinsurgency and stabilization strategy that gave me (and my colleague Kenneth Pollack) confidence—underscoring again that quantitative metrics must often be married with military and strategic judgment to reach bottom-line policy judgments in this field.[128] The science of war only goes so far.

By early 2008, things had improved much more. Progress was evident in a new pensions law, in amnesty legislation for some militia fighters, in an improved de-Baathification statute, and in a provincial powers act. Jason Campbell and I hazarded an estimate that Iraq's politics merited a "score" of roughly 5 on a scale of 0 to 11 (using 11 benchmarks for these purposes). This was an imprecise approach, subject to future revision, but it seemed the best way to gauge progress on issues that were both inherently important and topical within Iraq. We accorded the Iraqis a score of 0 for resolving the logjam over the disputed city of Kirkuk's future, for creating a permanent hydrocarbons law, and for passing a provincial election law in mid-2008. But the situation was still unmistakably improved relative to 2007 or earlier periods.

Alas, such progress was not durable in the years that followed—again underscoring the difficulty of counterinsurgency and stabilization campaigns, as well as the difficulty of reliably predicting their course.[129] Even progress that is visible and palpable may be reversible. As of 2020, it is probably still too soon to know if Iraqis will find a way to work across sectarian and other divides to take their united country forward.

Similarly, in Afghanistan, it has been difficult to make, and measure, progress.[130] In a series of articles in late 2019, the *Washington Post* coined the name Afghanistan Papers to describe a trove of interviews it uncovered through Freedom of Information requests in a manner designed to harken back to the Pentagon Papers scandal from the Vietnam era. It claimed that these documents demonstrated a pattern of deceit on the part of US policymakers who publicly exaggerated progress in Afghanistan when they knew and privately acknowledged that the mission was in fact failing.

I believe the *Post* went astray because it failed to appreciate the inherent complexity and imprecision associated with gauging progress (or the lack thereof) in this type of campaign. To be sure, wishful thinking afflicts public servants as much as other human beings. Policymakers did consistently *hope* that the nation's Afghanistan strategies (which were frequently modified) would work better than they generally did. To be more specific, they consistently hoped that the most recent modifications to strategy, in which they often had a hand, would work better than previous incarnations. Monday morning quarterbacking is fine, indeed appropriate and necessary, if we are to learn from history. But those conducting it should not conflate aspirational strategies that fall short of some or even most goals with deceitful disinformation campaigns designed to mislead the public and the Congress.

Conclusion: Subconscious versus Conscious Modeling

Modeling and simulation are essential to understanding modern military operations. Wargaming, in which different "players" take on the role of various parties to a crisis or conflict and then make various moves within a structure provided by a control team, is often helpful too. Sometimes, modeling and wargaming are even combined into a single integrated analytical exercise.

As Joshua Epstein has convincingly argued, whether we "model" mathematically and systematically, or anecdotally and impressionistically, *everyone* who forms an opinion on whether a given war should be fought and on which side would likely win is operating from some image, some set of expectations, of the likely course of battle.[131] What formal modeling does, simply, is require one to make assumptions transparent, and to apply some kind of historical, technological, or quantitative reasoning to the prediction business. Wargaming requires one to be attentive to the dynamics that arise when humans interact competitively.

The models and games need not be overly complex. Indeed, often the simpler ones do better because they tend to keep the analysis at a broad level, emphasizing assessments of the fundamentals of a fight rather than the technical details. Usually, in warfare, there are enough high-level uncertainties that there is more to be gained by analyzing, debating, and understanding them than by getting bogged down in the specific performance parameters of a large set of weapons as well as the computational codes of an elaborate algorithm. That said, complex models also have their utility—for example, for incorporating the effects of new weapons—so those who have the ability to employ complex algorithms as well as simple computational methods may benefit from doing both.

Models are also essential for force planning and defense budgeting purposes. How, for example, can the United States decide if it needs a military of 1 million or 1.35 million (the actual number today) or 2 million active-duty troops absent some sense of what would be required in various combat scenarios? To be sure, any such estimate is inevitably imprecise. Any decision on force size and posture is thus somewhat uncertain and depends on strategic judgment and risk mitigation as much as rigorous planning methodologies. But since decisions *must* be made, and budgets appropriated, methods for assessing what might be required in various contingencies are in fact essential.

Thus, while there is and will always be an art of war, there is an analytic science of war as well, and it must be a core element of any attempt to understand human combat.

The final chapters of this book turn to technology. Chapter 3 examines broad trends across many areas of military technology, including cyber and artificial intelligence, as well as robotics, directed energy, and stealth. Chapter 4 then turns to "deep dives" on nuclear weapons technology, space systems, and missile defense. This is not an exhaustive list of the scientific subjects that are prominent in modern defense planning, of course, But it includes several crucial subjects. In addition, it suggests a general approach to understanding science's role in military analysis—especially for the nonspecialist—that can be applied to other realms as well.

TECHNOLOGICAL CHANGE AND MILITARY INNOVATION

So far, this book has covered budgets, combat models, and other computational methods in modern defense analysis. This chapter and the next address what might be considered the science of war in a more literal sense, focusing on physics, engineering, and technology. They provide information on the contemporary state of technology and projections for the future. Beyond their specific and individual relevance for decisions on military investment, they have collective importance as well. Such assessments can help discern where the greatest vulnerabilities, and opportunities, exist in the defense capabilities and military plans of contemporary world powers. In addition, they provide grist for debates about whether warfare is likely to be revolutionized in coming years and decades—and, if so, in what ways. A sense of whether a "revolution in military affairs" (RMA) may be imminent or achievable is of fundamental importance for defense strategists—since one never wants to come second to a revolution. If an RMA is within reach, radical changes in defense resource allocation, military force structure, and warfighting concepts may be required. Because such change is never easy, conceptually or bureaucratically or politically, it is important to be vigilant and not to miss it when it is nigh.

How does an analyst or policy specialist wade into this complex world of actual military science—that is, the realm of physics and engineering on which so many practical decisions about military matters turn? Given the sophistication of the technologies involved, this would seem an impossible task for the generalist, or even for many scientists lacking specialized knowledge of certain aspects of military technical matters. But in another sense, it is a necessary task. Only by striving for answers to questions like whether missile defenses can work against contemporary and future threats, whether space weapons can provide useful capabilities economically, and whether future warfare might be revolutionized can we reach decisions about proper defense resource allocation. Even more important, only in these ways can we avoid major surprises in future wars (or, to put it differently, profit from any surprises before adversaries can do so). Only in these ways can we understand the potential, and the limits, of arms control.

In my undergraduate days at Princeton, students could take a course called Physics for Poets. This chapter and the next are intended in that same spirit, with a focus on the physics and engineering of systems and technologies pertinent to military affairs, but with an attempt to focus on the basics and keep things as simple as possible.

Of course, this kind of primer cannot arm a generalist with all the information needed to resolve technical issues in military analysis and decision making. True scientists are clearly needed as well. It took Leo Szilard and Albert Einstein to warn President Roosevelt that nuclear weapons were possible, for example, and it also took experts to figure out when capabilities like radar, aerial flight, space flight, and laser sensors were within reach. To anticipate future breakthroughs, and help decide which technologies are worth pursuing, the Department of Defense has numerous expert scientific advisory groups and consultants today—ranging from the so-called JASON group and the Defense Science Board, to the main weapons laboratories run by DoD (like Lincoln Labs at MIT) and the military services as well as the Department of Energy, to many individual scientists or groups of scientists working either for the defense industry or for universities.

That said, some basic understanding of scientific and technical issues in defense policy is essential for the policymaker. Scientists cannot be asked to make all decisions concerning technology, since many decisions involve other matters too—the country's national security objectives, its resource constraints, its competing priorities, its arms control interests, and so on. Even a basic knowledge about key concepts and terminologies allows the generalist to engage in conversations and debates led by more technically expert individuals. If generalists are at least able to follow technical discussions, they can often discern the key assumptions behind science-based arguments—which are often not conclusive, or dispositive for policymaking, just because they are "scientific." Gaining basic knowledge and understanding can also help generalists and policymakers ask thoughtful questions. The ensuing discussion can test premises, detect uncertainty or inconsistency, and provoke debate that sharpens the focus of where uncertainty is greatest. In other words, basic scientific literacy among generalists helps create a vetting process that can often weed out sloppy, mistaken, or ideologically motivated arguments. It can also make generalists more able to appreciate the work of whistleblowers and dissidents from *within* the scientific community, and pay them heed when institutional and political forces may otherwise overwhelm them.[1]

This chapter addresses the following broad question: Where are the greatest opportunities—for the United States and allies, as well as their potential adversaries—in terms of military innovation between now and 2040? The flip side of this question, of course, is where can one expect the greatest vulnerabilities to develop or emerge? Both are at the heart of understanding whether a revolution in military affairs is achievable; even without any RMA, they must be asked if good decisions about modernization and innovation are to be made. The next chapter then bores down more intensively on three specific key areas of military technology: satellites, missile defense, and nuclear weapons.

My approach here is to attempt to look out roughly two decades into the future, extrapolating from today to gauge where technology may reach by that point. Such a time horizon allows opportunity for proper planning and innovation. Yet that time horizon is also short enough that existing trends in laboratory research can help us understand the future without indulging in rampant speculation. Since many defense systems take a couple decades to develop, it should not be an overly daunting task to gauge how the world might look, in terms of deployable military technology, twenty years from now. This approach is not foolproof, but if undertaken with the proper degree of acknowledged uncertainty, it can still be quite useful.

This chapter's category-by-category examination of military technology employs the same basic framework that I developed in my book published in 2000, *Technological Change and the Future of Warfare*. The core of that book was an analysis of ongoing and likely future developments in various categories of military-related technologies. My goal was to attempt to determine in which areas the pace of change was likely to be revolutionary over the following twenty years, versus high or moderate. These terms are somewhat notional and imprecise. That said, revolutionary change has a fairly clear meaning: a pace of progress that renders obsolete old weapons, tactics, and operational approaches while making fundamentally new ones possible.

The earlier analysis was a response to the popular hypothesis of the 1990s and early years of this century that an RMA was underway. Advocates of this view warned that if the United States failed to take advantage of new military opportunities to dramatically change how it built and equipped its forces and how it waged war with them, it could fall dangerously far behind adversaries. Advocates argued that defense budgets might need to be radically reshaped, in favor of technology development and away from traditional systems. Some believed that many combat units might need to be taken "off-line" and used instead to prototype and test new technologies. A number favored cutbacks in overseas presence and deterrence missions to free up resources for innovation. Analogies were drawn with the 1930s and 1940s, when blitzkrieg, amphibious warfare, aircraft carrier operations, long-range strategic bombardment, and finally nuclear weapons were all developed—ultimately largely determining the outcomes of World War II.[2]

In the earlier work, I sought to challenge numerous aspects of the notion that an RMA was underway in the 1990s. Instead, what seemed more plausible was a continuation of the rapid evolution in military technology and operations that had continued *ever since* World War II, producing breakthroughs like satellites, helicopters, modern jets, lasers, night-vision sensors, stealth aircraft, and precision-guided autonomous munitions (like cruise missiles), among many other things. Because the Department of Defense was already investing in research, development, testing, and evaluation (RDT&E) in these and many other areas, it was not obvious that revolution—rather than a continuation of rapid, incremental evolution—was the wiser philosophy. The department's default assumption, at least since World War II, is that it must investigate virtually any technology that could have major defense implications, whether or not the United States deploys each and every new gadget it can build, in order to ensure that it is at a minimum never blindsided by an adversary. This stood in contrast to earlier eras of a much smaller standing American military establishment.

The RMA movement of the 1990s and early years of the 2000s is part of what influenced Secretary of Defense Donald Rumsfeld first to try to cut back severely on US ground forces and then to insist on deploying only a small invasion force to Iraq in 2003. To take another recent example, RMA proponents who had observed American technology at work in Operation Desert Storm in 1991 predicted that NATO airpower could easily intimidate Serbian militias into stopping their deprivations against the Kosovar Albanian population in 1999. Such wrong predictions were partly due to misreading politics and personalities of the Balkans and the Middle East in those eras. But political misjudgment was compounded and reinforced by breathless expectations about military technology.

Beyond the political mistakes, the technological basis for such prognostication was always weak. It did not take a PhD in physics to know why, but it did take a methodology that broke down the problem into analytically manageable chunks. For example, in regard to Kosovo, a basic knowledge of military technology made it easy to understand that if NATO planes stayed above 15,000 feet altitude to reduce their vulnerability to air defenses, their ability to identify and target small Serb formations through the cloud cover prevalent in the Balkans in early spring would be severely limited. Basic science, coupled with Clausewitzian cautions about fog and friction in war, should have disabused American policymakers of any heady optimism about the likely course of the air war. There were also few technologies on the drawing boards in the years just before the Iraq and Afghanistan wars that augured well for foreign forces trying to find hostile opponents armed with small weaponry and immersed within large civilian populations. We all should have known such campaigns would likely still be hard, even in such an advanced age of technology. While some innovations like unmanned aerial systems and mine-resistant ambush-protected vehicles (MRAPs) were helpful in those wars, on balance there were few breakthroughs that radically eased the nature of those conflicts for American and allied forces. Yet some still predicted "cakewalks" for American and allied forces in those conflicts, based largely on a sense of the technologies and capabilities of the day.

My methodology for assessing future trends in military technology, and thus future prospects for major warfighting innovation, has three main elements. First, understand and invoke foundational concepts of physics, to understand the realm of the possible—and the limits of the possible. Second, examine the scientific, engineering, and defense literature on various types of technological research in each of a number of prominent areas of military technology. Finally, armed with the resulting initial estimates of the prospects for sector-by-sector military technological breakthroughs, consult with experts including at several of the nation's major weapons laboratories for their feedback. This last opportunity was afforded me by years of work in the field, and the connections provided by an organization like the Brookings Institution, but the first two parts of the methodology are available to all in future work as well.

Of course, technological opportunity does not immediately translate into military innovation and new capabilities. When it comes to combining technologies into systems and operational concepts that can be instrumental in fighting wars, the human dimension of organizational performance, influenced by the external combat environment as well as domestic and bureaucratic politics, introduces new variables into the mix. This is the crux of the debate about military innovation past, present, and future—as the writings of experts like Stephen Rosen, Thomas Ehrhard, Barry Posen, Stephen Biddle, and others attest. The RMA debate of the 1990s underscored the reality that, while technology can provide the raw materials for military revolutions, those revolutions must ultimately be sparked by entrepreneurship and organizational adaptation, requiring astute study and good judgment as to when new technological possibilities could translate into meaningful military capability. That is the reason, of course, that the stakes are so high. Nothing about the process is automatic, and nothing ensures convergence to the mean. Germany was able to see, and seize, the new opportunities in the late 1930s, for example, in a way that France demonstrably was not. The process of divining a new warfighting frontier, and then transforming it into tangible reality, often takes a decade or more—and, by the end of the process at least, it may take large amounts of money (in order to build new weapons and force structure). This was true historically, as with the inventions or transformations of blitzkrieg, integrated air defense, aircraft carrier operations, amphibious assault, anti-submarine warfare (ASW) systems, and the atomic bomb in the 1930s and 1940s. It remains true today.[3]

My assessment of trends in key areas of military-relevant technology is organized into four categories. The first is sensors, of many different types, which gather data of relevance to military operations. The second comprises the computer and communications systems that process and distribute that data. Third are major weapons platforms as well as key enabling technologies for those platforms. Fourth are other types of weapons systems and other technologies, many of them relatively new (see table 3.1).

TABLE 3.1.   Projected Advances in Key Deployable Technologies, 2020–2040

	MODERATE	HIGH	REVOLUTIONARY
SENSORS			
Chemical sensors		X	
Biological sensors		X	
Optical, infrared, and UV sensors	X		
Radar and radio sensors	X		
Sound, sonar, and motion sensors	X		
Magnetic detection	X		
Particle beams (as sensors)	X		
COMPUTERS AND COMMUNICATION			
Computer hardware			X
Computer software			X
Offensive cyber operations			X
System of systems/internet of things			X
Radio communications	X		
Laser communications		X	
Artificial intelligence/big data			X
Quantum computing		X	
PROJECTILES, PROPULSION, AND PLATFORMS			
Robotics and autonomous systems			X
Missiles	X		
Explosives		X	
Fuels	X		
Jet engines	X		
Internal combustion engines	X		
Battery-powered engines		X	
Rockets		X	

(continued)

TABLE 3.1. (continued)

	MODERATE	HIGH	REVOLUTIONARY
Ships	X		
Armor		X	
Stealth		X	
Satellites		X	
OTHER WEAPONS AND KEY TECHNOLOGIES			
Radio-frequency weapons	X		
Nonlethal weapons		X	
Biological weapons		X	
Chemical weapons		X	
Other weapons of mass destruction	X		
Particle beams (as weapons)	X		
Electric guns, rail guns		X	
Lasers		X	
Long-range kinetic energy weapons	X		
Nanomaterials		X	
3D printing/additive manufacturing		X	
Human enhancement devices and substances		X	

Note: The terms "moderate," "high," and "revolutionary" are subjective and somewhat imprecise. In general terms, technologies showing moderate advances might improve their performance by a few percent or at most a couple of tens of percent—in terms of speed, range, lethality, or other defining characteristics—between 2020 and 2040. Those experiencing high advances will be able to accomplish tasks on the battlefield far better than before—perhaps by 50 to 100 percent, to the extent improved performance can be so quantified. Finally, technology areas in which revolutionary advances occur will be able to accomplish important battlefield tasks that they cannot now even attempt.

In short, my overall prognostication is that technological change of relevance to military innovation may be faster and more consequential in the next twenty years than it has proved over the last twenty. Virtually all the technological areas considered here are receiving high-level attention, and substantial resources, from DoD leadership. It is entirely possible that the ongoing, rapid pace of computer innovation may make the next two decades more revolutionary than the last two. The dynamics in robotics and in cybersecurity discussed here may only accelerate. They may be more fully exploited by modern military organizations, and they will likely extend in important ways into the artificial intelligence realm as well. At least, an examination of the last twenty years would seem to suggest the potential for such an acceleration. That is particularly true in light of the fact that multiple countries (most notably China, but also Russia) now have the resources to compete with Western nations in military innovation. Some other areas of technology, perhaps most notably directed energy systems, hypersonic missiles, and certain types of advanced materials, could play important supplemental roles in making the next two decades a true period of military revolution, or at least of very fast and ongoing rapid transformation. Should such opportunities emerge, the Pentagon may indeed need to shift its funding priorities and other activities quickly to take advantage. But, again, it should be recalled that all these technologies are already receiving money, and attention, and the opportunity to "prove themselves" in laboratories and in some cases on test ranges as well. As such, most arguments about a need for urgent revolution and military transformation should probably still be taken with a grain of salt.

I remain wary that an RMA of a magnitude akin to that of the World War II era will occur—partly because nuclear weapons will continue to provide an ultimate deterrent, partly because the age of precision strike and of robotics (starting with cruise missiles) is already now roughly thirty years old by most measures. But the pace of innovation will surely be impressive, nonetheless. In any case, the methodology for assessing, and debating, the prospects of an RMA is more important than whatever I personally may prognosticate about the future. So to that methodology we now turn.

Sensors

In warfare, targets obviously need to be found and tracked in order to be attacked and destroyed. Other battlefield information is crucial too, such as that concerning terrain, weather, and the locations of civilian populations, key infrastructure, and friendly forces.

Sensors are the military technologies that provide information about all objects and individuals of potential battlefield significance. I briefly examine eight general types here. Three categories—radar and radio, optical/infrared/UV sensors, and magnetic detectors—make use of one type or another of electromagnetic radiation. Another type, sonar, involves sound in water. Particle beams are a fifth category. Biological sensors, chemical sensors, and nuclear materials detectors round out the list.

Begin with this last group of sensors, those for detecting weapons of mass destruction. Just as in the past two decades, progress over the next two seems likely to be gradual.

Current research on chemical weapons detection focuses on finding more trace amounts in a given fixed site, and on making detectors more portable and affordable, rather than on developing fundamentally different methods of detecting chemicals from a distance.[4] Sandia Lab's pulsed-discharge ionization detector is an example of such a technology. The chief dilemma in finding chemical weapons, related to the challenge for biological materials, is that to identify a chemical compound, one generally needs direct access to it, to employ a method of identification such as gas chromatography. Laser spectroscopy from a distance or other such methods of remote interrogation are not particularly promising for most battlefield applications; such means could generally work only if a chemical were released into the atmosphere.[5]

Biological weapons detectors are improving. To date, they have needed not only direct access to any pathogens to identify them but also enough time to watch the pathogens grow or otherwise reveal their identity through natural biological functions. Given advances in microbiology and genetics, it seems likely that much faster methods will be developed in the next two decades. By "seeing" a pathogen's DNA more quickly, methods of identification can be reduced in part to more digital and computational realms where computers can bring their enormous powers to bear and dramatically accelerate the identification process.

Still, progress seems likely to be moderate or moderately fast rather than revolutionary—at least in terms of its battlefield implications. In the short term, the Department of Homeland Security (DHS) is prototyping a two-tier biological detection sensor system, but it will still take up to fifteen minutes to detect and identify a relatively narrow range of potential pathogens at close-in range. That is not dramatically different from where technologies stood two decades ago, even if there has been considerable effort toward making systems somewhat more deployable and user-friendly.[6] For example, the basic BioWatch technology on which current systems are based largely reflects modifications to technology and concepts first deployed in 2003, shortly after the anthrax attacks that followed 9/11.[7] Some new ideas are being pursued. For example, Lawrence Livermore National Laboratory has created the Lawrence Livermore Microbial Detection Array that examines DNA directly (without requiring cultures) and searches for literally thousands of bacteria, viruses, and fungi. To date, however, it has been used for very specialized applications and is not at the basis of current DHS or DoD deployable systems; it also requires twenty-four hours to detect a pathogen.[8] Identifying organisms is inherently a complex business.[9] As a recent review article put it, "For further progress in the biosensors field we need revolutionary ideas in the development of novel target recognition strategies. . . . We also need new paradigms for the identification and detection of existing or emerging pathogenic microorganisms, unknown toxins and viral threat agents." Since even future biological pathogen detectors will require direct physical access to agents, their strategic role for intelligence or targeting from long ranges will remain limited, even if their tactical usefulness improves.[10]

Detection of nuclear materials remains difficult given the basic physics of the signature. Key nuclear materials in a weapon do not give off large amounts of radiation, and they can be shielded by materials like lead so that whatever they do emit is prevented from escaping to the general environment.

Nuclear forensics are improving, however, through a number of sophisticated chemical and computational methods. That can make it easier to determine where a given fissile material or waste product may have originated, through improvements in the materials used in sensors such as stilbene crystals.[11] But the processes still require being close enough to the materials that their relatively feeble radioactive signatures can be detected and distinguished from normal background radiation.[12] Thus, it is not surprising that the 2018 Nuclear Posture Review would aspire to "sustain and build upon" the 57,000 radiation detectors operating at US ports, border crossings, and key interior sites rather than to propose pursuit of any breakthrough technology. There is no alternative, and there almost surely will be no alternative, to proximate monitoring and interrogation.[13]

Next, consider sonar, an acronym taken from the phrase "sound navigation and ranging"—that is, the process of using underwater pressure or sound waves to detect objects beneath the surface of a given body of water. Sonar is a mature technology, with the basic concept and technologies involved similar today to what they have been for decades.

Still, sonar is improving gradually, largely through better signals-processing capabilities and through expanded use of robotics to proliferate sensors. These trends could accelerate in the coming years.[14] One telling indicator of the expected progress in sonar is that, after decades when one might have already thought the method to be obsolete, dolphins may finally soon earn their retirement from the mine-warfare enterprise. The Knifefish, an unmanned underwater vehicle (UUV) using low-frequency synthetic-aperture sonar, may be among the pioneer vessels with this capability.[15] Low-frequency sonar, with lengthy receiver arrays that are physically separate from the emitter, is also showing promise for long-range active detection. Aided by the sophisticated signals-processing capabilities of modern computing, it is showing the potential to increase detection ranges against certain types of objects in at least some circumstances by up to an order of magnitude or so. The unclassified literature on the subject describes its capabilities in regard to finding fish, not enemy submarines, but advocates envision finding targets of interest 100 kilometers away or farther.[16]

Another concept being explored by the US Naval Undersea Warfare Center in Newport, Rhode Island, focuses on the physics of the water around mobile sonar sensors. The system uses a cavitator to change the flow of water near the sensors, reducing their exposure to noise and thus improving their sensitivity to an actual target signal.[17] Yet another sonar improvement being investigated would apply to shallow waters that are often noisy. By studying those waters at different times of year and understanding how sound ricochets through them, improvements can be made in how an actual signal of a specific vessel might be better separated from the noise.[18]

All that said, in regard to sonar's role in finding submarines, progress in making subs quieter has continued as well. A net assessment of sonar as a tool of anti-submarine warfare must therefore be less than bullish. It is for such reasons that the US Navy flatly declares, in an official document on sonar, that in previous eras passive sonar against noisy submarines could usually find them before they came within weapons-firing range of US assets, whereas today active sonar is needed to achieve the same early warning.[19] It is hard to find navy documents that suggest any radically different expectations about the future.

Consider the broad category of sensors employing the electromagnetic spectrum for their information. This includes visible light sensors such as lasers as well as ultraviolet and infrared sensors in the near-visible part of the spectrum; radio and radar; and magnetic detection methods.

A broad observation that can be offered about such sensors is that they will run head-on into basic physics in the future just as they have in the past. Despite the extremely impressive existing technologies that exploit these various kinds of electromagnetic radiation, the simple fact is that they are rapidly attenuated or blocked by a number of prevalent materials on earth. Water is perhaps the most significant. That means that most soil is also difficult to penetrate very far with any kind of sensor employing such radiation. Ultraviolet light, gamma rays, and X-rays fare even worse than visible light. Radar is also severely compromised by water, though extremely low-frequency (ELF) waves are a partial exception and can penetrate nearly ten times farther than visible light.[20] All of these kinds of radiation require a direct line of sight to any target. Radar curves modestly in the atmosphere, but it is the chief exception to this broad generalization, and only a partial one.

Metal is another unyielding barrier to electromagnetic radiation. Leaves, thin wood, and other materials with some water content may allow a certain modest transmission, but even here, there is no getting around the fact that any water content will rapidly attenuate radiation.[21]

There is impressive ongoing progress, though it needs to be viewed against these basic physical constraints on the plausible performance of future sensors. Laser sensor technology will continue to become smaller, cheaper, and thus more readily usable in multiple tactical systems on the battlefield.[22] For example, lasers are in use now not only in artillery like the Copperhead but also in mortar systems.[23] Laser radar, or lidar, will also to find new applications, such as helping robots and other unmanned systems "see."[24] It may become more commonly used in relatively shallow-water anti-submarine warfare, too.[25]

Similar progress is being observed with infrared technologies, which are becoming and will continue to become cheaper and more widely available as well.[26] Then there are various specific new applications. For example, optical sensors may soon be deployed within bullets to allow them to steer toward a target they have previously locked on, using small fins. They can do so even when wind or other perturbations affect flight trajectory.[27]

Magnetic detectors are improving, for example, with a number of new applications in small devices. However, the ability to find militarily significant objects in radically new ways appears to be advancing gradually. As one review article put it, "The development of magnetic sensor technology has been slow and gradual."[28] That can be expected to continue.

Magnetic detectors, as well as new uses of microwave devices and lasers, are also potentially useful in new concepts of anti-submarine warfare. Bioluminescence and wake-detection methodologies have also been investigated and some may remain of interest, including to Russia.[29] However, these methods seem unlikely to work at long range against deeply submerged submarines; their benefits are more likely to be tactical and local. One possible exception to this sweeping statement is wake-detection sensor systems, given the more inherently long-range phenomenology inherent in the basic concept of how the sensor operates. But by changing direction frequently, operating at greater depth at times, and otherwise avoiding straight-line steady movement under calm surface conditions, submarines may be able to take effective countermeasures.[30]

Radar is still making forward strides. For example, synthetic-aperture radar (by which the movement of a radar creates the effect of a much larger aperture system, once signals are integrated over a substantial distance) can now be used to detect moving objects. This development represents in effect a more clever exploitation of data that were already available, rather than a breakthrough in basic physics or engineering. Similarly, smaller radars can now be netted together to create the equivalent capability to that previously provided only by a larger system. That might, for example, allow a family of unmanned "Reapers" with Ground Moving Target Indicator capability to replace today's Joint Surveillance and Target Attack Radar System, among other such applications.[31]

In another recent application that continues to be refined (and to proliferate), radar altimeters can increasingly be used to optimize the detonation point of warheads to maximize their odds of destroying a given target—compensating for the computed inaccuracy of a given flight trajectory by last-minute adjustments to the height of burst of the ordnance. This technology is applicable, for example, to reentry vehicles carrying nuclear warheads.[32] Yet another new application of radar with implications that are still being developed is the use of small radar systems mounted on armored vehicles to detect and coordinate defenses against incoming threats. The Israeli Trophy system is an early example of this approach.[33]

Multispectral radar is also being more widely developed and applied. It is motivated in part by the desire to find stealth aircraft by surveying a wider range of radar frequencies, improving the sensitivity of receivers, and looking toward aircraft from a variety of angles (some of which may present less stealthy aspects of a given aircraft). That said, these improvements are most likely effective at shorter ranges. They do not eliminate the benefits of stealth altogether and will not do so. They certainly have not discouraged aircraft manufacturers from continuing to depend on stealth in cutting-edge systems despite its cost and complexity.[34] The improved radar systems are also likely to continue to be countered and challenged by computer-facilitated improvements in miniaturized decoys and jammers with increasingly autonomous capabilities, expendable and thus widely deployable given their small size.[35] In some cases, the sensors themselves are improving; in other cases like this, it is partly the ingenious combination of existing capabilities in new systems that produces the breakthrough.

Particle beams of various kinds as sensors are improving. For example, a pilot project at the Port of Boston uses a concept developed by two MIT physicists involving nuclear resonance fluorescence, which employs a neutron beam to interrogate cargo. It is able to discern objects inside closed containers much better than X-rays.

But the basic reality is that these active systems are inherently short-range in their phenomenology and their potential. That is because they must generate a high-energy beam that tends to disperse or be absorbed by numerous materials at fairly short ranges.

Systems like the MIT/Boston detector, noted earlier, still require proximate access to the objects being examined.[36]

The overall message on sensors: be realistic about breakthroughs. The laws, and constraints, of physics still rule.

Computers, Communications, and Robotics

Modern militaries, especially America's, have become extremely reliant on moving vast amounts of data around the battlefield as a normal part of operations. This has happened largely as the spread of computers, fiber-optic cables, and other technologies has gone unopposed by the likes of al Qaeda and the Taliban. The latter are enemies that, whatever their considerable strengths in other domains, are not able to compete on the high-technology battlefield with the United States, or disrupt its use of advanced data and communications systems.

These happy trends will not continue in any future warfare against more advanced militaries. To be sure, some new and exciting technologies may further aid tactical as well as theater-level and strategic communications. Laser communications systems, for example, could make an important difference, especially in space where clouds and other obstacles are not an impediment.[37] Frequency-hopping radios with advanced computers coordinating the dance from one frequency to another are increasingly capable. Even if the radio technology per se is fairly mature, better computers allow levels of performance that were not previously possible. And innovations from the commercial world of mobile communications and their advanced networks that allow for "network hopping" as well as other efficiencies will make the networks more robust and dependable against certain types of disruptions.

But the disruptions themselves will be much more threatening. Jamming, possible attacks on fiber-optic undersea cables as well as satellites (discussed more later), and cyberattacks on the software of the radios and other systems used for communications are all serious worries, to say nothing of high-altitude nuclear-induced electromagnetic pulse (EMP).[38] Even when communications systems within a small unit survive enemy attack, or find themselves outside the targeted zone of intense jamming, communications with central authority may suffer. It is because of such concerns, for example, that the army's Maneuver Warfare Center of Excellence at Fort Benning, Georgia, is examining concepts of future operations in which a brigade might be cut off from divisional or corps headquarters for an extended period, and have to function entirely on its own during that time.[39]

In regard to computers, rapid progress will likely continue. "Moore's law" may or may not hold quite as it now has for several decades; the capacity and speed of computers may no longer double every eighteen to twenty-four months. But rapid progress seems likely to continue. Around 1970, several thousand transistors could be built on a given chip; by 2000 the figure was roughly 10 million, and by 2015 or so it exceeded 1 billion.[40] Even if the pace of advance slows, it will not stop. And countless ways will continue to be invented to take advantage of all this computing capacity that is already available, with huge undeveloped potential in many areas.

For example, improved computing power can allow a multitude of satellites and other sensors to have their data synthesized automatically through various algorithms and artificial intelligence. This kind of effort may be further accelerated if the Department of Defense is successful in building up its relationships with Silicon Valley and other centers of computer excellence through innovations like the Defense Innovation Unit (Experimental) (DIUx).[41] These kinds of multiplatform networks can help mitigate the dangers associated with anti-satellite (ASAT) weapons attacking large, high-value military assets that previously had few if any backups.[42] The odds in favor of major breakthroughs in these technology areas are high for the next two decades.[43] Artificial intelligence systems are basically computers that can "learn" how to do things through a process of trial and error with some mechanism for telling them when they are right and when they are wrong—such as picking out missiles in photographs, or people in crowds, as with the Pentagon's "Project Maven"—and then applying what they have learned to diagnose future data.[44]

Largely as a result of the computer revolution, robotics will continue to improve dramatically.[45] Already, of course, self-driving vehicles are possible. Soon, a number are likely to be built for specific military purposes like tactical resupply on the battlefield; the army's "Wingman" may be one example.[46] Wingman is also being adapted to carry weapons at least for tests (albeit with real human soldiers in the decision-making loop).[47] And, of course, it may not end there. The former vice chairman of the Joint Chiefs of Staff, General Paul Selva, has recently argued that the United States could be about a decade away from having the capacity to build an autonomous robot that could decide when to shoot and whom to kill—though he also asserted that the United States had no plans actually to build such a creature.[48]

Other robotics with more specific functions surely will be built. They will include advanced sensor systems, often acting as networks or "swarms." In the air, they could also involve stealthier unmanned aerial vehicles (UAVs) with long range, usable as penetrating sensors, to give just one example.[49] On the sea, future robotics could include unmanned surface vessels for intelligence gathering, mine clearing, and possible local point defense against threats like fast-attack craft. Indeed, a RAND report in 2013 found there were already sixty-three unmanned surface vessels that had been developed and tested. Underwater robotic devices (UUVs), like DARPA's "Sea Hunter," could, for example, perform search functions associated with anti-submarine warfare and mine warfare.[50] It is already possible to talk somewhat precisely and realistically about how the US Navy's future fleet might include substantial numbers of large unmanned surface and underwater vessels; a team of researchers including Bryan Clark and Bryan McGrath has recently recommended a future fleet with forty of each, for example.[51] The navy is increasingly thinking of how to deploy its Littoral Combat Ships with families of unmanned ships and other robotics.[52] Some UUVs could have long persistence and low signature even within close proximity of an enemy's shores.[53] A $100,000 ocean glider recently crossed the Atlantic; promising concepts could cut that cost for UUVs by a factor of ten.[54]

Even if General Selva's terminator is not built, robotics will in some cases likely be given the authority to decide when to use force. This highly fraught subject requires careful ethical and legal oversight, to be sure, and the associated risks are serious. Yet the speed at which military operations must occur will create incentives *not* to have a person in the decision-making loop in many tactical settings.[55] Whatever the United States may prefer, restrictions on automated uses of violent force would also appear relatively difficult to negotiate (even if desirable), given likely opposition from Russia and quite possibly other nations.[56] Moreover, given progress in Russia and China, it is far from clear that the United States will be the lead innovator in artificial intelligence in the years ahead, with some warning that one or both of these countries may soon set the pace in AI—and thus also in warfighting robotics.[57]

For example, small robots that can operate as swarms on land, in the air, or in the water may be given certain leeway to decide when to wield their lethal capabilities. By communicating with each other and processing information about the enemy in real time, they could concentrate attacks where defenses are weakest in a form of combat that John Allen and Amir Husain call "hyperwar" because of its speed and intensity.[58] Other types of swarms could attack parked aircraft; even small explosives, precisely detonated, could disable wings or engines or produce secondary and much larger explosions. Many countries will have the capacity to do such things in the coming twenty years.[59] Even if the United States tries to avoid using such swarms for lethal and offensive purposes, it may elect to employ them as defensive shields (say, against North Korean artillery attack against Seoul) or as jamming aids to accompany penetrating aircraft. With UAVs that can fly ten hours and 100 kilometers now costing only in the hundreds of thousands of dollars, and quadcopters with ranges of a kilometer more or less costing in the hundreds of dollars, the trend lines are clear—and the affordability of using many drones in an organized way is evident.[60] Although defenses against such robotics will surely be built, too, at present they are underdeveloped against possible small UAV swarms.[61] And unless area defense allows for a certain part of the sky, sea, or land effectively to be swept clear of any robotics within a certain zone, it seems statistically likely that some offensive UAVs will survive a defense's efforts to neutralize them—meaning that their capabilities to act as a swarm, even if perhaps a weakened one, will probably remain.

Robotics with artificial intelligence may also deploy on the battlefield in close partnership with real humans. These robotics could be paired one for one, or in larger numbers, under the control and for the purposes of a single soldier or unit.[62]

With the progress in computers has, as noted, come far greater cyber vulnerability. By effectively building Achilles' heels into everything they operate, modern militaries—and modern societies writ large—have created huge opportunities for their potential enemies. The fact that everyone is vulnerable, in some sense, is no guarantee of protection. Deterrence of some actions is not impossible in cyberspace, but it is surely difficult, and likely to fail in many important situations.[63] Vulnerabilities may vary across countries based on different types of software employed in their military systems and different relative abilities of their respective offensive hacking units.

The United States undoubtedly possesses among the best, and probably the very top, offensive cyber capabilities on the planet. These could be used against the computer and networking capabilities of the militaries, as well as the broader economies and national infrastructural capabilities of other countries. Distressingly, however, the United States may also be among the most vulnerable, given how much it has computerized in modern times, often somewhat carelessly and often with software of questionable resilience.[64] A country figuring out how to integrate cyberattack plans that are temporarily crippling into an integrated operational concept may, even if still vulnerable to reprisal itself, be able to achieve dramatic success in the opening (and perhaps decisive) phases of a war. A military and a national infrastructure with key systems plugged into the internet, running on flawed software, and often employing a simple password system for user access rather than a two-factor authentication system is inherently vulnerable.[65] This is precisely the situation the United States and most of its major allies face today. Faced with such a situation, in a future conflict, an enemy is likely to roll the dice and attempt large-scale cyberattacks—even if, in crossing such a threshold, it opens itself up to inevitable retaliation in kind.[66]

Uncertainty abounds in the cyber domain. Software vulnerabilities that might exist at one time could be patched up subsequently. Indeed, methods for detecting and responding to intrusion proactively and quickly have improved dramatically in recent years; one example was Cyber Command's success in thwarting Russian attempts to interfere in the 2018 midterm elections in the United States.[67] But other vulnerabilities can and will continue to emerge. Those operating in the classified world may have a greater sense than I of the vulnerabilities and opportunities that the United States now faces due to cyber vulnerability. But even they generally cannot be sure. That is because cyber vulnerabilities are not static. They are always evolving in a game of measures/countermeasures, even faster than in other areas of military operations characterized by these kinds of dynamics, such as electronic warfare. In addition, the ripple effects of any cyberattack often cannot be easily foreseen even when specific vulnerabilities are understood. There may also be important path dependencies about how different types of failures might collectively affect a larger system. It is difficult to evaluate these possibilities by examining individual vulnerabilities alone.[68] On balance, though, the overall situation today is very worrisome in regard to the cyber systems of the private sector, the national civilian infrastructure (on which DoD depends in many ways), and the armed forces themselves. A Defense Science Board study in early 2017 asserted that virtually no major US weapon system had cyber systems that could be confidently viewed as resilient in the face of enemy attack.[69]

A separate type of problem related to the same basic phenomenon of ongoing progress in computers and electronics is the vulnerability of domestic infrastructure and of military weaponry to EMP from a high-altitude nuclear explosion. (US systems could also be vulnerable to severe solar storms of a type that can typically occur once a century or so.) These vulnerabilities may be growing because smaller and smaller electronics are progressively more vulnerable to a given electric insult, and because as the Cold War recedes in time, the perceived likelihood of an EMP attack may decline. American strategists, military services, and weapons manufacturers may delude themselves into a false sense of perceived invulnerability, believing that an EMP attack would be seen as tantamount to a direct nuclear attack against populations and hence too risky. It is debatable whether all adversaries would in fact make such a calculation; as such, US vulnerabilities in this area could easily grow further.[70]

Communications systems are also highly vulnerable to jamming from sophisticated electronic-warfare technologies. Digital electronics are amplifying and accelerating these challenges, to the point where in recent years some Department of Defense research and development documents have prioritized electronic warfare as among the most rapidly changing and threatening of technological developments.[71]

Overall, military "nervous systems" appear quite vulnerable—today and in the future.

Projectiles, Propulsion, and Platforms

Lumping together major vehicles, ships, aircraft, rockets, missiles, and the various engines and fuels that propel these large platforms, what can we usefully prognosticate about their likely progress over the next two decades? Many of the new capabilities that will be in the field in 2040 are already foreseeable—and programmatically planned—even today. Thus, prognostication is not so hard in some ways, particularly for major weapons platforms of the type emphasized in this section.

Perhaps the long time required to design, test, build, and field major weapons platforms is in part a flaw of the US weapons acquisition system. However, it is also not clear that platform technology is advancing so quickly as to require a more supple and fast-moving process. As former deputy secretary of defense William Lynn argued in a forum at Brookings in 2015, the Department of Defense may get a mediocre grade for "anything touched by Moore's Law," given that electronics and computers are advancing so fast, but it arguably does pretty well in regard to bending metal and building vehicles, ships, and planes.[72] In any case, for many large platforms, even modest progress in the speed of acquisition efforts would not change the fact that most systems that will be in service in the 2040s are already being researched today.

To begin this quick survey, consider first transport aircraft. They are likely to improve, but only modestly and gradually. Various possible innovations in areas such as structural materials for fuselages and wings, as well as engine technology, may improve performance—but typically by 10 to 25 percent, not 50 to 100 percent, in terms of various key metrics.[73]

Progress in missiles is ongoing. Today's air-to-air missiles, for example, can now range 200 miles and reach speeds of Mach 6, in some cases.[74] The most interesting developments in coming years are likely in the realm of hypersonic vehicles (those exceeding Mach 5, like the air-to-air missiles just noted) that may become capable of longer-range or even global strike operations over the time frame of interest in this book.[75] That could put any target on Earth within reach within an hour of decision and launch. They would likely employ scramjet and/or boost-glide technologies, which are expected to become substantially more affordable and capable. Scramjets use a rocket to attain high speeds, then an air-breathing engine to sustain the speed; boost-glide systems attain rapid speeds at high altitudes, then glide to target. While the United States will likely develop important new capabilities in this realm, so could China and Russia and perhaps other states. Indeed, as of early 2018, according to US under secretary of defense for research and engineering Michael Griffin, China has done twenty times as many hypersonic tests to date as has the United States.[76] Weapons are now starting to be tested in the realm of Mach 8 to Mach 10 (6,000 or more miles an hour).[77] Maneuverable and homing reentry vehicles are already a reality on some types of ballistic missiles (for example, on Chinese missiles that could be targeted against ships in the western Pacific). They will likely continue to improve and gain greater usage.[78]

Prototypes are also being developed for an aircraft with a combined conventional turbine engine with dual-mode ramjet/scramjet propulsion. The former would be used early in flight; the latter would kick in at higher speeds. Indeed, hypersonic aircraft reaching Mach 6 (in contrast to today's fighters in the Mach 2+ range) may become a possibility in the coming twenty years. In other words, they may become as fast as today's air-to-air missiles, especially if pilots can be left out of the cockpits and scramjet technology can be made affordable for them. Whether such systems truly wind up proving feasible, affordable, and effective in combat remains to be seen.[79]

Consider ground vehicles, and several key trends in their underlying technologies. In engines for cars and light trucks, efficiency as measured in horsepower per volume of engine size has improved roughly a third this century so far, roughly the same pace per decade as in the latter quarter of the twentieth century.[80] Tank engines have progressed at similar proportionate rates.[81] A 2014 paper by a well-known expert in the field projected progress of 2 to 5 percent in each of a dozen or so major elements of the functioning of an engine in the years ahead—hardly insignificant, especially if combined, but not revolutionary in character either.[82]

As for armor for heavy combat vehicles, most of the main innovations in widespread use today—depleted uranium armor, explosive-reactive armor, ceramic materials—were developed in the late twentieth century. Today's newer concepts involve ideas such as laser defenses, perhaps more than ideas about armor itself. Progress will also occur by adopting recent innovations in armor more broadly and widely across key military vehicles.[83] This pace of innovation may, however, be roughly matched by progress in ordnance used to attack armor, including the greater introduction of nanomaterials into explosives as well as the expanded use of explosively formed penetrators (which focus their power in a given direction for greater effect).

Next, consider large rockets. Any discussion here must begin with a sober realization that despite various predictions of revolutionary change in the 1990s, progress has been slow. Costs per pound of payload placed into orbit have remained similar to what they have been since the days of the Saturn rockets and Apollo program.[84] Many of the systems still in operation—Atlas, Delta IV, Athena, Minotaur, Pegasus, Taurus—were already in use in the 1990s; some even employ Minuteman or "Peacekeeper"/MX surplus missiles, often built in the 1970s and 1980s, as boosters.[85] To be sure, much greater progress could well loom, as reusable rockets show promise through the efforts of firms like SpaceX and Blue Sky. It is plausible that reusable rockets may ultimately cut costs by 50 percent or more (given the relative fraction of rocket cost attributable to the rocket body and main guidance systems, which are in principle reusable, versus the fuel and other specific preparations required anew for each launch, which are not). Space X claims that its huge Falcon Heavy rocket will cut costs by more than 75 percent relative to the Delta IV, for example.[86] But skepticism about the higher possible savings is warranted, especially in light of the dramatically exaggerated savings that have been promised in previous eras of rocket modernization, as with the Expendable Launch Vehicle of the 1990s. Indeed, a net cost reduction of 25 percent would be perhaps a more realistic (and still impressive, if attained) goal for the foreseeable future.[87]

Where there has been significant recent progress in space technology, it has largely been in making payloads smaller through use of miniaturized satellites, and also in integrating these satellites together into systems of systems. In recent years, this trend has been particularly significant in commercial and civilian markets, in functional areas such as communications for remote areas of the planet, low-resolution Earth observation, and weather forecasting.[88] Militaries can greatly benefit from these developments as well, for example, in creating more resilient communications networks that are less vulnerable to a small number of ASAT weapon attacks against large individual platforms. In addition, proliferation of small Earth-observation satellites allows more continuous tracking of larger objects on Earth (such as North Korean long-range missiles).[89] For example, Planet is a company that operates a fleet of nearly 200 small satellites, in the five-kilogram range, with roughly three-meter resolution, and some thirty ground stations to receive data. This fleet of satellites is able to map the entire surface of the Earth daily, taking more than 1 million images from its constellation. Large-data analytics can then compare the same regions from day to day to look for militarily significant changes.[90] Certainly these trends, offshoots of the computer and robotics revolutions, will continue into the future.

Missile defenses are also improving, though gradually (as discussed more fully in chapter 4). Consider first kinetic or "hit-to-kill" technology. Systems using an interceptor to destroy a threatening payload from a missile launch have become fairly reliable against short-range and intermediate-range ballistic missiles in the midcourse parts of their flight trajectories. Longer-range systems are getting better but less dramatically, to date. The US midcourse system, with interceptors based in Alaska and California, has finally achieved its first true intercept against a long-range missile. It has an overall test record of about 50 percent success, though most tests have been against shorter-range simulated threats.[91] Further progress is expected. With expected improvements to the kill vehicle, and to sensor networks including the Sea-Based X-Band Radar and Long-Range Discrimination Radar, midcourse missile defense seems likely to achieve reasonably good performance capabilities against simple threats in coming decades.[92] Other countries may achieve good capabilities, too.[93]

In broad terms, however, while midcourse defenses will improve against a given fixed threat, they still suffer from fundamental limitations that probably make them a mediocre long-term answer to the ballistic missile challenge. Decoys need not be particularly complicated to fool even advanced sensors because they can always mimic the heat and radar cross section of actual warheads. If need be, warheads (and decoys) can even be placed within Mylar balloons to disguise them in the vacuum of space during midcourse flight. This remains as true today as in the great countermeasure debates of earlier decades, since physics has not changed since then.[94] Moreover, maneuverable warheads are also feasible, particularly for more advanced powers.[95]

Boost-phase defenses should work increasingly well over the next twenty years, particularly against a small coastal country like North Korea where the United States and allies could station various platforms within close range of plausible launch sites. It is very difficult to do this from space, given the "absentee ratios" of satellites in low-Earth orbit. But airborne drones carrying interceptors or lasers, or interceptors based on ship or land, might be effective in such situations, especially given ongoing progress in laser weapons as discussed in more detail later.[96]

A related topic is anti-satellite weapons. Whatever one's views about the desirability of limiting the latter weapons, given that many satellites help promote strategic stability, it will be increasingly hard to prevent development of ASATs in the future. It is implausible that a world with many advanced missile defense systems and space-launch capabilities can really avoid creating ASAT potential inadvertently. Indeed, that is already the case today. China, the United States, and Russia have all already either shot down low-Earth orbit satellites in recent years or demonstrated the inherent ability to do so, generally with their missile defense systems. China and Russia have continued to develop various kinds of ASAT capabilities to the extent that the former head of US Strategic Command, and current Vice Chairman of the Joint Chiefs of Staff, General John Hyten, has expressed worry about America's overall competitive position in space.[97] In the years ahead, systems that can carry out ASAT roles even in geosynchronous orbit could become more common. Indeed, a maneuvering satellite at such an altitude is already in effect a potential ASAT, since the replacement of its existing payload with explosives could turn it into a space mine with little difficulty.[98] Satellites can try to protect themselves against various types of electronic or directed-energy attack from standoff distances, to some extent. But in the end, redundancy of satellites seems a more realistic strategy for preserving meaningful access to space than any ban on ASATs or any direct defense against them.

Three more categories in this wide-ranging quick survey of platform-related technology are surface ships, submarines, and stealth aircraft. In regard to basic ship technology, the watchword remains evolutionary change, not revolution. That is especially true in terms of hydrodynamics, structural design, efficiency of movement, and speed. Yes, there have been and will be some exotic innovations. Certain newer vessels travel just above the water's surface, as with one variant of the US Navy's Littoral Combat Ship, based partly on innovations associated with the 1991 Fincantieri Destrier vessel. Some employ triple hulls, as with the trimaran variant of the Littoral Combat Ship, or capture their own wakes, as with the lesser-known Stiletto. Otherwise, however, basic physics continues to limit the performance of major vessels, based on the simple fact that drag is a nonlinear function of ship speed, growing faster than speed in proportionate terms.[99] Today's large warships travel at similar speeds to those of nearly a century ago. It is safe to say that no major plans or technologies that would change this basic situation are envisioned for the fleet of the next twenty years (and beyond).[100] A notional trimaran transport ship that might travel at fifty-five knots, if successfully developed, would require perhaps four to eight times as much power as today's large transport ships yet carry only one-fourth the payload—and that is if it even proves possible to develop.[101]

Submarine quieting continues to advance, through the classic methods of isolating machinery within a submarine, using anechoic materials on its surface, and further extending "snorkeling time" through air-independent propulsion and related methods. New ideas in submarine quieting involve using low-magnetism steels in the hull, to reduce detectability by magnetic detectors, or placing new coatings on submarines that could absorb or redirect sonar in order to reduce detectability by active sonar. If the Seawolf class of submarine really offered the potential for quieting that was sometimes purported in the unclassified literature—approaching a tenfold improvement in quietness—it seems plausible that such technologies could be engineered to be more economical in coming years, and thus to be used on more vessels.[102]

Regarding aircraft stealth, some important new concepts and approaches are in the works. Shapes of key parts of aircraft, such as intakes to engines and exhaust vents, continue to be refined, as drawings of the B-21 bomber suggest, for example. (The B-21, expected to have a radar cross section between that of a "metal bumblebee" and a golf ball, will not be supersonic, however, since the shape needed to make it stealthy is incompatible with stable high-velocity flight.)[103] Materials that can attenuate returns from lower-frequency radars (which do better at finding most types of stealth aircraft, at the price of being less accurate) are being investigated. They include so-called metamaterials, composite artificial materials assembled from various types of constituent elements like metals and plastics.[104] Electronic countermeasures that can cancel out radar returns from stealth aircraft are also evolving and improving. Materials that are less inclined to degradation or to heating (which produces potentially detectable infrared signature) are being researched, too.[105]

What are the likely trends in the submarine/ASW competition, as well as the net trend in the stealth-counterstealth competition over the next couple decades?[106] I would hazard the following broad and rough prognostications based on current capabilities and expected developments. In many water conditions and locations, the submarine probably can be said to enjoy a certain basic advantage over sensors that future trends in technology will be hard-pressed to alter. Quantum computing, in some minds, offers the potential to find the submarine's wake like a needle in a haystack, through sustained monitoring and analyzing of ocean surface conditions. Beyond the enormous challenges and costs involved in making quantum computing really work,[107] this seems incredulous under all but the most benign sea conditions. Sensors would have to survive enemy attacks at interruption; submarines would have to maintain a steady course and not avail themselves of countermeasures; sea conditions would probably have to be very calm such that the random effects of wind, waves, and other objects in the water on surface conditions did not camouflage the submarine signature. And for those able to pay for stealth aircraft, such planes will likely continue to have the edge over radar systems and other sensors tracking to find and track them. Yet the sensor technology is improving fast enough that this could be an interesting competition to watch.

Other Technologies

Finally, there is a category of miscellaneous technologies that deserve mention. They range from nonlethal weapons of various kinds, to biological pathogens and other weapons of mass destruction, to lasers and particle beams, to rail guns and long-range kinetic strike systems, to enabling technologies such as nanomaterials and additive printing or 3D manufacturing.

Start with nonlethal weapons. Most of the concepts recommended as feasible and deployable even twenty years ago, such as cable to incapacitate ship propellers, slippery substances to make passage on bridges difficult, and acoustic weapons to disable enemy foot soldiers, appear not to have received significant attention or resources in the first two decades of the twenty-first century. There was some success in the 1999 Kosovo War in initially using graphite filament ordnance rather than explosives to disable electricity in Belgrade, and there have been a few other isolated examples of success as well—but not many.[108]

As the wars of the twenty-first century have demonstrated to date, lethal ordnance remains the coin of the realm for almost all tactical settings.[109] Whether it is stopping a suspicious truck that might contain a bomb, or incapacitating a shooter immersed within a civilian crowd, or creating a perimeter around a protected asset into which potential threats cannot be allowed access, lethal weaponry is still the default mechanism by which American forces and their allies and friends protect themselves.

There is some reason to think that could change considerably in coming years, however. For example, solid-state laser technology is coming of age and becoming deployable and affordable. Soon, mobile lasers may be able to disperse crowds, or incapacitate a given individual in a crowd, or disable a given vehicle, without a high risk of fatalities.[110]

Solid-state lasers can soon be expected to be capable of damaging or destroying many threatening systems on the tactical battlefield, in fact. Some of the most promising applications may be in maritime domains, for short-range defense of ships. Aircraft may also use them for protection against threatening missiles.[111] One such system, known as the Self-protect High Energy Laser Demonstrator (SHiELD) is to be prototyped in 2021 according to current plans.[112] Ground vehicles will surely use them against artillery, mortars, UAVs, and other proximate threats. In recent years, successful tests have been conducted against mortars and quadcopters, for example.[113] A key test is scheduled for 2022 with the High-Energy Laser Mobile Test Truck (involving a 100-kilowatt laser).[114] It is important to remember, however, the inherent limitations of such weapons even when they become available, in terms of range, power, number of kills per minute, and restrictions during bad weather.[115]

Consider next weapons of mass destruction. Most chemical and nuclear weapons technologies are fairly mature and evolving only modestly if at all. The Chemical Weapons Convention has limited research on chemical agents. Recent reports by the US intelligence community focus their sections on weapons of mass destruction on the use of sarin by the Syrian government, on violations of the Intermediate-Range Nuclear Forces Treaty by Russia, and on modernization of Chinese ballistic missiles and submarines. Underlying research on new chemical technologies is generally not a major subject of attention.[116] Even the Russian nerve agent Novichok used in the horrific 2018 attack on the Soviet double agent living in Britain was invented more than a quarter century ago.[117] The main exception to this assertion may be in the new category of drugs including opioids, fentanyl, and carfentanil—which behave in many ways like advanced chemical weapons, and could be employed that way in war.

The Nuclear Test Ban Treaty, though never ratified, has nonetheless been respected by the major nuclear powers since the 1990s and thereby impeded fundamental new work on nuclear explosives. Much nuclear research in the United States since then has gone into stewardship of the existing arsenal.[118] Much academic and scholarly writing about the bomb has emphasized nonproliferation, arms control, and disarmament rather than technical advancement.[119] Where some evolution has occurred, regrettably, has been in the sophistication of trade networks that have helped proliferators to access key technologies to build weapons in places such as Pakistan and North Korea.[120]

There was a flurry of interest in biological weapons after the 2001 anthrax attack in the United States. But, since then, public policy has focused more on naturally occurring biological pathogens, most notably Ebola, rather than on the development of biological warfare agents or protective capabilities.[121] To be sure, Ebola itself could be used as a weapon in the future, particularly by terrorist groups, though there is considerable debate as to how effective any such effort would likely be.[122] Perhaps a similar debate will now focus on coronaviruses.

The future may bring more radical changes, and graver dangers, in future biological weaponry. The core technical fundamentals for revolutionary developments are in place: in understanding and synthesizing DNA into viruses and other potential pathogens, and also in the ongoing difficulty of verifying compliance with the Biological Weapons Convention prohibition on research and development of pathogens.[123]

Consider several more technologies. Rail guns are making considerable strides.[124] They may soon replace traditional guns on some major ships. For example, they could extend direct-fire ranges of shipborne weapons to 100 miles or more, with round velocities at least twice that of traditional chemical-propelled ordnance.[125]

High-powered microwaves have some promise. However, uncertainties about whether they have successfully destroyed the electronics of a given enemy system, combined with inherently limited range (given that their power falls off inversely with the square of the distance from the weapon to its target), may limit their future roles unless the terminal defenses protecting a given asset can be reliably penetrated.[126]

Human performance enhancements of various types are sure to improve by 2040. Various types of exoskeletons show the ability to increase power of given limbs or joints, or to reduce the metabolic energy consumption required to create a certain amount of force or torque, by 25 percent or more.[127] Relatively safe medications like modafinil can keep people awake and at a high level of performance for up to two days; even more powerful and relatively safe medications seem likely to emerge over the next two decades.[128] These kinds of changes seem likely to happen in the competitive domain of warfare, whatever reservations a country like the United States may have had about them in the abstract. That said, it remains unclear how much difference they will really make if combatants on all sides of a given conflict have access to relatively comparable performance enhancers. Nor will any of the foreseeable advances make comic book heroes out of soldiers. People may run one or two miles per hour faster, stay awake a day longer, or lift 50 percent more weight. They will not learn to fly or leap tall buildings.

One more type of relevant technology is additive manufacturing, or 3D printing. It will be useful to militaries, to be sure. For example, it will help considerably in remote logistics operations, reducing the number of spare parts and other metallic or ceramic or related supplies that could be needed but would be difficult and costly to preposition.[129] It is less obvious that additive manufacturing will revolutionize most other areas of defense manufacturing.[130] And even on the battlefield, it will not change the fact that fuel and food and water will still need to be transported in massive amounts to deployed troops. So its likely effects on logistics operations, while important, may reduce supply requirements by 10 to 20 percent, not 50 to 75 percent. Still, especially when combined with improvements in battery and fuel cell and solar systems, some noticeable reductions in battlefield logistical footprints may become possible.[131] Most of all, though, for certain types of important and potent yet relatively simple technologies, like drones, 3D printing may allow mass production at economical rates—and thus the proliferation of innovations like robotic swarms on the future battlefield.[132]

In concluding this section, it may be useful to offer a brief word on some new materials that can go into the construction of various weapons platforms. Consider two broad categories—nanomaterials and "bespoke" materials. A recent survey of experts in materials found that so-called bespoke materials, exquisitely designed to have very specific chemical *and* atomic structures and compositions, are probably not on the horizon as major components of key military systems in a major way before 2040.[133]

Nanomaterials, with dimensions on the order of 1 one-billionth of a meter, are somewhat more significant and promising. They are already in use in some applications. Their promise is greatest in improving the power of explosives, the strength of materials, and the storage capacity of batteries. They may also be useful in manufacturing compounds at the molecular level through nanorobotics techniques. The degree to which they are introduced in widespread applications may be constrained by cost and other challenges associated with manufacturing them in large amounts. But they will likely improve the performance of certain types of capabilities—explosives, body armor, high-performance batteries—by as much as 50 to 100 percent, where cost considerations are not prohibitive.[134] Indeed, since their invention in 1991, lithium-ion batteries have continued to make rapid strides, and that progress will likely continue, largely as a result of the availability of such materials.[135]

Conclusion: Might a Revolution in Military Affairs Be in the Offing?

In the 1990s, much of the US strategic community was breathless about the so-called revolution in military affairs. I doubted at the time that a revolution was underway and would conclude today that in fact no broad-brush revolution has occurred since the Cold War ended. Old methods of combat and legacy systems have not been rendered fundamentally obsolete by progress in technology, in military organizations, or in operational concepts. The way we fight in a place like Iraq or Afghanistan is somewhat different than it was twenty years ago, but the continuities are more striking than the changes.

However, the RMA debate may now deserve fresh consideration, and the revolution may really happen this time. The period of 2020 to 2040 seems likely to experience significantly more change than the previous two decades in the character of warfare. For the period from 2000 to 2020, revolutionary technological change probably occurred only in various aspects of computers and robotics. For the next two decades, those areas will remain fast-moving, and they will be joined by various breakthroughs in artificial intelligence and the use of big data. The battlefield implications in domains such as swarms of robotic systems usable as both sensors and weapons may truly come of age. In addition, laser weapons, reusable rockets, hypersonic missiles, rail guns, unmanned submarines, biological pathogens, and nanomaterials may wind up advancing very fast. Peer rivals may exploit vulnerabilities in the United States' and other nations' cyber, satellite, and fiber-optic systems that previous enemies were unable to identify and attack. The sum total may or may not add up to a revolution. But the potential cannot be dismissed.

Moreover, the rise of China and return of Russia supercharge the competition and raise the stakes. The marriage of rapid technological progress with strategic dynamism and hegemonic change could prove especially potent. The return of great-power competition during an era of rapid progress in science and technology could reward innovators, and expose vulnerabilities, much more than has been the case in this century to date.

Some areas of military technology—most types of sensors, most types of major vehicles, most underlying technologies for nuclear and chemical weapons of mass destruction—seem unlikely to change dramatically. But perhaps a true military revolution of sorts will occur even without such developments. The key question, as always, will be how these individual technology trends interact synergistically with each other, and how military organizations as well as political leaders innovate to employ them on the battlefield.

SPACE, MISSILE DEFENSE, AND NUCLEAR WEAPONS

Three Case Studies in the Science of War

The previous chapter chapter surveys a wide range of military technologies, with a particular eye toward assessing whether collectively they can be used to revolutionize warfare in the coming years and decades. This chapter delves much deeper into three areas—nuclear weapons, space and satellites, and missile defense. These are among the subjects in military technology that are both simple enough to be accessible to the generalist, and important and enduring enough that they can be expected to remain relevant for policymakers well into the future. The approach used here, with an emphasis on fundamental concepts of how things work or "why things are," to quote best-selling author Joel Achenbach, also suggests a methodology for diving deeper into other key areas of defense technology. When the immutable laws of physics can be invoked to help understand a technology, as with these subjects, the resulting insights are likely to be durable. That makes them of long-term policy usefulness, as well.

Some examples of how a sound understanding of basic military principles and technologies can inform policy debate may illustrate these points. Take the missile defense debate of the 1980s, shortly after Ronald Reagan's "Star Wars" speech of 1983 in which he announced his Strategic Defense Initiative (SDI). Whatever the broader strategic benefits of SDI may have ultimately been, many of the technical goals advanced by its partisans could be debunked—or shown to be very expensive and rather improbable—by basic physical reasoning. For example, putting lasers in low-Earth orbit to shoot down warheads could be shown to require dozens of lasers (because of the Earth's rotation, meaning a given satellite would not stand still over a given point on the planet's surface). With each of those lasers requiring a mirror effectively equivalent to that of the Hubble telescope just to steer the beam, to counter the inevitable effects of diffraction, costs could be placed into the many tens of billions for just the initial deployment of the system (even assuming its technical feasibility). Analysis about possible countermeasures that an attacker could use to fool a defense suggested that any country capable of building an advanced nuclear-tipped ballistic missile inventory could defeat defenses relying on exoatmospheric intercept. These arguments did not shut the door on all possible uses for missile defense, by any means, but they were sobering for those who wanted to believe that defense could trump offense in the nuclear realm.

Basic physics also explains why nuclear weapons are hard to make—and also why they are very hard to find *before* they detonate, but rather hard to conceal (even at faraway locations) when they do explode. It explains why space is a very good place to carry out some, though certainly not all, military functions—and also that it is and will likely remain a rather expensive, and difficult, place to deploy any payload of substantial weight. These kinds of broad deductions do not answer all salient questions about the technologies in question, of course, but they are often surprisingly useful.

The Military Uses of Space

Space is a region from which the United States now does far more than monitor, and target, nuclear weapons and missiles. During much of the Cold War, the superpowers treated space as an arena of "cooperative restraint," in author James Clay Moltz's words.[1] They created arms control treaties in the 1960s that prevent nuclear deployments or explosions in space while tolerating each other's reconnaissance satellites. They ultimately based numerous additional arms control treaties on the verification capabilities that satellites could provide—though of course those same intelligence capabilities were also used to help develop war plans.

Much has changed in recent decades. In addition to traditional reconnaissance and early-warning missions, space is now the place from which the United States coordinates its conventional wars in real time. Information on battlefield targets is sometimes acquired there; information about these targets and most other data flow through space to allow rapid, high-volume, and dependable transmissions. And with the return of great-power military competition in recent years, space is now increasingly contested, as well.

Space and the purposes to which it can be put for military activities constitute a good place to begin this chapter. Several basic principles of the national security space subject are grounded in immutable principles of physics that, once understood, can provide a long-standing guide to many policy questions that arise in this crucial domain. A number of things about military operations in and from space do indeed change with improving technologies, and reinvigorated military competition between the great powers, but many others do not.

A Brief Primer on Space, Orbits, and Satellites

Space is home to a wide range of military and civilian satellites, not to mention vast amounts of debris that can interfere with satellite operations (see Table 4.1). Most satellites move around Earth at distances ranging from 200 kilometers to about 36,000 kilometers (see figure 4.1). This region is divided into three main bands. Most satellites in low-Earth orbit (LEO) are several hundreds of kilometers above the surface of the Earth, up to roughly 1,500 kilometers.[2] Geosynchronous orbit (GEO) is the outer band for most satellites; it is about 36,000 kilometers or 22,300 miles above the surface of the Earth.[3] At that altitude, a satellite's revolution around the Earth takes twenty-four hours (four minutes less, actually, in accordance with the actual duration of one rotation of the Earth). If positioned over the equator, the satellite hovers above the same spot on Earth continuously and is further described as geostationary. Medium-Earth orbit (MEO) is essentially everything in between LEO and GEO; MEOs are concentrated between altitudes of roughly 10,000 and 20,000 kilometers above the surface of Earth.[4]

Low-Earth orbits begin just above Earth's atmosphere, which is generally considered to end at an altitude of about 100 kilometers, and extend out to a couple

TABLE 4.1.   Satellite Quick Facts

Total number of operating satellites: 2,666
United States: 1,327
Russia: 169
China: 363
Other: 807
LEO: 1,918
MEO: 135
Elliptical: 59
GEO: 554
Total number of US satellites: 1,327
Civil: 30
Commercial: 935
Government: 170
Military: 192

Sources: Union of Concerned Scientists, "Satellite Quick Facts," Cambridge, Mass., April 2020, https://www.ucsusa.org/resources/satellite-database. On debris, there is some useful information from the European Space Agency (https://www.esa.int/Our_Activities/Space_Safety/Space_Debris/Space_debris_by_the_numbers).

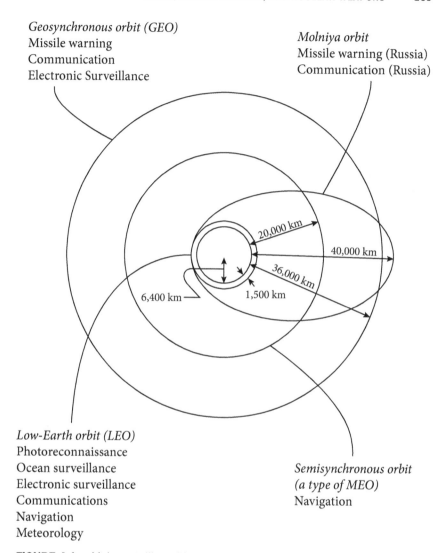

Geosynchronous orbit (GEO)
Missile warning
Communication
Electronic Surveillance

Molniya orbit
Missile warning (Russia)
Communication (Russia)

20,000 km

40,000 km

36,000 km

6,400 km

1,500 km

Low-Earth orbit (LEO)
Photoreconnaissance
Ocean surveillance
Electronic surveillance
Communications
Navigation
Meteorology

*Semisynchronous orbit
(a type of MEO)*
Navigation

FIGURE 4.1. Major satellite orbit types.

Source: Ashton Carter, "Satellites and Anti-satellites: The Limits of the Possible," International Security 10, no. 4 (Spring 1986): 49.

thousand kilometers. It is in this range where the International Space Station (about 250 miles, or 400 kilometers) and Hubble telescope (about 350 miles, or 565 kilometers) are found. The altitude of LEOs is less than the radius of Earth (which is about 6,400 kilometers, or 4,000 miles). In other words, if one viewed low-altitude satellites from a distance, they would appear quite close to Earth, relative to the size of the Earth itself. The dimensions of GEOs are large relative to the size of Earth, though they are still small relative to the distance between Earth and the moon, about 380,000 kilometers.

Earth's gravitational field, together with the speed and direction of movement of a satellite, establish the parameters for that satellite's orbit. Once these physical parameters are specified, the orbit is determined and trajectories are predictable, unless and until a maneuvering rocket is subsequently fired.

Satellites in LEOs take as little as ninety minutes to complete a tour around the planet. As noted earlier, GEOs take twenty-four hours. Satellites in close-in circular orbits move at nearly eight kilometers per second; those in GEO move at about three kilometers per second. Those following MEOs have intermediate speeds and periods of revolution about Earth.

Most satellite orbits are generally circular, though a number are elliptical. Some are highly elliptical—passing far closer to Earth in one part of their orbit than in another. Satellites may move in polar orbits, passing directly over the North Pole and South Pole once in every revolution around Earth. Alternatively, they may orbit continuously over the equator, as do GEO satellites, or may move along an inclined path falling somewhere between polar and equatorial orientations.

Placing satellites into orbit is a highly challenging enterprise. They must be accelerated to very high speeds and properly oriented in the desired orbital trajectories. Modifying a satellite's motion is difficult once the rocket that puts it into space has stopped burning; generally, the satellite's own small rockets are capable of only fine-tuning a trajectory, not changing it fundamentally. Even though satellites in GEO end up moving much more slowly than satellites in LEO, they must be accelerated to greater initial speeds (about 10.5 kilometers per second—close to the 11 kilometers per second or so needed to escape Earth's gravitational field altogether). That is because they lose a great deal of speed fighting Earth's gravity as they move from close-in altitudes to roughly 36,000 kilometers above the planet's surface. In fact, a three-stage rocket that could carry a payload of fifteen tons into LEO could transport only three tons into GEO. For that reason it typically costs two to three times as much per pound of payload to put a satellite into GEO as into LEO.

Even getting to LEO is difficult. For example, putting a payload into low-Earth orbit typically requires a rocket weighing 50 to 100 times as much as the payload. This math follows from the so-called rocket equation, essentially based on conservation of momentum principles, together with the power per pound of current fuels.[5] But costs have been coming down, and it is now possible to get a payload to LEO for as little as $1,000 to $2,000 a pound.[6]

Traditionally, satellites typically weighed from 2,000 pounds to 10,000 pounds, roughly speaking, implying launch costs of about $10 million for smaller satellites in LEO to $100 million for larger satellites in GEO. The large imaging satellites known as Lacrosse and KH-11 are each estimated to weigh about 30,000 pounds. In addition, most satellites have had dimensions ranging from 20 to 200 feet and power sources capable of generating 1,000 to 5,000 watts—though, again, imaging satellites would be expected to exceed these bounds.[7] Some satellites still do possess these kinds of dimensions, but a major trend in recent decades has been toward the proliferation of small satellites that operate as networks rather than individual and large assets. Combining that fact with reductions in launch costs per pound of payload, space is gradually becoming more accessible.

There are more than 2,000 working satellites in orbit today, as seen in table 4.1. About 1,300 are American, 300 Chinese, and 150 Russian. Of the total, more than 1,900 are in LEO. Roughly 125 are in medium-Earth orbit; some 550 are in GEO; and about 60 are in elliptical orbits of various sizes and orientations. Of the US total, more than 900 are commercial or civil, about 190 are military, and about 170 are other governmental satellites.[8]

Some of the more prominent US Air Force satellites, which total seventy-seven as of 2019, include the following. The most numerous type is the GPS satellite, of which there are now thirty-one in orbit. There are seven Wideband Global Satcom (WGS) and another seven Space-Based Infrared System (SBIRS) satellites. There are six Defense Satellite Communications System (DSCS) satellites. There are five of each of the following: Milstar (for robust communications), Defense Meteorological Satellite Program (DMSP), and the classified Defense Support Program (DSP) system. There are four more for Geosynchronous Space Situational Awareness (GSSAP) and for Advanced Extremely High Frequency (AEHF) communications. There are two Space Based Surveillance System (SBSS) satellites, and finally, a technology demonstrator.[9]

Since the space age began in the late 1950s, there have been more than 5,000 launches, putting a total of some 9,000 satellites in space overall. Of the 7,000 that are not operational, some 5,000 are still in orbit.[10] As noted, the vast majority of most countries' current satellites are in LEO or GEO.[11]

Often, the dividing line between military and civilian satellites is blurred. The United States uses GPS satellites for military and civilian purposes. It buys time on commercial satellites for military communications. The US military and intelligence services often purchase imagery from private firms, especially when relatively modest-resolution images (with correspondingly larger fields of view) are adequate. And some satellites provide weather data to the military as well as to other government agencies.

There are currently more than 22,000 objects in space that are large and visible enough to be tracked by the US space surveillance network. Since only about 2,000 are working satellites, most can be thought of as junk or debris, and the number is only likely to grow. There are perhaps 34,000 objects—all the known ones plus an estimated 12,000 more—with diameters of at least ten centimeters (about four inches), and nearly 1 million specks larger than a centimeter.[12]

All that junk can be dangerous. In 1983, for example, a paint chip only 0.2 millimeters in diameter made a 4-millimeter dent in the *Challenger* space shuttle's windshield. Already by the start of the twenty-first century, a small satellite at an altitude of 800 kilometers had about a 1 percent chance annually of failure due to collision with debris.[13]

Unsurprisingly, nuclear explosions in space can be dangerous, too. They can affect the atmosphere below, creating huge amounts of ionization that fry electronics on Earth through what is called nuclear-induced electromagnetic pulse. They can destroy, largely through X-rays, unshielded and/or close-by satellites in space. And they can cause persistent effects by "pumping" the so-called Van Allen belts (one centered at about 3,500 kilometers above Earth and composed largely of protons, the other closer to 16,000 kilometers and made up mostly of electrons) with radioactive material that then damages nearby satellites for months or years. It is in large part for these reasons that the 1963 Partial (or Limited) Test Ban Treaty prohibits nuclear explosions in space and the 1967 Outer Space Treaty prohibits the deployment of nuclear weapons in space—though in wartime it can be questioned whether nation-states would honor their peacetime obligations in the same way they do now.[14]

As noted earlier, the United States also deploys high-resolution imaging satellites in the LEO zone. They are of two principal types: radar imaging satellites, historically known as Lacrosse or Onyx systems, and optical imaging satellites, known as Keyhole systems, such as the KH-11 and KH-11 follow-on or advanced satellites. According to unclassified reports, the Lacrosse radar satellites operate at roughly 600 to 700 kilometers above Earth, are capable of effective operations in all types of weather, and produce images with sufficient clarity to distinguish objects one to three meters apart. The KH satellites are capable of nighttime as well as daytime observations, by virtue of their abilities to monitor infrared as well as visual frequencies. They acquire information digitally and transmit it nearly instantaneously to ground stations. Their mirrors are nearly three meters in diameter, and they move in slightly elliptical orbits ranging from about 250 kilometers at perigee (point of closest approach to Earth) to 400 kilometers or more at apogee. Ground resolutions are as good as roughly fifteen centimeters (six inches) or even less under daylight conditions. They can take images about 100 miles to either side of their orbital trajectories, allowing a fairly wide field of view.[15] They do not work well through clouds, however.[16]

The United States puts most military payloads into orbit from launch facilities at Cape Canaveral in Florida and Vandenberg Air Force Base in California. It also operates a half dozen smaller sites for some payloads.[17]

All these satellites have together permitted a radical increase in data flow rates in recent conflicts—for example, from 200 million bits per second, already an impressive tally, in Operation Desert Storm in 1991 to more than ten times as much (2.4 gigabits per second) in Operation Iraqi Freedom by 2003.[18] Of course, underscoring the limitations of data, technology, and perhaps intelligence writ large, those greater amounts of information hardly produced a better outcome in 2003 than had been achieved in 1991.

As for tracking objects in space, today most countries conduct space surveillance using telescopes and radar systems on the ground. Only the United States has a system providing some semblance of global coverage (though its Southern Hemisphere capabilities are quite limited). Its monitoring assets are located in Hawaii, Florida, Massachusetts, England, Diego Garcia, Japan, and Australia.

As noted, and as discussed in chapter 3, progress in electronics and computers and improvements in miniaturized boosters have made possible smaller and smaller satellites in recent years, often operating in integrated networks.[19] These types of devices augur a whole new era in satellite technology. Beyond benign applications in communications, scientific research, and the like, one type of application could be small, stealthy space mines able to position themselves near other countries' satellites, possibly without being noticed, awaiting commands to detonate and destroy the latter. They could also use microwaves, small lasers, or even paint to disable or destroy certain satellites. Moreover, they could be orbited only as needed, permitting countries to develop anti-satellite (ASAT) capabilities without having to place weapons in space until they wished to use them.

Most devices known as microsatellites weigh 10 to 100 kilograms. Nanosatellites are smaller, weighing 1 to 10 kilograms. In recent years, experimental picosatellites—devices weighing less than 1 kilogram—have been orbited. As a result of all of this miniaturization, there are now twice as many satellites in space as there were fifteen years ago.

To continue with the topic of ASAT operations, the maneuvering capability needed to approach a larger satellite through a co-orbital technique is not particularly sophisticated. That is especially the case if there is no time pressure to attack quickly and the microsat can approach the larger satellite gradually. In June 2000, for example, the University of Surrey launched a five-kilogram nanosatellite on a Russian booster (that also carried a Russian navigation satellite and Chinese microsatellite). The nanosatellite then detached from the other systems and used an on-board propulsion capability to maneuver and photograph the other satellites with which it had been orbited. In early 2003, a thirty-kilogram US microsat maneuvered to rendezvous with the rocket that had earlier boosted it into orbit. These microsats were already near the satellites they approached, by virtue of sharing a ride on the same booster, making their job somewhat easier. But the principle of independent propulsion and maneuvering is being established. Larger maneuvering space mines quite likely are already within the technical reach of a number of countries; smaller ones may be soon.[20]

Conclusions and Policy Lessons

In summary, then, a few enduring realities about the physics and technology of space systems can be distilled, and a few general answers to the questions posed at the beginning of this section can be deduced:

- Space is a complex environment in which to work, difficult to master. Launch vehicles often fail; satellites remain challenging to build, as they require great precision in manufacture; satellites in orbit remain impractical to repair.
- However, countries willing to develop expertise in space can certainly be successful with time, at least for basic technologies, and they can rent commercial assets even if they cannot field their own.
- Space is definitely already militarized, through the increasing use of satellites for real-time targeting and other such tactical warfighting purposes, a process led by the United States in the post–Cold War era (before that time, while the superpowers used satellites for nuclear targeting purposes and very limited communications, they did not have the capacity to create "reconnaissance strike complexes" to conduct real-time operations making heavy use of space assets).
- Space may or may not become formally weaponized in coming years, in the sense of weapons being placed in orbit. But ASAT weapons already exist.[21] In addition, missile defense systems will continue to have inherent capability against low-Earth orbit satellites. The use of the navy's Aegis ballistic missile defense capability, employing a Standard SM-3 Block IA missile launched from a Ticonderoga-class cruiser, to shoot down an errant satellite at an altitude of 153 miles in February 2008, underscored this point. Only small software changes were required to make the intercept possible.[22] Similar capabilities are surely inherent in the midcourse defense system based in California and Alaska; China and Russia have capabilities in this domain as well.
- In addition, as microsatellites proliferate and become more advanced and maneuverable, their inherent ability to become effective ASAT weapons (by having their scientific payloads replaced by ordnance) will grow.
- These realities make many types of space arms control unverifiable, though it may still be feasible to place limits on certain kinds of *actions or*

activities (such as debris-causing explosions and collisions) if not actual capabilities.[23]

- Low-Earth orbits in particular are also vulnerable to nuclear detonations. Nuclear bursts can destroy satellites at hundreds of kilometers from a detonation point, typically from X-rays; some satellites could even be affected at distances of 20,000 to 30,000 kilometers by a large blast, assuming limited shielding of the satellite.[24] In addition, a LEO nuclear burst could leave low-altitude space inhospitable to satellites (through "pumping" of the Van Allen radiation belts found at several thousand kilometers' altitude) for an extended period. Unhardened LEO satellites with expected lifetimes of five to fifteen years might last only a few months or less under such conditions.[25]

- Space is an expensive place in which to operate, with huge inefficiencies in using chemically fueled rockets to place objects in orbit.

- Yet certain military functions, notably in regard to communications and reconnaissance, are efficiently conducted from space despite the burdens of placing objects in orbit. Even though costs are high, benefits are greater still. Early-warning and communications satellites in geosynchronous orbit, and GPS satellites in MEO, are cases in point.

(Ballistic) Missile Defense

Missile defense was among the most polarizing and contentious issues in American defense policy for decades. It remains controversial today, if perhaps somewhat less so—and also remains expensive, to the tune of more than $10 billion a year in the Pentagon budget, spent through the Missile Defense Agency as well as the individual military services.[26] It also is central in understanding any military balance involving the United States and China, Russia, North Korea, or Iran, as well as a number of other countries.

Missile defense involves at least three major categories of threats: ballistic missiles, cruise missiles, and (in the future) hypersonic missiles (which would not go faster than ballistic missiles but would have some capacity for maneuver). The emphasis here is on the first, though some elements of ballistic missile defense systems can also be used against the other kinds of offensive technologies.

Indeed, from a broader military planning perspective, it is increasingly important that the other types of missile threats be prioritized as well. Hypersonic missiles, for example, can fly low (in the upper parts of the Earth's atmosphere) for much of their trajectories and can take evasive maneuvers at high speeds. Thus, different interceptors, as well as a space-based sensor network to track them throughout flight, may be needed once that threat becomes truly serious. The sections on hypersonics in chapter 3 further explain and highlight this important type of new capability, one that the United States is working hard to develop as an offensive weapon of its own.[27]

Several programs are at the core of the missile defense effort in the United States today. They include the Patriot missile defense system for ground-based defense against missiles in the final or "terminal" stage of flight, the Terminal High-Altitude Area Defense (THAAD) for ground-based defense against threats of moderate range, the navy's Aegis system that uses Aegis radars and Standard missiles against missiles of varying range, and the Alaska/California midcourse ground-based missile defense (GMD) system for continental defense against long-range missiles. The Patriot system does have capability against cruise missiles, in fairness—but it is worth underscoring that there is no real capability to protect the entire American homeland against cruise missiles unless an interceptor battery just happens to be in a place along the nation's borders where a cruise missile appears (and is serendipitously detected). These specific systems are fed information by various land-based, sea-based, and space-based sensor systems. Sophisticated data processing and command and control networks integrate and distribute the data and guide operations.

Basic Properties of Ballistic Missiles

Ballistic missiles are first accelerated by the combustion of some type of fuel, after which they simply follow an unpowered—or ballistic—trajectory. Their major components include rocket engines, fuel chambers, guidance systems, and warheads.

For shorter-range missiles, the weapons system usually consists of a single-stage rocket, which fires until its fuel is exhausted or shut off by a flight-control computer. The missile body and warhead often never separate from each other, flying a full trajectory as a large, single object.

For longer-range missiles, the system consists of two or three stages, or separate booster rockets, each with its own fuel and rocket engines. The rationale for this staging is to improve efficiency and thereby maximize the speed of the reentry vehicle or vehicles. Putting all the fuel for a long-range rocket in one stage would make for a very heavy fuel chamber and mean that the rocket would have to carry along a great deal of structural weight throughout the entire phase of boosted flight. That would lower the ultimate speed of the warhead or warheads, reducing their range. With staging, by contrast, much of the structural weight is discarded as fuel is consumed. That makes it possible to accelerate the payload to speeds sufficient to put it on an intercontinental trajectory. Long-range warheads must reach speeds of about 4.5 miles a second (roughly 7 kilometers a second), or almost two-thirds of the speed any object would need to escape the Earth's gravitational field entirely (roughly 7 miles, or 11 kilometers, a second).

On long-range missiles, including intercontinental ballistic missiles (ICBMs), warheads are usually released after boosting but while the rocket is still going up—that is, in the ascent phase of flight.[28] Releasing warheads from the missile is clearly necessary if multiple warheads with multiple aimpoints are to be used. It is also desirable, since large missile bodies are subject to extreme forces on atmospheric reentry that could throw them, and any warheads still attached to them, badly off course.

Warheads do not fly free and exposed. They are encased within reentry vehicles. These objects provide heat shields as well as aerodynamic stability for the eventual return into Earth's atmosphere. They protect the warheads from melting or otherwise being damaged by air upon reentry and also maximize the accuracy with which they approach their targets.

Missiles may be powered by solid fuel or liquid fuel. Modern ICBMs can use either type of fuel; Russian SS-18s use liquid fuel, for example, whereas modern US missiles use solid fuel.[29] Solid fuel is more convenient, since it can be kept continually within the missile, allowing the latter to be more quickly readied for launch.

Missile guidance must be exquisitely accurate. Warhead trajectories are determined by the boost phase, meaning that their course is set hundreds or thousands of miles before they reach their targets. To land within a few hundred meters or less of a target—as with today's systems—requires great precision in how long the rocket motors are fired and in what direction the rocket is steered. Generally, rockets use inertial guidance systems to measure the acceleration provided by the boosters at each stage of their burning. Computers then integrate those measurements to plot out a trajectory for the warheads; a feedback loop then corrects any inaccuracies in how the rockets have been firing, so that when they are shut off, the warheads' ballistic flight will take them halfway around the world and land them perhaps within a couple football fields of their designated aimpoint.

A missile can carry one or more large warheads, typically several hundred kilograms in weight in the current arsenals of advanced nuclear powers. It can also carry large numbers of bomblets, rather than warheads, if the weapon is not designed to cause a nuclear detonation. Such bomblets can carry conventional, chemical, or biological agents in smaller packages, distributing their aggregate effects over a larger area than a single warhead could. They could also carry radiological payloads—basically radioactive waste, designed not to explode but to contaminate, injure, and kill indirectly.

Warheads and bomblets can be designed to explode on impact, or when reaching a certain altitude, or after a certain time of flight. Bombs *not* designed to explode on impact that are accidentally dropped may or may not detonate when they hit the ground. Much depends on the details of their design and safety features; as a rule, modern US warheads would not explode under such circumstances, but simpler weapons could.

As mentioned earlier, a missile might carry more than one large bomb. If separate bombs from the same ICBM or submarine-launched ballistic missile (SLBM) can be steered to separate targets, they are described as multiple independently targetable reentry vehicles (MIRVs). Britain, France, Russia, and the United States have developed and deployed this technology.

MIRVs work in the following manner. All the warheads are initially within a "bus," or vehicle-sized object that separates from the rocket's third stage at the end of powered flight. The bus has mini–booster rockets of its own, which it can use to modify its position and speed before releasing a reentry vehicle containing a warhead. It can then reposition itself before releasing another reentry vehicle. Based on their minor differences in initial position and velocity, the warheads can then travel slightly different trajectories. Magnified by the effects of fifteen to twenty minutes of high-speed, long-distance flight, these minor changes in trajectory can translate into impact points distributed throughout a "footprint" perhaps 100 by 300 miles in size.[30]

A missile bus may also carry decoys. These are objects designed to resemble warheads when flying outside the atmosphere, thereby confusing the defense's sensors and preventing them from identifying the true warhead. In the vacuum of space, even extremely light decoys move at the same speed as heavy warheads if given the same initial speed; air resistance is clearly not a factor, and gravity acts equally on objects of all weights. That makes it straightforward to fool simple sensors during exoatmospheric flight. More advanced sensors that can gauge the size, shape, rotational motion, temperature, or radar reflectivity of an object may be able to distinguish warheads from decoys—unless the decoys become more sophisticated or unless the warheads are camouflaged to make them resemble decoys.

The Trajectory of a Ballistic Missile (and a Word on Hypersonics)

Ballistic flight is unpowered flight within the Earth's gravitational field. It is essentially the free fall of a fast-moving object. Once a rocket stops burning, the only forces acting on it—or any warheads or decoys released from it—arise from gravity or, upon atmospheric reentry, air resistance. That makes flight trajectories predictable and essentially parabolic with respect to the Earth's surface.

The first phase, or "boost phase," of a ballistic missile trajectory is powered flight. For shorter-range missiles, the boost phase occurs entirely within the Earth's atmosphere; for long-range missiles, it generally extends into space. Either way, during boost phase, the missile gains an upward as well as an outward or horizontal component to its velocity. For a long-range ICBM, the missile will usually be about 200 to 500 miles downrange of its launch point and have reached an altitude of about 125 to 300 miles at the end of its boost phase (see figures 4.2 and 4.3).[31]

Once boost phase is complete, the ascent phase follows. For existing ICBMs, the ascent phase begins outside the atmosphere.[32] (As noted previously, the atmosphere is generally considered to end at roughly 60 miles or 100 kilometers above the Earth's surface, even though in fact there is no true cutoff but instead an exponential decline, and some air molecules are found even above 100-mile altitude.) Upward flight ends at the trajectory's apogee, or highest point above the Earth. The missile then begins to accelerate back to Earth, in its descent phase. The exoatmospheric parts of ascent and descent are described as midcourse flight.

During exoatmospheric flight, the horizontal element of the velocity of the missile and any warheads or decoys remains constant. The vertical component of velocity is reduced by gravity, eventually slowing to zero, and then increasing in the opposite direction as the missile and any objects it has released return to Earth.

Finally, the missile and any objects it releases, including warheads, bomblets, and decoys, reenter the atmosphere—assuming that they reached a high enough altitude to have left it in the first place. Typically, missiles with ranges of 300 miles (about 500 kilometers) or more leave the atmosphere; those with shorter ranges do not.

Warheads, decoys, and structural elements of the missile slow down during reentry because of air resistance in a manner that depends on their weight, size, and shape. As a result of this air resistance, descending objects heat up; they are also subject to strong forces that may damage them structurally if they are not well built.[33]

Ballistic missile trajectories come in various shapes and sizes. A missile that flies a "minimum-energy trajectory" will travel the maximum distance given the speed at which its rocket burns out. It is the most efficient, for a given range. But missiles may also fly on what are known as lofted or depressed trajectories. Lofted trajectories are those on which the rocket's flight attains a higher altitude than a minimum-energy trajectory for the same horizontal range. Depressed trajectories, by contrast, stay closer to the Earth's surface than is normal for long-range flight. Both require greater speed, and hence more fuel, to cover the same distance relative to the Earth's surface.

Finally, a brief word on hypersonics. These can complicate greatly the missile defense effort because they travel at speeds much greater than those of traditional aircraft or cruise missiles but maneuver much more adroitly and unpredictably than ballistic missiles or classic ballistic missile warheads. (It is worth noting that it is also possible to build a maneuvering reentry vehicle [MaRV] for the atmospheric

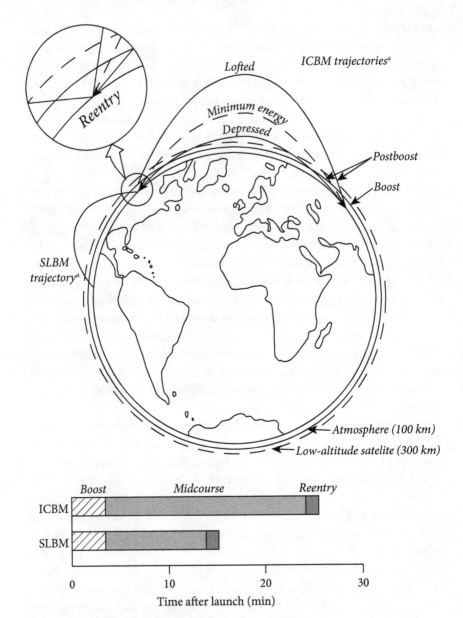

Lofted

ICBM trajectories[a]

Reentry

Minimum energy

Depressed

Postboost

Boost

SLBM trajectory[a]

Atmosphere (100 km)

Low-altitude satelite (300 km)

	Boost	Midcourse	Reentry
ICBM			
SLBM			

0   10   20   30

Time after launch (min)

FIGURE 4.2.   Ballistic missile profiles mapped against Earth.

Note: SLBMs can often go as far as ICBMs, over comparable time periods.

Source: Ashton B. Carter and David N. Schwartz, eds., *Ballistic Missile Defense* (Washington, D.C.: Brookings, 1984), 51.

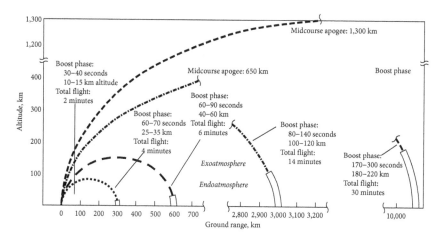

FIGURE 4.3. Trajectories of ballistic missiles.

Note: Short-range, medium-range, and intercontinental trajectories are shown.

Source: James M. Lindsay and Michael E. O'Hanlon, Defending America: The Case for Limited National Missile Defense (Washington, D.C.: Brookings, 2002).

descent of a ballistic missile warhead, but such MaRVs would only maneuver in the very final stages of the trajectory.) They can function in one of two ways: as an air-breathing "scramjet" or a "boost-glide" vehicle. The former operates in the high atmosphere as a very specialized kind of unmanned aircraft; the latter effectively bounces along the upper atmosphere, creating a plasma field around it due to its high speed. Both can be initially accelerated by ballistic missile over some portion of their flight.[34]

Basic Types of Missile Defenses

Missile defense systems should actually be thought of as complex networks, not simply the batteries that provide the final intercept against an actual threat. They include various types of sensors, sophisticated information and battle management systems, and then interceptors themselves.[35]

Someday, interceptors could in theory be replaced by directed-energy weapons such as lasers. In fact, such systems have been researched and developed already and, for certain very specific purposes like protection of individual aircraft, ships, or vehicles, are being deployed in some cases. But larger-scale area defenses do not yet benefit from directed-energy technology, and a weapon called the Airborne Laser was ultimately canceled because of limitations on its performance.

Historically, many missile defense interceptors from the early Cold War decades carried explosives near a target and then detonated the explosive. The payload was usually conventional; in the case of Russia's missile defense system, which remains deployed today, it could even be nuclear![36] But modern American systems such as the Alaska/California national missile defense system increasingly use "hit to kill" technology in which high-speed collisions between interceptor and warhead destroy the latter. Given the typical relative speeds of well over ten kilometers per second of these objects when they approach each other, any contact virtually guarantees the annihilation of both.

Most missile defense systems work in a fairly intuitive and step-by-step way. First a defense battery is "told" of a missile launch. The launch might first be detected by an early-warning satellite that senses the heat or infrared signal from the offensive missile's booster rockets. These satellites are generally in geosynchronous orbit—again, some 36,000 kilometers above the Earth's equator, and constantly positioned over the same location on the planet's surface.[37]

Long-range low-frequency radars might then acquire and track the incoming warhead while it is still far away from American airspace (especially for defenses against ICBMs).[38] In the case of today's American military, this sensor network includes launch detection satellites; the COBRA DANE radar at Shemya, Alaska; the Early Warning Radar systems in California, Massachusetts, the United Kingdom, and Greenland; forward-based X-band radars in Japan; Aegis Ballistic Missile Defense (BMD) destroyers; and the Sea-Based X-band Radar in the Pacific Ocean.[39] Many of these systems, as well as the interceptor missiles discussed in the following, are frequently being upgraded for improved performance under various potential combat conditions. It is worth underscoring, however, that they are vulnerable to attack—from unmanned aerial systems, commandos, helicopters, cyber methods— to a degree that existing policy has perhaps not properly acknowledged.[40]

Once the incoming object is at the proper distance, an interceptor missile is launched. Its trajectory is chosen to put it in the right place to meet the incoming threat; a computer linked to the radar makes the necessary computation.

After interceptor launch, the defense battery's radar continues to track the threat. But the same radar waves that it uses to do tracking (when they echo back toward the radar receiver) also can help the missile do precise, terminal homing. That is because many interceptor missiles have radar receivers of their own that can detect the reflected signals sent by their ground-based radar systems that are reflected by the incoming threat. When the system operates in this way, the process is called semiactive homing. Alternatively, if it is to operate outside the atmosphere, the kill vehicle may have infrared and/or electro-optical sensors for the final approach. These are passive systems that require no artificial signal; they look for the heat signature or reflected light from the incoming threat object. They would likely be blinded within the atmosphere by the heat created by their own missile's movement, but outside the atmosphere there is no such problem.

In older systems, at the proper moment, a ground control station then sends a radio signal to the interceptor, causing it to detonate a conventional-explosive warhead. The explosion then creates shrapnel that, if sufficiently close to the incoming warhead, should destroy that warhead. This is the basic way the Patriot missile defense system known as the Patriot PAC-2 functions.[41]

With hit-to-kill interceptors, the kill mechanism is different. For the United States, these systems include the army's Patriot PAC-3, the army's THAAD, the navy's Aegis-based programs using Standard missiles as interceptors, and the Alaska/California Ground-based MidCourse Defense (GMD) system. Equipped with many miniature boosters, they are intended to maneuver so well that they can collide directly with incoming threats, obviating the need for (and weight of) explosives. The United States now has 7 batteries of THAAD radar/interceptor systems (with 8 missiles per launcher, and rapidly reloadable), 60 batteries of Patriot (for the PAC-3, 16 missiles can fit on a launcher), 38 ships with Aegis radars capable of missile defense (headed to 60), and 44 Ground-based Interceptor (GBI) missiles (headed to 64).[42] Russia and China also have considerable ballistic missile defense capability, though the geographic extent of their deployments is generally smaller.[43]

The Alaska/California system is an example of what is sometimes called a midcourse missile defense against long-range ICBM or SLBM warheads. Such systems generally have fifteen to twenty minutes to work against ICBMs, which is one of their appeals. During that time, the exoatmospheric kill vehicle put into motion by the ground-based interceptor (blandly called the GBI) could travel thousands of miles, meaning that in theory it is practical to defend an entire land mass such as the United States with a single base or two or three of missiles, depending on the perceived threatening countries.

Several interceptors might be launched more or less simultaneously at a single threat, to account for the possibility of random failures. In principle, if the available time were sufficient, a first interceptor could be launched; a second, or third, would be launched only if previous efforts failed. This latter technique is called shoot-look-shoot defense. Perhaps more likely, several would be fired at once out of an abundance of caution.

Indeed, it could take four or five interceptors to reliably shoot down a single warhead, not only for midcourse systems but for most types of missile defense using interceptor rockets. That is the reason why the Clinton administration advertised its proposed 100-interceptor system as capable of destroying only a couple dozen warheads. Several problems could cause a given interceptor to miss. Rocket boosters can fail; for example, during the Cold War, superpower ICBMs were generally considered to have no more than 80 to 85 percent reliability.[44] Tests of most new missile defense systems have had much better track records of late—15 of 15 for the THAAD since 2006, 40 of 49 for the navy Aegis system, 11 of 19 for the Ground-based Midcourse Defense.[45] But, again, these tests were conducted under controlled conditions, and some of them tested only a certain aspect of a defense system's capabilities. In a real engagement, numerous things could go wrong, beyond the interceptor simply failing. For example, the kill vehicle could miss its target because of random error, a manufacturing defect, difficult battlefield conditions, enemy action, or some other cause. To obtain 99 percent confidence of a successful intercept, in this example, three interceptors each with an independent 80 percent chance of successful intercept would be needed per warhead, unless there was time to employ shoot-look-shoot methods. And as noted earlier, not all modern US systems have 80 percent reliability in their testing records.

Boost-phase defenses have an appeal that midcourse systems do not: they can in theory destroy a rocket before it releases multiple warheads, as well as any decoys designed to fool a defense. A major difficulty with boost-phase defenses, however, is that they must be based near the enemy missile launch point. That could be on land, at sea, or in the air—but it would need to be near the enemy missile launch points in any case. Since boost phase lasts only three to five minutes, or less for shorter-range missiles, an interceptor does not have much time and cannot cover much distance. As a result, it must begin its flight near its target. This problem can in principle be addressed for a small country like North Korea that borders US allies or international waterways, provided a viable and effective system for conducting boost-phase defense can be built. To date, the United States has not succeeded in finding one—whether in an airborne laser or an orbiting system of interceptors or a land-based or sea-based fast missile.

Boost-phase defense is even harder against missiles launched from countries with large land masses, like Russia or China. Against such potential adversaries, the only plausible location for effective boost-phase defenses would likely be in space—again, in theory, since space-based lasers or interceptors have proved very difficult to develop technically. Even if they could be, someday, a space-based interceptor would need to be in the right place at the time a missile was launched. It would not have much time to complete the intercept before the offensive booster stopped burning—at which point warheads could be released, and at which point the rocket would no longer present a large, bright, highly vulnerable target. So the defender would need to put interceptors in many different orbits, spacing them appropriately (the interceptors would be in constant motion relative to the Earth's surface). A simple calculation shows that only one out of several dozen interceptors might, by chance, be in the right place at the right time to intercept a given ICBM. The "absentee ratio" would likely be quite high. So even to have the capacity to intercept five to ten enemy missiles, several hundred interceptors could be needed.[46]

Laser-based defenses, which produce beams traveling at the speed of light, would also need to be located near missile launch points. Otherwise, their beams would be too weakened by the atmosphere, or by the inevitable spreading or "diffraction" of a light beam that occurs over distance even in the vacuum of space. The beams could also simply be blocked by the Earth's curvature.

Countermeasures

Missile defense technology is surely improving. But adversaries can adjust. Even relatively unsophisticated enemies would surely do everything in their power to make a defense's job as hard as possible—and they would probably have some fairly simple ways to do so.

One approach would be to fire more missiles than the defense has interceptors, saturating the defense and ensuring that some offensive weapons could not be intercepted. If the attacker had MIRV technology, saturating a midcourse or terminal defense would be even easier and require even fewer missiles. In a place like the western Pacific, where China could direct many hundreds of missiles (probably carrying conventional ordnance) against targets on Taiwan or Okinawa, for example, MIRVs would likely not even be necessary to achieve a saturation effect, as discussed in chapter 2.

Decoys can also confuse even fairly sophisticated defenses like today's current American capabilities.[47] Outside the atmosphere, air resistance will not separate out the generally lighter decoys from the heavier warheads.[48] In outer space, even extremely light decoys would fly the same trajectory as true warheads, so speed could not be used to distinguish the real from the fake. To mimic the infrared heat signature of a warhead, thereby fooling sensors that measure temperature, decoys could be equipped with small heat generators, perhaps weighing only a pound. To fool radars or imaging infrared sensors, warheads and decoys alike could be placed inside radar-reflective balloons that would make it impossible to see their interiors.[49] Decoys could also even be spun by small motors so that the balloons surrounding them rotated at the same speed as real warheads, in case the defense's radar was sensitive enough to pick up such motion.

Decoys like those just mentioned are not trivial to make, however—and might work only if repeatedly flight-tested. Balloons need to be inflated in outer space. Some type of mechanism needs to physically separate each decoy from its host vehicle as well—easy to do for Russia or the United States, Britain, or France, the countries that have mastered MIRV technology, but a bit harder for a country that has not. The associated technology is fairly simple, but making it work in the laboratory is not the same as making it work at high speed in outer space, after a high-acceleration trajectory through the Earth's atmosphere. (In fact, in late 2008 the United States conducted a missile defense test in which decoys failed to deploy properly.)[50]

The United States may also have some counters against certain kinds of decoys. For example, it is developing the Multi-Object Kill Vehicle so that a single interceptor may destroy more than one threatening object in a given "threat cloud."[51]

Making decoys work within the atmosphere against terminal systems like Patriot is harder. In principle, it can be done, but any decoys would have to overcome the effects of air resistance so as not to slow down more quickly than real warheads would. Decoys that could mimic warheads within the atmosphere therefore might need small booster rockets. Alternatively, they could be made small and dense, so that they would fly the same trajectories as heavier but larger warheads (since the rate of slowing from air resistance increases with an object's size as well as its weight), though in that case their radar signatures might give them away.

Countermeasures against boost-phase defenses are also possible, though they are relatively difficult to make. Boost phases could theoretically be shortened to minimize the time a defense would have to home in on the hot rocket booster. Against interceptors that would track a rocket's plume, contaminants could be put in the rocket fuel to make its plume asymmetrical and potentially lead interceptors that home in on the midpoint of the plume astray (unless the interceptors also had an additional sensor). Against lasers, a rocket could be rotated or be given a shiny external surface that would reflect most incoming light. Finally, rockets could also be launched from remote locations on cloudy days when infrared detection satellites might not detect their heat signatures immediately— reducing the time when boost-phase defenses could work.

In short, the missile defense job involves not only very advanced technologies but also a complex interaction between offense and defense. Moreover, the tools available to each side are different, and in many cases advantageous to an attacker. That does not make missile defense impossible, but it is a very difficult undertaking.

Conclusions and Policy Lessons

In the competition between ballistic missiles and missile defense systems, the offense enjoys the overall advantage, especially when nuclear weapons are involved (since they require a very high probability of successful intercept). But defensive technologies, especially hit-to-kill systems, have improved considerably. Thus, missile defense by a country like the United States against a country like North Korea may not be futile. The following points provide some additional detail to substantiate these broad conclusions:

- Modern interceptor rocket technologies, when juxtaposed with greater computing power and better sensors, offer meaningful new options for missile defense. The advent of hit-to-kill technology manifests a new accuracy and quickness in sensors, computing, and resulting course adjustment for small "kill vehicles."
- Countermeasures such as Mylar balloons released in outer space by a missile (along with the actual warhead or warheads) might well defeat a system such as the midcourse defense system of the United States (now featuring interceptor missiles based in Alaska and California). They can mimic the signature of actual warheads beyond the capacity of current sensors to distinguish real warheads from decoys.
- That said, releasing decoys (and having balloons properly inflate in space) requires some of the technologies used in building rockets with multiple independently targetable reentry vehicles (MIRVs) in the Cold War that were not trivial even for the superpowers to overcome. More-over, a country like North Korea may not have the political or diplomatic ability (or the excess rockets) needed to do enough tests to establish confidence that its procedures for releasing decoys really work.
- Boost-phase defenses that would destroy a rocket before it could release any warheads and decoys can overcome these countermeasures. But they may be vulnerable to certain other countermeasures. And most of all, they must generally be based near the potential adversary in advance of a conflict, given the short amounts of time available to do boost-phase intercept.
- Someday, space-based missile defenses may become possible in theory, providing an answer to the difficulties of having boost-phase defenses predeployed in the right places before a conflict. Advances in processing power and miniaturization could also make a concept like "brilliant pebbles" of Reagan-era "Star Wars" fame more feasible than in the past. The idea is to base small interceptors in space for ballistic missile defense, igniting their boosters when necessary to attack a ballistic missile or its warheads.
- That said, making a single brilliant pebble technically operable—already a daunting proposition—is a far cry from populating low-Earth orbit with enough of them to provide even a limited national missile defense capability. Because such pebbles would always be in motion relative to Earth, and because only a pebble that was near a ballistic missile at the time of launch could destroy it, at least several dozen pebbles would be needed in orbit for every missile that might need to be destroyed. In addition, the brilliant pebbles would not remain in orbit indefinitely; they probably would have to be replaced every ten years or so.[52]

Nuclear Weapons, Nuclear Testing, and Nuclear Proliferation

How hard is it for an extremist state or a terrorist group to get a nuclear bomb? How effective would any such bomb likely be in terms of reliability, deployability, and explosive power? Can the United States, nearly thirty years after it stopped actual nuclear tests, still be confident in its own nuclear arsenal? Is the Comprehensive Nuclear Test Ban Treaty (CTBT), currently in a state of legal limbo internationally since neither China nor the United States has ratified it, verifiable? Are there any concepts for new types of nuclear weapons that are worth considering?

To get at such questions, this section begins with a primer on how nuclear weapons work and then addresses several policy-related issues.

Basics of Nuclear Bombs

Nuclear bombs are roughly 1 million times more powerful than conventional explosives, per pound of fuel. Weapons typically weighing several hundred pounds, with at most a few dozen pounds of nuclear-explosive material, produce yields measured in the tens or hundreds of "kilotons" of TNT equivalent.

Luckily for the sake of preventing the spread of the bomb, the core materials for nuclear weapons do not exist in nature in usable form. Fission bombs, the simplest type, use either uranium (U-235) that has been "enriched," or plutonium (with Pu-239 the key isotope) created in a nuclear reactor and then "reprocessed," as their core material. Either one is capable of undergoing a chain reaction, meaning that once some atoms within a given mass of material begin to split or fission, they can cause an exponentially increasing number of atoms to themselves fission, in a process that accelerates extremely fast. Neutrons produced by the process of one atom splitting are sufficient in number, and typically endowed with the right amount of energy, that they can on average cause more than one atom to split themselves, assuming a sufficiently large amount of material is present in a condensed space. With *more than* one fission resulting on average from any previous one, the process escalates exponentially. The rate at which this occurs is fast enough that, if the materials are appropriately sized and shaped, they can create enormous numbers of fissions—and enormous energy—before the weapon blows itself apart.

As noted, one way to build a bomb is with enriched uranium or U-235—the scarcer isotope of the two found most in nature (the other being U-238, which makes up 99.3 percent of natural uranium). Bombs using a uranium chain reaction as their source of explosive energy cannot be built unless the concentration of U-235 is greatly increased through a process like centrifuge rotation or gaseous diffusion. First, typically, uranium metal is caused to bond with fluoride gas to form uranium hexafluoride; then that gas is manipulated in some way that tends to separate faster molecules from slower ones. The slightly lighter weight of U-235 means that on average molecules containing it have greater average speed than those with U-238. The process of separating faster molecules from slower ones must be employed several times since, as Maxwell-Boltzmann statistics show, any given gas has molecules with a wide range of speeds. Only after repeated efforts to distill out the faster molecules will the proportion of U-235 uranium move measurably toward the goal of 90 percent concentration. About twenty-five kilograms of U-235 are needed to build a simple bomb.

In a gun-assembly weapon, the uranium is formed into two main chunks (see Figure 4.4). Neither is large enough to generate a chain reaction itself, because when natural fissions occur in the uranium, the neutrons they generate generally escape from the mass into space, rather than encountering and being absorbed by new uranium atoms. So the chain reaction process never gets going. But when the two chunks are rapidly joined with the help of a conventional explosive, they produce a large enough mass to "go critical"—to create a critical mass of fissionable material that then leads to an accelerating nuclear chain reaction. If the uranium is partially surrounded with materials that tend to reflect neutrons—so any neutrons headed for the open tend to return to the uranium mass and have a chance at causing new fissions—and if it is also surrounded with a tamper that slows down the process of the explosion, allowing more time for new chain reactions to occur, the yield can be further enhanced.

Built in this way, the Hiroshima "Little Boy" bomb had a yield of some 15 kilotons (the equivalent of 15,000 tons of TNT). It annihilated a region with a radius of about one kilometer but also caused severe damage and injuries much farther out, to a distance of several kilometers.[53] Many victims died instantaneously from the X-rays, the blast, and the heat; many also died over ensuing months, and years, from injuries like radiation poisoning and associated cancers, with total fatalities reaching 200,000.[54] To underscore the power of nuclear explosives, that much energy was created by the complete fissioning of just half a kilogram of uranium, or 2 percent of the weapon's nuclear fuel. Despite such "imperfections," the bomb design concept was considered so reliable that it was never tested before use.[55]

For today's nuclear powers, however, the most common way to build a fission weapon is not with enriched uranium but with plutonium. Specifically, in the core of the weapon, a shell of plutonium is surrounded by conventional explosive. The explosive must be equipped with multiple detonators, so that it is simultaneously and symmetrically detonated all around the shell. It must also be shaped correctly so the explosive force applies equally across the surface of the plutonium. Such a modern weapon is in effect a more sophisticated and efficient derivative of the

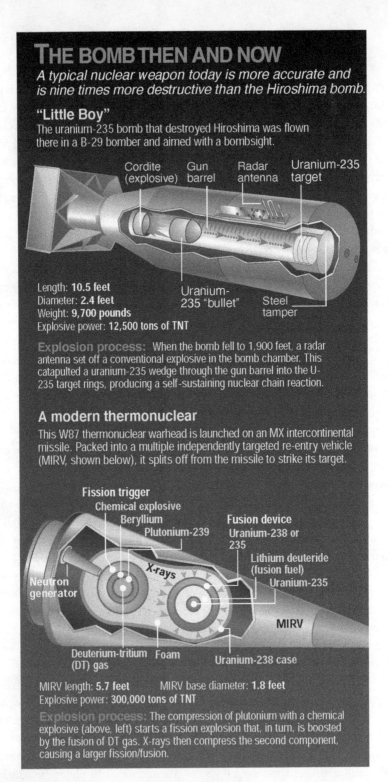

THE BOMB THEN AND NOW

A typical nuclear weapon today is more accurate and is nine times more destructive than the Hiroshima bomb.

"Little Boy"

The uranium-235 bomb that destroyed Hiroshima was flown there in a B-29 bomber and aimed with a bombsight.

Cordite (explosive)
Gun barrel
Radar antenna
Uranium-235 target

Length: **10.5 feet**
Diameter: **2.4 feet**
Weight: **9,700 pounds**
Explosive power: **12,500 tons of TNT**

Uranium-235 "bullet"
Steel tamper

Explosion process: When the bomb fell to 1,900 feet, a radar antenna set off a conventional explosive in the bomb chamber. This catapulted a uranium-235 wedge through the gun barrel into the U-235 target rings, producing a self-sustaining nuclear chain reaction.

A modern thermonuclear

This W87 thermonuclear warhead is launched on an MX intercontinental missile. Packed into a multiple independently targeted re-entry vehicle (MIRV, shown below), it splits off from the missile to strike its target.

Fission trigger
Chemical explosive
Beryllium
Plutonium-239

Fusion device
Uranium-238 or 235

Lithium deuteride (fusion fuel)
Uranium-235

X-rays

Neutron generator

MIRV

Deuterium-tritium (DT) gas
Foam
Uranium-238 case

MIRV length: **5.7 feet**   MIRV base diameter: **1.8 feet**
Explosive power: **300,000 tons of TNT**

Explosion process: The compression of plutonium with a chemical explosive (above, left) starts a fission explosion that, in turn, is boosted by the fusion of DT gas. X-rays then compress the second component, causing a larger fission/fusion.

FIGURE 4.4. Schematic of a thermonuclear weapon.

Source: U.S. National Security and Military/Commercial Concerns with the People's Republic of China (Washington, D.C.: Government Printing Office, 1999).

Nagasaki "Fat Man" concept, a bomb that had a yield of some twenty-one kilotons and killed 140,000.[56] (This type of weapon was tested once before use.) When the weapon is triggered, the shell is compressed, forming a sphere that attains critical mass. Roughly eight kilograms of plutonium (about twenty pounds) is adequate to serve as the core fuel for a relatively simple plutonium-based weapon.[57]

As with uranium bombs, the yield of these weapons can be enhanced considerably, for a given amount of fissile uranium or plutonium, if a neutron-reflecting material like uranium-238 or a beryllium or tungsten product is used to enclose the plutonium. Also, weapons can be made more efficient and deadly if neutron generators (designed to start the chain reaction more quickly) are used. In that way, the weapon does not depend entirely on random fissions to begin the explosion. Thus, the exponentially accelerating process can happen faster, allowing a greater yield before the weapon self-destructs. Polonium-210 is such a neutron-generating element.[58]

The yield of a weapon can be increased if a weapon is "boosted" by a mixture of deuterium and tritium gas injected inside the shell of the plutonium as the weapon is detonated. The gas absorbs neutrons and then undergoes a fusion process (atoms coming together to form new, heavier atoms). The fusion process itself generates energy. It also produces free neutrons—which in turn have a high likelihood of inducing more fissions from the plutonium. Again, the goal is to maximize the number of plutonium (or U-235) atoms that fission quickly, before the bomb essentially blows itself up and terminates the chain reaction process.

Methods such as use of neutron generators, use of neutron reflectors, and boosting can also reduce the amount of plutonium or uranium required to achieve a given explosive effect. In fact, we now know from unclassified sources that no more than four kilograms of plutonium, and perhaps twelve to fifteen kilograms of U-235, is considered adequate for the purposes of making modern US weapons.[59]

An even more advanced weapon is the thermonuclear or hydrogen bomb (see figure 4.4). Such a bomb includes a device like that just described as its "primary," which gets the whole explosion going through fission of U-235 or plutonium. In addition, it has a "secondary" stage, powered by X-rays from the first stage, that is designed to produce a large fraction of its energy from fusion. The primary creates temperatures and pressures that are high enough to create combustion of hydrogen isotopes that then turn into helium, releasing a huge amount of energy in the process. The yields of such thermonuclear weapons can be very large, hundreds of kilotons or even megatons. By contrast, even the most sophisticated and efficient fission bombs typically have yields limited to several dozen kilotons at most.

A thermonuclear weapon that is rebuilt to eliminate the secondary becomes a much-lower-yield but still dependable simple fission bomb. This concept is apparently behind the proposal in the Trump administration's 2018 Nuclear Posture

Review to develop a new low-yield sea-based nuclear warhead—and to do so without nuclear testing (even as the Trump administration reserved the right to resume testing at some future date should circumstances, in its view, so require).[60]

Even though the second stage of a thermonuclear bomb centers on the fusion process, it also typically generates some power by fission. The principal fuel, deuterium-tritium gas, is enclosed generally by a U-235 shell (some U-238 might also be used in the casing of the secondary). The former elements fuse; the latter absorb high-energy neutrons produced by the fusion process and split. So there is actually some fusion within the "fission" part of the bomb—due to boosting— and some fission within the "fusion" part.[61]

The nuclear materials discussed previously are all either hard to acquire or hard to work with. That fact underscores the degree to which building a nuclear bomb is challenging, even for some nation-states, and certainly for any terrorist groups that might make the attempt. They are dangerous to handle, and they must be well machined to function correctly within a weapon. A terrorist group or small nation might, however, have greater success stealing or buying a nuclear weapon. Some types weigh only about 100 pounds or even less and are man-portable, so if the right facility could be accessed, and any safety mechanisms on the warheads disabled, an extremist organization or country might acquire a usable nuclear weapon.[62]

High-performance nuclear weapons are also difficult to design and produce such that they have high reliability. Margins for error in such weapons are deliberately small, so that weapons may be of modest weight—to facilitate their deployment and delivery—yet have high yield. Specifically, in modern high-performance weapons, quite modest amounts of fissile material are used, so that the primary can be light (less fissile material implies less conventional explosive to assemble or compress it, so there is a double benefit). In a thermonuclear weapon, as long as the primary creates pressure and temperature conditions that are suitable to make hydrogen fuse, it has done its job; creating notably higher pressures and temperatures would be largely superfluous. But sophisticated warheads have less margin for error as a rule. In the past, the United States has encountered problems with its warheads as they aged and as their tritium, needed for boosting, decayed. Other problems have arisen with conventional explosives, as warheads aged, or when they encountered low-temperature conditions, as they would in the upper atmosphere or space in any actual delivery to target. The United States experienced these challenges even though it had the benefit of a grand total of more than 1,000 nuclear test explosions over nearly half a century of testing.[63]

The heyday of US nuclear testing was in the 1960s, when several dozen tests a year were typically performed. In this period, the United States built advanced and relatively lightweight thermonuclear warheads for delivery systems such as ballistic missiles in support of nuclear warfighting strategy.[64] When weight and yield performance were less of an issue, in the early nuclear years, it tested much less—only six times through 1950, in fact. That was partly because the early bomb designs proved successful in the July 1945 Trinity test as well as at Hiroshima and Nagasaki. Thus, on balance it must still be concluded that for groups able to get their hands on fissile material, the odds of it being turned into at least a crude, heavy, yet workable nuclear device are probably fairly high.[65]

As noted earlier in discussing casualties from the bombs dropped on Japan in 1945, nuclear weapons produce prompt effects as well as longer-term ones. The same is true of nuclear reactors—and nuclear reactor accidents. Fission, in a bomb or a reactor, produces a number of dangerous particles that decay spontaneously thereafter, emitting harmful high-energy particles whenever they do. One is cesium-135, with a half-life of 2.3 million years. Whatever amount of material one began with at the start of that time period, half will have decayed over the course of the 2.3 million years, and half will still remain. By contrast, for another fission product, cesium-137, the half-life is only 30 years. That material is quite potent initially but within a century or two is far less threatening. Broadly speaking, with such radioactive materials, there is never a precise period after which all is well and all is safe. It is a process of gradual natural decontamination, with relevant time periods measured in decades, centuries, and millennia.[66]

A related point: a nuclear bomb detonated in the atmosphere or at sea is relatively less harmful than one detonated on or near the surface of the Earth, in terms of radioactive fallout and its implications. That is because the fission products are quickly diluted to relatively harmless levels fairly quickly. That said, the combined radioactive effect of detonating hundreds of nuclear weapons in the atmosphere in the early decades of the nuclear age was considered to be concerning enough to help give rise to the Partial Test Ban Treaty of 1963.

This type of primer, while not adequate for answering questions such as whether North Korea or Iran can build a nuclear weapon to fit on a missile in the coming years, nonetheless can help inform some key policy debates. For example, consider the question of whether the nuclear test ban treaty, currently not in formal effect but nonetheless being respected by the major nuclear powers, can enhance American security.[67]

Is a Ban on Testing Verifiable?

On balance, the physics of nuclear detonations and of how they reverberate through the Earth's crust make it relatively straightforward to detect any nuclear explosion of meaningful size anywhere on Earth. That is why previous treaties limiting nuclear testing—the Partial Test Ban Treaty of 1963 (prohibiting tests in the atmosphere, oceans, and outer space) and the Threshold Test Ban Treaty of 1974 (limiting underground tests to a yield of 150 kilotons or less) are verifiable. If the Comprehensive Nuclear Test Ban Treaty of 1996 is ever ratified by enough countries to come into effect—a prospect that may be more distant now than it was twenty years ago—this fact will be relevant to ensuring compliance as well.[68] Even without such formal status for the CTBT, nuclear tests of any size can be reliably detected (such as those by India and Pakistan in 1998, most rather small, and by North Korea in 2006, 2009, 2013, 2016, and 2017).[69]

Large nuclear explosions in the atmosphere can generally be seen from space and can be detected subsequently through the radiation they create. If the detonations are underground, as is more common, they are still straightforward to identify—and within minutes or at most hours—via seismic monitoring and related means, provided they reach a certain size. In addition to the capabilities of individual nation-states, the Preparatory Commission for the Comprehensive Nuclear-Test-Ban Treaty Organization operates 50 main seismic sites and 120 auxiliary sites in a grand total of seventy-six countries, plus other kinds of stations that, for example, sample the air for contaminants possibly released into the atmosphere after an explosion. The organization is also supposed, if and when the CTBT every formally comes into effect, to have the capacity to do more precise on-site inspections.[70] Any weapon of kiloton power or above (the Hiroshima and Nagasaki bombs were in the 10-kiloton to 20-kiloton range) can be "heard" by US intelligence or international monitors in this way; in many parts of the world including known nuclear test sites, even much smaller explosions would be reliably detected. In other words, any weapon with significant military potential tested at its full strength is very likely to be noticed. American seismic arrays are found throughout much of Eurasia's periphery, for example, and even tests elsewhere could generally be picked up. Indeed, even though it either "fizzled" or was designed to have a small yield in the first place, with a yield of about 1 kiloton and thus well below those of the Hiroshima and Nagasaki bombs, the October 2006 North Korean test was detected and clearly identified as a nuclear burst.[71] Two of India's tests in 1998 were even smaller, yet were detected.[72]

There continue to be only two viable ways to reduce the chances of detection. First, one can test a device well below its intended military yield, through some type of modification of the weapon's physics. (Doing this may in fact make the device very different from the actual class of weapon it is designed to represent, meaning that sophisticated extrapolation will be needed to deduce how the actual weapon would behave based on the results of the detonation of the modified device.) Second, one can dig out a very large underground cavity into which a weapon can be placed, thereby "decoupling" the blast from direct contact with the ground and allowing it to weaken before it then reaches surrounding soil or rock and causes the Earth to shake. This latter approach is arduous. And it does not make a weapon totally undetectable; it simply changes the threshold yield at which it can be heard.[73]

A country that was very sophisticated in nuclear technology might be able to do a test of a modified device that escaped international detection by virtue of having its normal yield reduced through modifications to the basic physics of the weapon. For example, less plutonium or highly enriched uranium might be used. Or if it was an advanced type of weapon, less tritium might be used. But accomplishing such engineering feats would probably be beyond the means of a fledgling power. They are in fact difficult even for advanced nuclear powers. (In fact, this is much of the reason why the threshold test ban treaty that limits the power of any nuclear explosion allows tests up to 150 kilotons. It is hard to use very small explosions in the subkiloton range to verify the proper functioning of a sophisticated and powerful nuclear weapon.) Scientists can learn some things from artificially small explosions caused by modified devices—but probably not enough to give them high confidence that a weapon is reliable at its intended yield.

US nuclear verification capabilities have picked up the Indian, Pakistani, and North Korean nuclear tests—even the small, relatively unsuccessful ones—in the last decade and would be able to do so with high confidence for tests from those or other countries in the future. Verification capabilities are not airtight or perfect, but they are quite good.

Ensuring Stockpile Reliability without Testing

Most agree that the United States needs a nuclear deterrent well into the foreseeable future. Common sense would seem to support the position that, at some point at least, testing will be needed in the future to ensure the arsenal's reliability. How can one go 10 or 20 or 50 or 100 years without a single test and still be confident that the country's nuclear weapons will work? Equally important, how can one be sure that other countries will be deterred by an American stockpile that at some point will be certified only by the experiments and tests of a generation of physicists long since retired or dead? This concern is amplified by the fact that, as weapons expert and bomb designer Stephen Younger states, "All the weapons in the current American nuclear arsenal were designed to maximize the yield-to-weight ratio."[74] This means they were built for optimal performance more than reliability. Skepticism about the ability of the United States to sustain a reliable nuclear deterrent indefinitely into the future is part of why the US Senate voted against ratification of the CTBT in 1999.[75]

Some of this perception about the declining reliability of nuclear weapons might be welcomed in certain quarters.[76] Declining reliability might be interpreted as declining usability of the weapons, as well. But as a practical strategic and political matter, any test ban must still allow the United States to ensure 100 percent confidence in its nuclear deterrent into the indefinite future. Even if some uncertainty over the functioning of a certain percentage of the arsenal is tolerable, doubt about whether *any* part of it would function effectively would disrupt the core logic of deterrence—and also of *assurance* of American allies that they remain protected by a dependable US nuclear umbrella, a crucial element in dissuading some from developing their own nuclear weapons.[77]

Thankfully, a reasonable confidence in the long-term viability of the American nuclear arsenal should be possible without testing. To be sure, some would disagree with that statement. It is true that, with time, the reliability of a given warhead class may decline as its components age. In a worst case, it is conceivable that one category of warheads might in fact become flawed without our knowing it; indeed, this has happened in the past. But through a combination of monitoring, testing, and remanufacturing the individual components, conducting sophisticated experiments (short of actual nuclear detonations) on integrated devices, and perhaps introducing a new warhead type or two of extremely conservative design into the inventory, the overall dependability of the American nuclear deterrent can remain very good. With this kind of approach, there might be a modest reduction in the overall technical capacities of the arsenal, but still no question about its ability to exact a devastating response against anyone attacking the United States or its allies with weapons of mass destruction. The fact that the Trinity, Hiroshima, and Nagasaki bombs all worked on the first try and the fact that the United States now has more than 1,000 nuclear tests under its metaphoric belt, as well as a deep knowledge base and experimental capacity (short of actual nuclear tests) for conducting surveillance and stewardship of the stockpile, leave little doubt on this core point.

Consider first the issue of monitoring a given warhead type and periodically replacing components as needed. This is the key way the United States is maintaining its nuclear arsenal at present (its last test was in 1992). As an example, as noted earlier, a typical nuclear warhead has a shell of plutonium that is compressed by a synchronized detonation of conventional explosives that surround it. Making sure the explosion is synchronized along all parts of the explosive, so that the compression of plutonium is symmetrical, is critical if the warhead is to work. Over time, wires can age, detonators can age, and so forth. But these types of components can be easily replaced, and their proper functioning can be verified through simulations that make no use of nuclear material (and are thus allowable under a CTBT).

Things get a bit more complicated once the compression of the plutonium is considered. The interaction of the conventional explosive with the plutonium is a complex physical phenomenon that is highly dependent on not just the basic nature of the materials involved but also their shapes, their surfaces, and the chemical interactions that occur where they meet. Plutonium is not a static material; it is of course radioactive, and it ages in various ways with time. Conventional explosives age too, meaning that warhead performance can change with time.

To address these concerns, in theory one could simply rebuild the conventional explosives and the plutonium shells to original specifications every 20 or 30 or 50 years, avoiding the whole issue of monitoring the aging process by remanufacturing the key elements of the weapon every so often. In fact, one of the fathers of the hydrogen bomb, Richard Garwin, has recommended doing exactly that.[78] But others retort that previous processes used to cast plutonium and to manufacture chemical explosives have become outdated. For example, previous generations of plutonium shells, or "pits," were machined to achieve their final dimensions, but this produced a great deal of waste. The goal for the future has been to cast plutonium pits directly into their final shape instead (by heating the plutonium to molten form, forming it into proper shape, and then letting it cool). Doing so, however, would create a different type of surface for the pit that might interact slightly differently with the conventional explosive relative to the previous design. And even a slight difference might be enough to throw off the proper functioning of a very sensitive, high-performance, low-error-tolerance warhead. Similarly, the way high explosives are manufactured typically changes with time. Replacing one type with another has in the past affected warhead performance, even when that might not have been easily predicted.

So what to do? Garwin would argue that, for relatively small and shrinking nuclear arsenals, it is worth the modest economic cost and environmental risk (which is quite small by the standards of Cold War nuclear activities) to keep making plutonium pits and conventional explosives as we have done previously, even if the methods are outdated. That would ensure reliability by keeping future warheads virtually identical to those of the past. At least, it would minimize significant changes to them, particularly in the "physics package" of the weapons primary containing the fissile materials and tritium—where the most sensitive parts of the nuclear detonation occur. Mimicking past manufacturing processes should not be beyond the capacities of today's scientists. But Garwin's argument is not presently carrying the day, in part because of the view that there will inevitably be at least small differences in how warheads are built from one era to another even if attempts are made to avoid it.[79]

The Department of Energy has instead devoted huge sums of money to its science-based stockpile stewardship program, to understand as well as possible what happens within aging warheads and to predict the performance of those warheads once modified with slightly different materials in the future. It is a very good program, even as elements of it naturally remain debatable.[80] It is also more scientifically interesting—and thus more likely to attract good scientists into the weapons business in future years—than a program for stockpile maintenance that would do no more than rebuild weapons every few decades. But the science-based stockpile stewardship program still gives some people unease. For example, a key part of the effort is using elegant three-dimensional computer models to predict what will happen inside a warhead modified to use a new type (or amount) of chemical explosive based on computational physics. This is a very challenging process to model accurately. This method is good but perhaps not perfect.[81] It is for reasons such as these that many bomb designers are skeptical about a permanent CTBT—though many are not, provided that a robust, science-based stockpile stewardship program continue.[82]

A final way to ensure confidence in the arsenal is to design a new type of warhead, or perhaps use an old design that is not currently represented in the active US nuclear arsenal but that has been tested previously. This approach would seek to use "conservative designs" that allow for slight errors in warhead performance and still produce a robust nuclear yield. The conservative warhead could then take its place alongside other types of warheads in the arsenal, providing an added element of confidence. Taking this approach might lead to a somewhat heavier warhead (meaning the number that could be carried on a given missile or bomber would have to be reduced), or a lower-yield warhead (meaning that a hardened Russian missile silo might not be so easily destroyed, for example). This approach could also lead to less use of toxic materials such as beryllium and safer types of conventional explosives (that are less prone to accidental detonation) than is the case for some warheads in the current arsenal.[83]

It is for such reasons that the George W. Bush administration showed interest in a "reliable replacement warhead" concept.[84] Although controversial, the idea does have a certain logic as one element of a future American arsenal. In fact, it might even obviate the need to consider Garwin's idea, since it is quite clear that the United States could deploy such a warhead with extremely high confidence of its reliability.[85] Simple warhead designs are quite robust—again, recall that the Hiroshima bomb (a gun-assembly uranium device) was not even tested before being used.

The Case for New Nukes

Some have suggested that the United States may need future nuclear testing for new types of warheads to accomplish new missions. For example, in the 1980s, some missile defense proponents were interested in a space-based nuclear-pumped X-ray laser. That was never particularly practical. But the idea of developing a nuclear weapon that could burrow underground *before* detonating has gained appeal—not least because countries such as North Korea and Iran are responding to America's increasingly precise conventional weaponry by hiding key weapons programs well below the planet's surface.

One possible argument for such a warhead is to increase its overall destructive depth. In theory, the United States could modify the largest nuclear weapons in its existing stockpile to penetrate the Earth. This approach would roughly double the destructive reach of the most powerful weapons in the current arsenal, according to physicist Michael Levi.[86] But if an enemy can avoid weapons in the current arsenal, it could avoid the more powerful bombs by digging deeper underground.

Could Earth-penetrating weapons at least reduce the nuclear fallout from an explosion? They could not prevent fallout; given limits on the hardness of materials and other basic physics, no useful nuclear weapon could penetrate the Earth far enough to keep the radioactive effects of its blast entirely below ground But such weapons could reduce fallout. Relative to a normal bomb, it is possible to reduce the yield of an Earth-penetrating weapon tenfold while maintaining the same destructive capability against underground targets.[87] This would reduce fallout by a factor of ten as well.

That would be a meaningful change. But is it really enough to change the basic usability of a nuclear device? Such a weapon would still produce a huge amount of fallout. Its use would still break the nuclear taboo. It would still only be capable of destroying underground targets if their locations were precisely known, in which case there is a chance that conventional weapons or special forces could neutralize the site. American policymakers often reach different conclusions in answering this question. In fact, the George W. Bush administration sought to research a "robust nuclear Earth penetrator," but Congress would not provide the funding.[88]

It is worth noting that Russia, or another country, might consider the same pros and cons and reach a different conclusion. Moscow might see a nuclear test as a virtue, not a downside, of pursuing a new bomb design—making other countries think it is less hesitant to employ nuclear weapons in a conflict. Already, its official doctrine and statements have expanded the possible range of military uses to which it might put nuclear weapons.[89] The US Defense Intelligence Agency recently assessed that Russia is seeking to develop large-yield warheads with Earth-penetrating capabilities, in fact, and that it might be pursuing some kinds of nuclear-related tests (though not large-scale nuclear detonations) in that vein.[90] Russia, like nuclear-weapons states France and the United Kingdom, has signed and ratified the CTBT. But no country is obliged to comply with the treaty until China, the United States, Egypt, Iran, and Israel have also ratified it, and until India, Pakistan, and North Korea have all both signed and ratified.[91]

Conclusion and Policy Lessons

Nuclear weapons are complex devices that are expensive and difficult to produce. That is a fortunate fact of science. Some seventy-five years into the nuclear age, if it had been different on the technical front, many more countries and perhaps terrorist groups could have their own fission and/or fusion weapons. But the prevalence of nuclear material worldwide, the fact that numerous countries including Pakistan and North Korea already do possess nuclear weapons, and the limitations of international controls on the movement of nuclear technologies and materials nonetheless still make the present situation fraught with danger.

The focus here has been on the issues involved in building and testing a nuclear weapon. This is of relevance, among other things, for the nuclear testing debate. Specifically, how much would an international accord banning nuclear tests (and punishing any violators of the regime) complicate the challenges of would-be proliferators? On the other hand, assuming that nuclear weapons are still viewed as necessary for the foreseeable future, how much might a CTBT impinge on the reliability, credibility, and if desired the modernization of the American nuclear deterrent? Several observations flow from the preceding discussion. Like those presented in other sections of this chapter, they do not tend to put policy debates to rest or resolve them definitively. Rather, they establish some boundaries to the debate and help inform the choices at hand.

- Simple nuclear weapons are not inherently difficult to make, assuming that fissile materials are available and that a country has a respectable engineering and science tradition that, among other things, lends itself to precise manufacture of various components that must be built to fairly demanding specifications.
- To put it differently, midsize countries with good scientific and industrial capabilities can generally make nuclear weapons. Small, poor, technologically unsophisticated countries and terrorist groups probably cannot. Unfortunately, perhaps with help from others, North Korea has shown that it can, despite being rather small and poor.
- Even for midsize countries, however, obtaining fissile material to build a bomb is difficult. It requires time and considerable expense; it also generally requires some degree of international help and foreign technology.
- Even for those countries able to build simple fission bombs—something likely within the reach of almost any country that can get its hands on

enough U-235 or plutonium—making weapons capable of delivery by missile is hard. Given the need to be very efficient in the use of conventional explosives, casing, and other such materials (to keep weight down), it is not clear that such weapons can be developed without testing. This fact may be the chief technical argument on the positive side of the ledger when evaluating the CTBT.

- To put the point more bluntly, I am skeptical that North Korea can have any real confidence at this juncture, even after conducting six nuclear weapons tests since 2006, that it could deliver a warhead intercontinentally and then successfully detonate it over an American city.

- As for other aspects of such a treaty, a CTBT could be generally well verified. Only a very limited class of nuclear detonations—so small as to have quite modest military utility, especially for countries with fledgling nuclear research infrastructures—would have any realistic hope of evading detection.

- A CTBT would not deprive the United States of a nuclear deterrent under any plausible circumstances at any point in the future. That is to say, the United States could still credibly threaten powerful nuclear retaliation against an enemy with virtually complete technical confidence indefinitely into the future, if necessary by building simple bombs with greater weight and/or lower yield than warheads in today's arsenal.

- The detailed performance of some warheads could be cast into doubt under a CTBT, especially over a period of decades, and especially for high-performance, high-yield weapons that are designed and built with few margins for error.

- Finally, a CTBT could deprive the United States of a new type of nuclear warhead, specifically one able to penetrate deeply underground. There is a chance that such a warhead could be constructed by modifying existing weapons without testing, but it is not clear. The case for weapons such as Earth-penetrating warheads is in my judgment not strong; they cannot be made in a way that would prevent fallout. A broader policy judgment on their desirability requires considering the relatively modest (but nonetheless real) potential technical military advantages of any such new weapons against the harm to global nonproliferation efforts that any American resumption of nuclear testing could cause. In my view, testing to build such weapons is not worth it; however, that is admittedly a policy judgment informed by—but not immediately provable with—the technical assessments offered here.

Conclusion: Security Dilemmas, Wars of Choice, Uncertainty, and the Science of War

It is important that most foreign policy practitioners—indeed, even most public policy specialists writ large—have a basic understanding of the size, scope, and major characteristics of the American armed forces as well as other basic features of today's global security environment. The budgetary and human scale of the military and the consequences involved with its employment (or nonemployment) are simply too immense for this job to be outsourced to the generals or any other small group of experts. Moreover, the inherent interweaving of political and policy issues with military realities makes it impossible to create a clear red line separating civilian decision making from military execution, as Samuel Huntington might have wanted. War is so complex, and unpredictable, that it is not realistic to think we can simply first select a preferred policy objective and then task military organizations with the "technical" job of achieving it. Uncertainties over outcomes and costs are simply too great for that in the preponderance of important cases.

Understanding the Department of Defense and other nations' armed forces can be daunting given the enormity of these organizations and the sheer amount of detail. But if we seek to get the basics sound, and build a solid scaffolding of understanding of the fundamentals, the details tend to fall into place when they are needed. To paraphrase Clausewitz in conclusion, even if in war the simple things often prove hard, most of them are in fact fairly simple.

And to refer back to Sun Tzu, there is indeed an art of war that must be studied and mastered by strategists and policymakers; human passions, politics, history, and organizational dynamics are of central importance as well. But there is also a science of war. It involves methods of structured and computational analysis, as well as an understanding of physics and technology. The science of war is often not as exact as the term might sound. But if the purpose of analysis is to bound problems, rule out bad options, and understand trade-offs and uncertainties—rather than to arrive unambiguously at clear policy choices—its methods have much to offer.

The inherent inexactness of defense analytical methods has important implications for policy in the United States and abroad. Because predicting outcomes in war is *inevitably* difficult, as I contend in this book, it means that constructing adequate defenses, stable military balances of power, and robust means of national protection is fated to be a very difficult undertaking. To put it bluntly, two opposing countries or blocs of nations with roughly comparable military capabilities are generally *not* inherently safe from each other. Closely matched militaries can fight wars with lopsided outcomes—just as two outstanding football teams might produce either a close Super Bowl or a blowout. Too much depends on chance, on leadership, and on other intangibles. The security dilemma between nations does not arise just because intentions are hard to read—because one country's efforts to provide a solid defensive capability for itself can be misinterpreted by others as indicating offensive intentions. The security dilemma is in fact even more inherent in the nature of military organizations and of war. Simply achieving a strong defensive military capability tends to create offensive capabilities that could, with the right strategy and leadership, prove decisive against another state's armed forces. Certain elements of modern military power, like nuclear weapons, tend to dampen this phenomenon somewhat. But other aspects of modern technology, like uncertainty over the survivability of space, communications, and cyber systems, exacerbate the dangers. Policymakers need to be aware of this reality even as they also seek to develop military capabilities and budgets, as well as broader foreign policies, that make their nations secure.

For the United States, privileged by a favorable geostrategic position with two oceans and two big friends as neighbors, along with a strong nuclear deterrent and still-formidable industrial base, defense analytical methods can often help us discern if wars of choice should be fought in the first place. At a certain level, most US wars are in fact wars of choice, in the memorable phrase of the president of the Council on Foreign Relations, Richard Haass, because they generally occur far from home and do not directly implicate the territorial security of the nation.

Defense analytical methods are also crucial for the more mundane tasks of building defense programs and rightsizing defense budgets. They also are essential for fostering military innovation and recognizing the potential, or lack thereof, for military revolution at a given moment in history.

The science of war need not always be overly sophisticated. Simple back-of-the-envelope methodologies can generally provide substantial insight without requiring the churning of giant computer models or access to the classified data of official Pentagon studies. That means that generalists, outsiders, and individuals can play important roles in defense analytical debates even without legions of Department of Defense analysts at their beck and call. The latter have important roles, too, and can tackle some types of complex problems more effectively than lone scholars or staffers or senators. But much about war is inherently uncertain, and there is great danger in pretending otherwise. It is surprising how often "wiz kids" Enthoven and Smith's counsel, from half a century ago, to get it "roughly right" rather than "precisely wrong" proves to be the better part of wisdom in the field of security studies.

Notes

INTRODUCTION

1. Richard K. Betts, "The Grandiosity of Grand Strategy," *Washington Quarterly* 42, no. 4 (Winter 2020): 7–22.

2. On the World War I reference, see Barbara W. Tuchman, *The Guns of August* (New York: Bantam Books, 1980), 135.

3. By comparison with my 2009 book, *The Science of War*, this introduction and chapter 3 here are entirely new. Chapters 1, 2, and 4 cover related material but are restructured and updated relative to the earlier book.

4. Ploughshares Fund, "World Nuclear Weapon Stockpile," Washington, D.C., 2020, https://www.ploughshares.org/world-nuclear-stockpile-report.

5. Peter R. Lavoy, "Predicting Nuclear Proliferation: A Declassified Documentary Record," *Strategic Insights* 3, no. 1 (January 2004), https://fas.org/man/eprint/lavoy.pdf.

6. International Institute for Strategic Studies, *The Military Balance 2019* (Oxfordshire, U.K.: Routledge, 2019), 513–518.

7. China Power Project, Center for Strategic and International Studies, "What Does China Really Spend on Its Military?," Washington, D.C., 2019, https://chinapower.csis .org/military-spending.

8. International Institute for Strategic Studies, *The Military Balance 2020* (Oxfordshire, U.K.: Routledge, 2020), 528–534.

9. Office of the Under Secretary of Defense (Comptroller), "Defense Budget Overview: United States Department of Defense Fiscal Year 2020 Budget Request," March 2019, A-4, https://comptroller.defense.gov/Portals/45/Documents/defbudget/fy2020/fy2020 _Budget_Request_Overview_Book.pdf.

10. See Michael E. O'Hanlon, *The $650 Billion Bargain: The Case for Modest Growth in America's Defense Budget* (Washington, D.C.: Brookings, 2016), 1–21.

11. Michael E. O'Hanlon, *The Future of Land Warfare* (Washington, D.C.: Brookings, 2015), 150–154.

12. Ministry of Foreign Affairs of the Government of Armenia, "International Organisations: Collective Security Treaty Organization," Yerevan, Armenia, 2018, https://www .mfa.am/en/international-organisations/1.

13. Shanghai Cooperation Organisation, "Shanghai Cooperation Organisation," Beijing, September 2017, http://eng.sectsco.org/about_sco.

14. Lotta Themnér and Erik Melander, "Patterns of Armed Conflict, 2006–2015," in *SIPRI Yearbook 2016* (Oxford: Oxford University Press, 2016), https://www.sipri.org/sites /default/files/SIPRIYB16c06sII.pdf.

15. Lotta Themnar and Peter Wallensteen, "Armed Conflict, 1946–2013," *Journal of Peace Research* 51, no. 4 (2014), pcr.uu.se/research/ucdp/charts_and_graphs; Steven Pinker, *The Better Angels of Our Nature: Why Violence Has Declined* (New York: Penguin Books, 2012), 303–304; and Department of Peace and Conflict Research, Uppsala Conflict Data Program, "Number of Conflicts, 1975–2017," Uppsala University, Uppsala, Sweden, 2018, https://ucdp.uu.se/?id=1&id=1.

16. See "The Long and Short of the Problem," *Economist*, November 9, 2013, http:// www.economist.com/news/briefing/21589431-bringing-end-conflicts-within-states

-vexatious-history-provides-guide; and Department of Peace and Conflict Research, Uppsala Conflict Data Program, "Number of Deaths, 1989–2017," Uppsala University, Uppsala, Sweden, 2018, https://ucdp.uu.se/#/exploratory.

17. General Raymond Odierno (ret.) and Michael E. O'Hanlon, "Securing Global Cities," Washington, D.C., Brookings, 2017, 8, https://www.brookings.edu/research/securing -global-cities-2.

18. Center on International Cooperation, *Annual Review of Global Peace Operations 2013* (New York: Lynne Rienner, 2013), 9; and United Nations Peacekeeping, "Data," February 2019, https://peacekeeping.un.org/en/data.

19. See Bruce Jones, testimony Before the Senate Foreign Relations Committee, "U.N. Peacekeeping and Opportunities for Reform," December 9, 2015, http://www.brookings .edu/research/testimony/2015/12/09-un-peacekeeping-opportunities-jones.

20. Lise Morje Howard, *Power in Peacekeeping* (Cambridge: Cambridge University Press, 2019), 8.

21. RAND National Defense Research Institute Project, "Total Number of Terrorist Incidents" and "RAND Database of Worldwide Terrorism Incidents" (Santa Monica, Calif.: RAND, 2012), http://smapp.rand.org/rwtid/search.php.

22. See Response of Director of National Intelligence James Clapper to Question by Senator Dianne Feinstein, in "Transcript: Senate Intelligence Hearing on National Security Threats," *Washington Post*, January 29, 2014, http://www.washingtonpost.com/world /national-security/transcript-senate-intelligence-hearing-on-national-security-threats /2014/01/29/b5913184-8912-11e3-833c-33098f9e5267_story.html.

23. Max Roser, Mohamed Nagdy, and Hannah Ritchie, "Terrorism," University of Oxford, Oxford, England, 2018, https://ourworldindata.org/terrorism; and Erin Miller, "Trends in Global Terrorism," START Program, University of Maryland, College Park, Maryland, October 2019, https://www.start.umd.edu/sites/default/files/publications/local _attachments/START_GTD_TerrorismIn2018_Oct2018.pdf.

24. See "U.S. Constitution," http://constitutionus.com.

25. "The Origins of the Marine Corps," 2019, https://www.military.com/military -appreciation-month/origins-of-marine-corps-day.html.

26. National Archives Catalogue, "War Department. Office of the Secretary," Washington, D.C., 2018, https://catalog.archives.gov/id/10450628.

27. United States Coast Guard Historian's Office, "U.S. Coast Guard Historic Topics," Washington, D.C., 2019, https://www.history.uscg.mil/Complete-Time-Line/Time-Line -1900-2000/.

28. Stephen Brumwell, *George Washington: Gentleman Warrior* (New York: Quercus, 2012), 421.

29. John Quincy Adams, address to the US House of Representatives, July 4, 1821, https://millercenter.org/the-presidency/presidential-speeches/july-4-1821-speech-us -house-representatives-foreign-policy.

30. Farewell Address of George Washington, 1796, http://avalon.law.yale.edu/18th _century/washing.asp.

31. Henry Adams, *The War of 1812* (New York: Cooper Square Press, 1999), 3.

32. Adam Goodheart, *1861: The Civil War Awakening* (New York: Alfred A. Knopf, 2011), 159–160.

33. Nathaniel Philbrick, *The Last Stand* (New York: Viking, 2010), 41.

34. Edward M. Coffman, *The Regulars: The American Army, 1898–1941* (Cambridge, Mass.: Harvard University Press, 2004), 3–4.

35. See Michael Beschloss, *Presidents of War: The Epic Story, from 1807 to Modern Times* (New York: Crown Books, 2018); and Robert Kagan, *Dangerous Nation: America's*

Foreign Policy from Its Earliest Days to the Dawn of the 20th Century (New York: Vintage Books, 2007).

36. Colonel Cole Kingseed, "Army Blues to Olive Drab: A Modern Fighting Force Takes the Field," in *The Army*, ed. Brigadier General Harold W. Nelson (Arlington, Va.: Army Historical Foundation, 2001), 212–213.

37. Russell F. Weigley, *The American Way of War: A History of United States Military Strategy and Policy* (Bloomington: Indiana University Press, 1973), 174–182, 223–241; Admiral James Stavridis (ret.), *Sea Power: The History and Geopolitics of the World's Oceans* (New York: Penguin, 2017), 172–175; Carl H. Builder, *The Masks of War* (Baltimore: Johns Hopkins University Press, 1989), 67–87; and Michael J. Green, *By More Than Providence: Grand Strategy and American Power in the Asia Pacific since 1783* (New York: Columbia University Press, 2017), 56–114.

38. Paul Kennedy, *The Rise and Fall of the Great Powers* (New York: Random House, 1987), 203.

39. U.S. Marine Corps, "Timeline," Washington, D.C., 2014, http://www.marines.com /history-heritage/timeline; and "U.S. Marine Corps," 2000, http://www.encyclopedia.com /topic/United_States_Marine_Corps.aspx.

40. Barry R. Posen, *Restraint: A New Foundation for U.S. Grand Strategy* (Ithaca, N.Y.: Cornell University Press, 2014), 135–175.

41. Michael D. Doubler, *I Am the Guard: A History of the Army National Guard, 1636– 2000* (Washington, D.C.: Department of the Army, 2001), 10–96.

42. Paula G. Thornhill, *Demystifying the American Military: Institutions, Evolution, and Challenges since 1789* (Annapolis, Md.: Naval Institute Press, 2019), 120; and Kingseed, "Army Blues to Olive Drab," 239.

43. See, for example, Michael E. O'Hanlon, *Healing the Wounded Giant: Maintaining Military Preeminence While Cutting the Defense Budget* (Washington, D.C.: Brookings, 2012), 11; and Office of Management and Budget, *Budget of the U.S. Government, Fiscal Year 2015: Historical Tables* (Washington, D.C.: Government Printing Office, 2014), 156.

44. See, for example, Alain C. Enthoven and K. Wayne Smith, *How Much Is Enough? Shaping the Defense Program, 1961–1969* (Santa Monica, Calif.: RAND, 2005), 1116; Builder, *The Masks of War*, 3–43; and Weigley, *American Way of War*, 167–359.

45. See, for example, Weigley, *American Way of War*; Robert P. Haffa Jr., *The Half War: Planning U.S. Rapid Deployment Forces to Meet a Limited Contingency, 1960–1983* (Boulder, Colo.: Westview Press, 1984); William W. Kaufmann, *Planning Conventional Forces, 1950–1980* (Washington, D.C.: Brookings, 1982); William P. Mako, *U.S. Ground Forces and the Defense of Central Europe* (Washington, D.C.: Brookings, 1983); Richard D. Lawrence and Jeffrey Record, *U.S. Force Structure in NATO: An Alternative* (Washington, D.C.: Brookings, 1974); and Joshua M. Epstein, *Strategy and Force Planning: The Case of the Persian Gulf* (Washington, D.C.: Brookings, 1987).

46. See, for example, Thornhill, *Demystifying the American Military*, 139–164; and David Fitzgerald, *Learning to Forget: U.S. Army Counterinsurgency Doctrine and Practice from Vietnam to Iraq* (Stanford, Calif.: Stanford University Press, 2013); on the modern U.S. Army, see also Frederick W. Kagan, *Finding the Target: The Transformation of American Military Policy* (New York: Encounter Books, 2006).

47. See, for example, Christopher Bowie, Fred Frostic, Kevin Lewis, John Lund, David Ochmanek, and Philip Propper, *The New Calculus: Analyzing Airpower's Changing Role in Joint Theater Campaigns* (Santa Monica, Calif.: RAND, 1993); Eric V. Larson, Derek Eaton, Michael E. Linick, John E. Peters, Agnes Gereben Schaefer, Keith Walters, Stephanie Young, H. G. Massey, and Michelle Darrah Ziegler, *Defense Planning in a Time of Conflict: A Comparative Analysis of the 2001–2014 Quadrennial Defense Reviews, and Implications*

for the Army (Santa Monica, Calif.: RAND, 2018); William W. Kaufmann, *Glasnost, Perestroika, and U.S. Defense Spending* (Washington, D.C.: Brookings, 1990); Richard K. Betts, *Military Readiness: Concepts, Choices, Consequences* (Washington, D.C.: Brookings, 1995); and Michael E. O'Hanlon, *Defense Strategy for the Post-Saddam Era* (Washington, D.C.: Brookings, 2005).

48. See, for example, Stavridis, *Sea Power*.

49. Office of the Under Secretary of Defense (Comptroller), "Department of Defense Budget, Fiscal Year 2020: R, D, T, and E Programs (R-1)," March 2019, ii, https://comptroller .defense.gov/Portals/45/Documents/defbudget/fy2020/fy2020_r1.pdf.

50. See, for example, Ashton B. Carter and William J. Perry, *Preventive Defense: A New Security Strategy for America* (Washington, D.C.: Brookings, 1999).

51. See James Steinberg and Michael E. O'Hanlon, *Strategic Reassurance and Resolve: U.S.-China Relations in the 21st Century* (Princeton, N.J.: Princeton University Press, 2014).

52. Secretary of Defense Jim Mattis, "Summary of the 2018 National Defense Strategy," Department of Defense, Washington, D.C., January 2018, https://dod.defense.gov /Portals/1/Documents/pubs/2018-National-Defense-Strategy-Summary.pdf.

53. See "A Conversation with the Chief of Staff of the Air Force," Brookings Institution, Washington, D.C., February 19, 2019, https://www.brookings.edu/events/a-conversation -with-the-chief-of-staff-of-the-air-force.

54. See Alexander E. M. Hess and Robert Serenbetz, "15 Biggest Employers in the World," *USA Today*, August 24, 2014, https://www.usatoday.com/story/money/business /2014/08/24/24-7-wall-st-biggest-employers/14443001; Ruth Alexander, "Which Is the World's Biggest Employer?," BBC News, March 20, 2012, https://www.bbc.com/news /magazine-17429786; "The World's 30 Biggest Employers," *LoveMoney.com*, London, September 14, 2017, https://www.lovemoney.com/gallerylist/67573/the-worlds-30-biggest -employers; and Office of the Under Secretary of Defense (Comptroller), "National Defense Budget Estimates for FY 2020," Department of Defense, Washington, D.C., May 2019, 263–265, https://comptroller.defense.gov/Portals/45/Documents/defbudget/fy2020/FY20 _Green_Book.pdf.

55. Thornhill, *Demystifying the American Military*, 25.

56. Office of the Under Secretary of Defense (Comptroller)/Chief Financial Officer, "Defense Budget Overview: Fiscal Year 2021 Budget Request," Washington, D.C., March 2019, A-1 through A-10, https://comptroller.defense.gov/Portals/45/Documents /defbudget/fy2021/fy2021_Budget_Request_Overview_Book.pdf.

57. Janet Nguyen, "The U.S. Government Is Becoming More Dependent on Contract Workers," *Marketplace*, January 17, 2019, https://www.marketplace.org/2019/01/17/rise -federal-contractors; Moshe Schwartz, John F. Sargent Jr., and Christopher T. Mann, "Defense Acquisitions: How and Where DoD Spends Its Contracting Dollars," Congressional Research Service, Washington, D.C., July 2, 2018, https://fas.org/sgp/crs/natsec /R44010.pdf; and Russell Rumbaugh and Heidi M. Peters, "Defense Primer: DoD Contractors," Congressional Research Service, Washington, D.C., February 10, 2017, https:// fas.org/sgp/crs/natsec/IF10600.pdf.

58. See Charles A. Stevenson, *Secdef: The Nearly Impossible Job of Secretary of Defense* (Washington, D.C.: Potomac Books, 2007), 8–10.

59. Department of Defense, "DoD Organizational Structure," Washington, D.C., 2018, https://virginiaptap.org/wp-content/uploads/2018/03/DoD-Face-Chart-20180222 .pdf.

60. The NSC's core membership includes the president, vice president, secretary of state, secretary of defense, secretary of the Treasury, and national security adviser. See Executive Office of the President, "National Security Council," Washington, D.C., 2019, https://www.whitehouse.gov/nsc.

61. Joint Chiefs of Staff, "About the Joint Chiefs of Staff," Department of Defense, Washington, D.C., 2019, https://www.jcs.mil/About.

62. Thornhill, *Demystifying the American Military*, 27.

63. See, for example, Peter R. Mansoor, *Surge: My Journey with General David Petraeus and the Remaking of the Iraq War* (New Haven, Conn.: Yale University Press, 2013), 40–54; Bob Woodward, *Obama's Wars* (New York: Simon and Schuster, 2010), 234–240; Martin S. Indyk, Kenneth G. Lieberthal, and Michael E. O'Hanlon, *Bending History: Barack Obama's Foreign Policy* (Washington, D.C.: Brookings, 2012), 86–89; and Kurt M. Campbell and Michael E. O'Hanlon, *Hard Power: The New Politics of National Security* (New York: Basic Books, 2006), 52–57.

64. For good discussions of this subject, see Kori Schake and Jim Mattis, "A Great Divergence?," in *Warriors and Citizens: American Views of Our Military*, ed. Kori Schake and Jim Mattis (Stanford, Calif.: Hoover Institution Press, 2016), 9; Schake and Mattis, "Ensuring a Civil-Military Connection," in Schake and Mattis, *Warriors and Citizens*, 313–317; and James Fallows, "The Tragedy of the American Military," *The Atlantic*, January/February 2015, https://www.theatlantic.com/magazine/archive/2015/01/the-tragedy-of-the-american-military/383516/.

65. For more on this age-old debate, including views different from mine, see, for example, Samuel P. Huntington, *The Soldier and the State: The Theory and Politics of Civil-Military Relations* (Cambridge, Mass.: Harvard University Press, 1957); Morris Janowitz, *The Professional Soldier: A Social and Political Portrait* (New York: Free Press, 1960); and Samuel E. Finer, *The Man on Horseback: The Role of the Military in Politics* (London: Pall Mall Press, 1962).

66. See, for example, retired chairman of the Joint Chiefs of Staff Martin Dempsey, "Letter to the Editor: Military Leaders Do Not Belong at Political Conventions," *Washington Post*, July 30, 2016, https://www.washingtonpost.com/opinions/military-leaders-do-not-belong-at-political-conventions/2016/07/30/0e06fc16-568b-11e6-b652-315ae5d4d4dd_story.html.

67. William J. Lynn, "The Wars Within: The Joint Military Structure and Its Critics," in *Reorganizing America's Defense: Leadership in War and Peace*, ed. Robert J. Art, Vincent Davis, and Samuel P. Huntington (McLean, Va.: Pergamon-Brassey's, 1985), 168–204.

68. John Hamre, "Reflections: Looking Back at the Need for Goldwater-Nichols," Defense360 blog, Center for Strategic and International Studies, Washington, D.C., January 27, 2016, https://defense360.csis.org/goldwater-nichols-2016.

69. See US Department of Defense, "Chairman of the Joint Chiefs of Staff Marine Corps General Joseph F. Dunford, Jr.," Washington, D.C., 2019, https://www.defense.gov/our-story/meet-the-team/chairman-of-the-joint-chiefs-of-staff; and U.S. Code, Title 10 Section 151, http://uscode.house.gov/view.xhtml?req=granuleid:USC-prelim-title10-section151&num=0&edition=prelim.

70. "10 U.S. Code, Section 152—Chairman: Appointment, Grade and Rank," Legal Information Institute, Cornell Law School, Ithaca, N.Y., 2016, https://www.law.cornell.edu/uscode/text/10/152.

71. Bob Woodward, *The War Within: A Secret White House History, 2006–2008* (New York: Simon and Schuster, 2008), 363–364.

72. Greg Jaffe, Missy Ryan, and Josh Dawsey, "Trump Expected to Tap Army Chief as Next Chairman of the Joint Chiefs," *Washington Post*, December 7, 2018, https://www.washingtonpost.com/world/national-security/trump-expected-to-tap-army-chief-as-next-chairman-of-the-joint-chiefs/2018/12/07/dba7e8ea-fa3c-11e8-8c9a-860ce2a8148f_story.html?utm_term=.adf203f0c98b.

73. Department of Defense, "U.S. Department of Defense," Washington, D.C., 2019, https://archive.defense.gov/about.

74. For reflections on these commands and their global coverage, see Thomas P. M. Barnett, *The Pentagon's New Map: War and Peace in the Twenty-First Century* (New York: G. P. Putnam's, 2004).

75. Department of Defense, "Know Your Military: Combatant Commands," Washington, D.C., 2018, https://www.defense.gov/Know-Your-Military/Combatant-Commands.

76. Congressional Budget Office, "Costs of a Space Force," US Congress, Washington, D.C., 2019, www.cbo.gov; U.S. European Command, "About: Organization," Stuttgart, Germany, 2019, https://www.eucom.mil/about/organization; and U.S. Africa Command, "About the Command," Stuttgart, Germany, 2019, https://www.africom.mil/about-the -command.

77. See, for example, Dana Priest, *The Mission: Waging War and Keeping Peace with America's Military* (New York: W. W. Norton, 2003).

78. Department of Defense, "U.S. Cyber Command History," Washington, D.C., 2019, https://www.cybercom.mil/About/History; and Susan L. Marquis, *Unconventional Warfare: Rebuilding U.S. Special Operations Forces* (Washington, D.C.: Brookings, 1997).

79. See, for example, Andrew Feickert, "U.S. Special Operations Forces: Background and Issues for Congress," Congressional Research Service, Washington, D.C., October 2018, 1–2, https://fas.org/sgp/crs/natsec/RS21048.pdf.

80. Congressional Research Service, "General and Flag Officers in the U.S. Armed Forces: Background and Considerations for Congress," Washington, D.C., February 2019, https://fas.org/sgp/crs/natsec/R44389.pdf.

81. See Jeff Schogol, "Every Marine a Rifleman No More?," *Marine Corps Times*, May 7, 2017, https://www.marinecorpstimes.com/news/your-marine-corps/2017/05/07 /every-marine-a-rifleman-no-more.

82. Lee Hudson and Jen DiMascio, "Can the U.S. Air Force Add 74 Squadrons?," *Aviation Week and Space Technology*, October 1–14, 2018.

83. U.S. Air Force, "U.S. Air Force," Washington, D.C., 2019, https://www.af.mil/AF -Sites.

84. U.S. Marine Corps, "Organization of the United States Marine Corps," Department of the Navy, Washington, D.C., chap. 5, 5, https://www.marines.mil/Portals/59/Publications /MCRP%205-12D.pdf; 7th Air Force, "7th Air Force," Osan Air Force Base, Republic of Korea, 2019, https://www.7af.pacaf.af.mil/About-Us; U.S. Army, "Official Directory of Army Websites," Washington, D.C., 2019, https://www.army.mil/info/a-z; and Sam La-Grone, "U.S. 2nd Fleet Declares Operational Capability Ahead of Major European Exercise," *U.S. Naval Institute News*, May 29, 2019, https://news.usni.org/2019/05/29/u-s-2nd -fleet-declares-operational-capability-ahead-of-major-european-exercise.

85. U.S. Army, "Organization: Who We Are," Washington, D.C., 2019, https://www .army.mil/info/organization.

86. See, for example, U.S. Air Force, "U.S. Air Force."

87. Office of the Director of National Intelligence, "U.S. Intelligence Community Budget," Washington, D.C., 2019, https://www.dni.gov/index.php/what-we-do/ic-budget; and Office of the Director of National Intelligence, "Members of the IC," Washington, D.C., 2019, https://www.dni.gov/index.php/what-we-do/members-of-the-ic.

88. For an excellent book about the standards, values, and culture of the modern American military, see, for example, Thomas E. Ricks, *Making the Corps* (New York: Simon and Schuster, 1997).

89. Kim Parker, Anthony Cilluffo, and Renee Stepler, "6 Facts about the U.S. Military and Its Changing Demographics," Pew Research Center, Washington, D.C., April 2017, http://www.pewresearch.org/fact-tank/2017/04/13/6-facts-about-the-u-s-military-and -its-changing-demographics; and Shanea Watkins and James Sherk, "Who Serves in the U.S. Military? The Demographics of Enlisted Troops and Officers," Heritage Foundation,

Washington, D.C., August 2008, https://www.heritage.org/defense/report/who-serves-the-us-military-the-demographics-enlisted-troops-and-officers.

90. Richard L. Fernandez, "The Warrant Officer Ranks: Adding Flexibility to Military Personnel Management," Washington, D.C., Congressional Budget Office, 2002, 8, https://www.cbo.gov/sites/default/files/cbofiles/ftpdocs/32xx/doc3287/warrantofficer.pdf.

91. See, for example, U.S. Marine Corps, "MCINCR—Marine Corps Base Quantico," Washington, D.C., 2019, https://www.quantico.marines.mil/About/Mission-and-Vision.

92. Kristy N. Kamarck, "Goldwater-Nichols and the Evolution of Officer Joint Professional Military Education (JPME)," Congressional Research Service, Washington, D.C., January 2016, https://fas.org/sgp/crs/natsec/R44340.pdf.

93. See U.S. Army and U.S. Marine Corps, *Counterinsurgency Field Manual* (Chicago: University of Chicago Press, 2007).

94. Judith Hicks Stiehm, *The U.S. Military: A Basic Introduction* (New York: Routledge, 2012), 26–29.

95. Stiehm, 26–29.

96. See Michael E. O'Hanlon, *The Future of Land Warfare* (Washington, D.C.: Brookings, 2015), 196, taken from Department of the Army, "America's Army: The Strength of the Nation," Washington, D.C., November 2014.

97. Stiehm, *The U.S. Military*, 38–39; and William M. Arkin, Joshua M. Handler, Julia A. Morrissey, and Jacquelyn M. Walsh, *Encyclopedia of the U.S. Military* (New York: Ballinger, 1990), 775–838.

98. Leo Shane III, "Congress Is Giving the Officer Promotion System a Massive Overhaul," *Militarytimes.com*, July 25, 2018, https://www.militarytimes.com/news/your-military/2018/07/25/how-officers-are-promoted-will-get-its-biggest-overhaul-in-decades-heres-what-that-means-for-the-military.

99. See Commission on Military Compensation and Retirement Modernization, "Final Report," Washington, D.C., 2015, 1–21, https://apps.dtic.mil/dtic/tr/fulltext/u2/a625626.pdf; and Department of Defense, "Military Compensation," Washington, D.C., 2019, https://militarypay.defense.gov/Pay/Retirement; and Mike Meese and Military.com, "Upcoming Changes to Military Retirement System Explained," *Military.com*, 2019, https://www.military.com/benefits/military-pay/upcoming-changes-to-military-retirement-system-explained.html.

100. Eleventh Quadrennial Review of Military Compensation, "Final Report," Washington, D.C., June 2012, xv–xvii, https://militarypay.defense.gov/Portals/3/Documents/Reports/11th_QRMC_Main_Report_FINAL.pdf; and Brendan Stickles, "How the U.S. Military Became the Exception to America's Wage Stagnation Problem," Brookings Institution, Washington, D.C., November 29, 2018, https://www.brookings.edu/blog/order-from-chaos/2018/11/29/how-the-u-s-military-became-the-exception-to-americas-wage-stagnation-problem.

101. Todd Sandler and Keith Hartley, *The Economics of Defense* (Cambridge: Cambridge University Press, 1995), 167.

102. M. B. Pell and Joshua Schneyer, "Military Survey Finds Deep Dissatisfaction with Family Housing on U.S. Bases," Reuters, February 13, 2019, https://www.reuters.com/article/us-usa-military-survey/military-survey-finds-deep-dissatisfaction-with-family-housing-on-u-s-bases-idUSKCN1Q21GR.

103. Blue Star Families, "Military Family Lifestyle Survey, 2018," Encinitas, Calif., February 2019, 15, https://bluestarfam.org/wp-content/uploads/2019/02/2018MFLS-ComprehensiveReport-DIGITAL-FINAL.pdf; and comments of Holly Petraeus, at a panel discussion entitled "What Is the Impact of Persistent Military Spouse Unemployment?," Brookings Institution, Washington, D.C., October 21, 2019, https://www.brookings.edu/events/what-is-the-impact-of-persistent-military-spouse-unemployment.

104. See Amy Ebitz, "Why Would a Woman Want to Be a U.S. Marine?," Brookings Institution, Washington, D.C., February 28, 2019, https://www.brookings.edu/blog/order-from-chaos/2019/02/28/why-would-a-woman-want-to-be-a-u-s-marine.

105. Harvey M. Sapolsky, Eugene Gholz, and Caitlin Talmadge, *U.S. Defense Politics: The Origins of Security Policy*, 3rd ed. (New York: Routledge, 2017), 84.

106. America's Promise Alliance, "U.S. Military Demographics," Washington, D.C., 2019, https://www.americaspromise.org/us-military-demographics.

107. Kenneth W. Kizer and Suzanne Le Menestrel, eds., *Strengthening the Military Family Readiness System for a Changing American Society* (Washington, D.C.: National Academies Press, 2019), S-4 through S-5, https://www.nap.edu/catalog/25380/strengthening-the-military-family-readiness-system-for-a-changing-american-society.

108. George M. Reynolds and Amanda Shendruk, "Demographics of the U.S. Military," Council on Foreign Relations, New York, April 24, 2018, https://www.cfr.org/article/demographics-us-military.

109. Jim Golby, Lindsay P. Cohn, and Peter D. Feaver, "Thanks for Your Service: Civilian and Veteran Attitudes after Fifteen Years of War," in *Warriors and Citizens: American Views of Our Military*, ed. Kori Schake and Jim Mattis (Stanford, Calif.: Hoover Institution Press, 2016), 109–113; and Leo Shane III, "Troops See Rising Political Tension in the Ranks, Poll Shows," *Militarytimes.com*, October 17, 2018, https://www.militarytimes.com/news/pentagon-congress/2018/10/17/troops-see-rising-political-tension-in-the-ranks-poll-shows.

110. See, for example, Remarks of Under Secretary of the Army Ryan McCarthy at the Brookings Institution, Washington, D.C., March 14, 2018, www.brookings.edu.

111. Courtney Dock, "Military Families Are a Key to the Overall Readiness of the Force," *Militarytimes.com*, October 10, 2018, https://www.army.mil/article/212249/military_families_are_a_key_to_the_overall_readiness_of_the_force; Charlsy Panzino, "'Warrior Caste': Is a Public Disconnect Hurting Military Recruiting Efforts?," *Militarytimes.com*, January 18, 2018, https://www.militarytimes.com/news/your-army/2018/01/19/warrior-caste-is-a-public-disconnect-hurting-military-recruiting-efforts; and Kathy Roth-Douquet and Frank Schaeffer, *AWOL: The Unexcused Absence of America's Upper Classes from Military Service—and How It Hurts Our Country* (New York: HarperCollins, 2006).

112. General Stanley A. McChrystal (ret.) and Michael E. O'Hanlon, "How a Focus on National Service Can Unify Our Divided Country," *The Hill*, March 2, 2019, https://www.brookings.edu/blog/order-from-chaos/2019/03/05/how-a-focus-on-national-service-can-unify-our-divided-country.

113. Amy Bushatz, "Troop Divorce Rate Unchanged; Marriage Rate Continues to Fall," *Military.com*, March 21, 2018, https://www.google.com/amp/s/www.military.com/daily-news/2018/03/21/troop-divorce-rate-unchanged-marriage-rate-continues-fall.html/amp.

114. Center for Deployment Psychology, "Suicide in the Military," Uniformed Services University of the Health Sciences, Bethesda, Md., 2018, https://deploymentpsych.org/disorders/suicide-main; "Shocking Military Suicide Rates and Identifying the Signs," *U.S. Veterans Magazine*, September 2017, https://www.usveteransmagazine.com/2017/09/shocking-military-suicide-rates-identifying-signs; and "VA Suicide Prevention Program: Facts about Veteran Suicide," Department of Veterans Affairs, Washington, D.C., July 2016, https://www.va.gov/opa/publications/factsheets/Suicide_Prevention_FactSheet_New_VA_Stats_070616_1400.pdf.

115. Dave Philipps, "This Is Unacceptable: Military Reports a Surge of Sexual Assaults in the Ranks," *New York Times*, May 2, 2019, https://www.nytimes.com/2019/05/02/us/military-sexual-assault.html.

116. Gallup, "Military and National Defense," Washington, D.C., 2019, https://news.gallup.com/poll/1666/military-national-defense.aspx.

117. See, for example, Stephen G. Brooks and William C. Wohlforth, *America Abroad: Why the Sole Superpower Should Not Pull Back from the World* (Oxford: Oxford University Press, 2016); on the history of the base network, see Robert E. Harkavy, *Bases Abroad: The Global Foreign Military Presence* (Oxford: Oxford University Press, 1989).

118. Department of Defense, "Base Structure Report—Fiscal Year 2018 Baseline," Washington, D.C., 2018, 1–20, https://www.acq.osd.mil/eie/Downloads/BSI/Base%20Structure%20Report%20FY18.pdf.

119. Office of the Under Secretary of Defense (Comptroller), "National Defense Budget Estimates for Fiscal Year 2020" ("Green Book"), Department of Defense, Washington, D.C., May 2019, https://comptroller.defense.gov/Portals/45/Documents/defbudget/fy2020/FY20_Green_Book.pdf.

120. Office of Economic Adjustment, "Defense Spending by State, Fiscal Year 2017," Department of Defense, Washington, D.C., March 2019, http://oea.gov/dsbs-fy2017.

121. R. William Thomas, G. Wayne Glass, Barbara Hollinshead, and Christopher Williams, "The Economic Effects of Reduced Defense Spending," Congressional Budget Office, Washington, D.C., February 1992, 33–41, https://www.cbo.gov/sites/default/files/102nd-congress-1991-1992/reports/1992_02_theeconomiceffectsofreduceddefence.pdf.

122. Department of Defense, "Department of Defense Infrastructure Capacity," Washington, D.C., October 2017, https://fas.org/man/eprint/infrastructure.pdf; Government Accountability Office, Letter, "Military Base Realignments and Closures: Updated Costs and Savings Estimates from BRAC 2005," Washington, D.C., June 2012, https://www.gao.gov/assets/600/592076.pdf; Department of Defense, "DoD Base Realignment and Closure: FY 2018 Budget Estimates," Washington, D.C., May 2017, https://comptroller.defense.gov/Portals/45/Documents/defbudget/FY2018/budget_justification/pdfs/05_BRAC/FINAL_FY18_BRAC_Summary_Book.pdf; and Government Accountability Office, "Military Bases: Analysis of DoD's 2005 Selection Process and Recommendations for Base Closures and Realignments," Washington, D.C., July 2005, https://www.gao.gov/new.items/d05785.pdf.

123. Department of Defense, "Base Structure Report—Fiscal Year 2018 Baseline," 7–18.

124. See Department of Defense, "Military and Civilian Personnel by Service/Agency by State/Country," Washington, D.C., December 2018, https://www.dmdc.osd.mil/appj/dwp/dwp_reports.jsp.

125. Department of Defense, "Military and Civilian Personnel by Service/Agency by State/Country"; Michael E. O'Hanlon, *The Science of War* (Princeton, N.J.: Princeton University Press, 2009).

126. See Paul Kennedy, *Engineers of Victory: The Problem Solvers Who Turned the Tide in the Second World War* (New York: Random House, 2013).

127. Department of Defense, *Conduct of the Persian Gulf War: Final Report to Congress* (Washington, D.C.: Department of Defense, April 1992), F-1, F-2, F-26.

128. Thomas A. Keaney and Eliot A. Cohen, *Gulf War Air Power Survey Summary Report* (Washington, D.C.: Government Printing Office, 1993), 210.

129. Frances M. Lussier, *Replacing and Repairing Equipment Used in Iraq and Afghanistan: The Army's Reset Program* (Washington, D.C.: Congressional Budget Office, September 2007), 1–5.

130. Ochmanek, et. al., *To Find, and Not to Yield* (Santa Monica, Calif.; RAND, 1998), 27; Bowie et al., *The New Calculus*, 30–33; Keaney and Cohen, *Gulf War Air Power Survey Summary Report*, 210–213; and Christopher J. Bowie, *The Anti-access Threat and*

Theater Air Bases (Washington, D.C.: Center for Strategic and Budgetary Assessments, 2002), 15–16.

131. Government Accountability Office, "Prepositioned Stocks: DoD Needs Joint Oversight of the Military Services' Programs," Washington, D.C., January 2019, https://www.gao.gov/assets/700/696707.pdf; U.S. Marine Corps, "Maritime Pre-positioning Force," *Marines.com*, Washington, D.C., 2019, https://www.candp.marines.mil/Organization/MAG TF/Maritime-Pre-Positioning-Force-MPF; and Association of the U.S. Army, "Army Prepositioned Stocks: Indispensable to America's Global Force Projection Capability," AUSA, Washington, D.C., December 2008, https://www.ausa.org/sites/default/files/TBIP-2008 -Army-Prepositioned-Stocks-Indispensable-to-Americas-Global-Force-Projection -Capability.pdf.

132. General David Berger, "Commandant's Planning Guidance," U.S. Marine Corps, Washington, D.C., July 2019, 5, https://www.hqmc.marines.mil/Portals/142/Docs/%20 38th%20Commandant%27s%20Planning%20Guidance_2019.pdf?ver=2019-07-16 -200152-700.

133. See David Arthur, *Options for Strategic Military Transportation Systems* (Washington, D.C.: Congressional Budget Office, September 2005), 8, 14; Rachel Schmidt, *Moving U.S. Forces: Options for Strategic Mobility* (Washington, D.C.: Congressional Budget Office, February 1997), 13; Federation of American Scientists, "C-141B Starlifter," Washington, D.C., 1999, www.fas.org/man/dod-101/sys/ac/c-141.htm (accessed February 19, 2008); U.S. Air Force, "Fact Sheet: C-17 Globemaster III," Washington, D.C., May 2014, https://www.af.mil/About-Us/Fact-Sheets/Display/Article/1529726/c-17-globemaster-iii/; U.S. Air Force, "Fact Sheet: KC-10 Extender," Washington, D.C., May 2014, https://www.af .mil/About-Us/Fact-Sheets/Display/Article/104520/kc-10-extender; U.S. Air Force, "Fact Sheet: C-5 Galaxy," Washington, D.C., February 2018, https://www.af.mil/About-Us/Fact -Sheets/Display/Article/104492/c-5-abc-galaxy-c-5m-super-galaxy; and "Boeing 747 Long-Range Jetliner," February 2008, www.aerospaceweb.org/aircraft/jetliner/b747/ (accessed February 19, 2008). Maximum takeoff weights (and maximum cargo capacities) are roughly 290 tons (and 85 tons) for the C-17, 295 tons (and 85 tons) for the KC-10, and 420 tons for the C-5 (about 140 tons). The most recent fuel burn rates I have found are 7 tons/hour for the C-17, 8.6 tons/hour for the KC-10, and 10.3 tons/hour for the C-5. Unrefueled ranges are 2,750 miles for the C-17 (with 82-ton payload), 4,400 miles for the KC-10 (85-ton payload), and 5,500 miles for the C-5 (60-ton payload).

134. Robert W. Button, John Gordon IV, Jessie Riposo, Irv Blickstein, and Peter A. Wilson, *Warfighting and Logistic Support of Joint Forces from the Joint Sea Base* (Santa Monica, Calif.: RAND, 2007), 99–101; and Colonel Timothy M. Laur and Steven L. Llanso, *Encyclopedia of Modern U.S. Military Weapons* (New York: Berkley Books, 1995), 116–120, 150.

135. U.S. Air Force, "Air Force Fact Sheet: C-130 Hercules," May 2006, www.af.mil /factsheets/factsheet.asp?id=92 (accessed December 14, 2007); and conversation with Lt. Col. William Knight, U.S. Air Force (and Congressional Research Service fellow, 2007–2008), January 2, 2008. The C-130H's weight when empty is 85,000 pounds; its maximum takeoff weight is 155,000 pounds; its maximum fuel loading is 60,000 pounds

136. Arthur, *Options for Strategic Military Transportation Systems*, 5, 8, 14.

137. Schmidt, *Moving U.S. Forces*, 80.

138. This estimated capacity for sustained delivery from airlift and sealift together is not to be confused with a metric commonly used for airlift in particular, million ton miles per day (MTM/D). The United States presently has nearly 60 MTM/D of airlift capacity—defined as the sum of all airlifters' payload, times their average speed, times their average number of sustainable hours of flight per day, all divided by 2 to account for the

fact that the planes must fly back empty (more or less) to load up again for another trip. See Arthur, *Options for Strategic Military Transportation Systems*, 8–9. See also U.S. Air Force, "Fact Sheet: KC-10 Extender"; U.S. Air Force, "Fact Sheet: C-5"; and U.S. Air Force, "Fact Sheet: C-17 Globemaster III."

139. Schmidt, *Moving U.S. Forces*, 48–54, 80–81; and Department of Defense, *Conduct of the Persian Gulf War: Final Report to Congress* (Washington, D.C.: Department of Defense, April 1992), F-26.

140. Schmidt, *Moving U.S. Forces*, 48.

141. Arthur, *Options for Strategic Military Transportation Systems*, x, xii, 3, 5.

1. DEFENSE BUDGETING AND RESOURCE ALLOCATION

1. Office of Management and Budget, *Historical Tables: Budget of the U.S. Government, Fiscal Year 2009* (Washington, D.C.: Government Printing Office, 2008), 137.

2. Taking the budget years 1951–1990 as the duration of the Cold War, I used table 6–11 in the Comptroller's "Green Book" cited later to calculate the average (in 2020 dollars) of discretionary and mandatory outlays for the Department of Defense. The result was just under $500 billion ($497 billion, to be precise). Adding in Department of Energy nuclear weapons costs and a few other small expenses yields the ballpark figure of $525 billion, for overall national defense outlays, defined formally as the 050 account. See Office of Management and Budget, *Historical Tables: Fiscal Year 2020*, https://www .whitehouse.gov/omb/historical-tables, 123–130; and Office of the Under Secretary of Defense (Comptroller), *Defense Budget Estimates for FY 2020* (Washington, D.C.: April 2019), 100–160, 250–255, https://comptroller.defense.gov/Portals/45/Documents/defbudget/fy2020 /FY20_Green_Book.pdf.

3. Elbridge Colby, "How to Win America's Next War," *Foreign Policy*, May 5, 2019, https://foreignpolicy.com/2019/05/05/how-to-win-americas-next-war-china-russia -military-infrastructure/.

4. Office of Management and Budget, "Budget of the United States Government, Fiscal Year 2020," February 2019, 111–115, https://www.whitehouse.gov/wp-content/uploads /2019/03/budget-fy2020.pdf; Federal Reserve Bank of St. Louis, "State and Local Government Current Expenditures," April 2019, https://fred.stlouisfed.org/series/SLEXPND; and Under Secretary of Defense (Comptroller), *National Defense Budget Estimates for FY 2020*, 268, https://comptroller.defense.gov/Portals/45/Documents/defbudget/fy2020/FY20 _Green_Book.pdf; Raymond Hall, David Mosher, and Michael O'Hanlon, *The START Treaty and Beyond* (Washington, D.C.: Congressional Budget Office, 1991).

5. To be more specific, about 90 percent of outlays for personnel take place in the first year and almost all the remainder in the second. About 45 percent of outlays for O&M take place in the first year (averaging across the services, and excluding costs for pay and fuel). Almost 40 percent occur in year two, about 10 percent in year three, and small amounts in years four and five. Procurement dollars are spent more slowly—only about 5 to 20 percent in year one, 25 to 35 percent in year two, 20 to 30 percent in year three, 10 to 20 percent in year four, and smaller amounts in the next three to four years. For RDT&E, the figures are roughly 30 to 50 percent in year one, 40 to 50 percent in year two, 10 to 15 percent in year three, and small amounts thereafter. See Under Secretary of Defense (Comptroller), *National Defense Budget Estimates for FY 2009* (Washington, D.C.: Department of Defense, March 2007), 54–55; and Under Secretary of Defense (Comptroller), *National Defense Budget Estimates for FY 2020*, 70–72.

6. See, for example, Committee for a Responsible Federal Budget, "Better Budget Process Initiative," Washington, D.C., 2019, https://www.crfb.org/project/better-budget-process -initiative.

7. Congressional Budget Office, "Frequently Asked Questions," Washington, D.C., 2019, https://www.cbo.gov/faqs.

8. Keith Hall, "The Role of the Legislature in the U.S. Budget Process," Congressional Budget Office, June 2018, https://www.cbo.gov/publication/54133; Congressional Budget Office, "History," Washington, D.C., 2019, https://www.cbo.gov/about/history; Allen Schick, *The Federal Budget: Politics, Policy, Process*, 3rd ed, (Washington, D.C.: Brookings, 2007), 14–27; Philip G. Joyce, *The Congressional Budget Office: Honest Numbers, Power, and Policymaking* (Washington, D.C.: Georgetown University Press, 2011); USA.GOV, "Budget of the U.S. Government," Washington, D.C., October 2019, https://www.usa.gov/budget.;

9. Harvey M. Sapolsky, Eugene Gholz, and Caitlin Talmadge, *U.S. Defense Politics: The Origins of Security Policy*, 3rd ed. (New York: Routledge, 2017), 61.

10. Office of the Under Secretary of Defense, "Assistant Secretary of Defense for Strategy, Plans, and Capabilities," Department of Defense, Washington, D.C., 2019, https://policy.defense.gov/OUSDP-Offices/ASD-for-Strategy-Plans-and-Capabilities; and Shawn Brimley, "Getting the Pentagon's Next National Defense Strategy Right," *War on the Rocks*, May 24, 2017, https://warontherocks.com/2017/05/getting-the-pentagons-next-national-defense-strategy-right.

11. M. Thomas Davis, *Managing Defense after the Cold War* (Washington, D.C.: Center for Strategic and Budgetary Assessments, 1997), 1–3.

12. Office of Management and Budget, "Budget of the United States Government, Fiscal Year 2020: Historical Tables," Washington, D.C., March 2019, 96, 121, 136–137, https://www.govinfo.gov/content/pkg/BUDGET-2020-TAB/pdf/BUDGET-2020-TAB.pdf; and Office of the Under Secretary of Defense (Comptroller), "2021 Defense Budget Overview," Washington, D.C., February 2020, A-1 through A-10, https://comptroller.defense.gov/Portals/45/Documents/defbudget/fy2021/fy2021_Budget_Request_Overview_Book.pdf; and President Donald J. Trump, "A Budget for America's Future: Fiscal Year 2021," Washington, D.C., February 2020, 109–128, https://www.whitehouse.gov/wp-content/uploads/2020/02/budget_fy21.pdf.

13. Office of Management and Budget, "Budget of the United States Government, Fiscal Year 2021: Historical Tables," Washington, D.C., February 2020, 88–121, https://www.whitehouse.gov/wp-content/uploads/2020/02/hist_fy21.pdf.

14. Sapolsky, Gholz, and Talmadge, *U.S. Defense Politics*, 120.

15. U.S. Senate Historical Office, "Official Declarations of War by Congress," U.S. Senate, Washington, D.C., 2019, https://www.senate.gov/pagelayout/history/h_multi_sections_and_teasers/WarDeclarationsbyCongress.htm;

16. Jennifer K. Elsea and Matthew C. Weed, "Declarations of War and Authorizations for the Use of Military Force: Historical Background and Legal Implications," Congressional Research Service, April 2014, https://fas.org/sgp/crs/natsec/RL31133.pdf.

17. Jonathan Masters, "U.S. Foreign Policy Powers: Congress and the President," Council on Foreign Relations, March 2017, https://www.cfr.org/backgrounder/us-foreign-policy-powers-congress-and-president; Council on Foreign Relations, "Backgrounder: Balance of U.S. War Powers," New York, 2013, https://www.cfr.org/backgrounder/balance-us-war-powers; and Micah Zenko, *Between Threats and War: U.S. Discrete Military Operations in the Post–Cold-War World* (Stanford, Calif.: Stanford University Press, 2010), 163.

18. Office of the Under Secretary of Defense (Comptroller)/CFO, "Fiscal Year 2020 Budget Request: Briefing Slides," U.S. Department of Defense, March 2019, https://comptroller.defense.gov/Portals/45/Documents/defbudget/fy2020/fy2020_Budget_Request.pdf; and Congressional Budget Office, "Funding for Overseas Contingency Operations and Its Impact on Defense Spending," Washington, D.C., October 2018, 16, https://www.cbo.gov/system/files?file=2018-10/54219-oco_spending.pdf.

19. Office of the Under Secretary of Defense (Comptroller), "2021 Defense Budget Overview," A-1 through A-10; and Trump, "A Budget for America's Future."

20. Schick, *Federal Budget*, 258.

21. Under Secretary of Defense (Comptroller)/Chief Financial Officer, "Defense Budget Overview: United States Department of Defense Fiscal Year 2020 Budget Request," Washington, D.C., March 2019, A-5, https://comptroller.defense.gov/Portals/45 /Documents/defbudget/fy2020/fy2020_Budget_Request_Overview_Book.pdf.

22. William G. Gale, *Fiscal Therapy: Curing America's Debt Addiction and Investing in the Future* (New York: Oxford University Press, 2019), 47–48.

23. Congressional Budget Office, "Funding for Overseas Contingency Operations and Its Impact on Defense Spending," 8.

24. Richard Spencer, "The Navy in an Era of Great Power Competition," discussion at Brookings Institution, Washington, D.C., October 23, 2019, https://www.brookings .edu/events/the-navy-in-an-era-of-great-power-competition/.

25. Office of the Under Secretary of Defense (Comptroller), "Department of Defense Budget, Fiscal Year 2020: R,D,T, and E Programs (R-1)," March 2019, iii, https://comptroller .defense.gov/Portals/45/Documents/defbudget/fy2020/fy2020_r1.pdf.

26. Hall, Mosher, and O'Hanlon, *The START Treaty and Beyond*, 62, 135; and Stephen I. Schwartz, ed., *Atomic Audit: The Costs and Consequences of U.S. Nuclear Weapons since 1940* (Washington, D.C.: Brookings, 1998), 3.

27. See Office of the Under Secretary of Defense (Comptroller)/Financial Management, "Operation and Maintenance Overview, Budget Estimates, Fiscal Year 2019," Department of Defense, Washington, D.C., 2018, 418, https://comptroller.defense.gov /Portals/45/Documents/defbudget/fy2019/fy2019_OM_Overview.pdf.

28. Office of Economic Conversion, Department of Defense, "Defense Spending by State, Fiscal Year 2018," Department of Defense, Washington, D.C., 2019, 16, https://www .oea.gov/sites/default/files/defense-spending-rpts/FY2018-Defense-Spending-by-State -Report_0_0.pdf.

29. Sapolsky, Gholz, and Talmadge, *U.S. Defense Politics*, 140–157.

30. Moshe Schwartz, "Defense Acquisitions: How DoD Acquires Weapon Systems and Recent Efforts to Reform the Process," Congressional Research Service, May 23, 2014, https://fas.org/sgp/crs/natsec/RL34026.pdf.

31. Schwartz, "Defense Acquisitions."

32. Office of Economic Conversion, Department of Defense, "Defense Spending by State, Fiscal Year 2018," 16; and Department of Energy, "National Laboratories," Washington, D.C., 2020, https://www.energy.gov/national-laboratories.

33. Office of the Under Secretary of Defense (Comptroller)/Chief Financial Officer, "Defense Budget Overview," 4-3, https://comptroller.defense.gov/Portals/45/Documents /defbudget/fy2020/fy2020_Budget_Request_Overview_Book.pdf.

34. Stephen Daggett, "Costs of Major U.S. Wars," Congressional Research Service, Washington, D.C., 2010, https://fas.org/sgp/crs/natsec/RS22926.pdf.

35. It may be of interest that prior to Desert Storm, CBO estimated that war costs could be roughly $55 billion to $170 billion, as expressed in 2020 dollars. Actual costs were, as noted, about $115 billion in 2020 dollars, with just under 90 percent paid by friends and allies. Congressional Budget Office, "Costs of Operation Desert Shield," CBO Staff Memorandum, Congressional Budget Office, Washington, D.C., January 1991, 120; and Department of Defense, *Conduct of the Persian Gulf War: Final Report to Congress* (Washington, D.C.: Department of Defense, 1992), P-2.

36. Steven M. Kosiak, "The Global War on Terror (GWOT): Costs, Cost Growth and Estimating Funding Requirements," Testimony, Senate Budget Committee, Washington, D.C., February 6, 2007, www.csbaonline.org.

37. Amy Belasco, "The Cost of Iraq, Afghanistan, and Other Global War on Terror Operations Since 2001," Congressional Research Service, Washington, D.C., 2014, 6, https://fas.org/sgp/crs/natsec/RL33110.pdf; and Congressional Budget Office, "Funding for Overseas Contingency Operations and Its Impact on Defense Spending."

38. Watson Institute, "Costs of Wars," Brown University, November 2018, https://watson.brown.edu/costsofwar/figures/2018/budgetary-costs-post-911-wars-through -fy2019-59-trillion; and Department of Defense, "Casualty Status," Washington, D.C., May 2019, https://dod.defense.gov/News/Casualty-Status.

39. Kosiak, "The Global War on Terror," 3–6.

40. Elise Castelli, "Study: Intel Contract Employees Costly," *Defense News*, September 1, 2008, 24.

41. Matthew Goldberg, *Logistics Support for Deployed Military Forces* (Washington, D.C.: Congressional Budget Office, October 2005), 27–44; and Daniel Frisk and R. Derek Trunkey, *Contractors' Support of U.S. Operations in Iraq* (Washington, D.C.: Congressional Budget Office, August 2008), 1, 8, 13 (of 22), www.cbo.gov/ftpdocs/96xx/doc9688 /MainText.3.1.shtml (accessed August 20, 2008). There were about 190,000 contractors in Iraq in early 2008—just under 40,000 Americans, about 70,000 Iraqis, and about 80,000 third-country nationals. In most other wars, the United States had about 1 contractor for every 5 troops; in Korea, the ratio was 1 to 2.5.

42. See, for example, Office of the Under Secretary of Defense (Comptroller), "National Defense Budget Estimates for 2020," Department of Defense, Washington, D.C., May 2019, 104, https://comptroller.defense.gov/Portals/45/Documents/defbudget/fy2020 /FY20_Green_Book.pdf.

43. Michael J. Lostumbo et al., *Overseas Basing of U.S. Military Forces: An Assessment of Relative Costs and Strategic Benefits* (Santa Monica, Calif.: RAND, 2013), https://www .rand.org/pubs/research_reports/RR201.html.

44. Eric Labs, "Crew Rotation in the Navy: The Long-Term Effect on Forward Presence," Congressional Budget Office, Washington, D.C., October 2007, 5, https://www .cbo.gov/sites/default/files/110th-congress-2007-2008/reports/10-31-navy.pdf.

45. Congressional Budget Office, "The U.S. Military's Force Structure: A Primer," Washington, D.C., July 2016, https://www.cbo.gov/sites/default/files/114th-congress -2015-2016/reports/51535-fsprimer.pdf.

46. Quoted in Deborah Clay-Mendez, Richard L. Fernandez, and Amy Belasco, *Trends in Selected Indicators of Military Readiness, 1980 through 1993* (Washington, D.C.: Congressional Budget Office, 1994), 1, citing the definition from the Joint Chiefs of Staff, *The Dictionary of Military and Associated Terms*, JCS Publication 1 (Washington, D.C.: Department of Defense, 1986).

47. Richard K. Betts, *Military Readiness: Concepts, Choices, Consequences* (Washington, D.C.: Brookings, 1995), 43–62.

48. Betts, 115–143.

49. To give some historical perspective, in 1990, the air force budgeted for 19.5 hours per air crew per month of flying, and the navy for 24. In 2008/2009, the respective figures were down to roughly 14 and 18 per month. The decline was gradual; about half occurred during the Clinton years, the other half during the George W. Bush years. See Tamar A. Mehuron and Heather Lewis, "Defense Budget at a Glance," *Air Force Magazine*, April 2008, 61.

50. Daniel Dale, "Factcheck: Trump Exaggerates on Munitions Shortage," October 9, 2019, https://www.cnn.com/2019/10/09/politics/trump-munitions-shortage-fact-check /index.html.

51. Steven Lee Myers, "What War-Ready Means, in Pentagon's Accounting," *New York Times*, September 4, 2000, A11.

52. Betts, *Military Readiness*, 87–114.

53. Under Secretary of Defense (Comptroller) Tina W. Jonas, "Summary Justification: Fiscal Year 2009 Budget Request," Department of Defense, Washington, D.C., February 4, 2008, 14.

54. Department of Defense, *Quarterly Readiness Report to the Congress, April–June 2000* (Washington, D.C.: Department of Defense, August 2000).

55. Todd Harrison, "The Air Force of the Future: A Comparison of Alternative Force Structures," Center for Strategic and International Studies, Washington, D.C., October 2019, 9–10, https://csis-prod.s3.amazonaws.com/s3fs-public/publication/191029_Harri son_AirForceoftheFuture_WEB_v4.pdf?1Oe1zqS6wXgIn79yfyY7pmTlrYMgkgFO.

56. See Frances M. Lussier, *Structuring the Active and Reserve Army for the 21st Century* (Washington, D.C.: Congressional Budget Office, 1997), 3. At that time, for example, the active army had 176,000 soldiers in combat units, another 136,000 in deployable support units, and 183,000 in institutional and other nondeployable categories. For the National Guard, the respective numbers in the three categories were 175,000, 152,000, and 40,000; for the army reserves, they were zero, 139,000, and 69,000 respectively.

57. Congressional Budget Office, "The U.S. Military's Force Structure: A Primer," 10–12.

58. Congressional Budget Office, "Long-Term Implications of the 2020 Future Years Defense Program," Washington, D.C., August 2019, https://www.cbo.gov/publication/55500.

59. Amy Belasco, *Paying for Military Readiness and Upkeep: Trends in Operation and Maintenance Spending* (Washington, D.C.: Congressional Budget Office, September 1997), 5, 14; Allison Percy, *Growth in Medical Spending by the Department of Defense* (Washington, D.C.: Congressional Budget Office, September 2003), 2; Congressional Budget Office, "Trends in Spending by the Department of Defense for Operation and Maintenance," Washington, D.C., January 2017, 1–2, 10–12, https://www.cbo.gov/sites/default /files/115th-congress-2017-2018/reports/52156-omchartbook.pdf; and Congressional Budget Office, "Operating Costs of Aging Air Force Aircraft," Washington, D.C., September 2018, https://www.cbo.gov/publication/54113.

60. Hall, Mosher, and O'Hanlon, *The START Treaty and Beyond*, 139–140.

61. Lane Pierrot and Gregory T. Kiley, *The Long-Term Implications of Current Defense Plans* (Washington, D.C.: Congressional Budget Office, January 2003), 43; and Testimony of Christopher Jehn, "Procurement Costs to Maintain Today's Military Forces," Congressional Budget Office, Washington, D.C., September 2000, 6, https://www.cbo.gov /system/files/2018-10/procurement-costs.pdf.

62. See, for example, Office of the Under Secretary of Defense (Comptroller), "Program Acquisition Cost by Weapon System, Fiscal Year 2020 Budget Request," Washington, D.C., March 2019, https://comptroller.defense.gov/Portals/45/Documents/defbudget/fy2020/fy 2020_Weapons.pdf.

63. See Department of Defense, "Comprehensive Selected Acquisition Reports, Summary Tables," March 2018, https://media.defense.gov/2018/Apr/03/2001898705/-1/-1/1/DECEM BER-2017-SAR-PRESS-RELEASE.PDF; and Government Accountability Office, "Weapon Systems Annual Assessment: Knowledge Gaps Pose Risks to Sustaining Recent Positive Trends," Washington, D.C., April 2018, https://www.gao.gov/assets/700/691473.pdf.

64. For convenience, here are the GDP deflators listed in the DoD Comptroller's "Green Book," in five-year increments, with 2020 as a base and its dollars equal to 1.0: for 2015, 0.915; for 2010, 0.838; for 2005, 0.759; for 2000, 0.679; for 1995, 0.626; for 1990, 0.552; for 1985, 0.474; for 1980, 0.362; for 1975, 0.251; for 1970, 0.185—or, put differently, $1 in 1970 was worth what $5.40 is today.

65. The greatest inefficiencies occur when a production line is sized, scaled, and built for a certain total procurement buy, only to have that buy reduced in numbers thereafter. But

there are penalties even when a production line can be redesigned for a smaller procurement lot. For example, according to one estimate based on CBO data and other sources, a hypothetical two-thirds reduction in the air force's planned purchase of F-35 Lightning II aircraft (also known as the joint strike fighter), from roughly 1,700 planes to 500, suggested a 15 percent unit price increase. And a cut in the F-22 purchase from the intended 340 to about 125 was estimated to increase unit costs some 40 percent. See Michael O'Hanlon, "The Plane Truth," *Brookings Policy Brief* No. 53 (Washington, D.C.: Brookings, September 1999), 6.

66. See R. William Thomas, *Effects of Weapons Procurement Stretch-Outs on Costs and Schedules* (Washington, D.C.: Congressional Budget Office, 1987), 17–18.

67. Pierrot and Kiley, *Long-Term Implications of Current Defense Plans*, 44–46; Rachel Schmidt, *An Analysis of the Administration's Future Years Defense Program for 1995 through 1999* (Washington, D.C.: Congressional Budget Office, January 1995), 41–44; and Adam Talaber, *The Long-Term Implications of Current Defense Plans and Alternatives: Summary Update for Fiscal Year 2006* (Washington, D.C.: Congressional Budget Office, October 2005), 20–22. In the latter report, CBO estimates that total DoD investment costs (development plus procurement) might be about 15 percent more than anticipated, allowing for the risk of growing costs—but this calculation includes all acquisition including ongoing production of systems for which costs are already well understood. For new systems, thus, average cost increases are typically 25 percent (or more) in both development and procurement phases.

68. Lane Pierrot and Jo Ann Vines, *A Look at Tomorrow's Tactical Air Forces* (Washington, D.C.: Congressional Budget Office, January 1997), 84–89.

69. See, for example, John J. Mearsheimer, *The Tragedy of Great Power Politics* (New York: W. W. Norton, 2001).

70. See, for example, Stephen Peter Rosen, *Winning the Next War: Innovation and the Modern Military* (Ithaca, N.Y.: Cornell University Press, 1991); for a more wary take on military revolutions, see Stephen Biddle, *Military Power: Explaining Victory and Defeat in Modern Battle* (Princeton, N.J.: Princeton University Press, 2004).

71. For a skeptical take on this argument, see Michael E. O'Hanlon, *The Future of Land Warfare* (Washington, D.C.: Brookings, 2015).

72. See Barry R. Posen, *Restraint: A New Foundation for U.S. Grand Strategy* (Ithaca, N.Y.: Cornell University Press, 2014), 146–147.

73. Clearly many weapons are kept longer than two or three decades, but in that event they typically require major refurbishment at some point. So it is generally, to good approximation, reasonable to assume likely longevities of twenty to thirty years, depending on the type of equipment.

2. GAMING AND MODELING COMBAT

1. Robert Dallek, "Power and the Presidency, From Kennedy to Obama," *Smithsonian Magazine*, January 2011, http://www.smithsonianmag.com/history/power-and-the-presidency-from-kennedy-to-obama-75335897; Jonathan Masters, "U.S. Foreign Policy Powers: Congress and the President," Council on Foreign Relations "Backgrounder," March 2, 2017, https://www.cfr.org/backgrounder/us-foreign-policy-powers-congress-and-president; and James M. Lindsay, "Congress and Foreign Policy: Why the Hill Matters," *Political Science Quarterly* 107 (Winter 1992–1993): 607–628.

2. See, for example, Representative Les Aspin and Representative William Dickinson, *Defense for a New Era: Lessons of the Persian Gulf War* (New York: Brassey's, 1992); Michael E. O'Hanlon, *The Art of War in the Age of Peace: U.S. Military Posture for the Post–Cold War World* (Westport, Conn.: Praeger, 1992); and William W. Kaufmann, *Assessing the Base Force: How Much Is too Much?* (Washington, D.C.: Brookings, 1992).

3. See Caitlin Talmadge, *The Dictator's Army: Battlefield Effectiveness in Authoritarian Regimes* (Ithaca, N.Y.: Cornell University Press, 2015); and Kenneth M. Pollack, *Armies of Sand: The Past, Present, and Future of Arab Military Effectiveness* (Oxford: Oxford University Press, 2019).

4. For one of the most vivid and engaging illustrations of this fact, for a number of special operations raids from World War II as well as Vietnam and also the Israeli Entebbe mission, see William R. McRaven, *Spec Ops—Case Studies in Special Operations Warfare: Theory and Practice* (New York: Ballantine Books, 1996).

5. See, for example, Williamson Murray and Allan R. Millett, "Introduction: Military Effectiveness Twenty Years After," in Williamson Murray and Allan R. Millett, *Military Effectiveness*, vol. 1, *The First World War*, new ed. (Cambridge: Cambridge University Press, 2010), xiii–xxi.

6. By "roughly comparable military capabilities," I mean a situation in which neither side is estimated to exceed the other's capabilities by more than 50 percent. See Requirements and Resources Directorate, U.S. Army Concepts Analysis Agency, *Combat History Analysis Study Effort (CHASE): Progress Report* (Washington, D.C.: Army Concepts Analysis Agency, 1986), 3–20, cited in Joshua M. Epstein, "Dynamic Analysis and the Conventional Balance in Europe," *International Security* 12, no. 4 (Spring 1988): 156.

7. Richard K. Betts, *Surprise Attack* (Washington, D.C.: Brookings, 1982), 5–16.

8. Epstein, "Dynamic Analysis and the Conventional Balance in Europe," 156.

9. See, for example, Brendan R. Gallagher, *The Day After: Why America Wins the War but Loses the Peace* (Ithaca, N.Y.: Cornell University Press, 2019).

10. Nese F. DeBruyne, "American War and Military Operations Casualties: Lists and Statistics," Congressional Research Service, Washington, D.C., updated September 2019, 7, https://www.everycrsreport.com/reports/RL32492.html#_Toc20320999; and "Recent Trends in Active-Duty Military Deaths," Congressional Research Service, Washington, D.C., May 2019, 1, https://fas.org/sgp/crs/natsec/IF10899.pdf.

For aircraft in particular, recent accident rates including all services have totaled seventy to eighty "Class A Mishaps" a year, where the aircraft suffers $2 million or more in damage or someone is killed or disabled as a result of the incident. See Tara Copp, "The Death Toll for Rising Aviation Accidents: 133 Troops Killed in Five Years," *Military Times*, April 8, 2018, https://www.militarytimes.com/news/your-military/2018/04/08/the-death-toll-for-rising-aviation-accidents-133-troops-killed-in-five-years. Accident rates in training were generally higher a generation ago, at the time of Desert Shield/Storm—during which eighty-six fixed-wing aircraft were lost or damaged, a rate of one aircraft loss for every 1,800 sorties. That is not quite as low as during peacetime training, but it is not dramatically higher either. See Thomas A. Keaney and Eliot A. Cohen, *Gulf War Air Power Survey Summary Report* (Washington, D.C.: Government Printing Office, 1993), 61–62.

Or, to take another perspective, focusing on the workhouse F-16: its rate of "Class A Mishaps" per 100,000 flying hours was 4.55 in 1991, the year of Operation Desert Storm (and most of Operation Desert Shield as well). The ten-year average from 1985 to 1994 was 4.3. In other words, adding wartime loss rates on top of normal peacetime training accidents had only a small noticeable effect on the mishap rate. For the F-15 and A-10, mishap rates per flight hour in 1991 were actually less than in the years just before and after. See Air Force Safety Center, "Aviation Statistics," Washington, D.C., 2019, https://www.safety.af.mil/Portals/71/documents/Aviation/Aircraft%20Statistics/F-16.pdf.

11. Tara Copp, "Is Military Aviation Getting Any Safer? New Mishap Data Shows Mixed Results," *Military Times*, April 8, 2019, https://www.militarytimes.com/news/your-military/2019/04/09/is-military-aviation-getting-any-safer-new-mishap-data-shows-mixed-results/.

12. For a good explanation of TACWAR, see Francis P. Hoeber, *Military Applications of Modeling: Selected Case Studies* (New York: Gordon and Breach Science Publishers, 1981), 132–142.

13. Michael R. Gordon and General Bernard E. Trainor, *The Generals' War: The Inside Story of the Conflict in the Gulf* (Boston: Little, Brown, 1995), 457; Department of Defense, *Conduct of the Persian Gulf War: Final Report to Congress* (Washington, D.C.: Department of Defense, April 1992), A-3 through A-11; Congressional Budget Office, "Costs of Operation Desert Shield," CBO Staff Memorandum, U.S. Congress, Washington, D.C., January 1991, 15; and DeBruyne, "American War and Military Operations Casualties."

14. See, for example, David Schlapak and Michael Johnson, "Reinforcing Deterrence on NATO's Eastern Flank: Wargaming the Defense of the Baltics," RAND, Santa Monica, Calif., 2016, https://www.rand.org/pubs/research_reports/RR1253.html.

15. Daniel S. Marciniak, "Naval War College Reenacts Jutland Wargame," Naval History and Heritage Command, May 2016, https://www.history.navy.mil/news-and-events /news/2016/may/naval-war-college-reenacts-jutland-wargame-.html.

16. Stephen Peter Rosen, *Winning the Next War: Innovation and the Modern Military* (Ithaca, N.Y.: Cornell University Press, 1991), 69–71.

17. Major Jeff Wong, "Inter-war Period Case Studies—Germany, Japan, and the United States," Center for International Maritime Security, Washington, D.C., May 2017, http:// cimsec.org/interwar-period-gaming-today-conflicts-tomorrow-press-start-play-pt-2 /31712.

18. Rosen, *Winning the Next War,* 71–75.

19. George Packer, "Alternative Realities," *New Yorker,* October 23, 2006, https://www .newyorker.com/magazine/2006/10/30/alternative-realities?verso=true.

20. David A. Shlapak and Michael Johnson, "Reinforcing Deterrence on NATO's Eastern Flank: Wargaming the Defense of the Baltics," RAND, Santa Monica, Calif., 2016, https://www.rand.org/pubs/research_reports/RR1253.html.

21. Jim Lacey, "How Does the Next Great Power Conflict Play Out? Lessons from a Wargame," April 22, 2019, https://warontherocks.com/2019/04/how-does-the-next-great -power-conflict-play-out-lessons-from-a-wargame.

22. See, for example, John J. Mearsheimer, "Why the Soviets Can't Win Quickly in Central Europe," *International Security* 7, no. 1 (Summer 1982), reprinted in *Conventional Forces and American Defense Policy,* ed. Steven E. Miller (Princeton, N.J.: Princeton University Press, 1986), 121–157; Barry R. Posen, "Measuring the European Conventional Balance: Coping with Complexity in Threat Assessment," *International Security* 9, no. 3 (Winter 1984/85), reprinted in Miller, *Conventional Forces and American Defense Policy,* 79–120; Epstein, "Dynamic Analysis and the Conventional Balance in Europe," 154–165; Eliot A. Cohen, "Toward Better Net Assessment: Rethinking the European Conventional Balance," *International Security* 13, no. 1 (Summer 1988): 50–89; Steven J. Zaloga and Malcolm Chalmers, "Is There a Tank Gap? Comparing NATO and Warsaw Pact Tank Fleets," *International Security* 13, no. 1 (Summer 1988): 5–49; and Lutz Unterseher, "Correspondence: The Tank Gap Data Flap," *International Security* 13, no. 4 (Spring 1989): 180–187.

23. For a good explanation and critique of the Lanchester equations, see Joshua M. Epstein, *Strategy and Force Planning: The Case of the Persian Gulf* (Washington, D.C.: Brookings, 1987), 146–155.

24. For an explanation of the advantages of simpler, more transparent models, see Zalmay Khalilzad and David Ochmanek, "Rethinking US Defence Planning," *Survival* 39, no. 1 (Spring 1997): 43–64.

25. Posen, "Measuring the European Conventional Balance," 106; and William P. Mako, *U.S. Ground Forces and the Defense of Central Europe* (Washington, D.C.: Brookings, 1983), 36–37.

26. To compute ADE scores for various militaries in order to make these ADE comparisons, a system known as the WEI-WUV method is often employed. American qualitative advantages show up partly in the ADE scores, but even more in the exchange ratio. See U.S. Army Concepts Analysis Agency, War Gaming Directorate, *Weapon Effectiveness Indices/Weighted Unit Values III* (Bethesda, Md.: CAA, 1979).

It is also possible, however, to use a modified approach to scoring static inputs. Rather than employ the WEI-WUV system, a method such as TASCFORM can be employed (the name of which derives from The Analytical Sciences Corporation, which created this database or formula). TASCFORM shows a much greater advantage for Western equipment over alternatives such as Soviet weaponry. In such a situation, if TASCFORM is used rather than WEI/WUV scoring, the exchange ratio would be less lopsided in the United States' favor (since much of the American advantage would have already been captured in the ADE scores). See Lane Pierrot, *Structuring U.S. Forces after the Cold War: Costs and Effects of Increased Reliance on the Reserves* (Washington, D.C.: Congressional Budget Office, 1992), 46–53; and O'Hanlon, *The Art of War in the Age of Peace*, 67.

27. Epstein, "Dynamic Analysis and the Conventional Balance in Europe," 155–158; and Joshua M. Epstein, *Conventional Force Reductions: A Dynamic Assessment* (Washington, D.C.: Brookings, 1990), 51–65.

28. Trevor N. Dupuy, *Attrition: Forecasting Battle Casualties and Equipment Losses in Modern War* (Fairfax, Va.: HERO Books, 1990), 139.

29. See, for example, Epstein, *Strategy and Force Planning*, 63–88, 117–125; and Epstein, *Conventional Force Reductions*, 48–80. It is worth noting that once breakthroughs occur, motorized armies can generally advance 10 to 60 kilometers a day depending on factors such as terrain and any residual resistance (in fact, even in the nineteenth century, armies sometimes averaged 10 to 20 kilometers of progress a day). Against strong resistance, attackers more frequently average moving 1 to 5 kilometers a day, depending on the quality and preparedness of the defense and related factors. See Trevor N. Dupuy, *Numbers, Predictions, and War: The Use of History to Evaluate and Predict the Outcome of Armed Conflict*, rev. ed. (Fairfax, Va.: HERO Books, 1985), 16, 213–214; and Jeffrey Record, "Armored Advance Rates: A Historical Inquiry," *Military Review* 53, no. 9 (September 1973): 63–66.

30. Posen, "Measuring the European Conventional Balance," 105.

31. Despite various army reorganizations, and a greater emphasis over time on the brigade rather than the division as the key element of force structure, these numbers have not changed appreciably in decades. See Congressional Budget Office, "The U.S. Military's Force Structure: A Primer," Washington, D.C., July 2016, 24–25, https://www.cbo.gov/sites/default/files/114th-congress-2015-2016/reports/51535-fsprimerbreakoutchapter2.pdf.

32. See Tami Davis Biddle, *Rhetoric and Reality in Air Warfare: The Evolution of British and American Ideas about Strategic Bombing, 1914–1945* (Princeton, N.J.: Princeton University Press, 2002), 289–301.

33. Keaney and Cohen, *Gulf War Air Power Survey Summary Report*, 65, 199; and General Accounting Office (now the Government Accountability Office), *Operation Desert Storm: Evaluation of the Air Campaign* (Washington, D.C.: GAO, June 1997), GAO/NSIAD-97-134, 166.

34. Benjamin S. Lambeth, *NATO's Air War for Kosovo: A Strategic and Operational Assessment* (Santa Monica, Calif.: RAND, 1992), 35, 62–66; Ivo H. Daalder and Michael E. O'Hanlon, *Winning Ugly: NATO's War to Save Kosovo* (Washington, D.C.: Brookings, 2000), 135–143; and Anthony M. Schinella, *Bombs without Boots: The Limits of Airpower* (Washington, D.C.: Brookings, 2019), 87–89, 290.

35. Joshua M. Epstein, "War with Iraq: What Price Victory?," Briefing Paper, Brookings Institution, December 1990.

36. Gordon and Trainor, *The Generals' War*, 355–380.

37. Congressional Budget Office, "Costs of Operation Desert Shield," 15; and Dupuy, *Attrition*, 73–74, 131.

38. See Directorate for Information Operations and Reports, "Persian Gulf War: Desert Shield and Desert Storm," Department of Defense, December 15, 2001, web1.whs. osd.mil/mmid/casualty; Department of Defense, *Conduct of the Persian Gulf War*, M-1.

39. See also, Lawrence Freedman and Efraim Karsh, *The Gulf Conflict, 1990–1991: Diplomacy and War in the New World Order* (Princeton, N.J.: Princeton University Press, 1993), 409.

40. JSTARS was first used in Desert Storm; it can scan a region of twenty or more kilometers on a side when in broad-sweep mode. See James F. Dunnigan, *How to Make War: A Comprehensive Guide to Modern Warfare for the Post–Cold War Era*, 3rd ed. (New York: William Morrow, 1993), 154–155.

41. Stephen Biddle, "The Past as Prologue: Assessing Theories of Future Warfare," *Security Studies* 8, no. 1 (Autumn 1998): 1–74.

42. Stephen Biddle, "Victory Misunderstood: What the Gulf War Tells Us about the Future of Conflict," *International Security* 21, no. 2 (Fall 1996): 139–179.

43. See Keaney and Cohen, *Gulf War Air Power Survey Summary Report*, 21, 58–64, 155; and Aspin and Dickinson, *Defense for a New Era*, 1–41; for data on Arab-Israeli wars, see Posen, "Measuring the European Conventional Balance," 113; and Dupuy, *Numbers, Predictions, and War*, 118–139.

44. Pollack, *Armies of Sand*, 143–308.

45. See Hanlon, *The Art of War in the Age of Peace*, 67.

46. Keaney and Cohen, *Gulf War Air Power Survey Summary Report*, 105–106; and General Accounting Office, *Operation Desert Storm*, 8–10, 105–107, 146–148, 157–159.

47. Civilian casualty estimates based on briefing by William Arkin of Greenpeace to Gulf War Air Power Survey project members, October 31, 1991, cited in Keaney and Cohen, *Gulf War Air Power Survey Summary Report*, 75; for military casualty estimates, see Keaney and Cohen, 107.

48. Keaney and Cohen, 104–117, 203.

49. Airpower used in isolation is not always so effective; see Schinella, *Bombs without Boots*.

50. Epstein, *Strategy and Force Planning*, 113; and Frances M. Lussier, *Replacing and Repairing Equipment Used in Iraq and Afghanistan: The Army's Reset Program* (Washington, D.C.: Congressional Budget Office, 2007), xi.

51. Posen, "Measuring the European Conventional Balance," 104.

52. See Dupuy, *Attrition*, 104–132; see also Dupuy, *Numbers, Predictions, and War*; and Trevor N. Dupuy, *Understanding War: History and Theory of Combat* (New York: Paragon Books, 1987).

53. Dupuy, *Attrition*, 76.

54. Dupuy, 146–151.

55. Dupuy, 149.

56. Trevor N. Dupuy, *If War Comes, How to Defeat Saddam Hussein* (Fairfax, Va.: HERO Books, 1991), 104; Congressional Budget Office, "Costs of Operation Desert Shield," 15.

57. See Robert L. Goldich, "Casualties and Maximum Number of Troops Deployed in Recent U.S. Military Ground Combat Actions," Congressional Research Service, October 8, 1993; Brig. Gen. Robert H. Scales, *Certain Victory: The U.S. Army in the Gulf War* (Washington, D.C.: Brassey's, 1994), 32–35; International Institute for Strategic Studies, *The Military Balance 1989–1990* (Washington, D.C.: Brassey's, 1989), 26–27, 199; Susan L. Marquis, *Unconventional Warfare: Rebuilding U.S. Special Operations Forces* (Washington, D.C.: Brookings, 1997), 187–201; and Ronald H. Cole, "Operation Just Cause

Panama," Joint History Office, Office of the Chairman of the Joint Chiefs of Staff, Department of Defense, Washington, D.C., 1995, 65, https://nsarchive2.gwu.edu/NSAEBB/NSAEBB443/docs/area51_22.PDF.

58. See Statement of General James R. Harding, Director, Inter-American Region, Office of the Secretary of Defense, Before the Subcommittee on Western Hemisphere Affairs of the House Foreign Affairs Committee, July 30, 1991, www.nexis.com/research/search/submitViewTagged.

59. I have simplified Dupuy's method considerably. He employs factors to account for terrain, surprise, weather, and so on. More important, the way in which relative power differentials enter into his equations is not quite linear in the way I have suggested. But his method has an arbitrary quality about it at times as well; for example, he adds a "sophistication factor" in addition to mobility, firepower, and combat effectiveness coefficients to account for the quality of one military over another. It is unclear why so many different such factors are needed to explain similar phenomena, or how one selects the proper value for each. By contrast, his methodology for computing power is relatively straightforward. For more exact information on how power ratios enter into his calculations, see Dupuy, *Attrition*, 124–127, 146–152.

60. Some of my ideas here first appeared in Michael O'Hanlon, "Why China Cannot Conquer Taiwan," *International Security* 25, no. 2 (Fall 2000): 51–86.

61. See U.S. Marine Corps, "Operational Maneuver from the Sea," *Marine Corps Gazette*, June 1996.

62. See, for example, Phillip C. Saunders, Arthur S. Ding, Andrew Scobell, Andrew N. D. Yang, and Joel Wuthnow, eds., *Chairman Xi Remakes the PLA: Assessing Chinese Military Reforms* (Washington, D.C.: National Defense University Press, 2019); and State Council Information Office of the People's Republic of China, "China's National Defense in the New Era," Beijing, 2019, http://www.andrewerickson.com/2019/07/full-text-of-defense-white-paper-chinas-national-defense-in-the-new-era-english-chinese-versions/.

63. For the purpose of simplicity in illustrating the methodology, this part of the analysis focuses on PRC-Taiwan combat and does not consider the impact of US military intervention in support of Taiwan.

64. Office of the Secretary of Defense, "Annual Report to Congress: Military and Security Developments Involving the People's Republic of China 2019," Department of Defense, Washington, D.C., 2019, 44–48, https://media.defense.gov/2019/May/02/2002127082/-1/-1/1/2019_CHINA_MILITARY_POWER_REPORT.pdf.

65. Technically, a circular error probable is not exactly the expected or average miss distance. It is in effect the median miss distance—the radius of a circle that would include half the landing points of a given type of missile fired repeatedly at a given target (real or imaginary). See Richard L. Elder, "An Examination of Circular Error Probable Approximation Techniques," Air University, Maxwell Air Force Base, Montgomery, Alabama, 1986, https://apps.dtic.mil/dtic/tr/fulltext/u2/a172498.pdf.

66. See, for example, David A. Shlapak, David T. Orletsky, Toy I. Reid, Murray Scot Tanner, and Barry Wilson, *A Question of Balance: Political Context and Military Aspects of the China-Taiwan Dispute* (Santa Monica, Calif.: RAND, 2009), 31–44.

67. Shlapak et al., 35–45.

68. More generally, if one wishes to calculate the single-shot probability of kill, which is equal to 1 minus the single-shot probability of survival, the formula $SSPK = 1 - e^{(-LR*LR/1.44*CEP*CEP)}$ captures the essence of the math. In other words, the single-shot probability of kill of a missile/warhead with a given lethal radius against the target in question (LR) and a given circular error probable is the number 1 minus the natural number e taken to the power of $(-LR^2/1.44CEP^2)$. As an example, if $LR = 50$ meters and $CEP = 100$ meters, or for any other case where the lethal radius is half the CEP, then $SSPK = 0.16$. As another example,

if $LR = 200$ meters and $CEP = 100$ meters, or for any other case where the lethal radius is twice the CEP, then $SSPK = 0.93$. If the lethal radius is three-fourths of the CEP, then $SSPK = 0.33$; if the lethal radius is 50 percent greater than the CEP, then $SSPK = 0.79$.

69. See, for example, David Shlapak, "Projecting Power in a China-Taiwan Contingency: Implications for USAF and USN Collaboration," in *Coping with the Dragon: Essays on PLA Transformation and the U.S. Military*, ed. Stuart E. Johnson and Duncan Long (Washington, D.C.: National Defense University, December 2007), 90.

The US experience against Iraq in Desert Storm in 1991 provides a good window into how hard it is to shut down an enemy's air force. Coalition aircraft averaged dozens of strike sorties a day against Iraqi airfields during the war's first week, yet did not stop the Iraqi air force from flying about forty sorties a day. That was at a time when coalition aircraft completely ruled the skies, moreover. In the airfield attacks, British planes were dropping advanced runway-penetrating weapons, precisely and from low altitude. They carried some thirty bomblets apiece, each bomblet consisting of two charges: a primary explosive to create a small hole in the runway, and a second explosive to detonate below its surface, causing a crater of ten to twenty meters' width (depending largely on soil conditions). A standard attack would have used eight aircraft, each dropping two weapons, to shut down a standard NATO-length runway of 9,000 feet by 150 feet—a difficult mission, given the need to drop the weapons at precise and quite low altitudes.

See Keaney and Cohen, *Gulf War Air Power Survey Summary*, 56–65; General Accounting Office, *Operation Desert Storm*, 209–212; and Christopher S. Parker, "New Weapons for Old Problems," *International Security* 23, no. 4 (Spring 1999): 147; Duncan Lennox, ed., *Jane's Air-Launched Weapons* (Surrey: Jane's Information Group, August 1999), issue 33; and Christopher M. Centner, "Ignorance Is Risk: The Big Lesson from Desert Storm Air Base Attacks," *Airpower Journal* 6, no. 4, (Winter 1992): 25–35, www.airpower.maxwell .af.mil/airchronicles/apj/centner.html; and personal communication from Dave C. Fidler, Wing Commander Air 1, British Embassy, Washington, D.C., April 14, 2000.

70. See International Institute for Strategic Studies, *The Military Balance 2019* (Oxfordshire, U.K.: Routledge, 2019), 259–260; Office of the Secretary of Defense, "Annual Report to Congress: Military and Security Developments Involving the People's Republic of China 2019," 32–37, 85–89, 115; Department of Defense, *FY04 Report to Congress on PRC Military Power: Annual Report on the Military Power of the People's Republic of China* (2004), 40; and International Institute for Strategic Studies, *The Military Balance 2005/2006* (Colchester: Routledge, 2005), 270–276.

71. Shlapak et al., *A Question of Balance*, 119.

72. International Institute for Strategic Studies, *The Military Balance 2019*, 308.

73. See Dunnigan, *How to Make War*, 284–292.

74. Wendell Minnick, "Washington Establishes Military Hotline with Taipei," *Jane's Defence Weekly*, October 29, 2003, 14.

75. Michael D. Swaine, *Taiwan's National Security, Defense Policy, and Weapons Procurement Processes* (Santa Monica, Calif.: RAND, 1999), 60.

76. Office of the Secretary of Defense, "Annual Report to Congress: Military and Security Developments Involving the People's Republic of China," 32.

77. For historical perspective, see James A. Huston, "The Air Invasion of Holland," *Military Review* 32, no. 5 (September 1952): 13–27; and Gerard M. Devlin, *Paratrooper! The Saga of U.S. Army and Marine Parachute and Glider Combat Troops during World War II* (New York: St. Martin's Press, 1979).

78. Robert Dalsjo, Christofer Berglund, and Michael Jonsson, "Bursting the Bubble: Russian A2/AD in the Baltic Sea Region: Capabilities, Countermeasures, and Implications," FOI, Stockholm, Sweden, March 2019, 45–64, https://www.foi.se/rest-api/report /FOI-R-4651-SE.

79. J. Michael Cole, "How Taiwan Can Defend Its Coastline against China," June 30, 2019, https://nationalinterest.org/feature/how-taiwan-can-defend-its-coastline-against-china-64861.

80. This is a simplified version of Hughes's formula; see Capt. Wayne P. Hughes Jr. (U.S. Navy, retired), *Fleet Tactics and Coastal Combat*, 2nd ed. (Annapolis, Md.: Naval Institute Press, 2000), 268.

81. Hughes, 275–276.

82. A very good history is Martin Middlebrook, *The Falklands War* (South Yorkshire: Pen and Sword Books, 2012).

83. Lon O. Nordeen, *Air Warfare in the Missile Age*, 2nd ed. (Washington, D.C.: Smithsonian Institution Press, 2010), 201–203; and *Jane's Naval Review 1987* (London: Jane's Publishing, 1987), 124.

84. Shlapak et al., *A Question of Balance*, 98–99.

85. Ship losses are discussed in the text. As for aircraft attrition, Taiwan has well over 100 surface-to-air missile batteries with ranges of tens of kilometers—more than enough to have some coverage near all of its 20 to 30 large airfields and 5 major ports (the kinds of places where PRC paratroopers might do the most good, seizing assets that could then be used to deploy PRC reinforcements). In addition to its air force, it also has hundreds of antiaircraft guns and many smaller surface-to-air missile batteries that use high-quality modified Sidewinder and Sparrow missiles.

86. Office of Technology Assessment, *Proliferation of Weapons of Mass Destruction* (Washington, D.C.: Office of Technology Assessment, 1993), 45–67.

87. Dupuy, *Attrition*, 58; and Anthony H. Cordesman and Abraham R. Wagner, *Lessons of Modern War*, vol. 2, *The Iran-Iraq War* (Boulder, Colo.: Westview Press, 1990), 518.

88. See Victor A. Utgoff, *The Challenge of Chemical Weapons: An American Perspective*, (London: Palgrave MacMillan, 1990), 148–188; and Dupuy, *Attrition*, 58.

89. Cordesman and Wagner, *The Lessons of Modern War*, vol. 2, *The Iran-Iraq War*, 205–206; and Daniel L. Byman and Matthew C. Waxman, "Kosovo and the Great Air Power Debate," *International Security* 24, no. 4 (Spring 2000): 37–38.

90. James C. Mulvenon, Murray Scot Tanner, Michael S. Chase, David Frelinger, David C. Gompert, Martin C. Libicki, and Kevin L. Pollpeter, *Chinese Responses to U.S. Military Transformation and Implications for the Department of Defense* (Santa Monica, Calif.: RAND, 2006), 116–120.

91. Bernard D. Cole, "Right-Sizing the Navy: How Much Naval Force Will Beijing Deploy?," in *Right-Sizing the People's Liberation Army: Exploring the Contours of China's Military*, ed. Roy Kamphausen and Andrew Scobell (Carlisle, Pa.: Strategic Studies Institute, Army War College, 2007), 541–542.

92. For discussion of Chinese writings on the subject, see Roger Cliff, Mark Burles, Michael S. Chase, Derek Eaton, and Kevin L. Pollpeter, *Entering the Dragon's Lair: Chinese Antiaccess Strategies and Their Implications for the United States* (Santa Monica, Calif.: RAND, 2007), 66–73. Among other naval force modernizations, China now has many modern attack submarines in its fleet, and it is also expected to acquire ocean reconnaissance satellites (early versions of which it already reportedly possesses) as well as communications systems capable of reaching deployed forces in the field in the next five to ten years. See Office of the Secretary of Defense, *Military Power of the People's Republic of China, 2008: Annual Report to Congress* (Washington, D.C.: Department of Defense, 2008), www.defenselink.mil/pubs/pdfs/China_Military_Report_08.pdf, 4, 27 (accessed March 20, 2008); subsequent annual reports; and Michael McDevitt, "The Strategic and Operational Context Driving PLA Navy Building," in Kamphausen and Scobell, *Right-Sizing the People's Liberation Army*, 499.

93. Eric Heginbotham, Michael Nixon, Forrest E. Morgan, Jacob L. Heim, Jeff Hagen, Sheng Li, Jeffrey Engstrom, Martin C. Libicki, Paul DeLuca, David A. Shlapak, David R.

Frelinger, Burgess Laird, Kyle Brady, and Lyle J. Morris, *The U.S.-China Military Scorecard: Forces, Geography, and the Evolving Balance of Power, 1996–2017* (Santa Monica, Calif.: RAND, 2015), 75–84.

94. Heginbotham and others, 83.

95. Heginbotham and others, 75–88.

96. Roger Cliff, John Fei, Jeff Hogen, Elizabeth Hogue, Eric Heginbotham, and John Stillion, *Shaking the Heavens and Splitting the Earth: Chinese Air Force Employment Concepts in the 21st Century* (Santa Monica, Calif.: RAND, 2011), xxiii, 209–215; and Heginbotham et. al., *The U.S.-China Military Scorecard*, 149–150.

97. See Congressional Budget Office, *U.S. Naval Forces: The Sea Control Mission* (Washington, D.C.: Congressional Budget Office, 1978).

98. For an earlier discussion of how to think about such calculations, see letters by Lyle Goldstein and William Murray and by Michael O'Hanlon, "Correspondence: Damn the Torpedoes: Debating Possible U.S. Navy Losses in a Taiwan Scenario," *International Security* 29, no. 2 (Fall 2004): 202–206.

99. Heginbotham and others, *The U.S.-China Military Scorecard*, 184–198.

100. For analyses that remain mostly applicable today, see Owen Cote, *The Future of Naval Aviation* (Cambridge, Mass.: MIT Security Studies Program, 2006), 34–37, http://web.mit.edu/ssp/; Owen Cote and Harvey Sapolsky, *Antisubmarine Warfare after the Cold War* (Cambridge, Mass.: MIT Security Studies Program, 1997), 13; and Tom Stefanick, *Strategic Antisubmarine Warfare and Naval Strategy* (Lexington, Mass.: Lexington Books, 1987), 35–49.

101. M. Taylor Fravel, *Active Defense: China's Military Strategy since 1949* (Princeton, N.J.: Princeton University Press, 2019).

102. Desmond Ball, "China Pursues Space-Based Intelligence Gathering Capabilities," *Jane's Intelligence Review*, December 2003, 36–39.

103. Michael E. O'Hanlon, *Neither Star Wars Nor Sanctuary: Constraining the Military Uses of Space* (Washington, D.C.: Brookings, 2004), 91–104; Bill Gertz, "Chinese Missile Has Twice the Range U.S. Anticipated," *Washington Times*, November 20, 2002, 3; Barry Watts, *The Military Uses of Space: A Diagnostic Assessment* (Washington, D.C.: Center for Strategic and Budgetary Assessments, 2001); Bob Preston, Dana J. Johnson, Sean J. A. Edwards, Michael Miller, and Calvin Shipbaugh, *Space Weapons, Earth Wars* (Santa Monica, Calif.: RAND, 2002); and Benjamin Lambeth, *Mastering the Ultimate High Ground: Next Steps in the Military Uses of Space* (Santa Monica, Calif.: RAND, 2003).

104. Caitlin Talmadge, "Closing Time: Assessing the Iranian Threat to the Strait of Hormuz," *International Security* 33, no. 1 (Summer 2008): 90–97.

105. See Michael J. Mazarr, Gian Gentile, Dan Madden, Stacie L. Pettyjohn, and Yvonne K. Crane, "The Korean Peninsula: Three Dangerous Scenarios," RAND, Santa Monica, California, 2018, https://www.rand.org/content/dam/rand/pubs/perspectives/PE200/PE262/RAND_PE262.pdf; and David Axe, "North Korea's Deadly Artillery 'Has the Potential to Affect Millions of South Korean Citizens,'" November 18, 2018, https://nationalinterest.org/blog/buzz/north-koreas-deadly-artillery-has-%E2%80%9Cpotential-affect-millions-south-korean-citizens%E2%80%9D-36427.

106. Based on the Iran-Iraq War experience, as well as basic ballistics and blast information, warheads from a missile with several hundred kilograms of explosive might kill ten to twenty people on average, in a typical city, though of course the potential exists for much more devastation depending on where the explosion occurs. Artillery and mortar rounds, with warheads about one-tenth that size (say seven to twenty-five pounds of explosive, as noted earlier) would have about one-fifth the lethal effect. (The lethal area of an explosive varies roughly with the two-thirds power of explosive yield. So an eightfold reduction in

power produces a fourfold decrease in lethal area—and hence expected casualties.) The lethal radii for weapons in this range could be 30 to 50 meters for mortar rounds and artillery shells, and 100 meters or more for typical missile warheads. See Cordesman and Wagner, *The Lessons of Modern War*, vol. 2, *The Iran-Iraq War*, 364–368; U.S. Army, *Field Manual 5-34: Engineer Field Data* (Washington, D.C., September 1987), 4-1; Dunnigan, *How to Make War*, 124–125; and Janne E. Nolan, *Trappings of Power: Ballistic Missiles in the Third World* (Washington, D.C.: Brookings, 1991), 68–69. I also thank Colonel Thomas Lynch of the US Army for information on artillery via private correspondence, March 17, 2008.

107. For a good concise history of early targeting and force planning ideas, see Desmond Ball, "The Development of the SIOP, 1960–1983," in Desmond Ball and Jeffrey Richelson, *Strategic Nuclear Targeting* (Ithaca, N.Y.: Cornell University Press, 1986), 57–83.

108. See Bruce G. Blair, *Strategic Command and Control: Redefining the Nuclear Threat* (Washington, D.C.: Brookings, 1985); and Bruce G. Blair, *Global Zero Alert for Nuclear Forces* (Washington, D.C.: Brookings, 1995).

109. See Scott D. Sagan, *The Limits of Safety: Organizations, Accidents, and Nuclear Weapons* (Princeton, N.J.: Princeton University Press, 1993).

110. See Barry R. Posen, *Inadvertent Escalation: Conventional War and Nuclear Risks* (Ithaca, N.Y.: Cornell University Press, 1991).

111. Matthew Bunn and Kosta Tsipis, "The Uncertainties of a Preemptive Nuclear Attack," *Scientific American*, November 1983.

112. David Mosher, "Appendix B: Exchange Calculations," in Raymond Hall, David Mosher, and Michael O'Hanlon, *The START Treaty and Beyond* (Washington, D.C.: Congressional Budget Office, 1991), 143–165. Other examples include the Soviet SS-19 with a lethal radius of 300 meters, the U.S. Minuteman IIIA with a lethal radius of 185 meters, and the U.S. D5/Mark 5 (Trident II SLBM) warhead with a lethal radius of 210 meters.

With the lethal radius in hand, one can then calculate the single-shot survival probability for a silo attacked by a given warhead. First, square the lethal radius of the warhead (that is, take it to the second power, or multiply it by itself). Then square the circular error probable of the warhead and multiply the resulting number by 1.44, and then make it negative. Take the ratio of the first term (the square of the lethal radius) to the second (the negative of 1.44 times the square of the circular error probable). That overall expression is then the power to which the naturally occurring number e is taken. In short, single shot survival = [exp][−LRsquared/1.44CEPsquared], where LR = lethal radius and CEP = circular error probable.

113. Samuel Glasstone, ed., *The Effects of Nuclear Weapons*, rev. ed. (Washington, D.C.: Government Printing Office, 1962), 134–135, 156–176; Mosher, "Appendix B: Exchange Calculations," 159; and David Ochmanek and Lowell H. Schwartz, *The Challenge of Nuclear-Armed Regional Adversaries* (Santa Monica, Calif.: RAND, 2008), 7. Bombers would likely be damaged once struck by two to four pounds per square inch of overpressure or more.

114. Andrew F. Krepinevich Jr., *The Army and Vietnam* (Baltimore, Md.: Johns Hopkins University Press, 1986), 177–214; and Robert S. McNamara, *In Retrospect: The Tragedy and Lessons of Vietnam* (New York: Vintage Books, 1995), 169–177, 210–212, 220–223, 233–247, 262–263, 282–293.

115. Neil Sheehan, *A Bright Shining Lie: John Paul Vann and America in Vietnam* (New York: Vintage Books, 1988), 201–265.

116. See Michael Fitzsimmons, "Hard Hearts and Open Minds? Governance, Identity, and the Intellectual Foundations of Counterinsurgency Strategy," *Journal of Strategic Studies* 31, no. 3 (2008), 337–365; and Jacqueline L. Hazelton, "The 'Hearts and Minds' Fallacy: Violence, Coercion, and Success in Counterinsurgency Warfare," *International Security* 42, no. 1 (Summer 2017): 80–113. On the surge in Iraq, see Peter R. Mansoor,

Surge: My Journey with General David Petraeus and the Remaking of the Iraq War (New Haven, Conn.: Yale University Press, 2013), especially 36–39; and Kimberly Kagan, *The Surge: A Military History* (New York: Encounter Books, 2009).

117. General David H. Petraeus, Lt. General James F. Amos, and Lt. Colonel John A. Nagl, *The U.S. Army/Marine Corps Counterinsurgency Field Manual* (Chicago: University of Chicago Press, 2007), 23.

118. James Dobbins, John G. McGinn, Keith Crane, Seth G. Jones, Rollie Lal, Andrew Rathmell, Rachel Swanger, and Anga Timilsina, *America's Role in Nation-Building from Germany to Iraq* (Santa Monica, Calif.: RAND, 2003), xvii.

119. Michael E. O'Hanlon, *Saving Lives with Force* (Washington, D.C.: Brookings, 1997), 38–42; and James T. Quinlivan, "Force Requirements in Stability Operations," *Parameters* 25, no. 4 (Winter 1995–1996): 59–69.

120. Seth G. Jones, Jeremy M. Wilson, Andrew Rathmell, and K. Jack Riley, *Establishing Law and Order after Conflict* (Santa Monica, Calif.: RAND, 2005), 19; James Dobbins et al., *America's Role in Nation-Building*; and James Dobbins, Seth G. Jones, Keith Crane, Andrew Rathmell, Brett Steele, Richard Teltschik, and Anga Timilsina, *The UN's Role in Nation-Building: From the Congo to Iraq* (Santa Monica, Calif.: RAND, 2005).

121. Virginia Page Fortna, *Does Peacekeeping Work? Shaping Belligerents' Choices after Civil War* (Princeton, N.J.: Princeton University Press, 2008).

122. Lise Morje Howard, *Power in Peacekeeping* (Cambridge: Cambridge University Press, 2019).

123. Angel Rabasa, Lesley Anne Warner, Peter Chalk, Ivan Khilko, and Paraag Shukla, *Money in the Bank: Lessons Learned from Past Counterinsurgency (COIN) Operations* (Santa Monica, Calif.: RAND, 2007), ix–xv, 1–4.

124. David Galula, *Counterinsurgency Warfare: Theory and Practice* (New York: Praeger, 2005), 70–86.

125. Krepinevich, *The Army and Vietnam*, 172–177.

126. Petraeus, Amos, and Nagl, *U.S. Army/Marine Corps Counterinsurgency Field Manual*, 1–52; Steven Metz, *Learning from Iraq: Counterinsurgency in American Strategy* (Carlisle, Pa.: Army War College Strategic Studies Institute, 2007), 1–30; and Thomas E. Ricks, *Fiasco: The American Military Adventure in Iraq* (New York: Penguin, 2006), 149–202.

127. My profuse thanks to Adriana Lins de Albuquerque, Nina Kamp, Jason Campbell, and Ian Livingston for all they did to create and sustain this project, as well as the Afghanistan and Pakistan indices, over the years.

128. Michael E. O'Hanlon and Kenneth M. Pollack, "A War We Just Might Win," *New York Times*, July 30, 2007, https://www.nytimes.com/2007/07/30/opinion/30pollack.html.

129. Gallagher, *The Day After*.

130. Michael O'Hanlon, "What the Washington Post Gets Wrong about the United States and Afghanistan," December 13, 2019, https://www.lawfareblog.com/what-washington-post -gets-wrong-about-united-states-and-afghanistan.

131. See Joshua M. Epstein, *Measuring Military Power: The Soviet Air Threat to Europe* (Princeton, N.J.: Princeton University Press, 1984), xxv–xxvi.

3. TECHNOLOGICAL CHANGE AND MILITARY INNOVATION

1. For a very good discussion of this issue, see Frank von Hippel, *Citizen Scientist* (New York: Touchstone, 1991), xi–xv.

2. For a thoughtful example, see Andrew F. Krepinevich, "Cavalry to Computer: The Pattern of Military Revolutions," *National Interest*, no. 37 (Fall 1994): 30–42, https://www .jstor.org/stable/42896863.

3. See, for example, H. A. Feiveson, *Scientists against Time: The Role of Scientists in World War II* (Bloomington, Ind.: Archway, 2018); Thomas P. Ehrhard, *Air Force UAVs:*

The Secret History (Arlington, Va.: Mitchell Institute, 2010), http://notreally.info/transport /drones/aars/pdf/MS_UAV_0710.pdf; Montgomery C. Meigs, *Slide Rules and Submarines: American Scientists and Subsurface Warfare in World War II* (Honolulu: University Press of the Pacific, 2002); Barry R. Posen, *The Sources of Military Doctrine: France, Britain, and Germany between the World Wars* (Ithaca, N.Y.: Cornell University Press, 1984); Krepinevich, "Cavalry to Computer"; Williamson Murray, "Thinking about Revolutions in Military Affairs," *Joint Forces Quarterly*, no. 16 (Summer 1997), file:///C:/Users/MOHANLON/Downloads/ADA354177.pdf; and Stephen Peter Rosen, *Winning the Next War: Innovation and the Modern Military* (Ithaca, N.Y.: Cornell University Press, 1991).

4. See, for example, "Livermore Researchers Develop Battery-Less Chemical Detector," Lawrence Livermore National Laboratory, April 6, 2011, https://www.llnl.gov/news/liver more-researchers-develop-battery-less-chemical-detector; Sue Holmes, "Researching New Detectors for Chemical, Biological Threats," Sandia Labs News Releases, Albuquerque, New Mexico, September 5, 2013, https://share-ng.sandia.gov/news/resources/news_releases/threat _detectors/#.WiBKufnyupo; and Cory Nealon, "New Sensing Tech Could Help Detect Diseases, Fraudulent Art, Chemical Weapons," June 1, 2015, https://phys.org/news/2015-06-tech -diseases-fraudulent-art-chemical.html.

5. Joey Cheng, "Small, Deep-UV Lasers Could Detect Biological and Chemical Agents on the Battlefield," *Defense Systems*, March 24, 2014, https://defensesystems.com/articles/2014 /03/24/darpa-luster-chem-bio-detection.aspx.

6. Science and Technology Directorate, Department of Homeland Security, "Detect to Protect Bio-aerosol Detection Systems," Washington, D.C., April 2016, https://www.dhs .gov/sites/default/files/publications/Detect%20to%20Protect%20Bio-Aerosol%20Detec- tion%20Systems_0.pdf.

7. Joint Testimony of Reginald Brothers, PhD, Under Secretary for Science and Technology U.S. Department of Homeland Security and Kathryn H. Brinsfield, MD, MPH, Assistant Secretary for Health Affairs and Chief Medical Officer U.S. Department of Homeland Security Before the U.S. House of Representatives Committee on Homeland Security Subcommittee on Emergency Preparedness, Response, and Communications, Washington, D.C., February 11, 2016, http://docs.house.gov/meetings/HM/HM12 /20160211/104326/HMTG-114-HM12-Wstate-BrinsfieldK-20160211.pdf.

8. Stephen Wampler, "LLNL Biodetection System Bound for Space," Lawrence Livermore National Laboratory, April 28, 2016, https://www.llnl.gov/news/llnl-biodetection -system-bound-space.

9. Kim E. Sapsford, Christopher Bradburne, James B. Delehanty, and Igor L. Medintz, "Sensors for Detecting Biological Agents," *Materials Today* 11, no. 3 (March 2008): 38–49, http://www.sciencedirect.com/science/article/pii/S136970210870018X.

10. Jeffrey Kirsch, Christian Siltanen, Qing Zhou, Alexander Revzin, and Aleksandr Simonian, "Biosensor Technology: Recent Advances in Threat Agent Detection and Medicine," *Chemical Society Reviews*, issue 22 (2013), https://pubs.rsc.org/en/content/articlelanding/2013 /cs/c3cs60141b#!divAbstract.

11. See Allan Chen, "Revealing the Presence of Hidden Nuclear Materials," *Science and Technology Review*, January/February 2017), 18–22.

12. Michael Levi, *On Nuclear Terrorism* (Cambridge, Mass.: Harvard University Press, 2007); and Elizabeth Keegan, Michael J. Kristo, Kaitlyn Toole, Ruth Kips, and Emma Young, "Nuclear Forensics: Scientific Analysis Supporting Law Enforcement and Nuclear Security Investigations," *Analytical Chemistry* 88, no. 3 (2016): 1496–1505, http://pubs .acs.org/doi/abs/10.1021/acs.analchem.5b02915.

13. Secretary of Defense Jim Mattis, *Nuclear Posture Review 2018* (Washington, D.C.: Department of Defense, February 2018), 67, https://www.defense.gov/News/SpecialReports /2018NuclearPostureReview.aspx.

14. John Keller, "New Era Dawns in ASW as Manned and Unmanned Submarines Team for Bistatic Sonar," *Military and Aerospace Electronics*, October 24, 2017, http://www .militaryaerospace.com/articles/print/volume-28/issue-10/news/news/new-era-dawns -in-asw-as-manned-and-unmanned-submarines-team-for-bistatic-sonar.html.

15. "Retirement in Sight for Mine-Hunting Dolphins," *Aviation Week and Space Technology*, January 28, 2013, http://aviationweek.com/awin/retirement-sight-mine-hunting -dolphins.

16. Nicholas Makris, "New Sonar Technology Reveals City-Size Schools of Fish," *IEEE Spectrum*, July 26, 2011, https://spectrum.ieee.org/energy/environment/new-sonar-technology -reveals-citysize-schools-of-fish.

17. Technology Partnership Office, "NUWC Division Newport Commercialization Opportunities," Naval Undersea Warfare Center Division Newport, Newport, Rhode Island, 2012, http://www.navsea.navy.mil/Portals/103/Documents/NUWC_Newport/Techpartner ing/CommercializationOpportunities2012.pdf.

18. Daniel Perry, "Navy Researchers, Reservists Evaluate Novel Passive Sonar Surveillance Methods," U.S. Naval Research Laboratory, February 20, 2013, https://www.nrl .navy.mil/media/news-releases/2013/navy-researchers-reservists-evaluate-novel-passive -sonar-surveillance-methods.

19. U.S. Navy Fleet Forces Command, "Sonar," U.S. Navy, Washington, D.C., 2017, http://www.public.navy.mil/usff/environmental/Pages/Sonar.aspx.

20. J. D. Jackson, *Classical Electrodynamics*, 2nd ed. (New York: John Wiley, 1975), 290–292.

21. Duncan Brown, "Joint Staff J-7 Sponsored Science, Technology, and Engineering Futures Seminar," NSAD-R-14-051, Johns Hopkins University Applied Physics Laboratory, Laurel, Md., July 2014, 15.

22. Mark Sullivan, "Apple Is Working Hard on an IPhone Rear-Facing 3D Laser for AR and Autofocus: Source," *Fastcompany.com*, July 12, 2017, https://www.fastcompany .com/40440342/apple-is-working-hard-on-an-iphone-8-rear-facing-3d-laser-for-ar-and -autofocus-source.

23. Audra Calloway, "Army Developing Laser-Guided, Precision Mortar," March 3, 2017, www.army.mil/article/183491/army_developing_laser_guided_precision_mortar; and Robert Sherman, "M712 Copperhead," Federation of American Scientists, Washington, D.C., https://fas.org/man/dod-101/sys/land/m712.htm.

24. Christopher V. Poulton and Michael R. Watts, "MIT and DARPA Pack Lidar Sensor onto Single Chip," *IEEE Spectrum*, August 4, 2016, spectrum.ieee.org/tech-talk/semiconduc tors/optoelectronics/mit-lidar-on-a-chip.

25. Graham Templeton, "A Deeper Look into Lasers, Particle Beams, and the Future of War," *Extreme Tech*, April 25, 2013, https://www.extremetech.com/extreme/153585-a -deeper-look-into-lasers-particle-beams-and-the-future-of-war; Weilin Hou, "Blue-Green Laser Communications Critical Technologies for Anti-submarine Warfare and Network Centric Operations," *International Defence, Security, and Technology*, September 8, 2017, http://idstch.com/home5/international-defence-security-and-technology/technology /photonics/blue-green-laser-communications-and-lidar-critical-technologies-for-anti -submarine-warfare-and-network-centric-operations; and Peter Coates, "LIDAR: An Anti-submarine Warfare Sensor," *Submarine Matters*, January 16, 2014, http://gentleseas.blogspot .com/2014/01/lidar-anti-submarine-warfare-sensor.html.

26. Dexter Johnson, "Infrared Technology on the Cheap with Nanostructured Gratings," *IEEE Spectrum*, May 26, 2016, https://spectrum.ieee.org/nanoclast/semiconductors /optoelectronics/infrared-technology-on-the-cheap-with-nanostructured-gratings.

27. Annabs Sanchez, "Watch DARPA's New Self-Guided Bullets Turn in Mid-flight, Following Their Target," *Futurism* March 17, 2016, futurism.com/wanteds-curved-bullet-now

-a-reality; and Benjamin Sutherland, "Military Technology: Wizardry and Asymmetry," in *Megatech: Technology in 2050*, ed. Daniel Franklin (London: Profile Books, 2017), 132.

28. Pavel Ripka and Michal Janosek, "Advances in Magnetic Field Sensors," *IEEE Sensors Journal* 10, no. 6 (June 2010): 1108–1116, http://ieeexplore.ieee.org/document/5443656/?reload=true.

29. Norman Polmar and Edward C. Whitman, "Russia Poses a Nonacoustic Threat to U.S. Subs," *Proceedings*, October 2017, 26–30, https://www.usni.org/magazines/proceedings/2017-10/russia-poses-nonacoustic-threat-us-subs.

30. See also "Optical Underwater Acoustic Sensor," in Technology Partnerships Office, Naval Undersea Warfare Center Division Newport, "NUWC Division Newport Commercialization Opportunities," U.S. Navy, Washington, D.C., 2012, http://www.navsea.navy.mil/Portals/103/Documents/NUWC_Newport/Techpartnering/CommercializationOpportunities2012.pdf.

31. Lara Seligman, "U.S. Air Force's Future Battlefield Edge Hinges on MQ-9 Reaper," *Aviation Week and Space Technology*, March 12–25, 2018, 23–24.

32. Keir A. Lieber and Daryl G. Press, "The New Era of Counterforce: Technological Change and the Future of Nuclear Deterrence," *International Security* 41, no. 4 (Spring 2017): 20–40.

33. Joseph Trevithick, "The U.S. Army Buys Israeli Trophy System So Its Tanks Can Blast Incoming Projectiles," *The Drive*, September 29, 2017, http://www.thedrive.com/the-war-zone/14748/us-army-buys-israeli-trophy-system-so-its-tanks-can-blast-incoming-projectiles.

34. V. K. Saxena, "Stealth and Counter-stealth: Some Emerging Thoughts and Continuing Debates," *Journal of Defence Studies*. 6, no. 3 (July 2012): 19–28, https://idsa.in/jds/6_3_2012_StealthandCounterstealthSomeEmergingThoughtsandContinuingDebates_VKSaxena; and Gabriel Dominguez, "China Develops Photonics-Based Radar," *Jane's Defence Weekly*, June 28, 2017, 16.

35. Angus Batey, "Miniature Electronics and Antennas Open the Door to New Set of Decoys," *Aviation Week and Space Technology*, September 4–17, 2017, 40–43; Bryan Clark, Mark Gunzinger, and Jesse Sloman, "Winning in the Gray Zone: Using Electromagnetic Warfare to Regain Escalation Dominance," Center for Strategic and Budgetary Assessments, Washington, D.C., 2017, 23–26, http://csbaonline.org/research/publications/winning-in-the-gray-zone-using-electromagnetic-warfare-to-regain-escalation/publication.

36. Robert Draper, "They Are Watching You—and Everything Else on the Planet," *National Geographic*, February 2018, https://www.nationalgeographic.com/magazine/2018/02/surveillance-watching-you.

37. David W. Young, Hugh H. Hurt, Joseph E. Sluz, and Juan C. Juarez, "Development and Demonstration of Laser Communications Systems," *Johns Hopkins APL Technical Digest* 33, no. 2 (2015), www.jhuapl/techdigest; George Leopold, "Laser Comms from Space Gets Another Test," *Defense Systems*, February 17, 2017, https://defensesystems.com/articles/2017/02/17/spacelaser.aspx; and Sydney J. Freedberg Jr., "Say It with Lasers: $45 Million DoD Prize for Optical Coms," *Breaking Defense*, May 30, 2017, https://breakingdefense.com/2017/05/say-it-with-lasers-45m-dod-prize-for-optical-coms.

38. U.S. Army, "Techniques for Tactical Radio Operations," ATP 6-02.53, January 2016, http://www.apd.army.mil/epubs/DR_pubs/DR_a/pdf/ARN3871_ATP%206-02.53%20FINAL%20WEB.pdf; David Axe, "Failure to Communicate: Inside the Army's Doomed Quest for the 'Perfect' Radio," Center for Public Integrity, Washington, D.C., May 19, 2014, https://www.publicintegrity.org/2012/01/10/7816/failure-communicate-inside-armys-doomed-quest-perfect-radio; and James Hasik, "Avoiding Despair about Military Radio Communications Is the First Step towards Robust Solutions," realcleardefense.com,

July 24, 2017, https://www.realcleardefense.com/articles/2017/07/24/avoiding_despair_about
_military_radio_communications_is_the_first_step_towards_robust_solutions_111884
.html.

39. Briefing at the Army's Maneuver Warfare Center of Excellence, Fort Benning, Georgia, December 13, 2017.

40. M. Mitchell Waldrop, "The Chips Are Down for Moore's Law," *Nature*, February 9, 2016, http://www.nature.com/news/the-chips-are-down-for-moore-s-law-1.19338; see also Rose Hansen, "A Center of Excellence Prepares for Sierra," *Science and Technology Review*, March 2017, 5–11.

41. Jacquelyn Schneider, "Swiping Left on Silicon Valley: New Commercial Analogies for Defense Innovation," *War on the Rocks*, May 16, 2017, https://warontherocks.com /author/jacquelyn-schneider.

42. Brown, "Joint Staff J-7 Sponsored Science, Technology, and Engineering Futures Seminar," 32–33.

43. James Somers, "Is AI Riding a One-Trick Pony?," *MIT Technology Review*, September 29, 2017, www.technologyreview.com/s/608911/is-ai-riding-a-one-trick-pony.

44. Lt. Gen. Jack Shanahan, "Project Maven Brings AI to the Fight against ISIS," *Bulletin of the Atomic Scientists*, November 2017, https://thebulletin.org/project-maven -brings-ai-fight-against-isis11374; and Phil Stewart, "Deep in the Pentagon, a Secret AI Program to Find Hidden Nuclear Missiles," Reuters, June 5, 2018, www.reuters.com/article /us-usa-pentagon-missiles-ai-insight/deep-in-the-pentagon-a-secret-ai-program-to-find -hidden-nuclear-missiles-idUSKCN1J114J?utm_source=Twitter&utm_medium=Social.

45. For a good general overview of this subject and related matters that goes beyond the military sphere, see Darrell M. West, *The Future of Work: Robots, AI, and Automation* (Washington, D.C.: Brookings, 2018).

46. Thomas B. Udvare, "Wingman Is the First Step toward Weaponized Robotics," *Army AT&L*, January–March 2018, 86–89; Hector Montes, Lisbeth Mena, Roemi Fernandez, and Manuel Armada, "Energy Efficiency Hexapod Walking Robot for Humanitarian Demining," *Industrial Robot* 44, no. 4 (2016), www.emeraldinsight.com/doi/pdfplus/10 .1108/IR-11-2016-0281; Robert Wall, "Armies Race to Deploy Drone, Self-Driving Tech on the Battlefield," *Wall Street Journal*, October 29, 2017, www.wsj.com/articles/armies -race-to-deploy-drone-self-driving-tech-on-the-battlefield-1509274803; and Scott Savitz, "Rethink Mine Countermeasures," *Proceedings*, July 2017, www.usni.org/print/91134.

47. Udvare, "Wingman Is First Step toward Weaponized Robotics," 86–89.

48. Matthew Rosenberg and John Markoff, "The Pentagon's 'Terminator Conundrum': Robots That Could Kill on Their Own," *New York Times*, October 25, 2016, nyti. ms/2eApcwz.

49. Austin Long and Brendan Rittenhouse Green, "Stalking the Secure Second Strike: Intelligence, Counterforce, and Nuclear Strategy," *Journal of Strategic Studies* 38, nos. 1–2 (2015): 38–73.

50. Paul Scharre, *Army of None: Autonomous Weapons and the Future of War* (New York: W.W. Norton, 2018); Anika Torruella, "USN Seeks to Fill SSN Shortfalls with Unmanned Capabilities," *Jane's Defence Weekly*, July 5, 2017, 11; and Scott Savitz, Irv Blickstein, Peter Buryk, Robert W. Button, Paul DeLuca, James Dryden, Jason Mastbaum, Jan Osburg, Philip Padilla, Amy Potter, Carter C. Price, Lloyd Thrall, Susan K. Woodward, Roland J. Yardley, and John M. Yurchak, *U.S. Navy Employment Options for Unmanned Surface Vehicles* (Santa Monica, Calif.: RAND, 2013), xiv–xxv.

51. Bryan Clark and Bryan McGrath, "A Guide to the Fleet the United States Needs," *War on the Rocks*, February 9, 2017, warontherocks.com/2017/02/a-guide-to-the-fleet-the -united-states-needs.

52. Kris Osborn, "Navy Littoral Combat Ship to Operate Swarms of Attack Drone Ships," *Warrior Maven*, March 28, 2018, https://www.themaven.net/warriormaven/sea/navy-littoral -combat-ship-to-operate-swarms-of-attack-drone-ships-cSVfXZfBME2bm1dTX1tsIw.

53. Shawn Brimley, "Arresting the Erosion of America's Military Edge," Center for a New American Security, December 2015, 17, https://s3.amazonaws.com/files.cnas.org /documents/While-We-Can-151207.pdf?mtime=20160906082559.

54. T. X. Hammes, "The Future of Conflict," in R. D. Hooker Jr., ed., *Charting a Course: Strategic Choices for a New Administration* (Washington, D.C.: National Defense University Press, 2016), 25–27.

55. Rosenberg and Markoff, "The Pentagon's 'Terminator Conundrum.'"

56. Patrick Tucker, "Russia to the United Nations: Don't Try to Stop Us from Building Killer Robots," *Defense One*, November 21, 2017, www.defenseone.com/technology/2017/11 /russia-united-nations-dont-try-stop-us-buying-killer-robots/142734; and "Special Report: The Future of War," *The Economist*, January 27, 2018, 4.

57. Elsa B. Kania, "Battlefield Singularity: Artificial Intelligence, Military Revolution, and China's Future Military Power," Center for a New American Security, Washington, D.C., November 2017, https://www.cnas.org/publications/reports/battlefield-singularity -artificial-intelligence-military-revolution-and-chinas-future-military-power.

58. John Allen and Amir Husain, "On Hyperwar," *Proceedings*, July 2017, www.usni .org/print/91129; Jules Hurst, "Robotic Swarms in Offensive Maneuver," *Joint Forces Quarterly* 87, no. 4 (2017): 105–111; Graham Warwick, "Powerful Pairing," *Aviation Week and Space Technology*, November 27–December 10, 2017, 35–36; and Graham War-wick, "Swarm Enabler," *Aviation Week and Space Technology*, April 3–16, 2017, 31–32.

59. Hammes, "The Future of Conflict," 25–27.

60. Ben Knight, "A Guide to Military Drones," *Deutsche Welle*, June 30, 2017, http:// www.dw.com/en/a-guide-to-military-drones/a-39441185.

61. Kelsey Atherton, "As Counter-UAS Gains Ground, Swarm Threat Looms," *Aviation Week and Space Technology*, March 26–April 8, 2018, 36–37.

62. Alexander Kott, "The Artificial Becomes Real," *Army AT&L*, January–March 2018, 90–95.

63. Joseph S. Nye Jr., "Deterrence and Dissuasion in Cyberspace," *International Security* 41, no. 3 (Winter 2016/2017): 44–71.

64. David E. Sanger and Nicole Perlroth, "U.S. Escalates Online Attacks on Russia's Power Grid," *New York Times*, June 15, 2019, https://www.nytimes.com/2019/06/15/us /politics/trump-cyber-russia-grid.html?action=click&module=Top%20Stories&pgtype =Homepage; Nigel Inkster, "Measuring Military Cyber Power," *Survival* 59, no. 4 (August– September 2017): 32; and Lieutenant Commander Damien Dodge, "We Need Cyber-space Damage Control," *Proceedings*, November 2017, 61–65.

65. Tunku Varadarajan, "Report from the Cyberwar Front Lines," *Wall Street Journal*, December 29, 2017, https://www.wsj.com/articles/report-from-the-cyberwar-front -lines-1514586268.

66. Erica D. Borghard and Shawn W. Lonergan, "The Logic of Coercion in Cyberspace," *Security Studies* 26, no. 3 (2017): 452–481; and Travis Sharp, "Theorizing Cyber Coercion: The 2014 North Korean Operation against Sony," *Journal of Strategic Studies* 40, no. 7 (2017), dx.doi.org/10.1080/01402390.2017.1307741; David D. Kirkpatrick, "British Cyber-security Chief Warns of Russian Hacking," *New York Times*, November 14, 2017, https:// nyti.ms/2JqzGCF; and Nicole Perlroth, "Hackers Are Targeting Nuclear Facilities, Homeland Security Department and FBI Say," *New York Times*, July 6, 2017, https://nyti.ms/2tRVPNq.

67. Richard A. Clarke and Robert K. Knake, *The Fifth Domain: Defending Our Country, Our Companies, and Ourselves in the Age of Cyber Threats* (New York: Penguin, 2019);

and Ellen Nakashima, "At Nations' Request, U.S. Cyber Command Probes Foreign Networks to Hunt Election Security Threats," *Washington Post*, May 7, 2019, https://www.washingtonpost.com/world/national-security/at-nations-request-us-cyber-command-probes-foreign-networks-to-hunt-election-security-threats/2019/05/07/376a16c8-70f6-11e9-8be0-ca575670e91c_story.html.

68. Michael Frankel, James Scouras, and Antonio De Simone, "Assessing the Risk of Catastrophic Cyber Attack: Lessons from the Electromagnetic Pulse Commission," Johns Hopkins University Applied Physics Laboratory, Laurel, Md., 2015, https://pdfs.semanticscholar.org/bda9/16313363cf775f9a06dd8d5195caf6a60c63.pdf; Robert McMillan, "Cyber Experts Identify Malware That Could Disrupt U.S. Power Grid," *Wall Street Journal*, June 12, 2017, https://www.wsj.com/articles/cyber-experts-identify-malware-that-could-disrupt-u-s-power-grid-1497271444; and Clarke and Knake, *The Fifth Domain*, 159–161, 187–196.

69. Defense Science Board, "Task Force on Cyber Deterrence," Washington, D.C., February 2017, https://www.acq.osd.mil/dsb/reports/2010s/DSB-CyberDeterrenceReport_02-28-17_Final.pdf.

70. Brown, "Joint Staff J-7 Sponsored Science, Technology, and Engineering Futures Seminar," 17–24; and, for a good overview, see Sukeyuki Ichimasa, "Threat of Cascading 'Permanent Blackout' Effects and High Altitude Electromagnetic Pulse (HEMP)," *NIDS Journal of Defense and Security*, no. 17 (December 2016): 3–20.

71. Assistant Secretary of Defense for Research and Engineering, "DoD Research and Engineering Enterprise," Department of Defense, Washington, D.C., May 2014, 3, https://www.acq.osd.mil/chieftechnologist/publications/docs/ASD(R&E)_Strategic_Guidance_May_2014.pdf.

72. Proceedings of a panel discussion at Brookings, "Acquisition Reform: Increasing Competition, Cutting Costs, and Out-innovating the Enemy," Washington, D.C., April 13, 2015, https://www.brookings.edu/events/acquisition-reform-increasing-competition-cutting-costs-and-out-innovating-the-enemy.

73. Thomas S. Grose, "Reshaping Flight for Fuel Efficiency: Five Technologies on the Runway," *National Geographic*, April 23, 2013, news.nationalgeographic.com/news/energy/2013/04/130423-reshaping-flight-for-fuel-efficiency; and Lara Seligman, "Future Fighter," *Aviation Week and Space Technology*, September 4–17, 2017.

74. Jeffrey Lin and P. W. Singer, "China Is Testing a New Long-Range, Air-to-Air Missile That Could Thwart U.S. Plans for Air Warfare," *Popular Science*, November 22, 2016, https://www.popsci.com/china-new-long-range-air-to-air-missile.

75. See Richard P. Hallion and Curtis M. Bedke with Mark V. Schanz, "Hypersonic Weapons and U.S. National Security: A 21st Century Breakthrough," Mitchell Institute for Aerospace Studies, Air Force Association, Arlington, Va., November 2015, file:///C:/Users/mohanlon/AppData/Local/Microsoft/Windows/INetCache/Content.Outlook/GWM1LT5A/2015%20Hallion-Bedke-Schanz%20Hypersonics%20Weapons%20%20US%20Security%20Mitchell%20Inst%2012-9-15.pdf.

76. Daniel Wasserbly, "Eyeing China, Hypersonic Technology Is U.S. DoD's Top Development Priority," *Jane's Defence Weekly*, March 14, 2018, 4.

77. Robert Haffa and Anand Datla, "Hypersonic Weapons: Appraising the 'Third Offset,'" American Enterprise Institute, Washington, D.C., April 2017, aei.org/publications/hypersonic-weapons-appraising-the-third-offset; Kyle Mizokami, "The U.S. and Australia Conducted a Secretive Hypersonic Missile Test," *Popular Mechanics*, July 18, 2017, www.popularmechanics.com/military/research/a27384/us-australia-hypersonic-missile-test; Guy Norris, "Boeing's Hyper Hope," *Aviation Week and Space Technology*, January 29–February 11, 2018, 20–21; and Guy Norris, "Prime Time: With Tripled High-Speed Research Budget, U.S. Air Force Spells Out Its Operational Hypersonic Needs," *Aviation Week and Space Technology*, August 14–September 3, 2017, 57–58.

78. Richard D. Fisher Jr., "Chinese Resurgence: Beijing Returns to Larger Defense Budgets," *Aviation Week and Space Technology*, December 25, 2017–January 14, 2018, 56.

79. Guy Norris, "Hypersonic Skunk," *Aviation Week and Space Technology*, June 12–25, 2017, 26.

80. Gurpreet Singh, "Overview of the DOE Advanced Combustion Energy R&D Program," Department of Energy, Washington, D.C., June 16, 2014, https://www.energy.gov /sites/prod/files/2014/09/f18/ace_rd_overview_2014_amr.pdf; Jerald A. Caton, "Maximum Efficiencies for Internal Combustion Engines: Thermodynamic Limitations," *International Journal of Engine Research* 19, no. 10 (October 2017), http://journals.sagepub.com/doi/pdf /10.1177/1468087417737700.

81. Alec Wahlman and Brian M. Drinkwine, "The M1 Abrams: Today and Tomorrow," *Military Review* 94, no. 6 (November–December 2014), http://www.armyupress.army .mil/Portals/7/military-review/Archives/English/MilitaryReview_20141231_art006.pdf.

82. John B. Heywood, "Improving Engine Efficiency and Fuels: An Overview," Conference Presentation, Baltimore, Md., February 2014, https://crcao.org/workshops/2014AFEE /Final%20Presentations/Day%201%20Intro%20Presentations/I1-1%20Heywood,%20 John%20-%20Presentation%20[Compatibility%20Mode].pdf.

83. Chun Hong Kelvin Yap, "The Impact of Armor on the Design, Utilization and Survivability of Ground Vehicles: The History of Armor Development and Use," Naval Postgraduate School, Monterey, Calif., 2012, http://dtic.mil/dtic/tr/fulltext/u2/a567418.pdf; and Sydney J. Freedberg Jr., "Milley's Future Tank: Railguns, Robotics, and Ultra-light Armor," *Breaking Defense*, July 27, 2017, https://breakingdefense.com/2017/07/railguns-robotics -ultra-light-armor-general-milleys-future-tank.

84. Paul B. Rehmus, *Alternatives for Future U.S. Space-Launch Capabilities* (Washington, D.C.: Congressional Budget Office, 2006), 11, 19, https://www.cbo.gov/sites/default /files/109th-congress-2005-2006/reports/10-09-spacelaunch.pdf; see also Peter B. de Selding, "SpaceX's New Price Chart Illustrates Performance Cost of Reusability," *Space News*, May 2, 2016, http://spacenews.com/spacexs-new-price-chart-illustrates-performance -cost-of-reusability.

85. Nathan Daniels, "Current Space Launch Vehicles Used by the United States," American Security Project, Washington, D.C., April 2014, https://www.americansecurityproject .org/wp-content/uploads/2014/05/218841132-Current-Space-Launch-Vehicles-Used-by -the-United-States.pdf.

86. Adam Mann, "Heavy-Lift Rocket Poised to Boost Space Science," *Science* 359, no. 6374 (January 26, 2018): 376–377.

87. Mike Wall, "SpaceX Rocket Could Be 100-Percent Reusable by 2018, Elon Musk Says," *Space.com*, April 10, 2017, www.space.com/36412-spacex-completely-reusable -rocket-elon-musk.html; and Todd Harrison, Andrew Hunter, Kaitlyn Johnson, and Thomas Roberts, "Implications of Ultra-Low-Cost Access to Space," Center for Strategic and International Studies, March 2017, 5–6, csis.org/analysis/implications-ultra-low-cost -access-to-space.

88. Lucien Rapp, Victor Dos Santos Paulino, and Adriana Martin, "Satellite Miniaturization," Sirius Chair, University of Toulouse, Toulouse, France, 2015, http://chaire-sirius .eu/wp-content/uploads/2015/07/Note-SIRIUS-Satellite-Miniaturization.pdf.

89. David E. Sanger and William J. Broad, "Tiny Satellites from Silicon Valley May Help Track North Korea Missiles," *New York Times*, July 6, 2017, https://nyti.ms/2uPyTM5; and Zachary Keck, "North Korea's New ICBMs: How Well Can American Intelligence Track Them?," *National Interest*, August 6, 2017, http://nationalinterest.org/blog/the-buzz/north -koreas-new-icbms-how-well-can-american-intelligence-21801.

90. Michael Bold, "Very Small Satellites, Very Big Deal," *Army AL&T*, January–March 2018, 229–237. Planet had raised almost $200 million in capital as of early 2018,

suggesting individual satellite costs of under $1 million. See also Robert Draper, "They Are Watching You," *National Geographic*, February 2018, 41–45.

91. Daniel Wasserbly, "U.S. Homeland Missile Defence System Scores First ICBM Target Intercept," *Jane's Defence Weekly*, June 7, 2017, 4; and Thomas Karako, Ian Williams, and Wes Rumbaugh, "Missile Defense 2020: Next Steps for Defending the Homeland," Center for Strategic and International Studies, Washington, D.C., April 2017, 53–54, 73–78.

92. Statement of General Lori J. Robinson, Commander, United States Northern Command, Before the Senate Armed Services Committee, April 6, 2017, 8–10, http://www.northcom.mil/Portals/28/NC%202017%20Posture%20Statement%20Final.pdf?ver=2017-04-06-110952-160; and Karako, Williams, and Rumbaugh, "Missile Defense 2020," 93–96.

93. See, for example, Gabriel Dominguez and Neil Gibson, "China Develops 'Ultra-fast Interceptor,'" *Jane's Defence Weekly*, June 7, 2017, 8.

94. See Andrew M. Sessler, John M. Cornwall, Bob Dietz, Steve Fetter, Sherman Frankel, Richard L. Garwin, Kurt Gottfried, Lisbeth Gronlund, George N. Lewis, Theodore A. Postol, and David C. Wright, *Countermeasures: A Technical Evaluation of the Operational Effectiveness of the Planned U.S. National Missile Defense System* (Cambridge, Mass.: Union of Concerned Scientists, 2000); and James M. Lindsay and Michael E. O'Hanlon, *Defending America: The Case for Limited National Missile Defense* (Washington, D.C.: Brookings, 2001), 94–99.

95. National Air and Space Intelligence Center, "Ballistic and Cruise Missile Threat," Wright-Patterson Air Force Base, Ohio, June 2017, 8, fas.org/irp/threat/missile/bm-2017.pdf.

96. See, for example, David E. Sanger and William J. Broad, "Downing North Korean Missiles Is Hard. So the U.S. Is Experimenting," *New York Times*, November 16, 2017, https://nyti.ms/2hGs7r5.

97. Gabriel Dominguez, "U.S. Risks Losing Advantage in Space to China and Russia, Warns STRATCOM Chief," *Jane's Defence Weekly*, December 13, 2017, 6.

98. Peter L. Hays, "United States Military Uses of Space: Issues and Challenges," in *Space and Security: Trends and Challenges*, ed. Yoshiaki Sakaguchi (Tokyo: National Institute for Defense Studies, 2016), 23; Massimo Pellegrino and Gerald Stang, "Space Security for Europe," Report no. 29, EU Institute for Security Studies, Paris, France, July 2016, 24; and Michael E. O'Hanlon, *Neither Star Wars nor Sanctuary: Constraining the Military Uses of Space* (Washington, D.C.: Brookings, 2004), 61–117.

99. See "M80 Stiletto," *Naval Technology*, 2017, http://www.naval-technology.com/projects/m80-stiletto; "Littoral Combat Ship," *Naval Technology*, 2017, http://www.naval-technology.com/projects/littoral; and Milan Vego, "No Need for High Speed," *Proceedings*, September 2009, 46–50, https://usnwc2.usnwc.edu/getattachment/fd318cca-90c7-4221-8f3f-946e8ec07e05/VEGO-NO-NEED-FOR-HIGH-SPEED-PROCEEDINGS-SEPT—2009.aspx.

100. Michael O'Hanlon, *Technological Change and the Future of Warfare* (Washington, D.C.: Brookings, 2000), 80; and United States Navy Fact File, "Destroyers DDG," U.S. Navy, 2017, http://www.navy.mil/navydata/fact_display.asp?cid=4200&tid=900&ct=4.

101. David Arthur, "Options for Strategic Military Transportation Systems," Congressional Budget Office, Washington, D.C., September 2005, 27, https://www.cbo.gov/sites/default/files/109th-congress-2005-2006/reports/09-27-strategicmobility.pdf.

102. Julian E. Barnes, "A Russian Ghost Submarine, Its U.S. Pursuers and a Deadly New Cold War," *Wall Street Journal*, October 20, 2017, https://www.wsj.com/articles/a-russian-ghost-submarine-its-u-s-pursuers-and-a-deadly-new-cold-war-1508509841; and William Herkewitz, "This Camouflage Coating Hides Submarines from Sonar," *Popular Mechanics*, March 27, 2015, www.popularmechanics.com/military/navy-ships/news/a14800/this-camouflage-coating-hides-submarines-from-sonar.

103. Jerry Hendrix and James Price, "Higher, Heavier, Farther, and Now Undetectable?," Center for a New American Security, Washington, D.C., June 2017, 54–55, cnas. publications/reports.

104. Brown, "Joint Staff J-7 Sponsored Science, Technology, and Engineering Futures Seminar," 8–9.

105. Kris Osborn, "The U.S. Air Force Is Doing All It Can to Keep the B-2 Bomber Stealth," nationalinterest.org, June 6, 2017, http://nationalinterest.org/blog/the-buzz/the -us-air-force-doing-all-it-can-keep-the-b-2-bomber-21020.

106. Dan Katz, "Shaping Things to Come," *Aviation Week and Space Technology*, September 18–October 1, 2017, 64–67.

107. Tom Garlinghouse, "Quantum Computing: Opening New Realms of Possibilities," *Discovery: Research at Princeton Magazine*, February 2020, 12–17.

108. See, for example, Richard L. Garwin, W. Montague Winfield, and the Independent Task Force on Nonlethal Weapons, *Nonlethal Technologies: Progress and Prospects* (New York: Council on Foreign Relations, 1999), 1–31; Benjamin S. Lambeth, *NATO's Air War for Kosovo: A Strategic and Operational Assessment* (Santa Monica, Calif.: RAND, 2001), 42; and Ivo H. Daalder and Michael E. O'Hanlon, *Winning Ugly: NATO's War to Save Kosovo* (Washington, D.C.: Brookings, 2000), 145.

109. Dan Lamothe, "The U.S. Military Has Pain Rays and Stun Guns. So Why Aren't They Being Used?," *The Week*, August 7, 2014, http://theweek.com/articles/445332 /military-pain-rays-stun-guns-why-arent-being-used.

110. David Hambling, "Raytheon's New Radar Tech Could Realize the Pentagon's Pain Ray," *Popular Mechanics*, April 4, 2016, www.popularmechanics.com/military/research /a20264/raytheons-gallium-nitride.

111. Aaron Mehta, "Inside the 'Foundational' Future Technologies of the World's Largest Defense Company," *Defense News*, October 19, 2017, https://www.c4isrnet.com/show -reporter/ausa/2017/10/19/inside-the-foundational-future-technologies-of-the-worlds -largest-defense-company; Doug Cameron, "Pentagon Makes New Push to Put a Laser Weapon on a Fighter Jet," *Wall Street Journal*, December 8, 2017, www.wsj.com/articles /pentagon-makes-new-push-to-put-a-laser-weapon-on-a-fighter-jet-1512756505; and Kris Osborn, "Navy Develops Laser Weapon Prototypes for Destroyers, Cruisers—Maybe Carriers," *Scout*, April 2, 2017, www.scout.com/military/warrior/story/1625939-navy-accelerates -warship-fired-laser-weapons.

112. Valerie Insinna, "Coming in 2021: A Laser Weapon for Fighter Jets," *Defense News*, November 7, 2017, https://www.defensenews.com/air/2017/11/07/coming-in-2021 -a-laser-weapon-for-fighter-jets.

113. Michael Holthe, "Precision Fires Tilt the Field," *Army AL&T*, January–March 2018, 64–72.

114. Graham Warwick, "High-Energy Laser Weapons," *Aviation Week and Space Technology*, December 25, 2017–January 14, 2018, 77; and Kip R. Kendrick, "When Beams Combine," *Army AL&T*, January–March 2018, 70.

115. Brown, "Joint Staff J-7 Sponsored Science, Technology, and Engineering Futures Seminar," 14–15.

116. Daniel R. Coats, Director of National Intelligence, "Worldwide Threat Assessment of the U.S. Intelligence Community," Testimony Before the Senate Select Committee on Intelligence, May 11, 2017, https://www.dni.gov/files/documents/Newsroom/Testimonies /SSCI%20Unclassified%20SFR%20-%20Final.pdf.

117. See, for example, Will Englund, "What a Brave Russian Scientist Told Me about Novichok, the Nerve Agent Identified in the Spy Attack," *Washington Post*, March 12, 2018, https://www.washingtonpost.com/news/worldviews/wp/2018/03/12/what-is-novichok-the -russian-nerve-agent-and-the-scientist-who-revealed-it/?utm_term=.f7a478ed98b7.

118. Stephen M. Younger, *The Bomb: A New History* (New York: HarperCollins, 2009); and James E. Doyle, *Renewing America's Nuclear Arsenal: Options for the 21st Century* (London: International Institute for Strategic Studies, 2017), 24–28, 82–83.

119. Richard L. Garwin and Georges Charpak, *Megawatts and Megatons: A Turning Point in the Nuclear Age?* (New York: Alfred A. Knopf, 2001); Harold A. Feiveson, Alexander Glaser, Zia Mian, and Frank N. von Hippel, *Unmaking the Bomb: A Fissile Material Approach to Nuclear Disarmament and Nonproliferation* (Cambridge, Mass.: MIT Press, 2014); and Arnie Heller, "Stockpile Stewardship at 20 Years," *Science and Technology Review*, July 2015, 2015, https://str.llnl.gov/july-2015/verdon.

120. Robert Einhorn, "Non-proliferation Challenges Facing the Trump Administration," *Arms Control and Non-proliferation Series*, Paper 15, Brookings Institution, Washington, D.C., 2017, vi.

121. It is striking how many of the review articles on biological weapons and warfare turned up by standard searches were written in the last years of the twentieth century or 2001 and 2002. There has generally been much less literature since, it would appear. See, for example, SIU School of Medicine, "Overview of Potential Agents of Biological Terrorism," Southern Illinois University, Carbondale, Ill., 2017, https://www.siumed.edu/im/overview-potential-agents-biological-terrorism.html; and John B. Foley, "A Nation Unprepared: Bioterrorism and Pandemic Response," *Interagency Journal* 8, no. 2 (2017): 25–33.

122. Stephen Hummel, "Ebola: Not an Effective Biological Weapon for Terrorists," Combating Terrorism Center at West Point, September 29, 2014, www.ctc.usma.edu/posts/ebola-not-an-effective-biological-weapon-for-terrorists.

123. Kai Kupferschmidt, "Labmade Smallpox Is Possible, Study Shows," *Science* 357, no. 6347 (July 14, 2017), http://science.sciencemag.org/content/357/6347/115; John D. Steinbruner, *Principles of Global Security* (Washington, D.C.: Brookings, 2000), 175–193; and C. Raina MacIntyre, "Biopreparedness in the Age of Genetically Engineered Pathogens and Open Access Science: An Urgent Need for a Paradigm Shift," *Military Medicine* 180, no. 9 (September 2015), https://www.ncbi.nlm.nih.gov/pubmed/26327545.

124. Andrea Shalal, "U.S. Military Sees More Use of Laser, Microwave Weapons," Reuters, July 28, 2015, https://www.reuters.com/article/us-usa-military-arms/u-s-military-sees-more-use-of-laser-microwave-weapons-idUSKCN0Q22HH20150728.

125. Geoff Fein, "U.S. Navy Recharges Railgun Development Effort," *Jane's Defence Weekly*, June 14, 2017, 12; and Ronald O'Rourke, "Navy Lasers, Railgun, and Hypervelocity Projectile: Background and Issues for Congress," Congressional Research Service, June 9, 2017, fas.org/sgp/crs/weapons/R44175.pdf.

126. Brown, "Joint Staff J-7 Sponsored Science, Technology, and Engineering Futures Seminar," 17–21.

127. Juanjuan Zhang, Pieter Fiers, Kirby A. Witte, Rachel W. Jackson, Katherine L. Poggensee, Christopher G. Atkeson, and Steven H. Collins, "Human-in-the-Loop Optimization of Exoskeleton Assistance during Walking," *Science* 356, no. 6344 (June 23, 2017): 1280–1283.

128. Javier Gonzalez, "Go Pills for Black Shoes?," *Proceedings*, July 2017, www.usni.org/print/91128.

129. Argie Sarantinos-Perrin, "A New Dimension of Acquisition," *Army AL&T*, January–March 2017, 83–87.

130. David Rotman, "The 3-D Printer That Could Finally Change Manufacturing," *MIT Technology Review*, April 25, 2017, https://www.technologyreview.com/s/604088/the-3-d-printer-that-could-finally-change-manufacturing; Rose Hansen, "A New Composite-Manufacturing Approach Takes Shape," *Science and Technology Review*, June 2017, 16–10; and "Printing Things Everywhere," *The Economist*, July 1, 2017, 15.

131. Brown, "Joint Staff J-7 Sponsored Science, Technology, and Engineering Futures Seminar," 35–38.

132. T. X. Hammes, "3-D Printing Will Disrupt the World in Ways We Can Barely Imagine," *War on the Rocks*, December 28, 2015, https://warontherocks.com/2015/12/3-d -printing-will-disrupt-the-world-in-ways-we-can-barely-imagine.

133. Brown, "Joint Staff J-7 Sponsored Science, Technology, and Engineering Futures Seminar," 9–10.

134. Bjorn Hogberg, "Remote Control of Nanoscale Devices," *Science* 359, no. 6373 (January 19, 2018): 279; Hammes, "The Future of Conflict," 23–24; and Brown, "Joint Staff J-7 Sponsored Science, Technology, and Engineering Futures Seminar," 9–10.

135. Christopher Mims, "The Battery Boost We've Been Waiting for Is Only a Few Years Out," *Wall Street Journal*, April 1, 2018, https://www.wsj.com/articles/the-battery-boost-weve -been-waiting-for-is-only-a-few-years-out-1521374401; and Robert F. Service, "Lithium-Sulfur Batteries Poised for Leap," *Science* 359, no. 6380 (March 9, 2018): 1080–1081.

4. SPACE, MISSILE DEFENSE, AND NUCLEAR WEAPONS

1. James Clay Moltz, *The Politics of Space Security*, 3rd. ed. (Stanford, Calif.: Stanford University Press, 2019).

2. See, for example, Paul B. Stares, *Space and National Security* (Washington, D.C.: Brookings, 1987), 15–19; and Union of Concerned Scientists, "UCS Satellite Database," Cambridge, Mass., January 2019, https://www.ucsusa.org/nuclear-weapons/space-weapons /satellite-database#.XG6yv3RKiUk.

3. NASA, "What Is an Orbit?," Washington, D.C., 2017, https://www.nasa.gov /audience/forstudents/5-8/features/nasa-knows/what-is-orbit-58.html.

4. See Ashton B. Carter, "Satellites and Anti-satellites: The Limits of the Possible," *International Security* 10, no. 4 (Spring 1986): 50–52; and David Wright, Laura Grego, and Lisbeth Gronlund, *The Physics of Space Security: A Reference Manual* (Cambridge, Mass.: American Academy of Arts and Sciences, 2005), 40–46.

5. See Curtis D. Cochran, Dennis M. Gorman, and Joseph D. Dumoulin, eds., *Space Handbook*, 12th rev. ed. (Montgomery, Ala.: Air University Press, 1985), 2-1 through 3-50.

6. Harry W. Jones, "The Recent Large Reduction in Space Launch Cost," 48th International Conference on Environmental Systems, Albuquerque, N.M., July 2018, file:///C:/ Users/mohanlon/Downloads/ICES_2018_81.pdf.

7. Michael E. O'Hanlon, *Neither Star Wars nor Sanctuary: Constraining the Military Uses of Space* (Washington, D.C.: Brookings, 2004), 34.

8. Union of Concerned Scientists, "UCS Satellite Database."

9. Amanda Miller and Arie Church, "ICBMs and Spacecraft in Service over Time," *Air Force Almanac*, June 2019, 58.

10. See Union of Concerned Scientists, "UCS Satellite Database"; Tamar A. Mehuron, "2007 Space Almanac: The U.S. Military Space Operation in Facts and Figures," *Air Force Magazine*, August 2007, 82.

11. Barry D. Watts, *The Military Uses of Space: A Diagnostic Assessment* (Washington, D.C.: Center for Strategic and Budgetary Assessments, 2001), 50.

12. See European Space Agency, "Space Debris," Paris, January 2019, https://www .esa.int/Our_Activities/Space_Safety/Space_Debris/Space_debris_by_the_numbers.

13. Peter L. Hays, *United States Military Space: Into the Twenty-First Century* (Montgomery, Ala.: Air University Press, 2002), 133; and Joel R. Primack, "Debris and Future Space Activities," in *Future Security in Space: Commercial, Military, and Arms Control Trade-Offs*, Occasional Paper 10, ed. James Clay Moltz (Monterey, Calif.: Monterey Institute of International Studies, 2002), 18–20.

14. Bruce G. Blair, *Strategic Command and Control: Redefining the Nuclear Threat* (Washington, D.C.: Brookings, 1985), 205–206; Carter, "Satellites and Anti-satellites," 89–92; Watts, *Military Uses of Space*, 99; and O'Hanlon, *Neither Star Wars nor Sanctuary*, 68–69.

15. The ability of a satellite to image places on Earth not directly below it is limited by three factors: first, the ability of its camera or lens to swivel; second, the need of the user for a certain minimum degree of resolution in the image (which often makes images taken at longer range less useful); and, third, the curvature of the Earth, which blocks distant regions from view. This last constraint is generally the most binding. To calculate the maximum range, for low-altitude satellites, the formula is: radar horizon = square root of (diameter of Earth × altitude of satellite). This follows directly from the Pythagorean theorem, drawing a right triangle with one side the radius of the Earth, a second side the distance from the satellite in question to the farthest point on Earth's surface within its view, and a third side from the center of the Earth to the satellite (this latter segment is the triangle's hypotenuse). Using symbols, we can write more compactly $RH = \sqrt{(DA)}$. Since the diameter of the Earth is about 8,000 miles, a satellite at 200 miles' altitude can therefore "see" out about 1,250 miles (and an aircraft at just under 8 miles' altitude can see about 250 miles).

16. "Outlook/Specifications: Spacecraft," *Aviation Week and Space Technology*, January 15, 2007, 176–178, and January 28, 2008, 170–172; Watts, *Military Uses of Space*, 42–43, 78; Craig Covault, "Secret NRO Recons Eye Iraqi Threats," *Aviation Week and Space Technology*, September 16, 2002, 23; Jeffrey T. Richelson, *America's Secret Eyes in Space: The U.S. Keyhole Spy Satellite Program* (New York: Harper and Row, 1990), 130–132, 186–187, 206–208, 227, 236–238; O'Hanlon, *Neither Star Wars nor Sanctuary*, 42–53; and Justin Ray, "Next Round of U.S. Optical Spy Satellites to Start Launching in 2018," *Spaceflight Now*, May 1, 2015, https://spaceflightnow.com/2015/05/01/next-round-of-u-s-optical-spy -satellites-to-start-launching-in-2018.

17. Mehuron, "2007 Space Almanac," 84.

18. Thomas A. Keaney and Eliot A. Cohen, *Gulf War Air Power Survey Summary Report* (Washington, D.C.: Government Printing Office, 1993), 193; Department of Defense, *Kosovo/Operation Allied Force After-Action Report* (Washington, D.C.: Department of Defense, 2000), 46; William B. Scott, "Milspace Comes of Age in Fighting Terror," *Aviation Week and Space Technology*, April 8, 2002, 77–78; and Patrick Rayerman, "Exploiting Commercial SATCOM: A Better Way," *Parameters*, Winter 2003–2004, 55.

19. Comments of General Paul Selva at the Brookings Institution, June 28, 2019, https://www.brookings.edu/events/the-future-of-u-s-defense-strategy-a-conversation -with-general-paul-j-selva.

20. Todd Harrison, Kaitlyn Johnson, and Thomas G. Roberts, "Space Threat Assessment 2019," Center for Strategic and International Studies, Washington, D.C., 2019, 10–13, https://aerospace.csis.org/wp-content/uploads/2019/04/SpaceThreatAssessment2019 -compressed.pdf; and O'Hanlon, *Neither Star Wars nor Sanctuary*, 86–87.

21. Harrison, Johnson, and Roberts, "Space Threat Assessment 2019."

22. Jon Rosamond, "USN Admiral Says Satellite Kill Was 'One-Time Event,'" *Jane's Defence Weekly*, March 26, 2008, 8.

23. Transcript of "Assessing Space Security: Threat and Response," Brookings Institution, Washington, D.C., July 31, 2019, https://www.brookings.edu/events/assessing-space -security-threat-and-response.

24. Blair, *Strategic Command and Control*, 201–207; Ian Steer and Melanie Bright, "Blind, Deaf, and Dumb," *Jane's Defence Weekly*, October 23, 2002, 21–23; Donald Rumsfeld, *Report of the Commission to Assess United States National Security Space Management and Organization* (Washington, D.C.: January 11, 2001), 21–22; Carter, "Satellites and Anti-satellites"; and Watts, *Military Uses of Space*, 99.

25. Dennis Papadopoulos, "Satellite Threat Due to High Altitude Nuclear Detonations," briefing slides presented at Brookings on December 17, 2002, cited by permission of the author.

26. Office of the Secretary of Defense, "2019 Missile Defense Review," Washington, D.C., 2019, 40–43, https://media.defense.gov/2019/Jan/17/2002080666/-1/-1/1/2019-MISSILE-DEFENSE-REVIEW.PDF

27. Thomas Karako, "The Missile Defense Review: Insufficient for Complex and Integrated Attack," *Strategic Studies Quarterly*, Summer 2019, https://www.airuniversity.af.edu/Portals/10/SSQ/documents/Volume-13_Issue-2/Karako.pdf.

28. David R. Tanks, *National Missile Defense: Policy Issues and Technological Capabilities* (Cambridge, Mass.: Institute for Foreign Policy Analysis, 2000), 3.3.

29. Curtis D. Cochran, Dennis M. Gorman, and Joseph D. Dumoulin, eds., *Space Handbook* (Maxwell Air Force Base, Ala.: Air University Press, 1985), 3.27–3.30.

30. Thomas B. Cochran, William M. Arkin, and Milton M. Hoenig, *Nuclear Weapons Databook*, vol. 1, *U.S. Nuclear Forces and Capabilities* (Pensacola, Fla.: Ballinger, 1984), 107.

31. Tanks, *National Missile Defense*, 3.3.

32. See John Tirman, ed., *The Fallacy of Star Wars* (New York: Vintage Books, 1984), 52–65.

33. For more, see Stephen Weiner, "Systems and Technology," in *Ballistic Missile Defense*, ed. Ashton B. Carter and David N. Schwartz (Washington, D.C.: Brookings, 1984), 49–97; and Robert G. Nagler, *Ballistic Missile Proliferation: An Emerging Threat* (Arlington, Va.: System Planning Corporation, 1992), 52–65.

34. James M. Acton, *Silver Bullet? Asking the Right Questions about Conventional Prompt Global Strike* (Washington, D.C.: Carnegie Endowment, 2013), 1–6; and Steve Trimble and Guy Norris, "Pole Position," *Aviation Week and Space Technology*, July 1–14, 2019, 34–36.

35. For more, see David B. H. Denoon, *Ballistic Missile Defense in the Post–Cold War Era* (Boulder, Colo.: Westview Press, 1995), chaps. 3–5; and Department of Defense, "The Strategic Defense Initiative: Defense Technologies Study," reprinted in *The Star Wars Controversy*, ed. Steven E. Miller and Stephen Van Evera (Princeton, N.J.: Princeton University Press, 1986), 291–322.

36. Office of the Secretary of Defense, "2019 Missile Defense Review."

37. See Thomas Karako, Ian Williams, and Wes Rumbaugh, "Missile Defense 2020: Next Steps for Defending the Homeland," Washington, D.C., 2017, https://csis-prod.s3.amazonaws.com/s3fs-public/publication/170406_Karako_MissileDefense2020_Web.pdf?rgfZJOoY5AJY5ScsfZQW8z7Bn7dtSlrr.

38. See J. C. Toomay, *Radar Principles for the Non-specialist* (Mendham, N.J.: SciTech, 1998), 1–64.

39. Office of the Secretary of Defense, "2019 Missile Defense Review."

40. Karako, "The Missile Defense Review."

41. For more information, see the website of the Federation of American Scientists at www.fas.org.

42. See Office of the Secretary of Defense, "2019 Missile Defense Review," 42–50; Missile Defense Agency, "Terminal High-Altitude Area Defense," Department of Defense, Washington, D.C., 2019, https://www.mda.mil/system/thaad.html; and "Patriot Missile Long-Range Air-Defence System," *Army Technology*, London, Verdict Media, 2019, https://www.army-technology.com/projects/patriot.

43. For China, see, for example, Eric Heginbotham, Michael Nixon, Forrest E. Morgan, Jacob L. Heim, Jeff Hagen, Sheng Li, Jeffrey Engstrom, Martin C. Libicki, Paul DeLuca, David A. Shlapak, David R. Frelinger, Burgess Laird, Kyle Brady, and Lyle J. Morris, *The U.S.-China Military Scorecard* (Santa Monica, Calif.: RAND, 2015), 248–249.

44. David Mosher and Michael O'Hanlon, *The START Treaty and Beyond* (Washington, D.C.: Congressional Budget Office, 1991), 148.

45. Arms Control Association, "U.S. Missile Defense Programs at a Glance," Washington, D.C., 2019, https://www.armscontrol.org/factsheets/usmissiledefense; and Missile Defense Agency, "Ballistic Missile Defense Intercept Flight Test Record," Washington, D.C., April 2019, https://www.mda.mil/global/documents/pdf/testrecord.pdf.

46. Mosher and O'Hanlon, *The START Treaty and Beyond*, 167–171.

47. Brad Roberts, *The Case for U.S. Nuclear Weapons in the 21st Century* (Stanford, Calif.: Stanford University Press, 2016), 87.

48. See Andrew M. Sessler, John M. Cornwall, Bob Dietz, Steve Fetter, Sherman Frankel, Richard L. Garwin, Kurt Gottfried, Lisbeth Gronlund, George N. Lewis, Theodore A. Postol, and David C. Wright, *Countermeasures: A Technical Evaluation of the Operational Effectiveness of the Planned U.S. National Missile Defense System* (Cambridge, Mass.: Union of Concerned Scientists, April 2000), 42; and Ballistic Missile Defense Organization, *Report of the Panel on Reducing Risk in Ballistic Missile Defense Flight Test Programs*, Department of Defense, February 27, 1998, 56 (also known as the Welch report), https://www.armscontrol.org/act/2000-07/report-national-missile-defense-independent-review-team.

49. See the testimony of Richard L. Garwin and David C. Wright, "Ballistic Missiles: Threat and Response," Hearings Before the Senate Committee on Foreign Relations, 106th Cong., 1st Sess. (Washington, D.C.; Government Printing Office, 2000), 74–90.

50. Ann Scott Tyson, "U.S. Shoots Down Missile in Simulation of Long-Range Attack," *Washington Post*, December 6, 2008, A2.

51. Office of the Secretary of Defense, "2019 Missile Defense Review," xv.

52. Wright, Grego, and Gronlund, *Physics of Space Security*, 98–100.

53. Samuel Glasstone, ed., *The Effects of Nuclear Weapons*, rev. ed. (Washington, D.C.: US Atomic Energy Commission, 1962), 196–274.

54. Richard Rhodes, *The Making of the Atomic Bomb* (New York: Simon and Schuster, 1986), 714–735; and Michael Levi, *On Nuclear Terrorism* (Cambridge, Mass.: Harvard University Press, 2007), 35–38, 52.

55. Richard L. Garwin and Georges Charpak, *Megawatts and Megatons: A Turning Point in the Nuclear Age?* (New York: Alfred A. Knopf, 2001), 34–35, 48–59.

56. Rhodes, *Making of the Atomic Bomb*, 737–741; and National Nuclear Security Administration Nevada Field Office, "United States Nuclear Tests: July 1945 through September 1992," Las Vegas, Nevada, September 2015, vii, https://www.nnss.gov/docs/docs_LibraryPublications/DOE_NV-209_Rev16.pdf.

57. Edwin Lyman and Frank N. von Hippel, "Reprocessing Revisited: The International Dimensions of the Global Nuclear Energy Partnership," *Arms Control Today*, April 2008, 9.

58. Garwin and Charpak, *Megawatts and Megatons*, 58–61.

59. Harold A. Feiveson, Alexander Glaser, Zia Mian, and Frank N. von Hippel, *Unmaking the Bomb: A Fissile Material Approach to Nuclear Disarmament and Nonproliferation* (Cambridge, Mass.: MIT Press, 2014), 36–42.

60. Department of Defense, "Nuclear Posture Review," January 2018, 54–63, https://media.defense.gov/2018/Feb/02/2001872886/-1/-1/1/2018-NUCLEAR-POSTURE-REVIEW-FINAL-REPORT.PDF.

61. Garwin and Charpak, *Megawatts and Megatons*, 58–65.

62. Graham Allison, *Nuclear Terrorism: The Ultimate Preventable Catastrophe* (New York: Times Books, 2004), 43–53. Such weapons are actually sophisticated and difficult to design correctly, since they are close to a performance "cliff" where if anything malfunctions slightly, they could fail to attain critical mass and produce a significant nuclear yield. See Stephen M. Younger, *The Bomb: A New History* (New York: HarperCollins, 2009), 29.

63. Steve Fetter, *Toward a Comprehensive Test Ban* (Cambridge, Mass.: Ballinger, 1988), 72–78; and National Nuclear Security Administration Nevada Field Office, "United States Nuclear Tests."

64. For an illuminating study of the nuclear age and the evolution of perceived targeting requirements, see Janne E. Nolan, *Guardians of the Arsenal: The Politics of Nuclear Strategy* (New York: Basic Books, 1989).

65. Levi, *On Nuclear Terrorism*, 40–50; and National Nuclear Security Administration Nevada Field Office, "United States Nuclear Tests," xiii.

66. Garwin and Charpak, *Megawatts and Megatons*, 122–123.

67. Some of my arguments here first appeared in Michael O'Hanlon, "Resurrecting the Test-Ban Treaty," *Survival* 50, no. 1 (February–March 2008): 119–132.

68. Brad Roberts, "On Creating the Conditions for Nuclear Disarmament: Past Lessons, Future Prospects," *Washington Quarterly* 42, no. 2 (Summer 2019): 7–30.

69. Federation of American Scientists, "Pakistan Nuclear Weapons," Washington, D.C., 2002, https://fas.org/nuke/guide/pakistan/nuke.

70. Preparatory Commission for the Comprehensive Nuclear-Test-Ban Treaty Organization, "Seismic Monitoring," https://www.ctbto.org/verification-regime/monitoring-technologies-how-they-work/seismic-monitoring/.

71. Zhang Hui, "Revisiting North Korea's Nuclear Test," *China Security* 3, no. 3 (Summer 2007): 119–130.

72. Garwin and Charpak, *Megawatts and Megatons*, 306.

73. Fetter, *Toward a Comprehensive Test Ban*, 107–158.

74. Younger, *The Bomb*, 217.

75. Younger, 149–150.

76. For a good discussion of this issue, see Fetter, *Toward a Comprehensive Test Ban*, 95–102.

77. See Keith B. Payne, *The Great American Gamble: Deterrence Theory and Practice from the Cold War to the Twenty-First Century* (Fairfax, Va.: National Institute Press, 2008), 409–448.

78. America's Defense Monitor Interview with Richard Garwin, April 3, 1999, http://www.cdi.org/adm/1235/Garwin.html; and Garwin and Charpak, *Megawatts and Megatons*, 352–354.

79. Jonathan Medalia, "The Reliable Replacement Warhead Program: Background and Current Developments," *CRS Report for Congress*, RL32929 (July 2007), 4–9.

80. A. Fitzpatrick and I. Oelrich, "The Stockpile Stewardship Program: Fifteen Years On," Federation of American Scientists, April 2007, www.fas.org/2007/nuke/Stockpile_Stewardship_Paper.pdf (accessed January 9, 2008).

81. "At the Workbench: Interview with Bruce Goodwin of Lawrence Livermore Laboratories," *Bulletin of the Atomic Scientists*, July/August 2007, 46–47.

82. Younger, *The Bomb*, 148–149, 184–186.

83. National Nuclear Security Administration, "Reliable Replacement Warhead Program," March 2007, www.nnsa.doe.gov/docs/factsheets/2007/NA-07-FS-02.pdf.

84. Walter Pincus, "New Nuclear Warhead's Funding Eliminated," *Washington Post*, May 24, 2007, A6.

85. John R. Harvey, "Nonproliferation's New Soldier," *Bulletin of the Atomic Scientists*, July/August 2007, 32–33; and Medalia, "The Reliable Replacement Warhead Program."

86. Michael A. Levi and Michael E. O'Hanlon, *The Future of Arms Control* (Washington, D.C.: Brookings, 2005), 28.

87. Michael A. Levi, "Dreaming of Clean Nukes," *Nature* 428 (April 29, 2004): 892.

88. Roberts, *The Case for U.S. Nuclear Weapons in the 21st Century*, 24–25.

89. William J. Perry, *My Journey at the Nuclear Brink* (Stanford, Calif.: Stanford University Press, 2015), 187–190.

90. Lt. Gen. Robert P. Ashley Jr., "Russian and Chinese Nuclear Modernization Trends," Hudson Institute, Washington, D.C., May 29, 2019, https://www.dia.mil/News/Speeches-and-Testimonies/Article-View/Article/1859890/russian-and-chinese-nuclear-modernization-trends.

91. Nuclear Threat Initiative, "Comprehensive Nuclear-Test-Ban Treaty," Washington, D.C., July 2018, https://www.nti.org/learn/treaties-and-regimes/comprehensive-nuclear-test-ban-treaty-ctbt.

Index